Expert Performance in Sports

Advances in Research on Sport Expertise

Janet L. Starkes, PhD
McMaster University

K. Anders Ericsson, PhD
Florida State University

Editors

Human Kinetics

Library of Congress Cataloging-in-Publication Data

Expert performance in sports : advances in research on sport expertise /
Janet L. Starkes, K. Anders Ericsson, editors.
   p. cm.
Includes bibliographical references and index.
  ISBN 0-7360-4152-4 (Hard Cover)
  1. Sports sciences. 2. Physical education and training. I. Starkes,
Janet L. II. Ericsson, K. Anders (Karl Anders), 1947-
  GV558 .E96 2003
  796'.01--dc21

            2002152294

ISBN: 0-7360-4152-4

Acquisitions Editor: Judy Patterson Wright, PhD; **Managing Editor:** Amanda S.
Ewing; **Copyeditor:** Scott Jerard; **Proofreader:** Erin Cler; **Indexer:** Daniel Connolly;
Permission Manager: Dalene Reeder; **Graphic Designer:** Fred Starbird; **Graphic
Artist:** Denise Lowry; **Photo Managers:** Leslie A. Woodrum and Kareema McLendon;
Cover Designer: Nancy Rasmus; **Photographer (cover):** © Empics; **Photographer
(interior):** © Human Kinetics, except as otherwise noted; photo on page 275 © John
Salmela; photo on page 295 © Sian Beilock; photo on page 461 of K. Anders Ericsson by
John Sheretz © 2002 CASBS; **Art Manager:** Kelly Hendren; **Illustrator:** Accurate Art;
Printer: Edwards Brothers

Printed in the United States of America   10 9 8 7 6 5 4 3 2 1

Human Kinetics
Web site: www.HumanKinetics.com

United States: Human Kinetics; P.O. Box 5076; Champaign, IL 61825-5076
800-747-4457
e-mail: humank@hkusa.com

Canada: Human Kinetics; 475 Devonshire Road Unit 100; Windsor, ON N8Y 2L5
800-465-7301 (in Canada only)
e-mail: orders@hkcanada.com

Europe: Human Kinetics; 107 Bradford Road; Stanningley
Leeds LS28 6AT, United Kingdom
+44 (0) 113 255 5665
e-mail: hk@hkeurope.com

Australia: Human Kinetics; 57A Price Avenue; Lower Mitcham, South Australia 5062
08 8277 1555
e-mail: liahka@senet.com.au

New Zealand: Human Kinetics; P.O. Box 105-231, Auckland Central
09-523-3462
e-mail: hkp@ihug.co.nz

Contents

Part V   The Great Debate: Is a General Theory 345 of Expert Performance Achievable?

Acknowledgments

Chapter 3: This article was, in part, prepared while the author was a Fellow at the Center for Advanced Study in the Behavioral Sciences. I am grateful for the financial support provided by the John D. and Catherine T. MacArthur Foundation, Grant #32005-0 and by the FSCW/Conradi Endowment Fund of Florida State University Foundation. The author wants to thank Ray Amirault and Len Hill for their valuable comments on an earlier draft of this chapter.

Chapter 4: This chapter was supported in part by the Social Sciences and Humanities Research Council of Canada (SSHRC #410-1999-0525 and SSHRC #410-2002-0235).

Chapter 6: The male adult tennis research was supported in part by a grant from the International Tennis Federation.

Chapter 10: This research was supported by research grants from the Social Sciences and Humanities Research Council of Canada, the Canadian Foundation for Innovation, and the Ontario Innovation Trust, awarded to J. Starkes.

Chapter 11: This chapter was supported in part by a standard research grant 410-99-0525 of the Social Sciences and Humanities Research Council of Canada (SSHRC).

Chapter 13: The Netherlands Organization for Scientific Research (NWO) is gratefully acknowledged for funding this project. The research was conducted while both David Jacobs and Raoul Huys were supported by a grant from the Foundation for Behavioral and Educational Sciences of this organization, the first (#575-12-070) being awarded to Claire Michaels and the second (#425-202-01) to Peter Beek.

Chapter 15: This article was, in part, prepared while the author was a Fellow at the Center for Advanced Study in the Behavioral Sciences. I am grateful for the financial support provided by the John D. and Catherine T. MacArthur Foundation, Grant #32005-0 and by the FSCW/Conradi Endowment Fund of Florida State University Foundation. The author thanks Ray Amirault for his valuable comments on an earlier draft of this chapter.

Foreword

An Olympic gold medal is the most recognized symbol of athletic success and represents the pinnacle of athletic expertise. Yet very few athletes ever make it to the Olympic Games, and fewer still make it to the podium. What does it take to get there? Physical, technical, and tactical skills; psychological and emotional skills; genetic factors; training and practice; access to quality coaching, equipment, and facilities; and access to international competition (i.e., the resources to afford international travel and competition) are all important factors. However, many athletes have all of these elements but can't seem to achieve the highest levels of performance in a consistent and stable manner. Does something get in the way? What is missing?

I spoke to a group of young athletes after the 1998 Winter Olympic Games in Nagano. I shared with the group that over the previous four years, for every decision I made, I asked myself, *Will this affect my getting the gold medal?* If it would affect my chances of winning, I made the appropriate decision; and if it wouldn't affect my chances, I went with whatever was easiest, categorizing the decision as unimportant. My goal affected every big decision I made: the car I drove (I chose an SUV so that I could make the long drives to hockey practice in the New Brunswick snow), the job I took (the schedule had to be flexible in the winter), and where I lived (it had to be close to the rink and the gym). This thinking influenced even the little decisions, such as whether I should go camping with my friends on the weekend (I would miss two training sessions if I went) and what I should eat for dinner (even if I wasn't hungry, I needed food to refuel after a training session). The kids were shocked. They could not believe that an athlete lives this way. I was surprised because I couldn't understand how an athlete could *not* live this way.

Like many Olympians, I arranged my life so that I could train, practice, and compete at my sport. It's not that I ignored other elements of life. I went to school and obtained a wonderful education. In fact, I am back at school working at an MBA part-time. I worked as a professor and a sport administrator. I volunteered my time to assist sport organizations, and I made time for friends and family, though not as much time as I would have liked. But as the Elvis Presley song goes, "you were always on my mind" describes exactly my approach to sport. Having had the opportunity to meet other Olympians, I can tell you that this determined focus on training, improving, and being the best you can be, regardless of the outcome, is a characteristic that many of the medalists have in common.

But it's not all about the medal. In fact, athletes who seem to have the most success think the least about the outcome. The focus is on the process and on being the best you can be on the day that it matters most. My team was not able to do that in Nagano, and we ended up with a silver medal. After this disappointment, I remember thinking that if I knew beforehand that I would end up with the silver medal and not the gold, I still would have done all the training. I decided to stay on for another four years, and at the 2002 Winter Olympics in Salt Lake City, we won the gold. Despite the many challenges, distractions, and adversity along the way, the difference was that we were able to focus on the journey so that we would be the best we could be on the night it mattered most, February 21, 2002. This is a real tribute to the 20 athletes who were on the team. In my own view, success is a journey. In many ways, this book is about the journey, not the outcome.

Therese Brisson

Part I

Introduction

WELCOME TO THE STUDY of sport expertise. This book provides the most comprehensive and up-to-date analyses of what we currently know about developing expert athletes. We hope that the book is of benefit not just to researchers but to high-level athletes and coaches in their quest to become the best. We begin by outlining the format of the book and by providing a brief synopsis of each chapter.

Chapter 1

The Magic and the Science of Sport Expertise

■ ■ ■ ■ ■

Introduction to Sport Expertise Research and This Volume

Janet L. Starkes

Sport is unlike most human endeavors. It inspires poets and artists while it energizes armchair coaches and critics. A terrific run or a fantastic slam dunk has the power to enthrall, and it may even on occasion inspire great sentiment or a patriotic spirit. Sport is so prevalent and so much a part of our everyday lives that we take for granted the years of necessary preparation that underlie every great sporting feat. When one sees Marion Jones, Michael Jordan, Mario Lemieux, or Cal Ripken perform, we marvel at the fluidity, grace, and apparent ease with which they carry out seemingly impossible maneuvers. We don't stop to wonder, however, what role training, practice, mentors, and injury rehabilitation have played in getting the athlete to that moment.

Studying how athletes reach and stay at the pinnacle of their sport is the domain of sport expertise researchers. As researchers who follow the training and performance exploits of some of the best athletes in the world, we are a privileged group. We have the opportunity to work with and study athletes who devote much of their lives in pursuit of the dream of becoming the best. Few human endeavors exist to which people dedicate so much time, energy, resources, and effort—all with the goal of becoming quite simply the best they can be.

Sport expertise research comprises a little magic and a lot of science. The magic of sport expertise research includes observing awe-inspiring performances and pursuing their causes. The underlying questions that spur this research are age-old, and sport expertise researchers employ the scientific approach to try to provide answers. They include questions such as the following:

- How much of being the best is related to training, and how much is based on one's genetic, physical, and emotional makeup?
- In the quest to be the best, how important are coaches, competition, and access to facilities and resources?

This book accesses what information we currently have to try to answer these questions, and it proposes new ways of answering them. The reader should be aware of several unique aspects to this book, in addition to a brief outline of some of the milestone publications in sport expertise research, which should help elucidate the material.

In the last 15 years, researchers have made tremendous advances in our understanding of sport expertise, yet no one has ever written a book dedicated to this topic. This one is the first. One of the earliest edited collections of readings to address both theoretical and applied aspects of cognition in sport was by Straub and Williams (1984). Although this book was limited in the work it presented on sport expertise, it nevertheless was the first to give license to an examination of cognitive issues in sport. This precedence in the literature was somewhat surprising since the cognitive perspective had enjoyed support within psychology for at least 10 years by that time.

The Straub and Williams publication was followed by three special issues of the *International Journal of Sport Psychology (IJSP)*, which were all devoted to sport expertise research. The first issue was edited by Ripoll (1991), and it presented an impressive and eclectic range of articles: visual search strategies of expert athletes, early work on perceptual training, work on anticipation and visually guided locomotion, work on decision accuracy and speed in ball games, attentional styles, as well as Ripoll's own work on semantic and sensorimotor visual processing. A second issue of *IJSP*, edited by Abernethy (1994), focused on expert-novice differences in sport, and it also examined the huge diversity of experimental approaches used to assess performance differences in experts. This issue also presented a comprehensive look at the key themes and issues in sport expertise research to date. A third special issue, edited by Tenenbaum (1999), examined the development of expertise in sport through a debate on the contributions of nature and nurture. This special issue outlined the cognitive components associated with expert decision making and how these components develop. A certain number of the articles focused on the nature of the knowledge base required for making expert decisions.

In 1994, a special edition of the journal *Quest*, edited by Housner and French, examined expertise in sport and other physical activity domains from the perspectives of learning, performance, teaching, and coaching. Many of the articles in this volume were practical in their approach, and they had value for athletes and coaches.

Along the way, several books have contributed substantially to our basic understanding of expertise. Perhaps the most influential of these books are the edited works by Ericsson and Smith (1991), *Toward a General Theory of Expertise: Prospects and Limits*, and by Ericsson (1996), *The Road to Excellence: The Acquisition of Expert Performance in the Arts and Sciences, Sports, and Games*. For both books, Anders Ericsson brought together a group of 12 researchers from around the world, all of whom were working on various research issues surrounding expertise. The goal was to discuss their findings and to propose future research strategies. These research roundtables (the first in Berlin, the second in Florida) were successful and in each case led to an edited book. Although the books include only a minimal amount of research on sport per se, they have been extremely influential in the theoretical directions that currently drive sport expertise research. In 1995, Ericsson was invited to craft a state-of-the-field article on expertise for *Annual Review of Psychology*. This request is significant because it was the first time *Annual Review*, which typically reviews the "hot" or influential topics in psychology, had covered the area of expertise. The result was Ericsson and Lehmann's (1996) excellent summary of what was known about expertise to that point. The article is a valuable reference for those who want a historical approach to the study of expertise and a view of the most up-to-date research to that time.

Another edited book by Starkes and Allard (1993) narrowed the field of expertise from the broader context followed by Ericsson. The focus of this book was *motor* expertise, and sport was only one form of motor expertise examined in this book, which included many other venues, such as surgery, speech production, and video game performance. This book was the first of its kind to take a motor-behaviorist perspective on expertise, but once again, it was highly cognitive in its view.

Although no real primer on the area of expertise exists that may be of benefit, the goal of this book is somewhat different. We assume that the readers of this book will have a certain familiarity with psychological principles and with expertise research in general, and we hope that this volume will provide an overview of the most current and critical issues facing those who pursue sport expertise research. This book is aimed at graduate students and researchers in motor behavior, psychology, and sport psychology, as well as high-level performers and coaches who seek to have a better understanding of the road to expertise. It also serves as a reference text for those involved in or contemplating doing research on sport expertise.

One impetus to the creation of this book was the World Congress of the International Society for Sport Psychology, held in Skiathos, Greece, in 2001. Ericsson and Starkes were keynote speakers at that conference, and they organized two symposia on expertise in sport. Most of the authors in this book attended that conference and gave research presentations. In all, the conference hosted three symposia on sport expertise, in addition to many poster presentations. It was the largest collection of research ever presented on the topic of expertise in sport, and we feel it reflects the growing interest in this area.

One unique aspect of this book is the Experts' Comments section that follows each chapter. So often, we read about research on a topic, but we never hear how those directly involved view this research. In a small way, this section serves as our attempt to bridge the gap between sport expertise research and those who may benefit most from it—athletes and coaches. For this book, two world-class experts have contributed their responses to each chapter: Nick Cipriano and Therese Brisson.

Professor Nick Cipriano is both an academic and an international-level wrestling coach. Cipriano is a former international-level wrestler and world-renowned coach in freestyle and Greco-Roman wrestling. He has been a national-level coach in Canada for over 25 years, and he has coached at three Olympics (Seoul, Barcelona, and Atlanta). He has published extensively on wrestling technique and coaching, and he wrote the technical manuals for all coaches in Canada, up to the national level. He continues to coach athletes, from those in high school to those on the Olympic team, both men and women.

Our second expert is Dr. Therese Brisson. Dr. Brisson's academic training is in motor behavior, but more relevant to this task, she is an Olympic gold medalist (Salt Lake City), silver medalist (Nagano), and six-time World Champion in ice hockey. We can think of no one else better to comment on the relevance of the research in this text than our two world-class sport experts, and we thank them for their willingness to share their views and experience with us.

Part II: Where Are We and How Did We Get There?

Part II of this book begins with a chapter by Janelle and Hillman (chapter 2), who provide a comprehensive overview of what is currently known with regard to sport expertise and its various technologies and research paradigms. This chapter provides a historical background for those who wish to better understand the development of research in this area. Janelle and Hillman outline various critical issues that have not yet been examined (but need to be) if we are to understand the relative contributions of say, for example, nature versus nurture, in the development of skill. One unique contribution of the chapter is the examination of the role of cortical activation and gaze behavior (through electrophysiological measurement) in elucidating the altered brain structure of experts. Traditionally, these data have not been considered in conjunction with more cognitive aspects in the discussion of expert performance.

Chapter 3 is by Ericsson, and it is an important chapter both for novices and current researchers. For those new to the area, Ericsson provides an extensive introduction to memory research. He explains how the results from early studies and from more recent work in chess and music have shaped his thinking regarding memory. Ericsson's chapter is specifically significant for researchers, however, in that it provides the next theoretical leap for research in this area. He further defines deliberate practice, but he also discusses two major points: He suggests reasons why recreational athletes may continue to compete but not improve, and he poses questions related to the role of coaches and mentors. Throughout our book, readers will note that Ericsson, Krampe, and Tesch-Römer's paper (1993) has significantly influenced most sport expertise research since its publication. In the 1993 paper, Ericsson and colleagues proposed that deliberate practice was the primary determinant of expert performance and that extended amounts of practice spur biological adaptations that in turn are conducive to further improvements in performance.

Part III: Developing and Retaining Sport Expertise

Part III of the book presents a series of seven chapters, the first five of which are related to the development of sport expertise in athletes, referees, and judges. These are followed by a chapter on the efficacy of perceptual training to potentially speed up the acquisition process (chapter 9; Williams & Ward) and a chapter that considers how easy or difficult it is for experts to retain high-performance levels as they age (chapter 10; Starkes, Weir, & Young).

Often, researchers who examine the acquisition of expertise pose questions in the hopes of better understanding the influence of age, the role of coaches, the distinction of what functions are best acquired at what times, as well as the absolute levels of expert performance attained on representative tasks. Such questions include the following:

- Is it better for aspiring young athletes to focus on one sport or to experience many sports before they concentrate their training on just one?
- Are procedural skills developed before, after, or in tandem with declarative skill? How are they best developed?
- How does one's motor skill development interact with the development of strategies and tactics in a sport?
- What aspects of performance best reflect expert behaviors in a particular sport: anticipation, perceptual accuracy, decision speed, attentional focus, response selection, response consistency, strategy, and so on.
- Do coaches, sport referees, and judges exhibit domain-specific expertise in the same way athletes do?
- Why is it that athletes seem to have all the time in the world to respond and don't seem to be limited by the speed of the game?

- Once an athlete reaches expert levels of performance, how difficult is it to stay there?
- How does an athlete maintain motivation over the 10-plus years or 10,000-plus hours of practice required to attain expert performance levels?

Because training and practice are so integral to the attainment of expertise, researchers often pose questions to better understand the amount, type, and quality of practice that most likely lead to success. Here we see research questions such as these:

- How do the best coaches teach, critique, support, and motivate athletes?
- How much and what combination of training techniques should athletes engage in for various sports?
- How much and what sort of training activities are best for Master athletes, who hope to retain their high levels of performance?

Finally, given that the road to expertise is a long and arduous one, some researchers have begun to question whether there are ways in which we can potentially speed up this process. These questions address such issues as the following:

- Can we improve perceptual accuracy or decision speed through the use of perceptual- and decision-training programs?
- How can we best assess the value of these training programs, and how do we determine whether the learning they impart transfers to real-world game situations?
- If perceptual- and decision-training programs are proven useful, then at what age can athletes potentially benefit from them? What skill levels could they enhance? What proportion of overall practice should be devoted to them?

In part III, Côté, Baker, and Abernethy (chapter 4) track the career development patterns of several national and professional-level athletes in a number of sports. They examine the social influences that affect the development of expert athletes, and they analyze how the role of parents changes from their children's grade school years to high school years (the "sampling" through "investment" years). Côté (Côté, 1999; Côté & Hay, 2002) has proposed elsewhere a developmental model of expertise in which young children progress through three stages in their athletic development from childhood through adolescence. From ages roughly 7 to 12 (the "sampling years"), they begin sampling a diversity of sports, and they engage in a great deal of deliberate play. From 13 to 15 years, they begin the "specializing years," in which they reduce the number of pursued sport activities and thus spend more time devoted to one sport. Côté et al. find in support of this model a rapid decrease in the number of varied sport activities from 13 years of age and on. During the "investment years" (from ages 15 to 17), athletes devote their practice time to one or sometimes two sports, and the amount of deliberate practice increases dramatically. By age 17, these athletes average three sports, two of which are pursued as either cross-training or relaxation with the remaining sport pursued as a serious endeavor. The nonexperts, however, never do specialize in one sport, and they never increase the amount of deliberate practice.

Deakin and Cobley (chapter 5) further question our preconceptions of the role of practice and of coaching. First, they present evidence that athletes are precisely aware of what it is they need to practice to take them to the next level. However, when one monitors the practices of the athletes who belong to the "what and how much" group, one sees that even skilled athletes spend a considerable amount of time practicing the skills they already do well. The researchers question whether all practice is "deliberate" and whether it actually spurs improvements in performance. In contrast, they provide in the second part of the chapter evidence that coaches do indeed structure practices to maximize active time and preparation for the next impending competition. Deakin and Cobley provide an excellent practical format for examining how the intentions of a coach in creating a practice format may be tracked throughout the practice. This chapter illustrates new and innovative ways for researchers to examine practice and its structure.

In chapter 6, McPherson and Kernodle extend previous work (McPherson, 2000), and like earlier research, they employ verbal protocol techniques, a method for which McPherson is well known and continues to be one of the only researchers in sport to use it. Verbal protocol analysis is time consuming and laborious; however, it has the potential to shed important information about strategies and tactics that are unobtainable by any other means. It is a paradigm rich in information, and McPherson and Kernodle show to best advantage how this technique can explain game strategies and tactics as used by expert tennis players. The authors examine the problem representations and resultant response selections of novice, intermediate, and advanced tennis players. Among their findings, they note that professional players had more extensive, varied, sophisticated, and associated tactical concepts for planning patterns of moves and for building and updating play conditions than did either intermediate players, female experts, or youth experts. Although such findings may not seem that surprising, they also found that while 95.5% of shot selections may be accurate for skilled players, only 65% of shots were actually executed as planned. They suggest that young experts do not diagnose ongoing conditions in a match and cannot analyze their own skills very well. As a result, "current event profiles," or the diagnosis and updating of tactics throughout the game, are actually the last cognitive skill attained in the development of expertise. The last section of the chapter is of particular interest to coaches and athletes. McPherson and Kernodle speculate that the role of the instructor is to build response-selection knowledge and to offer suggestions on how this may be accomplished.

Ste-Marie's chapter (chapter 7) is a departure from most other expertise research to date. Although we understand a great deal about the structure of expertise in athletes, we know very little about the structure of knowledge and expertise in coaches, referees, and judges. Ste-Marie's work focuses on referees in rugby and on judges in gymnastics. Elsewhere (Ste-Marie, 1999; Ste-Marie & Lee, 1991), she has demonstrated that gymnastics judges do exhibit characteristics of expertise in their recognition and recall of gymnastics moves and errors made in competition. In this chapter, she employs an information-processing analysis of performance, and she suggests that referees and judges (like athletes) are able to circumvent the normal information-processing limits through various means. This ability makes their performances appear to be unconstrained by the amount of information they must process and by the speed with which decisions must be made during competition. She presents several examples of ways in which this objective may be accomplished.

In chapter 8, Tenenbaum presents a new model to explain the nature of decision making in athletes. There are two novel aspects to this model. First, it is equally applicable to athletes who are in "closed" sports, such as gymnastics and swimming, and to those who are in traditionally "open" sports, such as basketball, handball, or soccer. Second, in most models of expert performance, the affective side, or emotional side, of sport is rarely considered. Tenenbaum's model includes a view of affective response and its role on the attentional capabilities of high-level athletes.

Having covered the process of developing expertise and the characteristics of expert performers, this part of the book now shifts to consider how one might potentially speed the acquisition of expert performance. Williams and Ward (chapter 9) provide an excellent review of articles in the literature that attempt to demonstrate how to train athletes to use perceptual and cognitive skills in sport. The chapter is complete in this regard, and it offers an up-to-date view of the literature on training skill. A unique aspect of the chapter is the data that are presented on the use of perceptual training in young soccer players. This part of the chapter is extremely valuable for those contemplating the use of perceptual-training programs. It demonstrates some of the difficulties in running intervention programs, but it also illustrates the potential gains that can be made through such training.

Part III ends with chapter 10, written by Starkes, Weir, and Young. Previously, Starkes and colleagues had examined performance changes and the effects of aging in Master runners (Starkes, Weir, Singh, Hodges, & Kerr, 1999) and swimmers (Weir, Kerr, Hodges, McKay, & Starkes, in press). In this chapter, the authors examine performance by Master athletes as a way of determining what losses experts may expect in performance simply as a result of aging versus a decrease in practice. They present data from swimming and running, and they suggest that the traditional view of performance loss with aging may be substantially moderated by continued practice. However, this is not simply a story of "use it or lose it." The authors then provide lifetime training data on two athletes who began running at an early age and have continued to train past middle age. Through these case studies, they demonstrate that performance may not only be retained in old age but may continue to improve, if in fact one's training level also increases or if precisely "what" is practiced is better tailored to how one competes. In sum, this is a good-news story for older expert athletes.

Part IV: Novel Ways of Examining the Characteristics of Expertise and Related Theories

Part IV of the book is devoted to novel ways of examining the characteristics of expertise that have not yet been used but have shed new light on the questions posed earlier. Chapter 11, by Salmela and Moraes, examines cross-cultural issues in the sports of soccer and rhythmic gymnastics. They suggest that models proposed for the development of expertise in developed countries do not hold up well if one considers the case of young soccer players in developing countries such as Brazil. In developing countries, young athletes simply do not have the advantages of skilled coaching, access to good facilities, equal competition, and so on. Nevertheless, playing soccer may capture a child's interest in a way that motivates the child to practice endlessly. Perhaps their devotion is fostered by the hope of future economic gains or travel. Whatever the source, one cannot dispute the fact that economically disadvantaged countries do produce excellent athletes, yet the athlete's developmental profile rarely fits the models proposed by academics in developed countries. Salmela and Moraes use several converging techniques to examine this issue, and they provide surprising data on the development of expertise in economically challenged countries.

In general, we tend to take for granted in the study of sport expertise that experts in sport are simply "better at doing things" in their sport than are novices or lesser-skilled counterparts. Motor skills are obviously more refined, but so is performance on any of the cognitive tasks typically used to assess expertise, such as recall of player/position, game information recognition, speed of decision making, anticipation, visual search patterns, and so on (for reviews, see Goulet, Bard, & Fleury, 1989; Helsen & Starkes, 1999; Jannelle & Hillman, chapter 2 of this book; Starkes, Helsen, & Jack, 2001). Throughout the literature on sport expertise, few (if any) cases exist where expert performers are actually at a disadvantage relative to their lesser-skilled peers.

In chapter 12, however, Beilock, Wierenga, and Carr present the first evidence of a disadvantage for skilled athletes. They first begin with a comprehensive review of memory research and the paradigms that are employed to date. Next, they describe a study where skilled golfers are asked to putt toward a goal. The golfers are then asked to recall the procedures they employed to do so. What is interesting is that they cannot verbalize how they did it. They are able to provide either prescriptive information about what they need to do on the next shot or diagnostic feedback on what went wrong with the last shot, but they are not able to outline the actual procedural steps they took to make the previous shot. On the other hand, novices (in this case, those who have never played golf) are better at explaining their actions. What makes for an intriguing additional finding is that when a novel "S-shaped and weighted" putter is employed, experts once again regain the ability to provide procedural details. This factor suggests that the thousands and thousands of practice trials that go into the procedural learning of a motor skill eventually create an automatic procedural state, such that the details of procedures are no longer immediately accessible. This finding could potentially lead the way to a "metric for motor expertise." Presumably, the more skilled a movement becomes, the less accessible the information is about the underlying procedures. Perhaps in the future, the extent of "expertise induced amnesia" for procedures seen in experts may become a measure of automation in a motor skill.

In chapter 13, Beek, Jacobs, Daffertshofer, and Huys suggest that our view of sport expertise to date has been limited by the theoretical perspectives chosen to examine it. What has traditionally driven this research is either information processing or cognitive perspectives. The authors suggest, however, that the joint perspectives of ecological psychology and dynamical systems theory can offer new insights into the study of sport and movement skill. In the past, ecological psychology and dynamical systems have been criticized because of the difficulties the researchers have had in experimentally manipulating the variables to test such factors or even demonstrate their existence. One strength of the Beek et al. chapter is the sheer number of practical sport examples they provide that illustrate the principles espoused in both ecological psychology and dynamical systems theory.

Part V: The Great Debate: Is a General Theory of Expert Performance Achievable?

The final two chapters are an absolute must-read for anyone engaged in expertise research. In sport research, there is a division of thought about the potential value and attainability of a general theory of expertise that could accommodate the findings within sport expertise research. The different views of these two chapters represent the best scientific debate on this issue. Chapter 14, by Abernethy, Farrow, and Berry, takes a critical look at the expert-performance approach (Ericsson & Smith, 1991) and theory of deliberate practice (Ericsson, Krampe, & Tesch-Römer, 1993). They suggest that the approaches may not be able to handle the unique issues created in sport by the fact that one's response is always movement-based and temporally constrained. Although most of this book is cognitively oriented, the chapter by Abernethy et al. reminds us of several motor-learning principles. It also soberly reminds us about the complexities of creating a theory of expertise that encompasses not just the cognitive advantages and disadvantages afforded to high-level athletes, but the consequences of their skilled movement as well. The chapter brings us solidly back into the realm of motor control and motor learning as the basis of high-level performance. In the end, Abernethy et al. suggest the following: Because sport experts must engage in movement responses within strict temporal constraints and because they must also deal with the effects of physiological fatigue, any potential general theory of expertise must fully engage elements of motor control theory to be applicable to sport. For this reason, they are skeptical that a generalized theory of expertise is feasible. Along the way, they offer a spirited critique of the expert-performance approach that has to date influenced much of the sport expertise literature.

Part of the value of this book is the lively debate it encourages. This spirit of discussion is highlighted in chapter 15, Ericsson's rebuttal to Abernethy, Farrow, and Berry's argument of chapter 14. Ericsson acknowledges that the authors' assumptions may be widespread among researchers of motor control; therefore, he welcomes the opportunity to clarify his views on the expert-performance approach. He discusses how many of Abernethy's criticisms may be more correctly attributed to the general theory of expertise (Simon & Chase, 1973) and the human information-processing theory (Newell & Simon, 1972). He notes that the expert-performance approach (Ericsson & Smith, 1991) was actually developed to deal with many of the issues raised by the earlier and more general theories. The main point, however, that Ericsson focuses on is how the expert-performance approach, as he interprets it, differs from either traditional laboratory studies (that test general hypotheses about basic processes) or descriptive studies (that attempt to elicit basic processes by designed tasks in the laboratory). He then describes how the expert-performance approach makes a firm commitment to the study of complex behavioral phenomena and how these phenomena can be reproduced and analyzed under controlled conditions. Ericsson's clarifications on these issues are not found anywhere else in the literature, and they make fascinating and necessary reading for anyone involved in sport expertise research.

The book concludes with a brief epilogue, and we hope very much that you enjoy this volume. We feel that the book is an unprecedented resource and reference text, and that it provides a glimpse of future directions over the next 10 years for research on sport expertise.

Part II
Where Are We and How Did We Get There?

TO UNDERSTAND HOW our current knowledge of sport expertise evolved, we need to trace the historical routes of the study of expertise. Janelle and Hillman (chapter 2) take us on a journey to discover what is unique about expert athletes, and along the way, they introduce some of the more controversial recent issues related to the acquisition and training of skill. They provide the necessary background to understand existing findings, discuss some of the age-old dilemmas (such as the role of nature versus nurture), and bring us into the current realm. They point us toward the future by questioning what the rapidly expanding field of genetics may show with regard to talent. They also broaden our perspective of sport expertise by speculating on the role of motivation and emotion in sport. This chapter is an excellent primer to our volume, and it presents some new challenges for research in sport.

No one has influenced the current direction of expertise research more than Anders Ericsson. In chapter 3, he clarifies many of his terms and thoughts regarding the expert-performance approach (Ericsson & Smith, 1991) and the model of deliberate practice (Ericsson, Krampe, and Tesch-Römer, 1993). This chapter represents the next theoretical update in the literature: He speculates on why recreational athletes plateau in skill, and he provides more extensive analyses of what might constitute deliberate practice.

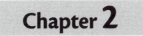

Chapter **2**

Expert Performance in Sport

■ ■ ■ ■ ■

Current Perspectives and Critical Issues

Christopher M. Janelle
Charles H. Hillman

False facts are highly injurious to the progress of science, for they often endure long; but false views, if supported by some evidence, do little harm, for every one takes a salutary pleasure in proving their falseness: and when this is done, one path towards error is closed and the road to truth is often at the same time opened.

—Charles Darwin, *The Descent of Man,* pp. 368-369

Though an avid hunter and occasional billiards player, Darwin likely did not place much emphasis on the development of sporting expertise when composing *On the Origin of Species* or *The Descent of Man.* However, the topic of expert sport performance has provided a fruitful battleground for the exchange of ideas and continued scientific advancement toward understanding the inherited and developed assets of superior athletes. On even casual consideration of the modern climate of athletic competition, it becomes readily obvious that Darwinian notions (survival of the fittest and species adaptation) are well represented in the microcosm of sport. In recent years, researchers have begun to unravel the mysteries of expertise. They have done so with increased attention on what it takes athletes to be the best, and they have done so despite (or maybe because of) diametrically opposed views that concern the development of superior achievement.

Expert athletes embody perhaps the most visible of all expert performers. They attract immense followings, enormous media attention, and the mutual admiration of coaches, fellow competitors, and teammates. This visibility is perhaps best exemplified by the fact that the most popular national and world events tend to surround sport competitions. The Olympic Games, the Super Bowl, Formula One racing events, the World Series of baseball, and World Cup soccer (among others) each provide examples of the massive popularity of sport and the immense opportunity to view expertise in action. However, despite being routinely observed, sport expertise is extremely difficult to characterize with a succinct list of requisite aptitudes. As such, the factors that predispose, describe, and lead to the emergence of the fittest athletes (in the Darwinian sense) remain largely unspecified, especially from a scientific standpoint.

Accounting for the qualities of the expert athlete necessitates a perspective that encompasses the inherent nature of sport as being diverse in task requirements and proficiencies. For example, to identify the common characteristics of expertise between an NFL quarterback and one of his offensive linemen could prove as futile as delineating the shared qualities of expertise between that offensive lineman and the conductor of the Boston Pops. In this chapter, we acknowledge such limitations, so we therefore identify and expound the generalizations made about experts in a variety of domains. We then present a discussion on the current state of theoretical development both in the general study of expertise as well as sport. Afterward, we examine sport-specific findings from several studies of expertise that were completed via a variety of tasks and simulations, and we also provide a synthesis of the existing expertise literature. Last, we make recommendations for specific research directions, which will provide systematic advancement in theory as well as applications for the selection and training of athletes.

Introduction to the Domains of Sport Expertise

Expert performance in sport can be defined as the consistent superior athletic performance over an extended period (Starkes, 1993). To obtain expert status, athletes must excel in no less than four domains: physiological, technical, cognitive (tactical/strategic; perceptual/decision-making), and emotional (regulation/coping; pyschological).

Expert Physiology

Physiological components of expertise include factors such as anaerobic power and aerobic capacity, muscle fiber type and distribution, body morphology and body segment size, height, flexibility, and general aesthetics (Wilmore & Costill, 1999). The physiological aspect of performance is unique to sport, whereas in other domains, it is typically of no concern. Physiological superiority has no real relevance in other expertise settings such as chess, music, electronics, mathematics, and computer programming. Likewise, the specific physiological necessities for expert achievement in various sports are as wide and varied as the sports themselves, and the distinctions can even be found among sports that require similar skill. For example, the physiological requirements for expertise in sprinting are quite different than those needed in a related movement pattern such as distance running.

Ample evidence exists to suggest that factors such as body morphology and muscle fiber type are malleable through extended practice and systematic training (e.g., Wilmore & Costill, 1999). However, sport and exercise physiologists agree that the degree of adaptability is indeed restricted and that the limits imposed are primarily genetically determined (e.g., Bouchard, Dionne, Simoneau, & Boulay, 1992; Bouchard, Malina, & Pérusse, 1997; Klissouras, 1997; Swallow, Garland, Carter, Zhan, & Sieck, 1998). As such, hereditary predispositions to physiological characteristics appear to be significant limiting factors to the overall level of expertise that may be acquired in sport. Although the research acknowledges the heritability of advantageous predispositions for certain sports, empirical documentation regarding the role of heredity as related to expertise is limited (e.g., Reilly, Bangsbo, & Franks, 2000). Given that this chapter is psychologically oriented, we will not give any additional attention to expert physiology, aside from a discussion of how it relates to other domains of expertise.

Technical Expertise

Technical expertise refers to the degree of sensorimotor coordination from which refined, efficient, and effective movement patterns emerge. Technical measures of technique and sport-skills tests include quantitative analysis, which includes assessment of the kinematics and kinetics of movement patterns. Qualitative indexes of technical expertise, such as artistic impression and aesthetic value, can be evaluated as well. In several sports, the technical aspects of the skill dictate the overall level of expertise, such as in gymnastics and figure skating, while in others they merely contribute to the overall quality of the movement.

Regarding the development of technical expertise, ample evidence exists to suggest that coordinated, refined, and efficient movement patterns emerge largely as a function of years of extended and systematic training, or deliberate practice (e.g., Ericsson & Lehman, 1996; Helsen Starkes, & Hodges, 1998; Starkes, 1993, 2000; Starkes, Deakin, Allard, Hodges, & Hayes, 1996). Over time, learners acquire skilled movement patterns that are less errant and more efficient, and the movements are performed with a high level of automaticity (e.g., Fitts & Posner, 1967; Logan, 1988; Schneider & Shiffrin, 1977; Singer, 2001).

Cognitive Expertise

Cognitive expertise can be broken down into two subdomains: tactical skills and decision-making abilities. The former comprises an athlete's global approach to a particular sport; the latter focuses more on an athlete's ability to make in-the-moment decisions.

Tactical and Strategic Knowledge

Tactical expertise is requisite for expert performance in virtually all achievement domains. Sport is unique, however, in that tactical knowledge involves not only the ability to determine what strategy is most appropriate in a given situation, but also whether the strategy can be successfully executed within the constraints of the required movements (e.g., McPherson, 1994; Starkes, 1993). Thus, tactical expertise in sport is quite different than nonmotor performance domains in that physiological and technical limitations constrain the strategic options available to sport performers.

Emanating from cognitive frameworks of information processing, the primary research methods employed to determine tactical expertise have been verbal protocol analysis and behavioral observation in practice and competitive sport settings (French & McPherson, 1999; French, Spurgeon, & Nevett, 1995; McPherson, 1993, 1994, 1999; McPherson & French, 1991). Through the collective study of the characteristics of expert memory, researchers have gleaned much information about the mechanisms of expert working memory, both short term and long term, as well as the organization of relevant domain-specific knowledge and retrieval processes.

Perceptual and Decision-Making Skill

Regardless of whether one is involved in self-paced or externally paced sport skills, expert athletes are capable of attending to and extracting the most relevant cues in the sport environment and can avoid attending to distracting or irrelevant cues. Perceptual skills include pattern recognition, the use and extraction of anticipatory cues, visual search strategies, and signal detection. Decision-making speed and accuracy is then based largely on the interpretive value of information acquired through perceptual skills and its appropriateness for effective response selection. Given the spectrum of literature in the mainstream sport expertise area, this domain has garnered the lion's share of research to date. Consequently, researchers can make several conclusions from this aggregate body of research with a significant degree of confidence. As will be presented later, the majority of research efforts in the perceptual and decision-making domain have indicated reliable differences between expert and nonexpert performers.

Emotional Expertise

Emotional expertise is divided into two arenas: emotional regulation and psychological skills. Emotional regulation involves exactly what it implies: an athlete's ability to monitor and exert some control over emotion. Psychological skills, however, include a broader range of factors, all of which may influence emotional readiness.

Emotional Regulation and Coping Strategies

When considering the sport context, even over the course of a single competition, one soon realizes that the gamut of possible emotions can be typically exhausted—from the elation and joy after a big play to the sadness, disappointment, and embarrassment that follow a poor performance. Emotions, and the capability to regulate them effectively, arguably account for a large portion of the variance in athletic performance. Despite the intuitive observation that sport is inherently emotional, a scientific understanding of the emotions of sport experts is virtually nonexistent. Studies of affective characteristics among elite performers tend to be largely descriptive and susceptible to self-report confounds. In addition, they typically do not involve comparisons to nonexpert samples. Needless to say, this domain of expertise warrants extensive future research.

Psychological Skills

In addition to acquiring the requisite skills as described in the aforementioned domains of expertise, the development of psychological skills is critical to expert performance. Psychological skills refer to performance-related determinants of expertise that include attributes such as motivation and goal-setting strategies; confidence-building and maintenance of a positive attitude; imagery and mental training; coachability considerations; and interpersonal skills. Relative to the large body of work that has been done on strategic and perceptual/decision-making aspects of expertise, few studies of these social-cognitive determinants of expert performance have been conducted, especially ones that compare experts and novices. In fact, rarely are these terms even mentioned in the reviews of expertise literature, aside from the references to the lack of research that describe how experts develop such skills.

Interactive Determinants of Expertise

When considering the various domains of expertise that must be achieved by today's elite athlete, one realizes that any weakness in one of them will significantly impede the athlete's capability to perform at the highest level. Expertise in one domain, however, can either facilitate or hinder the attainment of expertise in others. For example, social-cognitive factors such as motivation may largely influence the expression of the physiological characteristics deemed necessary for success in sport. That is, athletes who are highly motivated are more inclined to direct their efforts to the systematic physical training programs that will influence their physical and psychomotor capabilities. Likewise, the athletes' development of cognitive-behavioral skills enable them to achieve optimal performance. For instance, self-regulation through exposure to competitive challenges enables elite athletes to regulate emotional function and metacognitive strategies. Such skills also may be genetically influenced. Figure 2.1 represents a schematic representation that depicts the interactive nature of the domains of expertise.

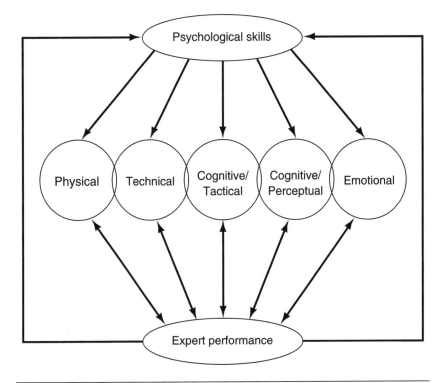

Figure 2.1   The domains of expertise in sport. Psychological skills influence the athlete's capability to perform components of each domain, with proficiencies in each domain interacting to dictate the overall level of sport expertise. The athlete's relative level of expertise suggests future alterations in psychological skill and preparation for sport participation, as well as specific improvements in each expertise domain.

Athletes associated with sport may find these introductory remarks intuitively obvious. As will become increasingly clear, however, the scientific study of sport expertise to date has been largely restrictive in attempts to describe and account for expertise phenomena. More specifically, the interactive effects of the components of sporting expertise have been neglected in favor of focusing on detached, independent, and solitary determinants of expertise, often in contrived settings. Similarly, mechanistic explanations of why and how these phenomena occur remain underdeveloped. Given the relatively recent emergence of expertise as a topic of scientific inquiry and its roots in cognitive psychology, the narrow scope of expertise research to date is understandable. However, the absence of a viable and inclusive theory to truly advance expertise research in a systematic manner has been prohibitive in this regard. In spite of this realization, researchers have made admirable efforts to provide a conceptual framework for the study of expertise, with an eye toward theory development and advancement of science in this intriguing area of study.

The Scientific Study of Experts

One might contend that arriving at a consensus among researchers, or at least a partial agreement on the nature of expertise, is not worth pursuing scientifically (Sternberg, 1996, 1998). Given the negative connotations that typically confront sport science scholars, the scientific study of sport expertise may be regarded with even less fanfare. However, our position is that the continued pursuit of knowledge regarding expertise is important for several philosophical, theoretical, practical, and ethical reasons. Perceptions of accomplishment, failure, and success are some of the most salient pieces of information on which people rely for a sense of self-worth, and such information is significantly shaped by the degree to which individuals perceive that they control their own destiny. Likewise, how and to whom training is structured may depend greatly on the existence of varying levels of perceived talent, work ethic, motivation, and cognitive or motor deficits (Detterman, Gabriel, & Ruthsatz, 1998).

Theoretical Foundations for the Study of Expertise

In explaining how experts in sport and other domains are capable of performing with remarkable levels of consistency and quality in their movements, theorists have attempted to describe the means by which expertise is achieved. They have attempted to do so primarily through orientations that would favor either a predominantly genetic perspective (talent and nature) or an environmental perspective (practice and nurture). At one end of the continuum, innate giftedness and talent would completely account for expert performance. The alternative viewpoint purports that expertise arises from (and is limited by) the accumulated duration of systematic training, regardless of any hereditary giftedness. Less restrictive than the former views is the notion that expertise arises as a consequence of some combination of both variables; that is, athletes arrive at expertise via both genetic and environmental interactions.

Considering contemporary literature, one would appear simplistic to attribute all variability in levels of expertise to innate talent. As would be expected, virtually no one adheres to this notion (Sternberg, 1998). Appearing equally radical is the suggestion that the opposite end of the continuum is exclusively the most viable theoretical account for the acquisition of expertise. Despite its counterintuitive nature, the latter alternative has been strongly advanced by prominent researchers (for a recent review, see Howe, Davidson, & Sloboda, 1998). At the crux of this approach is the notion that expertise is obtainable by virtually anyone and that expert performance, irrespective of innate "talent," will inevitably emerge through an extended period of "deliberate practice," typically either 10 years or 10,000 hours (Ericsson, Krampe, & Tesch-Römer, 1993).

The greatest opposition to this extreme "nurturist" perspective (and admittedly not on the opposite end of the continuum) has been presented by those who acknowledge the role of deliberate practice (or systematic training) and other environmental influences in achieving expertise; however, they recommend that innate hereditary factors impose influences on and limits to the level of acquirable expertise. This approach might best be described as an "interactionist" approach. Thus, recognizing that the strict "naturist" perspective has been all but abandoned, it appears that there are currently two prominent views that explain expertise, with each acknowledging the substantial role of practice.

The Common Denominator: Practice

Emerging from the "expertise approach" to determining what differentiates expert and nonexpert performers in their respective domains of excellence, a convincing corpus of evidence has been gathered to suggest that regardless of innate talent, hereditary predispositions, and genetic limitations, high levels of skill cannot be acquired without years of dedicated practice. Expert athletes progress toward excellence in much the same way as expert musicians (e.g., Lehmann, 1997; Sloboda & Howe, 1991), chess players (Charness, 1992; Charness, Krampe, & Mayr, 1996; Gobet & Simon, 1996, 1998), and scholars (cf. Simonton, 1999, 2000). Evidence suggests that experts adhere to a strict regimen of extended practice that is not necessarily coach developed. Such practice is characterized by structured activities that require effort and concentration, that do not immediately lead to financial or other extrinsic rewards, and that are not inherently enjoyable (Ericsson, Krampe, & Tesch-Römer, 1993; Starkes, 2000; Starkes, Helsen, & Jack, 2001). These general characteristics of deliberate practice have minor exceptions to their basic tenets, most notably that many components of deliberate practice are deemed by athletes as enjoyable (cf. Hodges & Starkes, 1996). However, the majority of findings have indicated that elite athletes in a variety of sport activities do practice, and they deliberately practice, more so than their relative nonexpert counterparts. As such, the importance of deliberate practice, as outlined by Ericsson and colleagues (1993), is generally agreed on.

Most would agree that although compelling and accurate, the finding that "those who practice more get better" is somewhat obvious. Driving this concern is the fact that knowing how much to practice really tells one very little about why people get better at what they do. What comes to mind is a phrase still popular among coaches and teachers, "practice makes perfect." The more recent adage, "perfect practice makes perfect," carries with it the underlying assumption that practicing incorrectly, or going through the motions, does not lead to gains in achievement. The notions of deliberate practice certainly capture the general idea that practice must be conducted structurally, systematically, and done effortfully and often. However, meaningful advances in expertise research must move beyond evaluation of how much practice is necessary and must move forward to understanding the *what* and the *how* of practice (e.g., Davids, 2000; Durand-Bush & Salmela, 2001; Singer & Janelle, 1999; Starkes, 1993; 2001). In other words, researchers need to be able to provide practical, real-world recommendations to aspiring expert athletes.

The Expertise Approach

As popularized by Ericsson and Smith (1991) and adapted and structured from the landmark work of Chase and Simon (1973a, 1973b) with chess experts, the expertise approach has been the primary driving force behind much of the research conducted in the area of expertise over the past two decades. Ericsson and Smith argue that the scientific identification of expert characteristics could be accomplished through a three-step process. The first step is for researchers to identify reproducible and superior task performances in the laboratory setting using representative tasks. Second, they must compile an index of data that reflect the cognitive processes that underlie superior performance and allow it to occur. During this second step, researchers may have to manipulate the environmental conditions under which expert performance is maintained so that they may identify critical differences as a result of task variations. As such, they may be able to uncover the mechanisms that govern and regulate experts' ability to demonstrate consistent high achievement. During the third step, the researchers provide explanations to account for how the mechanisms identified in the second step were acquired. By following this three-step process, it was implied that researchers could advance "toward a general theory of expertise" (Ericsson & Smith, 1991).

The expertise approach is favored by Ericsson and Smith (1991) when compared with other plausible methods for the investigation of outstanding performance (see table 2.1). On examination of table 2.1, however, we should point out the notable absence of "the primarily inherited and acquired" category, which thereby neglects a potentially viable alternative account for expertise. As such, the expertise approach has been criticized as being biased toward the detection and description of environmental influences on expert performance (e.g., Heller & Ziegler, 1998; Rowe, 1998).

■ Table 2.1
Different Approaches to Accounting for Outstanding Performance

Attribution	Construct	Research approach
Primarily inherited General abilities	Intelligence, personality	Correlation with personality profile, general intelligence
Specific abilities	Musical ability, artistic ability, bodybuilding	Correlation with measures of specific ability
Primarily acquired General learning and experience	General knowledge and cognitive strategies	Investigation of common processing strategies
Domain-specific training and practice	Domain- or task-specific knowledge	Analysis of task performance, that is the expertise approach

Reprinted from K. A. Ericsson, J. Smith, 1991, Prospects and limits of the empirical study of expertise: An introduction. In *Toward a general theory of expertise: Prospects and limits* (Cambridge, UK: Cambridge University Press). Reprinted with the permission of Cambridge University Press.

By favoring the expertise approach, researchers must recognize that the skills identified as task-specific and acquired are inherently the product of genetic and environmental interactions, which are undoubtedly embodied in any sample of experts. Acknowledging a genetic component, even among what appear to be clearly environmental influences on expert performance, the expertise approach has been invaluable in guiding the identification of expert characteristics in a variety of domains, not the least of which has been sport.

Sport-Specific Expertise As Developed Through Practice

With slight departures from Ericsson and Smith (1991), the expertise approach in its many forms has served as a source of guidance for the current literature that has been conducted to clarify the nature of expert performance and skill acquisition in sport. With few exceptions, expert-novice differences have been consistently identified in a number of skills and abilities. Findings from these areas are briefly summarized as follows.

Pattern Recognition, Memory, and Tactical Skills

The topic of memory has been the centerpiece of much of the expertise research to date. In chess, for example, domain-specific expert memory has consistently been shown to be superior to that of relative nonexperts, and the expert advantage is especially pronounced in structured situations. These findings have been replicated in a variety of sport domains, specifically when expert athletes have been confronted with structured game situations and plays. In sports as diverse as baseball (McPherson, 1993), volleyball (Allard & Starkes, 1980), soccer (Helsen & Pauwels, 1993; Williams, Davids, Burwitz, & Williams, 1993), and figure skating (Deakin, 1987; Deakin & Allard, 1992), athletes have demonstrated reliable advantages in recognition, recall, and retention in comparison to relatively nonexpert counterparts. Likewise, their attainment of an expert advantage in these types of tasks appears to be due to direct and repeated training in the task environment; that is, it is not acquirable solely from observational learning of the specific event (Allard, Deakin, Parker, & Rodgers, 1993; Williams & Davids, 1995).

Regarding the tactical or strategic requirements for expertise in sport, the work of McPherson (1993, 1994, 1999, 2000) and the work of French and colleagues (French, Spurgeon, & Nevett, 1995; French & Thomas, 1987) have largely confirmed the existence of an extensive declarative and procedural knowledge base. From this base, expert athletes are capable of extracting the most appropriate responses to meet specific environmental demands. It is a repertoire of facts and procedures from which expert athletes form tactical strategies and therefore increase the effectiveness of their decision making. Additionally, this knowledge base appears to be acquired over a substantial period of deliberate practice.

Knowing "what to do" and "how to do it" reflects the specific and unique demands of sport. The development of response execution and coordination proficiencies is critical in sport settings but is minimally important in other activities, such as chess. As such, the capability to execute a skill influences the tendency to rely on the skill as a tactical option in game situations. French et al. (1996) demonstrated that youth baseball participants will not choose an action as a response possibility when a particular skill cannot be physically executed. The implications of this finding cannot be overestimated when one considers the unique nature of sport expertise. The particular constraints imposed on developing experts are not completely attributable to psychomotor or cognitive input, but instead, they are limited by developmental, technical, and physiological factors.

Anticipatory Behaviors and Visual Search Strategies

Another primary area of interest to sport psychology researchers is the identification of expert-novice differences in the use and extraction of pertinent information for the purpose of anticipation. Researchers have used an array of methods to determine what information experts attend to and how they process it in advance so that they can execute the apparently effortless responses in situations that demand high precision, under restrictive time constraints and uncertain stimulus properties. Of these methods, the most popular have been occlusion paradigms, eye-movement registration techniques, and the manipulation of mental chronometry through the use of cost-benefit paradigms.

Early research by Abernethy and colleagues (e.g., Abernethy & Russell, 1987a, 1987b) examined how temporal and spatial occlusion of various cues affected the anticipation abilities of expert and novice badminton players. Temporal occlusion techniques indicated that expert players were more capable of using information presented earlier in the visual display than were novices. These studies also demonstrated that prediction accuracy was adversely affected for experts when critical aspects of the scene were spatially occluded, an effect not noticed for novices. Presumably, novices were less attuned to arm and racket orientations, which would have granted them prediction information. These findings were replicated with squash players (Abernethy, 1990). The pioneering work of Abernethy and colleagues, as well as earlier attempts (Isaacs & Finch, 1983; C.M. Jones & Miles, 1978), provided the foundation for further work in this area and highlighted the superior cue-extraction and utilization capabilities of expert performers in reactive settings.

Regarding eye-tracking studies, the results obtained are generally consistent with occlusion findings, despite occasional assertions to the contrary (e.g., Abernethy, 1990). The studies indicate a superior attunement to critical environmental cues among expert performers, as implied from their search patterns. Within the broad range of sport applications in which eye movements have been recorded, reliable differences have been identified between expert and novice athletes in both self-paced and externally paced tasks in fixation location, fixation duration, search order, and search rate. Generally, experts consistently demonstrate more efficient search strategies in laboratory simulations and real-world applications of eye-movement recordings. They fixate longer and more often on the most relevant cues in a given display, and they exhibit fixation patterns that maximize the capability to extract information from peripheral visual sources. These differences have emerged in a number of reactive sports (e.g., Goulet, Bard, & Fleury, 1989; Helsen & Pauwels, 1990, 1993; Ripoll & Fleurance, 1985; Shank & Haywood, 1987; Singer, Cauraugh, Chen, Steinberg, & Frehlich, 1996; Singer et al., 1998; Williams, Davids, Burwitz, & Williams, 1994). If one assumes a high degree of coupling between fixation location and cue utilization, then experts appear to be capable of extracting information from foveal and ambient visual fields to respond quickly and appropriately.

Expert-novice differences in search patterns have been identified and documented in self-paced tasks as well. Perhaps the first study to demonstrate these differences was published by Vickers (1992) who documented expertise differences in the performance of the golf putt. Later research focused on the "quiet eye period," a duration of time needed for accurate programming of motor responses. The quiet eye period takes place between the last fixation of a target and the initiation of the motor response (Vickers, 1996a). Reliable expert-novice differences in quiet eye period have been revealed in an increasing number of sports, such as basketball free-throw shooting (Vickers, 1996a, 1996b), small bore rifle shooting (Janelle et al., 2000; Janelle, Hillman, & Hatfield, 2000), and biathlon (Vickers, Williams, Rodrigues, Hillis, & Coyne, 1999). The consistent finding is that experts maintain a longer quiet eye period before the initiation of movement.

Recently, researchers have looked toward multimethod assessment of attentional allocation, perceptual processing, and information extraction. Efforts have therefore been made to determine whether occlusion paradigms, verbal report, and eye-tracking indexes mutually correspond. For example, Williams and Davids (1997, 1998) have studied the eye movements of expert and novice soccer players as compared to verbal report and occlusion data in 1-on-1, 3-on-3, and 11-on-11 soccer situations. Though largely congruent, the researchers noticed that eye-movement indexes of the most important information-gathering areas of the display were different than those that appeared more informative using occlusion techniques. Likewise, verbal reports were occasionally decoupled from eye-movement indications of attentional allocation. These differences were more pronounced for expert soccer players than for relative nonexperts. Therefore, researchers may benefit significantly by comprehensively describing expert attentional processing through the involvement of multiple assessment modes of data collection.

In addition to using eye-tracking systems and occlusion paradigms to infer attentional allocation, researchers can evaluate the orienting of attention and the potential costs and benefits through anticipation via the manipulation of expectations and conditional probabilities. A person's capability to switch attention from one source of information to another, in spite of preconceived probabilities and attentional biases, defines the "attentionally flexible" performer (Nougier & Rossi, 1999). Through variations of the classic cost-benefit paradigm (Posner, 1980), an expert advantage with regard to attentional flexibility has been documented (e.g., Nougier, Azemar, Stein, & Ripoll, 1992; Nougier, Ripoll, & Stein, 1989; Nougier & Rossi, 1999; Rossi & Zani, 1991; Tenenbaum, Stewart, & Sheath, 1999; Zani & Rossi, 1990). Experts are more resilient to incorrect a priori expectations and can therefore override dysfunctional automatic orienting processes more efficiently than can nonexperts.

In addition to the typical reaction time measures that are employed in this line of research, researchers can record event-related cortical potentials (ERPs) as an index of attentional processing. Intriguing work by Rossi and Zani (1991; Zani & Rossi, 1990) has demonstrated the specificity of expertise by showing that experts and novices process the same environmental stimuli differently. They compared expert trap shooters with expert skeet shooters. Trap shooting is a sport in which the stimulus characteristics are unpredictable, and skeet shooting has stimulus characteristics that are much more predictable. The two types of shooters differentially processed auditory signals in line with the domain-specific training to which they had been exposed in their particular sports. More specifically, trap shooters allocated increased attentional resources to the earlier, stimulus-driven stages of processing whereas skeet shooters used a more memory-driven mode of processing. Other ERP studies have demonstrated reliable differences between experts and relative novices in volleyball (Pesce Anzeneder & Bosel, in press) and in baseball (Radlo, Janelle, Barba, & Frehlich, 2001). These findings suggest a comparative ease by which experts are capable of minimizing attentional/anticipatory costs and thus maximizing benefits so as to improve performance. Psychophysiological performance profiling has been an increasing focus of several other research areas, and it is discussed in the next section.

The Psychophysiology of Expert Performance

During the past two decades, electroencephalography (EEG), as well as other psychophysiological measures (e.g., heart rate), have been used to identify differences between experts and novices during sport performance (for a recent review, see Hatfield & Hillman, 2001). The essential contributions of this work have been in the descriptive identification of the psychophysiological correlates of experts in sport and the comparative differences with those at lesser skill levels. A distinct advantage of the psychophysiological approach to understanding expertise lies in its capability to evaluate ongoing aspects of cognition, attention, and emotion in real time.

Much of the research that has examined skill-based differences in sport has come from the psychophysiological study of marksmen. From a psychophysiological perspective, marksmen provide an ideal sample in which to study expertise. Real-time data can be covertly collected in the absence of bioelectrical signal artifact as a result of movement, which typically prohibits this sort of data collection in other sports. Further, because these experts are highly attentive and visually focused during performance, they provide insight into the associated cortical mechanisms involved in this type of expertise behavior.

Initially, intrasubject hemispheric EEG differences were observed in elite marksmen during the preparatory period before shot execution (Hatfield, Landers, & Ray, 1984). Observed differences indicated that elite marksmen progressively relaxed the left hemisphere of their cortex before shot execution as measured by increased alpha power, which has been associated with one's verbal-analytic processes. The effect was not observed in the right hemisphere, which has been associated with one's visual-spatial processes. These two findings strongly suggest that these processes are germane to superior performance in marksmanship. This asymmetric pattern of alpha power observed during performance has been found to be quite robust, and it has been replicated in numerous other studies with marksmen (e.g., Hillman, Apparies, Janelle, & Hatfield, 2000;

Janelle et al., 2000) as well as in other sports (Crews & Landers, 1993; Landers et al., 1994).

In comparison with elite marksmen, research has also incorporated those with lesser skill levels to better understand underlying differences that accompany skill acquisition (Haufler, Spalding, Santa-Maria, & Hatfield, 2000; Janelle et al., 2000; Landers et al., 1994). Although these studies have utilized participants at various skill levels, researchers have arrived at consistent findings. Specifically, asymmetric EEG differences between the two cerebral hemispheres have not been observed to the same degree that is exhibited in elite marksmen, even after lesser skilled subjects have been trained for some period (Janelle et al., 2000; Landers et al., 1994). Interpretation of differences in hemispheric alpha asymmetry between elite and lesser skilled marksmen can be accounted for by two related phenomena: one, the efficient allocation of relevant neural resources that accompany expertise, and two, decreased performance states. As such, expertise in marksmanship is not only accompanied by the relative increased allocation of relevant neural resources (the right hemisphere), but also by the quieting of irrelevant resources (the left hemisphere).

Extending the concept of neural resource allocation during skilled performance, Hillman and his colleagues (2000) found intraexpert differences in alpha power during shot execution and rejection. Specifically, expert marksmen showed global increases in alpha power before their decision to reject a shot (when they pull away from the target without firing a shot) compared to the time just before shot execution. This finding suggests that a certain degree of relaxation (alpha power) is necessary during performance; after which, too much cortical relaxation may relate to performance decrements. Further, alpha power was found to increase progressively to the point of rejection, a finding not observed during shot execution. These data again speak to the adaptive nature of neural resource allocation during sport performance. Global increases in alpha power appear to relate to an inability to gather or utilize the necessary resources to accomplish the given task successfully. Interestingly, it appears as though in this case, the inefficient allocation of resources was recognized on a subjective level, which allowed the marksmen to reject the shot and begin the aiming period over again while trying to orchestrate a more successful mental set.

Recently, attention has been paid toward examining the relatedness of various cortical regions (EEG coherence) during marksmanship performance, with the assumption that increased relatedness reflects lesser skill levels. In terms of neural resource allocation, a greater amount of relatedness between two regions indicates decreased functional autonomy between those regions. Hence, the allocation of resources may be described as less efficient. Deeny, Hillman, Janelle, and Hatfield (2001) examined elite and lesser skilled marksmen with the a priori prediction that elite marksmen would show decreased cortical relatedness. Results supported the hypothesis and suggested that elite marksmen compared to lesser skilled marksmen exhibited increased psychomotor efficiency in terms of neural resource allocation. While these findings cannot be directly linked to behavioral performance (the marksmen's score), they are descriptive of differential cortical activation between elite and lesser skilled performers.

Sport scientists have also studied cortical ERPs during the period immediately preceding shooting tasks. Specifically, Konttinen and Lyytinen (1992) measured slow potential (SP) negativity (cortical activation related to stimulus processing) in national level marksmen. Results showed that increased negativity was found before the trigger pull and that less accurate shots were associated with even greater negativity. This finding suggests that the level of arousal preceding the poorer shots may have been excessive whereas a more efficient profile of cortical activation was associated with superior performance. Other work by Konttinen and Lyytinen (1993) and colleagues (Konttinen, Lyytinen, & Era, 1999) has supported their initial findings by demonstrating that intra–marksmen variability between superior and poorer shots exists in SP negativity. As a result, this variability affects performance. Further, Konttinen et al. (1999) compared elite Finnish Olympic team marksmen with nationally ranked shooters who did not have international competitive experience. They found increased SP positivity for poorer shots versus superior shots, which suggested that the positivity reflected the shooters' increased effort to inhibit irrelevant motor activity and thus override the SP negativity associated with arousal regulation. In other words, researchers observed a less efficient cortical profile during poorer performance. It is interesting that differences in cortical SP profiling associated with performance emerged in light of the slight differences in skill level between the two groups.

Anxiety, Emotion, and Expert Performance

Despite the inherent realization that anxiety and other affective states dramatically influence performance effectiveness, the exploration of expert-novice differences in this regard is in its infancy. Intuitively, it would appear that because experts are more capable of demonstrating superior performance than novices, they must be capable of dealing with affective states more appropriately than novices. However, at least two alternative explanations are viable for how experts and nonexperts respond to situational influences on performance. One, experts do not experience the degree of emotional activation that novices do; two, experts are capable of regulating emotional fluctuations with compensatory mechanisms to allow the maintenance of high-performance levels. Although empirical evidence is scarce, we will briefly describe and evaluate the relative contribution of each of these explanations (and potential others).

Predominant findings from descriptive studies of expert athletes indicate that the elite athlete tends to possess an elevated, vigorous mood state (e.g., Terry, 1995). However, despite findings that athletes are characterized by more positive mood states relative to nonathletic populations, the majority of extant research indicates that mood profiles are not effective in differentiating relative expertise levels (e.g., Terry, 1995). Recent research has applied the Individual Zones of Optimal Functioning (IZOF) model to study affective influences on performance, and it has been more fruitful in accounting for performance variation than have efforts to discriminate athletes of varying achievement levels (Hanin & Syrjä, 1995, 1996). As Gould and Tuffey (1996) and others have pointed out, however, the IZOF model is limited in explaining the mechanisms by which mood states, anxiety, or specific emotions influence performance.

Elite athletes appear to be both capable of regulating reactions to anxiety-producing stimuli as well as perceiving potentially threatening situations as either positive or challenging (e.g., Hardy, Jones, & Gould, 1996). The effects of anxiety and arousal on attentional processing have also received empirical evaluation (Janelle, Singer, & Williams, 1999; Murray & Janelle, 2000; Vickers, Williams, Rodrigues, Hillis, & Coyne, 1999; Williams, Vickers, Rodriques, & Hillis, 2000). Again, how these attributes differ as a function of expertise, as well as how these capabilities develop, has lacked scientific exploration. A rare exception is the work of Williams and Elliott (1999), who examined expert-novice differences in visual search characteristics and performance among karate athletes who participated in a simulated combat situation. Results indicated that although both groups exhibited notable shifts in visual attention as a function of anxiety, expert search patterns were more robust to the anxiety manipulation than were those of novices, thus indicating that experts are capable of maintaining consistency in attentional allocation in spite of emotional variability. These findings corroborate less mechanistic accounts that describe the emotional characteristics of expertise (e.g., Janelle, in press; J.G. Jones, Hanton, & Swain, 1994; Woodman & Hardy, 2001).

Psychological Skills

Early research efforts to determine the involvement of psychological skills among athletes of varying skill levels were initiated during the late 1970s with the influential work of Mahoney and Avener (1977), who studied psychological skill usage among successful and less successful gymnasts. Later work (Gould, Weiss, & Weinberg, 1981; Grove & Hanrahan, 1988; Highlen & Bennett, 1979; Orlick & Partington, 1988; Spink, 1990) followed a common purpose to describe skill level differences in the use of mental skills. Through a variety of self-report assessments (using several different instruments), the collective results of these investigations indicated that the following traits characterized the relatively more successful or higher skill level athletes: commitment to the sport and to quality training (including simulation training); goal setting; concentration and anxiety management; self-confidence; use of imagery and mental preparation; and mental training. However, the self-reported ratings, as well as questionable reliability and validity of some of the instruments used in these investigations, restrict the ability to make confident conclusions on psychological skill usage and how it may differ between elite and nonelite samples.

Later efforts have employed variations of the Ottawa Mental Skills Assessment Tool (OMSAT and OMSAT-3*) as a means to differentiate mental skill utility among athletes of differing skill levels. Notable studies in this area have included the work of Bota (1993), Stevenson (1999), Wilson (1999), and Durand-Bush, Salmela, and Green-Demers (in press). Collectively, across a variety of sports that range from synchronized skaters to hockey players, findings indicate a propensity among relatively elite athletes to score higher in commitment, goal setting, competition planning, self-confidence, stress reactivity, focusing, and refocusing. Moreover, results indicate that elite athletes use mental skills more than their nonelite counterparts in both training and competition (e.g., Wilson, 1999). Though valuable in describing what skills successful athletes employ in training and competition, literature in the psychological skills arena of expertise research has failed to examine the specific means by which these skills are implemented into the training and competitive setting, and it has also neglected to evaluate how these skills are developed.

Summary

The expertise approach, whether explicitly followed or implicitly present in research designs, has yielded valuable information concerning the development of expertise and has provided an indication of some of the mechanisms responsible for the expert advantage in sport. Expert sport performers in both self-paced and externally paced tasks develop a deeper, more intricate knowledge base by which to form representations of typical sport scenarios; they are more efficient and effective in recognizing and responding to structured game situations; they are more capable of matching appropriate strategies and tactics to game situations, which allows them to respond more effectively; they are more attuned to the richest informational sources provided in the visual scene, which enables them to make efficient and appropriate decisions; and their attentional and coordination capabilities appear to be less influenced by variations in affective states. Despite the wealth of scientific data derived from variations of the expertise approach, the current state of knowledge in the study of expertise is quite limited, with constraints on advancement potentially imposed by the nature and derivation of the expertise approach. As such, some areas of consideration for future research efforts are proposed as follows.

Critical Issues for Future Research

In the following section, we present a brief (and by no means exhaustive) summary of general topics and specific issues that have yet to be addressed or have not been fully resolved in the development of sport expertise. Indeed, developmental considerations for sport expertise, opportunities for deliberate practice, as well as coaching influences (among other topics) are areas of critical importance to our understanding of expertise. Given their extensive coverage in other sections of this book (see chapters 3, 4, 5, and 11), they have not been included here but certainly warrant further exploration.

The Development of Competitive Toughness and Emotional Regulation

In the context of our current understanding of expert performance, the relative contribution of competitive experiences has been largely de-emphasized in favor of general descriptions of the requirements for deliberate practice. Indeed, no known research to date has documented the amount of expert performance variance accountable by exposure to competitive settings. However, from an intuitive standpoint, one could certainly contend that to be effective in evaluative settings, the capability to compete has to be learned. Systematic and sport-specific training creates an athlete who is physically, technically, tactically, and perceptually capable of performing the requisite skills to consistently execute precise, consistent, efficient, and effective movements in benign settings. However, each of these performance components is inherently dependent on effective emotional regulation in the dynamic, often hostile sporting environment. Without competitive experience, it is difficult to imagine how anyone can acquire the self-regulatory capabilities to deal with the wide array of internal (emotional, cognitive) and external distractions that arguably cannot be experienced outside of the competitive arena.

Russell (1990) found that elite athletes progressively de-emphasized physical and technical components of performance while relying more on metacognitive skills. Though largely speculative, he suggests that novices and intermediate performers are less focused on these metacognitive skills in favor of physical and technical emphases. This prediction has been supported by Durand-Bush and Salmela (2001), who indicate that experience in the competitive setting is critical to the development of expertise in sport. Likewise, Cleary and Zimmerman (2001) and Jack, Kirshenbaum, Poon, Rodgers, and Starkes (1999) demonstrated that experts develop refined levels of metacognitive strategies. Whereas research has been done to determine the extent of deliberate practice that is needed for expertise, efforts should be undertaken to determine the amount and type of exposure to competition that is needed to hone competitive psychological skills. One might contend, in fact, that hours accumulated in competitive settings are a form of "deliberate experience" (where participants actively involve themselves in competition) and that such experience is necessary for experts to acquire the needed skills for effective performance in evaluative settings.

Critical Issues Related to Psychophysiology and Genetics

Though gaining in popularity over the past several years, the utilization of psychophysiological measures to study expert performance is underrepresented in the literature. The increasing implementation of psychophysiological assessment has occurred largely due to the increased comprehension of psychophysiological indexes and their relative affordability as compared to a decade ago. Some possibilities for implementation of psychophysiological research methods in the study of expert performance are outlined as follows.

Behavioral geneticists have typically focused on the relationship between general cognitive ability (g) and nonsport aptitude. Aside from g (and potentially related to g), genetic influences on the speed of information acquisition and processing might significantly influence sport expertise. These influences include attentional considerations and the influence of potential innate limitations, such as attention deficits and dyslexic learning disabilities. For example, despite the lack of attention devoted to understanding the influence of learning disabilities on sport performance, it is relatively safe to assume the following: Innate factors influence the way people process information in academic and social aspects of life; therefore, they also significantly affect sport performance. In fact, recent theory in this area has implicated the cerebellar regulation of a number of physiological factors that characterize those with dyslexia (e.g., Fawcett & Nicholson, 1995, 1999).

A wealth of information has recently emerged that examines expertise in performance domains other than sport, in addition to studies that regard the acquisition of skill by use of event-related brain potentials (ERPs) and neural imaging techniques (functional magnetic resonance imaging [fMRI] and magnetoencephalography [MEG]). Although these areas of research do not directly involve sport performance and although obvious differences between sport and other performance domains do exist, it still may be beneficial for researchers to gain an understanding of the basic mechanisms involved in skill acquisition and expertise. Most notably, Elbert and his colleagues (Elbert, Pantev, Wienbruch, Rockstroh, & Taub, 1995) compared changes in cortical plasticity (reorganization of the cerebral cortex) of string musicians and nonmusicians using magnetic source imaging. Results showed that the cortical representations of the digits of the left hand (the string hand) were "substantially enlarged" for string players compared to nonmusicians, but no such differences were observed for the right hand (the bow hand). Further, researchers observed a correlation between the age at which string players began playing their instrument and the magnitude of change in the cerebral cortex, with those beginning at a younger chronological age resulting in increased cortical plasticity.

Additional research on musical expertise by Münte, Kohlmetz, Nager, & Altenmüller (2001) used ERPs to measure differences between musical conductors, musicians (pianists), and nonmusicians on an auditory localization task. Their results suggest that conductors were able to allocate increased attentional resources to predetermined target locations in the environment when stimuli were presented both focally and peripherally. The increased spatial tuning observed in the peripheral environment is of great advantage and necessity to the musical conductors' developing expertise as they stand in front of large orchestras. It appears as though the many hours of deliberate practice that orchestras must engage in may also have an effect on the cortex of conductors that is adaptive in nature.

Animal models have also added insight into the biobehavioral development and acquisition of motor skill proficiency. For example, Isaacs and colleagues (Isaacs, Anderson, Alcantara, Black, & Greenough, 1992) examined angiogenic effects in the cerebellar cortex of adult female rats after one month of repeated training. They found that motor skill learning and aerobic exercise training distinctly affect the plasticity of the cerebellar cortex.

Taken together, the aforementioned research may appear to favor environmental influences on skill acquisition. However, it may also be plausible that the cortex is predisposed to specific neural adaptations in response to the specific constraints of a given environment. With future research geared toward identifying the variance explained by acquired characteristics and hereditary predispositions, psychophysiological approaches may prove to be extremely useful in delineating the mechanisms that underlie expert performance.

Influences on Practice Effectiveness

As mentioned, agreement exists regarding the need for long hours of practice to develop "talent." However, without acknowledging the variety of potential influences on the overall quality of the practice environment, as well as how to structure training so that practice can be maintained, it remains difficult to provide meaningful training recommendations (Davids, 2000; Singer & Janelle, 1999; Starkes, Helsen, & Jack, 2001). Issues that warrant attention in this category include the following: the motivation to devote long hours to training; the type of practice (versus the amount of practice) that is required to attain expert performance; the conditions that characterize "perfect practice"; the variable that permits expert performance in practice to transfer to competitive and evaluative domains; and the mechanisms by which long hours of deliberate practice might influence the development of expertise. Furthermore, research is notably scarce in issues that deal with the identification of expert psychological skills and how those skills are developed.

Similarly, much of practice time is currently spent in observation of others. Significant lessons can therefore be learned by observing peers (teammates) in the competitive setting. Performers who strive for expertise eventually have to practice a task systematically to learn and refine it to expert levels, but having the opportunity to learn through modeling arguably speeds the progression to skilled performance. However, with regard to the amount of time available for observational learning (see Starkes, Deakin, Allard, Hodges, & Hayes, 1996;

Helsen, Starkes, & Hodges 1998), especially in team sports where athletes have the opportunity to watch and learn from others, it is perhaps unrealistic to assume that careful attention to detail in these situations does not facilitate skill acquisition and eventual expertise. Furthermore, observing others' success in the competitive setting arguably provides the relative novice with the necessary conviction (self-efficacy) to believe that they too can be successful in the competitive arena (Bandura, 1997).

Summary

As may have become evident throughout this chapter, the absence of a specific, detailed, and testable theory has arguably compromised the ability to systematically advance the scientific study of expertise. The expertise approach, though providing a viable framework to guide expertise research over the past two decades, is not a theory per se of expertise. Likewise, it is inherently biased toward accounting for environmental influences (Heller & Zeigler, 1998; Rowe, 1998). Devaluing hereditary input to account for at least some of the variability in expert performance contradicts one of the most accepted foundational assumptions that concern the development and reorganization of human behavior and performance: the notion that over time, organisms evolve. They do so in accordance with specific adaptations to respond more appropriately and effectively in an ever-changing and dynamic environment. As such, they are also dependent on the particular experiences that are specific to one's culture and environment. By suggesting that inherent differences in innate predispositions to expertise do not exist, researchers therefore dismiss ideas that concern evolution and natural selection. Though not universally agreed on, the upper limits of human performance are largely dictated through years of evolution that have shaped and molded the potential for expertise among human beings.

A concept that is potentially lost in evolutionary arguments for expertise is that evolution reflects learning. Living organisms learn to adapt to meet the demands of their environment and to ensure that their offspring carry the genetic markers of these adaptations from one generation to the next. As such, adaptations as a result of deliberate practice will predispose the next generation for superior performance in those activities toward which their predecessors devoted most of their energy, effort, and training. As such, Hebb's (1949) statement that expertise "is a product of 100% nature and 100% nurture" is clearly accurate.

If we were to accept this argument, from where might a viable theory emerge in which the genetic and environmental contributions to expertise are illuminated? Contemporary theories of coordination and control of motor actions provide promising perspectives for the development of a comprehensive and practical theory of expert performance. Although traditional information-processing approaches to understanding skill acquisition remain prominent in cognitive psychology and elsewhere, a paradigm shift has arguably occurred in the field of motor behavior. It is a shift in which ecological accounts of coordination dynamics, invariants, affordances, and control parameters have replaced traditional cognitive terms, such as memory representations and response programming (for reviews, see Davids, Williams, Button, & Court, 2001; Williams, Davids, & Williams, 1999). Although stringent ecological accounts remain (or interpretations of them), far fewer restrictive orientations have emerged, which has led to the development of integrative frameworks in which traditional cognitive factors such as intention, attention, personality, and emotion act as control parameters that organize efficient movement patterns.

In 1994, Abernethy, Burgess-Limerick, and Parks reviewed differing approaches to the study of expertise and queried whether competing theoretical orientations would converge or diverge. Indeed, their recommendation that relative convergence would advance understanding of expert performance is beginning to be realized. Broadly considering the "state of the union" in the study of expertise, these integrative approaches hold perhaps the greatest promise for a workable theory. They account for the performing organism within the context of the environment while considering the task for which control must be exerted.

The notion of person, task, and environmental interactions was originally conceptualized by Newell (1986), but it has only recently been integrated in a way that may appeal to researchers who emanate from traditional cognitive perspectives as well as contemporary ecological approaches. Researchers will likely make closer approximations in forthcoming attempts to describe and explain expertise by comprehensively accounting for the respective influences on action by way of task and environmental constraints, in addition to organismic constraints that include hereditary influences. In contrast to the occasionally reductionist, self-confirming nature of expertise research to date, future research efforts will more than likely lead to the identification of the components of a general theory of expertise for sport. It will be a theory in which researchers consider the interactive and multiple influences on expertise, and it will comprise real and practical applications toward selection and training of aspiring expert athletes.

▬ EXPERTS' COMMENTS ▬

▪ Question

In this chapter, Jannelle and Hillman suggest that although expertise research has considered many of the "learned" factors associated with experts, we need to also consider how talent (or genetic factors) may play a role. How important is a coach's ability to "recognize talent" in determining who will eventually become an expert athlete?

▪ Coach's Perspective: Nick Cipriano

In the early stages of athletic development, no one can predict with a high degree of certainty which athletes will rise to the top and achieve excellence. Even in an extreme case, where a young athlete displays all the characteristics of greatness and is vastly superior to his or her peers, talent alone (in my experience) is a weak predictor of future success because the journey to expertise is such a long process. Moreover, because of the variance in physical maturation rates, it is entirely possible that the athlete who is seen as a talent at age 13 could well prove otherwise by age 16. Of course, the opposite is also true. One such example is Michael Jordan, perhaps the most celebrated basketball player of all time. He was cut from his high school basketball team because he did not display (according to his coach) what it was going to take to be successful. Fortunately, Jordan paid little attention to the coach who failed to recognize his persevering attitude. Through rigorous practice, Michael Jordan perfected his technical/tactical skills, which later propelled him to greatness. Michael Jordan's story is likely the most celebrated incident that provides the strongest support for Ericsson's theory of deliberate practice.

▪ Player's Perspective: Therese Brisson

Janelle and Hillman suggest that although research has considered many of the learned factors associated with experts, genetics (or genetic factors) may play a considerable role. Genetics plays an important but sometimes sad role in high-performance sport. For example, 50 years ago, the average size of the NHL hockey player was about 5' 7" and 150 lbs. Of course, today the average size is closer to 6' 0" and 200 lbs. Smaller players are the exception, not the rule. Interestingly enough, the average size of players in the women's event at the 1998 Olympics was 5' 6" and 150 lbs. Since then, in the women's game I have observed the trend toward bigger players (more players close to 6' 0" and 200 lbs. are appearing on national team rosters). I'm glad to have played when I did, because 10 years from now I would be too small to make the team (I'm 5' 7" and 150 lbs.)! Body size is something we can't do too much about, but it is an important factor in many sports.

Other important physical skills in hockey are speed and quickness, which are not synonymous. Many talented hockey players in Canada will never make the national team because they are simply not fast enough. I have noticed that with training, many athletes can improve their overall speed—they get faster. However, no matter how much training they do, they can't get quicker. Quick feet, quick hands, quick movement, and quick thinking are critical in hockey, yet quickness does not seem to be a trainable skill; it appears to be "hard-wired." This is where genetics can be a little sad because no matter how much training athletes do, they will never be quicker. After the window of opportunity passes by, quickness doesn't appear to be something we can do much about.

We know that many factors influence athletic performance. Physical skills; technical and tactical skills; psychological and emotional skills; training; nutrition; and access to good coaching, facilities, and equipment are all important. We actually know a lot about these things. Using historical information and regression analysis, we can even predict what time an athlete will need to win the gold medal at the 1,000 m long-track speed skating event at the 2006 Winter Olympics. However, we know very little about genetic factors and their influence on athletic performance. I would say that talent identification remains the biggest challenge in high-performance sport. We are simply not very good at identifying who will eventually be an expert performer. One of the reasons for this is that the pattern of skills necessary for success in grassroots sport can be quite different than the skill set necessary at the elite level. For example, in youth sport, the bigger, stronger children are usually the most successful. However, this is not necessarily the case in international competition. In my sport, all the athletes that get to the international level can skate, pass, and shoot. Most athletes all fall within a pretty similar range for strength, speed, and conditioning too. I have heard NHL players joke about players who excel in fitness testing. They are in such great shape but can't compete on the ice. A different skill set is required. The thing that separates the good players from the less talented is the ability to make good decisions under pressure. This is difficult to evaluate in 8- to 10-year-olds.

Chapter 3

Development of Elite Performance and Deliberate Practice

■ ■ ■ ■ ■

An Update From the Perspective of the Expert Performance Approach

K. Anders Ericsson

When elite athletes such as ice skaters, divers, and soccer players demonstrate their outstanding skills at public competitions, their performances often look exquisitely natural and gracefully effortless. To the casual observer, these exhibitions appear so extraordinary that it seems unlikely that most other performers—regardless of any amount or type of training—can ever achieve similar performance levels. It is tempting to view these amazing performances as a reflection of some unique, innate talent, which is required before anyone can achieve such a performance. Indeed, some athletes have body builds with the requisite flexibility, strength, and speed to suggest that they must have been born to be superior athletes. Some would even argue that these athletes seem to possess a general athletic ability that would allow them to excel in virtually any type of sport.

If general athletic ability and innate talents were the primary constraints on elite achievement, then one would naturally expect the same athletes to excel at a wide range of sports. For example, one would expect that an elite gymnast would be able to display similarly superior performance as a diver or an ice skater with a minimum of additional training. However, among contemporary athletes, such transfer of elite performance across domains of sport is rare. International level of performance has never (to my knowledge) been demonstrated across different sports without prior extended training. In the late 20th and early 21st centuries, athletes are able to attain international-level performance only in a few highly related events that are consistent with their current and past training. Is it even possible that the development of elite athletic performance can be fully explained as the results of extensive training?

In chapter 2 of this book, Janelle and Hillman provide a clear and comprehensive account of the ongoing discussion about the relative role of innate factors (genetics) versus training (environment) in attaining the highest levels of performance. They demonstrate that the scientific discussion has moved beyond arguing about the relative importance of genetics and environment for the development of performance. This chapter will therefore explore both environmentally induced mechanisms and genetic mechanisms, both of which influence and control the development and structure of expert performance.

If one favors a genetic account to explain why some select athletes can attain exceptional levels of performance, then researchers are now expected to demonstrate the influence of specific genes on the development of nerves, muscles, and other physiological systems of their bodies. In other words, which genes do only the select athletes possess as part of their DNA? Similarly, researchers who favor an account based on acquired skills need to identify the effects of specific types of practice. That is, what exact activities lead these select individuals to acquire the cognitive skills and the physiological adaptations to attain their superior performance? Researchers may even have to specify the particular stages of development. They may have to illustrate when the developing child and adolescent should engage in the practice and training because anatomical structures and physiological systems would theoretically be maximally modifiable during certain critical periods (Ericsson, 2002; Ericsson & Lehmann, 1996).

In this chapter, I sketch the development of accounts regarding expert performance. In an initial section on its historical background, I discuss how recent findings have led many researchers to question the traditional theories of expertise. Specifically, I examine how the dramatic effects of training and extended practice transformed the assumption that performance and cognitive processes were constrained by innately determined capacity. In the remainder of the chapter, I use the expert performance approach (Ericsson & Smith, 1991) as a framework to discuss how we can describe elite performance in each domain and how we can reproduce the associated superior performance under controlled conditions. I discuss advances in the analysis of the mechanisms that mediate the reliably superior performance of elite athletes. I also focus on our improved understanding of how athletes attain their detailed mechanisms and abilities in the course of their developing expert performance. In particular, I examine how the performance of individual athletes develops longitudinally over decades of engagement in activities in their domain of expertise.

Historical Background

The pioneering research on expertise and expert performance focused not on sport, but on world-class chess players and on how these players differed from skilled players in local chess clubs (de Groot, 1946/1978). In the 1970s and 1980s, Simon and Chase (1973) developed and formalized de Groot's framework and thus proposed a theoretical perspective that would eventually dominate the concepts of expertise in a range of domains. Simon and Chase's theory proposed that world-class chess players did not differ from less accomplished players in terms of their mental "hardware" or basic abilities and general capacities. In other words, experts were constrained by the same unmodifiable limits of short-term memory (STM) and speed of processing.

Simon and Chase generalized that the performance advantage of experts was attributed to their vast storehouse of knowledge and complex patterns (chunks), which they had accumulated during their many years of experience in their respective domains of activity, either in chess or sport. In a compelling series of studies, Chase and Simon (1973) showed the dramatic effect of the experts' complex domain-specific patterns of memory for chess configurations. When representative situations from chess games were briefly presented to subjects, the chess experts' memory was found to be vastly superior to that of beginning chess players. However, when the same chess pieces were randomly arranged to eliminate any meaningful patterns, the experts' significant memory advantage over the beginners virtually disappeared, and the expert players—now exhibiting performances similar to novices—could only recall around four or five chess pieces.

The finding that superior memory performance of experts is limited to familiar meaningful stimuli from the domain was later replicated in several other domains of expertise. In an influential series of studies (for a review, see Starkes & Allard, 1991), the expert-level athletes demonstrated superior memory over less skilled players when the situations reflected representative situations from actual games. However, memory for unstructured situations, such as the same players' walking back to the sidelines at intermissions, is not any better for experts than for less skilled players.

Simon and Chase's (1973) theory of expertise predicted a close association between individual players' proficiency of performance during actual games (the crucial attribute of expert performers) and the capacity of their memory for representative stimuli. Simon and Chase's theory assumed that expert performance, such as playing chess or soccer, was mediated by the same patterns and knowledge that mediated the superior memory for representative game situations. However, several studies failed to find a close correlation, and moreover, they even uncovered superior memory without superior performance and vice versa (superior performance without superior memory). These findings raise issues about the sufficiency of the pattern-recognition model proposed by Simon and Chase (1973), and these results therefore suggest that more complex mechanisms must mediate expert performance (for an extended discussion, see Ericsson, Patel, & Kintsch, 2000).

In a review of expert performance, Smith and I (Ericsson & Smith, 1991) concluded that the traditional theories of expertise (cf. Simon & Chase, 1973) and skill acquisition (cf. Fitts & Posner, 1967) could not fully account for the new and emerging evidence on complex mechanisms of memory and perception that mediate expert performance. These theories had particular difficulties in explaining how the identified complex mechanisms could be acquired within the fixed limits of memory and perception. In our review, we argue that when experts extend their training over months and years, they are able to acquire mechanisms that can either circumvent or simply change the basic limits on information processing. These processing limits appear to provide valid constraints in typical training studies that last only a few hours. When the training is extended for *hundreds* of hours, however, regular college students were shown to be able to improve their memory performance dramatically and actually acquire qualitatively different cognitive mechanisms, as will be shown in the next section.

Expanding Working Memory With Practice

A fundamental assumption of Simon and Chase's (1973) theory of expertise is that experts' and novices' performances are constrained by the general limit of short-term memory, which can hold no more than seven chunks (plus or minus two; Miller, 1956). In an early study, Chase and I (Chase & Ericsson, 1981; Ericsson, Chase, & Faloon, 1980) showed that with practice, subjects could alter this general limit of seven. In our study, we afforded a few "unexceptional" college students the opportunity to practice recalling series of auditorily presented digits. As a result of their practice, all of the students became exceptional with their short-term memory. Each student could perfectly recall over 20 digits, as can be seen in figure 3.1. Two of the students continued their training, and after several hundred hours of practice, they were able to recall over 80 digits. Every one of our trained students started the memory training experiment with normal memory capacity for a series of digits—they could accurately recall about seven digits (such as a typical phone number). We concluded that the students' exceptional memory must thus be directly attributable to training.

Most important, we studied how the thought processes of our students changed as their memory for digits increased. At the start of training, the students rehearsed the presented digits to themselves—the same way that nearly all adults do when remembering digits. However, after more practice, our students started to segment the presented digits into groups in an attempt to store the groups into long-term memory (LTM), thus creating associations to numerical patterns and preexisting knowledge. For example, several of them encoded three-digit groups as running times—357 would be 3 minutes and

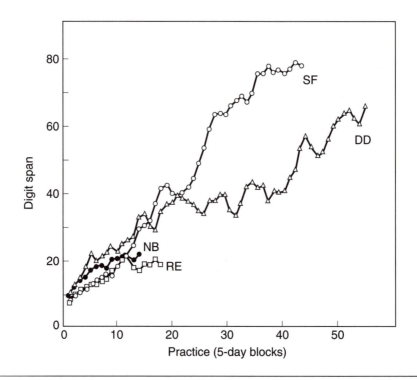

Figure 3.1 Ability to accurately reproduce series of rapidly presented digits (digit span) as a function of practice for four regular college students (whose initials are SF, RE, DD, and NB). The initial digit span for all students was about seven digits, which is the average memory performance of college students.

From W.G. Chase and K.A. Ericsson, Skilled memory. In *Cognitive skills and their acquisition* (Mahwah, NJ: Lawrence Erlbaum Publishing), 141-189. Adapted by permission of K.A. Ericsson.

57 seconds, a time just below the 4-minute mile. They also developed retrieval cues to encode the locations of the digit groups within the list so that they could recall all the digits in order (for a detailed description of the complex skills that the students developed to attain their exceptional memory, see Chase & Ericsson, 1981, 1982).

Chase and I collected the students' verbal reports on their thoughts during the trials of memory testing; we also designed experiments to test and validate the mechanisms that the students developed through practice. We thus demonstrated that it was possible to understand the development of exceptional ability in initially "unexceptional" subjects. We then went on to describe the acquisition of specific mechanisms as a function of continued training. Based on subsequent training studies by other investigators, our conclusion is that it is now reasonable to argue that motivated "average" adults can acquire exceptional levels of memory performance by acquiring memory skills for specific types of information. The specific structure of these acquired memory skills will vary among participants as a function of their prior knowledge and skill (Ericsson, 1988).

To assess if these findings could be extended beyond skills acquired in the laboratory, my colleagues and I discovered various individuals with exceptional memory in all walks of everyday life, including a waiter who could remember complete dinner orders from 20 customers without any written notes, and an exceptional person who had memorized over 40,000 digits of the mathematical constant pi. With many other scientists, we have tested musicians, chess players, actors, and many others with exceptional abilities, and we have been able to identify the cognitive mechanisms that mediate the superior memory performance of many experts from a wide range of domains (for a review, see Ericsson and Lehmann, 1996). In a recent review, Kintsch and I (Ericsson & Kintsch, 1995) showed that experts were able to acquire memory skills that allowed them to expand their working memory to engage in planning, reasoning, evaluation, and other demanding activities that involved working memory. Hence, experts are indeed able to develop their skills to provide for the working memory needed for their superior performance.

A Broader View of Limits to Improvement of Performance

The improvements in working memory along with numerous other findings raise doubt about the view that fixed capacities limit an individual's ability to reach the highest levels of performance. In fact, virtually all elements of the human body can change and adapt to induced demands, and these changes can be particularly dramatic when practice is initiated during childhood and adolescence. For example, a ballet dancer's ability to turn out the feet and the range of motion of a baseball pitcher's shoulder joint are both influenced by appropriate practice (Ericsson & Lehmann, 1996).

More general, when the cells of the human body are put under exceptional strain, a whole range of extraordinary physiological processes are activated in the body. For example, adults' bodies can recover from surgery, and broken bones can heal. Similarly, when adults donate one of their kidneys, the remaining kidney grows automatically in size by approximately 70% during the two weeks following surgery. When adults expose themselves to demanding and physiologically straining activities or when they challenge themselves to improve their performance by deliberate practice, they are eventually able to transcend the stable structure of abilities and capacities that mediate activities in everyday life (Ericsson, 1996, 2002). Later in this chapter, I discuss the empirical evidence for the marked modifiability of human characteristics as a result of extended practice.

Reviews of expert performance have, in my opinion, been unsuccessful in uncovering any evidence of innate talents that are critical to expert performance, including factors that could not be altered or circumvented with the subjects' executing of extended practice (for a discussion, see Janelle and Hillman in chapter 2 of this volume). An exception, however, is one's height, which no known practice activity can increase. Excluding height-related characteristics, recent reviews (Ericsson & Lehmann, 1996; Howe, Davidson, & Sloboda, 1998) have not uncovered any firm evidence that innate characteristics are required for healthy adults to attain elite performance. When appropriately designed training is maintained with full concentration on a regular basis for weeks, months, or even years, inborn unmodifiable characteristics do not appear to constrain anyone from reaching high levels of performance. At this time, no solid empirical evidence exists to prove otherwise. (Of course, the genetic exceptions of height and body size deem a clear advantage in, for example, the high jump and basketball, and a distinct disadvantage in, for example, gymnastics.)

Outline of the Remainder of the Chapter

If "basic" capacities, physiological characteristics, and performance can be so greatly modified through extended training, one cannot simply conclude that some characteristic is innately determined because it is either physiological or assumed to reflect a basic capacity. It is entirely possible that the characteristics necessary for elite performance can be shaped and changed through some type of training during the period of an athlete's development. Consequently, Smith and I (Ericsson & Smith, 1991) argue that these issues can only be resolved by studying the stable performances that experts have attained after many years of practice—a unique body of reproducible empirical phenomena. If we were to analyze the structure of the mechanisms that mediate these achievements, we could provide psychological scientists with insights into the potential degree of physiological adaptation and the human complexity of skilled mechanisms.

In the following sections, I first briefly sketch the expert performance approach, then I discuss the recent issues that have emerged in the last decade that are reflected in the contributions in this volume.

The Expert Performance Approach

The empirical analysis of the mechanisms that mediate expert performance is based on three steps (Ericsson & Smith, 1991). First, researchers study the naturally observable expert performance to capture the essence of domain expertise and to identify the representative tasks that would allow them to reproduce the performance in the laboratory. Second, the researchers analyze the captured superior performance with standard methodology from cognitive psychology, such as designed experiments with reaction times, eye-movement recordings, and verbal protocol analysis, to trace the mediating cognitive processes (cf. the earlier described work in the introductory section on exceptional memory). Finally, once researchers identify the mechanisms that mediate experts' superior performance, they can then assess whether different types of experience and practice activities explain the acquisition of these mechanisms and whether expert performers engage in these activities during the development of their performance.

Capturing Superior Performance of Experts Rather Than Studying Mere Behavior of Experts

The focus on expert-novice differences (Chi, Glaser, & Rees, 1982; Simon & Chase, 1973) led investigators to search for highly experienced and knowledgeable people, who were later defined to be *experts*. It was simply taken for granted that these experts would display superior performance on relevant tasks in their respective domains. What researchers rapidly discovered, however, was that "experts" with extended experience and specialized knowledge frequently did not show a performance advantage over others. For example, highly experienced psychotherapists are not more successful in treatment of patients than are novice therapists (Dawes, 1994). In addition, stock market experts and professional bankers are not able to forecast stock prices any more reliably than university teachers and students can (Stael von Holstein, 1972). In fact, a range of experts have failed to exhibit a performance advantage over novices when they have been presented representative tasks under controlled conditions (for a review, see Ericsson & Lehmann, 1996).

Of course, many domains of expertise exist where experts repeatedly show a level of performance that vastly surpasses beginners and novices. For example, elite runners and swimmers can finish races under standardized and controlled conditions much faster than others, even subelite athletes in the same domain (see Starkes, Weir, & Young, chapter 10). Expert golfers can putt more accurately than novices can (see Beilock, Wierenga, & Carr, chapter 12). Similarly, elite ice skaters and gymnasts can perform challenging jumps and difficult combinations that are completely outside the current ability of less accomplished athletes (see Deakin & Cobley, chapter 5).

On the other hand, some events in sport involve judges, such as gymnastics and diving. Ste-Marie (chapter 7) shows that expert judges and referees are more accurate in detecting mistakes and errors of performance than are athletes. However, an increasing body of evidence exists that demonstrates how judges are not completely reliable and even exhibit systematic biases. For example, research in the evaluation of music performance has shown that judges show surprisingly low agreements among each other and that they are influenced by irrelevant factors, such as the gender, physical attractiveness, and reputation of the performer (Gabrielsson, 1999). The problems with judges' ratings are consistent with the well-known biases found in the performance ratings of employees in business (Landy & Farr, 1980). Systematic biases in judged aspects of performance, owing to factors such as fame, reputation, and past performance, can never be recorded by objective measures; thus, they cannot be explained by the theoretical mechanisms proposed to mediate performance. In certain cases, these judgment biases can be avoided by simply hiding the identity of the performer to the judges. In other cases, researchers can seek *objective* measures by which to judge performance (rather than subjective measures), even when such measures may not capture all the available information.

A particular challenge exists when one tries to capture superior performance in domains such as chess, tennis, and fencing, where each game consists of sequences that rarely (if ever) repeat themselves in that exact form. In a path-breaking and innovative research effort, de Groot (1946/1978) addressed this problem by identifying certain challenging situations in representative games that required some type of action. After identifying the situations, de Groot presented the same situations to all the participants, and he observed their cognitive processes as they selected the most appropriate actions. Subsequent research has shown that this methodology provides the best available measure of chess skill that can predict performance in chess tournaments (Ericsson, Patel, & Kintsch, 2000). Researchers have applied a similar methodology to measure superior performance in representative situations in medical diagnosis, snooker, and a range of other domains (Ericsson, 1996), including team sports such as soccer (see Helsen & Starkes, 1999, and Williams & Ward, chapter 9).

The complexity of elite performance is clearly seen in team sports where team members frequently have different roles and different performance expectations yet also have an associated goal. For instance, soccer players all have a common goal (to win the game), but each has a different role (goalkeepers, defensive players, and offensive players) with different expectations (prevent the ball from entering the goal, prevent the opposing team from advancing, score as many goals as possible, respectively). The representative situations during game conditions differ as a function of each person's role within the team. Thus, it is likely that the mechanisms that mediate superior performance for an elite offensive player may differ from those of an elite defensive player in each one's detailed structure.

We do know, however, that the detailed mechanisms that mediate superior performance differ among most experts. Virtually all experts have some aspects of their performance that are stronger or weaker than other performers at the same level. For example, research has shown that at the highest levels, expert musicians differ markedly in their performance on different musical activities. Some musicians excel in accompanying singers and soloists, where they typically play music from the notes without prior preparation and practice; other musicians excel at performing well-rehearsed pieces as a solo performer consistent with their chosen professional specialization (Lehmann & Ericsson, 1996). When experts show individual differences in the measured performance for different types of essential domain-related activities, it becomes necessary to separately measure and analyze superior performance in these activities. If investigators were to measure a composite index of performance by averaging all the many types of activities, then to do so will reduce reliability and the ability of investigators to explain both the structure of the mechanisms that mediate superior performance and how these mechanisms are acquired.

In sum, the principal challenge of the expert performance approach is to identify the essence of expertise in a domain and then design representative tasks that allow expert performers to reproduce their superior performance consistently under standardized conditions. Ideally, it should be possible to administer the same measurement procedure to children and other beginners as well as to advanced experts so that the development of performance can be objectively measured in a longitudinal design. For example, we can collect performance data in many individual sports (such as the 100-meter sprint) and in other types of activities, including music (by listening to someone perform specific pieces) and chess (by observing a player select moves from unfamiliar positions). In other domains, such as team sports, it is more difficult to measure individual performance in general; it is especially challenging to measure the performance on the same or similar tasks. Only when it has been possible to measure the reproducibly superior performance in specific activities can one profitably proceed to the next steps of analysis, namely that of identifying the mediating mechanisms of that performance. The less reproducible and the less precise the measurement of the superior performance, the harder it is to identify and describe its mediating mechanisms and their attainment during the extended development.

Identifying the Mechanisms That Mediate Expert Levels of Performance

Once researchers can reproduce experts' superior performance on representative tasks that capture the expertise in the domain, the next challenge is to identify the specific processes that account for the experts' performance advantage over those less skilled. For this type of investigation, researchers employ a general research method that starts by examining the overall performance to either find complex cognitive mechanisms or isolate intermediate actions and steps that differentiate the expert performance.

Particularly relevant to the study of elite performance of motor activities is the decomposition of the overall time to complete an event. For example, one can examine the advantage of an elite sprinter over subelite sprinters during different phases of the event, such as the time necessary to get out of the blocks, the time to accelerate to max speed, and the time of sustained speed to the finish line. Researchers can likewise measure and examine the characteristics of expert golfers' putting and driving shots that are associated with their superior motor consistency (Ericsson, 2001).

Many differences of superior athletes' performance have also been linked to anatomical differences, such as differences in the joints of the baseball pitchers' throwing arms, the structure of hearts of long-distance runners, and the distributions of fast muscle fibers of sprinters (Ericsson & Lehmann, 1996). However, this line of research has shown that the most important differences are not at the lowest levels of cells or muscle groups, but at the athletes' superior control over the integrated and coordinated actions of their bodies. For example, with respect to their hitting action, elite golfers and racket players reveal their highest consistency at ball contact rather than across the entire hitting motion. Elite long-distance runners differ from subelite runners by their running economy (the metabolic efficiency of maintaining their race pace). Elite runners also report monitoring their internal states more closely and planning their race performance with more focus (for a review, see Masters & Ogles, 1998).

The most compelling scientific evidence for preserved cognitive control of expert performance comes from laboratory studies where the task is to generate the most appropriate action in representative game situations (Ericsson & Smith, 1991). In his pioneering work that introduced this methodology, de Groot (1946/1978) showed expert and world-class chess players unfamiliar chess positions and asked them to select the best next move while verbalizing their thoughts. He found that chess players first rapidly perceived and interpreted the chess position, then they accessed from memory interesting potential moves. These promising moves were then evaluated mentally by planning the consequences of each potential move. During the phase of planning and evaluation, chess players would find the best move and sometimes even discover new and better moves. In sum, as players acquire increased chess skill, they acquire better and more refined mental representations that allow them to evaluate and manipulate chess positions mentally. In a review of similar studies, Ericsson and Lehmann (1996) found a similar pattern of experts' solving representative tasks in a range of domains of expertise, such as medicine, computer programming, and games. When experts solve representative tasks, their think-aloud protocols contain verbalized thoughts that reveal how deliberate preparation, planning, reasoning, and evaluation mediate their superior performance.

In their pioneering research, McPherson and French traced the development of mental representations and planning in baseball and tennis players using think-aloud protocols (Ericsson & Simon, 1993). Nevett and French (1997) showed how school-age baseball players who performed at higher levels of expertise used an increase in planning and updating of game situations. In chapter 6, McPherson and Kernodle propose a theoretical framework that describes the structure of tennis players' mental representations, which are based on the players' verbal reports when confronting simulated game situations as well as engaging in actual tennis matches. They describe the professional tennis players' refined representations of game situations with associated action plans, then they trace the development of these representations (as a function of attained level of skill) all the way back to the rudimentary representations of novice players. Researchers have used a similar verbal-report methodology to study other types of perceptual-motor expertise, such as playing snooker (Abernethy, Neal, & Konig, 1994), where experts have been presented with representative situations and asked to respond while thinking aloud.

In most sporting events, the demand for rapid execution of highly practiced activities has led investigators away from collecting verbal reports of the athletes' thoughts. However, even the superior speed of expert performers appears to depend primarily on acquired representations, rather than a faster base speed of their motor system.

Of all the domains, the most extensively researched motor skill is *typing*. Many studies have found that the source of the expert typists' advantage is linked to the experts' ability to look ahead in the text beyond the word that they are currently typing (Salthouse, 1984). By looking farther ahead, they can prepare future keystrokes in advance by moving relevant fingers toward their desired locations on the keyboard. These preparatory movements have been confirmed by analysis of high-speed films of expert typists' finger movements during typing. Furthermore, when expert typists are restricted from looking ahead, their performance is reduced almost to the level of novice typists, who don't rely on looking ahead.

Similarly, the rapid reactions of athletes, such as hockey goalies, tennis players, and baseball batters, have been found to reflect acquired skills that involve anticipation of future events. For example, when skilled tennis players are preparing to return a serve, they study the movements of their opponent's leading up to contact between the ball and the racket, which allows them to identify the type of spin and the general direction. Given the ballistic and biomechanical nature of a serve, it is often possible for skilled players to make these judgments accurately. It is important to note that novice tennis players use an entirely different strategy. They usually initiate their preparations to return the ball once it is sufficiently close and they can see where it will bounce. Similarly, Ste-Marie (chapter 7) shows how gymnastics judges use their anticipatory skills to gain an advantage in evaluating rapid movements in performance routines. This evidence supports the hypothesis that expert athletes have a learned speed advantage (rather than a biological speed advantage) over their less accomplished peers (Abernethy, 1991; Starkes & Deakin, 1984; Williams & Ward, chapter 9).

Expert athletes do not simply acquire superior anticipation skills; they also acquire superior control over their motor actions. At increased levels of expertise, athletes such as figure skaters and gymnasts are able to perform more complex behavior (for example, a triple-axel jump for figure skaters). Furthermore, expert performers attain the ability to consistently reproduce the same motor actions. For instance, expert golf players are more consistent in executing the same putt or drive than are less skilled players (Ericsson, 2001). Similarly, skilled jugglers and other athletes intentionally vary their movements to discover how to increase their control (Beek, Jacobs, Daffertshofer, & Huys, chapter 13). Additionally, studies of expert musicians' representations have shown how they are able to control their performance in a flexible manner (Ericsson, 2002).

In sum, expert performance is mediated by acquired mental representations that allow the experts to anticipate, plan, and reason alternative courses of action. These mental representations provide experts with increased control of the aspects that are relevant to generating their superior performance. In chapter 8, Tenenbaum discusses the complex mechanisms that control perception, attention, and memory, which allow expert athletes to gain their performance advantage in dynamically changing game situations.

Scientific Accounts of the Acquisition of Expert Performance and Its Meaning Mechanisms

A complete scientific account of expert performance needs to be able to explain the following: the acquisition and development of typical and elite performance per domain, and the process of how only the elite performers develop more refined mechanisms and advanced adaptations that mediate their superior performance. Based on an earlier account (Ericsson, 1998), my proposal is that the development of typical, novice performance is prematurely arrested in an effortless automated form; experts, however, engage in an extended, continued refinement of mechanisms that mediate improvements in their performance. In other words, most amateurs do not improve their performance only because they have reached (in their minds) an acceptable level!

The Development of Typical Performance in Recreational and Everyday Activities

When adults are first introduced to an activity, such as golf and tennis, their primary goal is to reach some level of mastery that is sufficient to allow them to perform the activity at an acceptable level. As shown in figure 3.2, the development of these types of performances has been described in three phases (Anderson, 1982; Fitts & Posner, 1967). During the first phase of learning (the cognitive/associative phase), performers attempt to understand the task and form a mental representation of it and its associated procedures. They have to concentrate on the execution of each step to reduce gross mistakes. With more experience, their obvious mistakes become rare, the mediating steps become more tightly associated, and the performance appears smoother.

After some limited period of training and experience—frequently less than 50 hours for most recreational activities, such as skiing, tennis, and driving a car—people can attain an acceptable level of performance without much effortful attention. No longer does the person feel a need to concentrate as hard before. The goal was to reach as rapidly as possible a satisfactory level that is stable and "autonomous." At this point, they have reached the second phase, the autonomous phase. As their behavior gradually meets the performance demands, the execution of the skill is increasingly automated. After the learners pass through the cognitive/associative phase, they can generate a virtually automatic performance with a minimal amount of effort (see the gray/white plateau at the bottom of figure 3.2). This newfound automation, however, reduces one's conscious control and limits one's ability to make intentional, specific adjustments. When this final automatic phase has been reached, further experience will not be associated with any marked improvements, and the amount of accumulated experience will not be related to any new attained level of performance.

In contrast, expert performers counteract automaticity by developing increasingly complex mental representations so that they can attain higher levels of control of their performance and therefore remain

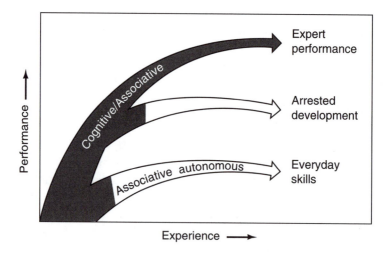

Figure 3.2 An illustration of the qualitative difference between expert performance and everyday activities during the course of improvement.

Adapted from K.A. Ericsson, 1998, "The scientific study of expert levels of performance: General implication for optimal learning and creativity" *High Ability Studies* 9:90. http://www.tandf.co.uk

within the cognitive/associative phases. At some point in their career, however, some experts eventually give up their commitment to seek excellence. They stop engaging in deliberate practice and focus only on maintaining their performance, which results in premature automation (and "arrested development"). Beilock et al. (chapter 12) give a full description of traditional models of skill acquisition and study the development of automaticity by contrasting the putting by expert golfers with novices who have no prior experience of putting and golf.

Theoretical frameworks, such as the dynamical systems theory (Beek et al., chapter 13), have proposed learning mechanisms that can account for skill acquisition as well as the typical development of children and young adolescents. When children start engaging in an activity, such as walking or running, they slowly discover the essential factors needed for control. One can similarly explain how they reach an acceptable level so that they can playfully engage in recreational activities with their peers. One important difference between children's developing proficiency in a recreational activity versus adults' (see the previous paragraph) is that children keep growing and their performance keeps improving with age. These changes do not just reflect physical maturation and increased strength and body size; studies have shown that their cognitive representation of the game situations improves as well (French et al., 1996; Williams & Ward, chapter 9).

In chapter 4, Côté, Baker, and Abernethy discuss how the role of activities related to popular sports (such as soccer and ice hockey) changes as children grow older. They found that older children increase their involvement, especially in progressively structured activities, such as playing recreational games of hockey and soccer. These activities, referred to as *deliberate play*, are constrained by rules and involve direct competition between individuals or teams. The desire to win games and competitions increases one's motivation to improve performance. For example, there are interesting anecdotes in the literature (Ericsson, 1996) about competitive children who actually seek out other children who are performing at a higher level. Some children even design competitive activities that provide feedback on their performance and opportunities for repetitions. By engaging in these additional activities, these children are able to improve their performance relative to that of their peers. Hence, it is important to distinguish between enjoyable recreation and other types of activities where engagement is motivated primarily by the desire to improve one's performance.

The Development of Expert Performance

Research on the development of expert performance has found that those who eventually become expert performers do not start out in a domain of expertise with an already exceptional level of performance as compared with their peers, when the benefits from earlier engagement in other related activities are considered (Bloom, 1985). The level of performance of future experts continues to improve during years and decades of active involvement in domain-related activities. Their performance typically peaks when they reach their late 20s, 30s, or early 40s—long after they have reached physical maturity at around age 18 (see Ericsson and Lehmann, 1996, for a review). In well-established domains of expertise, even the most "talented" cannot reach an international level in less than approximately a decade of experience and intense preparation. Hence, in stark contrast to the performance of everyday and recreational activities, the performance of experts continues to increase for years, and even decades.

The aspiring experts do not allow their cognitive representation of situations and methods in the domain to become as firmly settled as seen in amateurs, whose performances become increasingly effortless and eventually automated, as shown in figure 3.2. The skill acquisition of experts involves a continued search for how to improve their cognitive representations of the tasks and situations. Like the amateurs, they are able to disregard irrelevant stimuli and execute skilled actions based on their immediate representation of a situation. Unlike the amateurs, however, the experts remain in the cognitive phase while they continue to change their mental representations and make them increasingly refined. Experts can view these developed mechanisms as tools to gain higher levels of access to (and control over) relevant aspects of performance, whenever they so desire (Ericsson, 1996, 1998). These tools help the experts attain their highest levels of performance during competition and also help them to keep improving their performance during deliberate practice.

From retrospective interviews of international-level performers in several domains, Bloom and colleagues (Bloom, 1985; for a review, see Côté et al., chapter 4) showed that the developmental history of elite performers is fundamentally different from that of less accomplished performers and amateurs. Both future elite performers and their peers are typically introduced to their domains in a similar playful manner. As soon as the future elite performers show promise as compared to peers in the neighborhood, however, they are encouraged to seek out a teacher and initiate regular practice. Based on interview data, an argument was made by Bloom (1985) that access to sound training resources appears to be necessary to reach the highest levels.

To extend Bloom's and his colleagues' (1985) research and to further understand the development of differences among those with access to some of the best teachers and training resources, Krampe, Tesch-Römer, and I (Ericsson et al., 1993) tried to identify those training activities most closely associated with optimal improvement. Analyzing a review of laboratory studies of learning and skill acquisition during the last century, we found that improvement of performance was uniformly observed when people were given tasks with well-defined goals, were provided with feedback, and had ample opportunities for repetition. These deliberate efforts to increase one's performance beyond its current level involve problem solving and finding better methods to perform the tasks. When a person engages in a practice activity (typically designed by teachers) with the primary goal of improving some aspect of performance, we called that activity *deliberate practice*.

The importance of deliberate practice in attaining the highest levels of performance was first demonstrated in our study (Ericsson et al., 1993) of three groups of expert violinists who differed in level of attained music performance. We studied how these expert musicians spent their daily lives by interviewing them and having them keep detailed diaries for a week. Despite the fact that our expert violinists all spent about the same amount of combined time participating in all types of music-related activities, the two best groups were found to spend more time in solitary practice. When the experts practiced by themselves, they focused with full concentration on improving specific aspects of their music performance as identified by their master teachers, thus meeting the criteria for deliberate practice. The best group of young expert violinists spent around four hours every day, including weekends, in this type of solitary practice.

From retrospective estimates of practice, Ericsson and colleagues (1993) calculated the number of hours of deliberate practice that five groups of musicians at different performance levels had accumulated by a given age, as shown in figure 3.3. By the age of 20, the best groups of young and middle-aged violinists had spent over 10,000 hours of practice, which is 2,500 and 5,000 hours more than the two less accomplished groups of expert young violinists. This amount is 8,000 hours greater than that for amateur pianists of the same age. Even more interesting, the estimated amount of solitary practice was shown to be closely correlated with the objective speed of performance on a series of music-related tasks performed by amateur and expert pianists. Furthermore, greater amounts of solitary practice were reliably associated with faster speed of performing the tasks even when the data from only the expert pianists were analyzed.

In domains where the performance of experts is measured by solo performance on a representative task (such as in music, darts, and

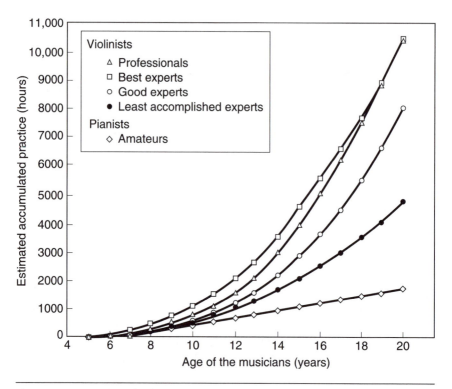

Figure 3.3 Estimated amount of time for solitary practice as a function of age for the middle-aged *professional* violinists (triangles), the *best* expert violinists (squares), the *good* expert violinists (empty circles), the *least accomplished* expert violinists (filled circles), and the *amateur* pianists (diamonds).

Adapted, by permission, from K.A. Ericsson, R.T. Krampe, and C. Tesch-Römer, 1993, "The role of deliberate practice in the acquisition of expert performance," *Psychological Review* 100: 363-406. Copyright © 1993 by the American Psychological Association. Adapted by permission.

individual sports), studies have found a consistent correlation between the level of attained performance and the amount and quality of solitary activities that meet the criteria of deliberate practice (for reviews, see Ericsson, 1996, 2002; Starkes, Deakin, Allard, Hodges, & Hayes, 1996). The same pattern of results has also been found in competitive games such as chess. Charness, Krampe, and Mayr (1996) showed that the amount of time of solitary study of chess games was the best predictor of attained chess-playing performance. Interesting enough, the amount of time that chess players played games did not explain any additional reliable variance. The distinction between deliberate practice and other types of domain-related activities for athletes, however, is more problematic (Starkes et al. 1996; Côté et al., chapter 4; Deakin & Copley, chapter 5). Research on team sports (Helsen, Starkes, &

Hodges, 1998; Starkes et al., 1996; Williams & Ward, chapter 9), such as soccer and field hockey, has shown a more complex picture when the duration of engagement in many types of domain-related activities has been associated with higher levels of achievement. In the following section, I attempt to develop a more precise description of deliberate practice that links the practice activity of individual performers to specific changes of the cognitive and physiological mechanisms that mediate improvements in performance.

In sum, the key challenge for aspiring expert performers is to avoid the arrested development associated with automaticity and the completed adaptation to the physiological demands of the current levels of activity (see figure 3.2). The expert performer actively counteracts such tendencies toward automaticity by deliberately constructing and seeking out training situations in which the set goal exceeds their current level of performance. They acquire mechanisms that are designed to increase their ability to monitor and control performance. In domains where strength, endurance, or flexibility is important, the expert performers keep pushing themselves during training to go beyond their current physiological adaptations to new and higher levels. The more time expert performers are able to invest in deliberate practice with full concentration, the further developed and refined their performance—thus, the observed correlation between the accumulated amount of solitary practice and attained performance (Ericsson, 1996).

Toward Detailed Causal Accounts of the Development of Expert Performance in Sport

The central assumption of the expert performance approach is that the development of expert performance occurs gradually, through incremental changes and refinements of the mediating mechanisms that through orderly accumulation lead to large observable differences in performance. Therefore, it should be possible, at least in principle, to describe the development of performance of each individual expert as a sequence of specific changes to their bodies and mediating mechanisms that ultimately combine with the mechanisms that explain the superior expert performance, as shown in figure 3.4. This framework proposes that reliable changes in the structure of performance have definite causes, such as developmental growth and adaptive responses to changes in practice activities. Each observable change in the structure of the mechanisms, as shown by the transitions in figure 3.4, must therefore be explained. Ultimately, a complete theory should be able to account for the development of all associated biological and cognitive mechanisms that contribute to the development of expert performance. The same theory must also be able to explain how induced stress from specific practice activities and genetic factors cause both physiological adaptations to the body and changes in the nervous system that explain observed increases in the experts' performance.

Detailed longitudinal descriptions that describe the development of expert performance for the 5 to 20 years in the domain are rare. Descriptions of the changes in the mediating mechanisms and the concurrent practice activities (as illustrated in figure 3.4) are not to my knowledge available. The best records consist of the detailed logs written by athletes on their practice and performance (Starkes et al., chapter 10), but we don't have the experimental assessment of the structure of their mediating mechanisms, which should be similar to those obtained for the different memory experts (Ericsson, 1988).

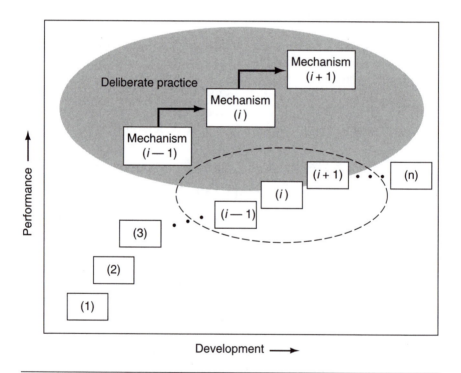

Figure 3.4   The acquisition of expert levels of performance is portrayed as a sequence of states where the performance is increased in gradual and incremental steps. Each *state* (stage of development/performance as indicated by a box with a number, such as 1, ..., *i*-1, *i*, *i*+1, ..., n) is mediated by associated *mechanisms* (deliberate practice), which are incrementally modified to generate the mechanisms of each subsequent state.

Lacking detailed concurrent records of the athletes' development and practice history, researchers have searched for the best available information and have thus asked athletes to retrospectively recall information. The retrospective approach has clear limitations: The accuracy of an athlete's memory after 5 to 20 years cannot be assumed, yet it has to be verified. Côté, Ericsson, and Beamer (2001), however, found that recalled levels of training during development met criteria of reliability and validity.

Studies using retrospective assessments show uniformly that elite athletes recall having engaged in more sport-related activity during their development, when compared with less accomplished peers. When Starkes et al. (1996) examined the development of reported weekly practice of future expert performers, they found that it increased gradually as a function of the number of years in the domain. However, it is well known that elite performers, especially athletes in team sports, are required by their coaches to participate in scheduled practice and that the amount of required weekly practice increases with the level of the team. Increased practice in those instances may thus be a consequence of being selected to play on a better team or being admitted to an international-level academy. However, evidence also exists that some young athletes engage in more solitary practice before they are recruited by elite teams, and thus in these cases, a higher initial level of practice may account for attained performance and their subsequent selection to the higher-level teams (Helsen et al., 1998). This finding is in agreement with research results from music, where the performers' higher levels of practice preceded their acceptance to a music academy. Similarly, those who reach high levels of performance in many domains of expertise, such as chess, music, and sports (Ericsson et al., 1993), have typically started practice at very young ages. Thus, they had the opportunity to accumulate more time for deliberate practice and on the average attain a higher level of skill than their peers who had later starting ages.

To advance our understanding beyond statistical correlations between reported amount of practice and levels of general performance, we need to search for causal mechanisms (preferably, biological) that can explain how expert performers attain the specific characteristics of superior performance by their engaging in particular practice activities. The greatest success in developing such detailed causal models has been made in improving physical performance and its associated physiological characteristics. We will discuss this area of research before we address the cognitive mechanisms that mediate performance.

Improving the Physiological and Anatomical Mechanisms That Mediate Performance

The human body is constantly trying to protect its homeostasis with its preferred temperature range and its ample supply of oxygen, water, and energy to every cell of the body. When people engage in physical activities, the metabolic rate of their muscles increases, which means that their bodies consume the supply of oxygen and energy at unusually high rates. To reestablish and preserve homeostasis, the body activates various countermeasures (negative feedback loops), that increase rates of breathing, overall metabolism, and blood circulation. However, when people push themselves beyond the comfort zone (Ericsson, 2001, 2002) and engage in sustained strenuous physical activity, they challenge the homeostasis sufficiently enough to induce a strained bodily state, with oxygen concentrations outside the acceptable range, which eventually yield biochemical waste products. The biochemical compounds lead to an expression of genes in the cells' DNA that initiates bodily reorganization and change. For example, it is well documented that adults have to engage in intense aerobic exercise to improve their aerobic fitness (Robergs & Roberts, 1997). Specifically, young adults have to exercise at least a couple of times each week, for at least 30 minutes per session, with a sustained heart rate that is 70% their maximal level (around 140 beats per minute for a maximal heart rate of 200). These activity levels lead to extreme conditions for some of the involved cells. For example, sustained activity in the muscles leads to low levels of oxygen in the capillaries that surround the critical muscles, which, in turn, trigger the growth of new capillaries (angiogensis). Similarly, improvements of strength and endurance require that people continue overloading (i.e., increase intensity, frequency, or duration on a weekly basis) and that they keep pushing the associated physiological systems outside the comfort zone to stimulate physiological growth and adaptation (Ericsson, 2001, 2002).

The numerous physiological and anatomical characteristics that distinguish the elite performers have been shown to be adaptations to the demands induced by their regular practice. For example, the larger heart size of endurance runners emerges only after years of extended intense practice. It continues to grow in response to continued challenge (higher levels of practice), but it eventually reverts back toward average size when the athletes stop their engagement in above-average physical exercise (Ericsson & Lehmann, 1996). Many examples also exist where practice during certain critical developmental periods can irreversibly change the course of one's development. For example, ballet dancers' ability to turn out their feet and baseball pitchers' ability to stretch back with their throwing arm are linked to practice overload at a certain age. These movements are established when the children's bones become calcified at around 8 to 10 years of age. Compelling evidence also supports that brain development can be changed at a critical developmental period when children engage in early practice with musical instruments (Ericsson & Lehmann, 1996). Starkes et al. (chapter 10) provide compelling evidence for the role of deliberate practice in attaining and maintaining the strength, endurance, and flexibility of older Master athletes who sustain an exceptional level of performance.

The anatomical and physiological characteristics of expert performers (with the exception of height and body size, as noted earlier) can be explained as the results of a long series of adaptations induced by biochemical responses to the strain induced by specific practice activities. These biochemical signals trigger the expression of previously inactive genes of the cells' DNA that guide the physiological changes. Given that all healthy people seem to have every critical gene as part of their cells' DNA, the effects of these genes cannot provide genetic explanations of individual differences in attained performance.

This general framework can account for individual differences in terms of the amount, type, and intensity of practice in terms of the strain that it induces on the physiological systems. For example, lengthy engagement in some training activity has minimal effect unless it overloads the physiological system sufficiently to lead to associated gene expression and subsequent changes (improvements) of mediating systems. Hence, logging many hours of practice at low levels of intensity is likely to allow the body to adapt to exactly that— namely, improvement in one's ability to exert low levels of intensity for extended periods of time. It is equally important to recognize that there is an optimal level for straining the targeted system. If the strain exceeds the systems' capabilities, it may result in irreparable damage to the tissue. To monitor and maintain the strain in the optimal range, athletes need to exert control and sustain full concentration. Furthermore, this account of improvement emphasizes the need for rest, whereby the body can engage in its restoration and physiological transformation and when athletes can recuperate so that they can engage with full concentration during the next practice session (Ericsson et al., 1993). Finally, to optimize deliberate practice, coaches need to help athletes design training programs that identify the best order for targeting physiological systems for improvement. Coaches can also motivate the athletes to push themselves as well as encourage them to seek rest to retain equilibrium on a daily basis (Salmela & Moraes, chapter 11).

Toward an Account of the Development of the Mental Aspects of Performance

The acquisition of most types of expert performance can be viewed as the sequential mastery of increasingly higher levels of performance through the acquisition of more complex and refined cognitive mechanisms, as is illustrated in figure 3.4. Performers with a given level of skill are already able to successfully complete certain tasks, such as an ice skater's single-rotation jump, but there are other specific tasks that the same performers cannot complete reliably or even at all, such as a double rotation during the same jump (and definitely a triple or quadruple rotation). To progress to higher levels, the performers need to practice and focus on the not-yet-attained and challenging tasks that define the desired superior level of performance (cf. the criteria of deliberate practice, Deakin & Cobley, chapter 5). This section describes how experts gradually attain mastery of increasingly difficult tasks and how the essential role of cognitive mechanisms and representations monitor and control the integration of complex behavior during learning. This section also focuses on how some types of practice activity lead to effective refinement of the mediating representations and associated improvements in expert performance.

Acquisition of Increasingly Difficult and Complex Motor Activities

In many types of sports, including gymnastics, figure skating, and platform diving, it is possible to rank the difficulty of movement combinations. Coaches and teachers instruct the performers to master the easiest movements first, then the basic movements, nearly always in their order of complexity and difficulty. In all of these domains, guidance and instruction are crucial, and no performer reaches elite levels without the help of coaches and teachers. These domains typically demonstrate a close relation between different individuals' overall achievement and the most difficult movement that they have mastered.

The training in these domains is centered on helping the athletes attain mastery of the complex movement sequences performed during competitions. When the young athletes start working with coaches, they perform the simplest movement sequences first with a focus on execution of fundamentals. The importance of acquiring fundamental posture and movement patterns is implied by the finding that the world-class rhythmic gymnasts started their careers by studying classical ballet as children (Beamer, Ericsson, Côté, & Baker, 2001). In contrast, rhythmic gymnasts at the national level started with less structured, playful gym activities.

As the athletes' mastery increases, the coaches select more challenging movements, in addition to raising expectations for artistic beauty and expression. When athletes try to learn new and difficult movement sequences, their initial attempts will almost certainly be unsuccessful. Eventual mastery therefore involves the athletes' removing weaknesses by changing the execution and control of their performance. Continued attempts for mastery require that the athlete always try to correct specific weaknesses, preserve the established aspects, and stretch the performance beyond its current level. This type of deliberate practice requires full attention and complete concentration, but even with such maximal effort, athletes will experience some kind of failure. These failures are aversive because they often lead to falls that can be quite painful on the ice or gym floor.

Deliberate practice for improving performance therefore requires that athletes extend themselves with full concentration, but the difficulty of the attempted tasks will (in spite of those efforts) probably still lead to initial failure and painful falls. It is indeed interesting then that Deakin and Cobley (chapter 5) found that the ice skaters spend a considerable portion of their limited practice time on already mastered jump combinations, rather than work on the not-yet-mastered combinations with the largest room for improvement. However, they also found that with increasing level of attained skill, skaters spent more time on jumps and other challenging activities that had the potential to improve their performance. These findings are consistent with studies where music students and musicians are observed as they engage in practice. As the skill level of the musicians increases, so does a similar progression toward increased quality of practice, where the expert-level musicians engage in problem solving and rely on specialized training techniques to master the remaining challenges (Chaffin & Imreh, 1997; Ericsson, 2002; Gruson, 1988; Nielsen, 1999).

In related domains, such as ballet and music, performers move through a similar progression of increasingly difficult tasks where the guidance of a teacher is often critical for acquisition of fundamentals and continued development to success. Despite these domains that are dependant on mentors, however, domains do exist where large improvements in performance can be attained without teachers.

Acquisition of Superior Speed of Motor Activities

In sports such as swimming, skiing, and tennis, the task conditions for competitions remain similar at all levels of performance. The experts' major type of superiority over less skilled performers involves strength and power (see section on improvements of physiological and anatomical mechanisms, p. 72), as well as their ability to control and reproduce their actions more accurately than novices. In this section, the focus is aptly on the experts' ability to initiate and complete series of actions faster than novices can. The earlier discussed speed advantage of experts can generally be attributed to their ability to anticipate the need for particular actions so that they can prepare such actions in advance.

The extensive research on typing provides the best evidence on how speed of performance can be increased through deliberate practice by refining the representations of future actions. The key finding is that one's typing speed is not fixed. Typists can systematically increase their speed by pushing themselves for as long as they can maintain full concentration, which is typically some 15 to 30 minutes per day (for untrained typists). While pushing themselves to type at a faster speed—typically around 10 to 20% faster than their normal speed— typists strive to improve their anticipation, in part by extending their gaze somewhat farther ahead.

The faster tempo also serves to uncover keystroke combinations that are comparatively slow and poorly executed. Typists then practice these specific combinations in special exercises and incorporate them in the typing of regular text, all of which ensures that any modifications typists make can be integrated into the representations of all other movement sequences that mediate regular typing. By successively eliminating weaknesses, typists can increase their average speed and practice at a rate that is still 10 to 20% faster than the new average typing speed.

The general approach of finding methods to push performance beyond its normal level—even if that performance can be maintained only for a short time—offers performers the potential to identify and correct weaker components and enhance anticipation, which will ultimately allow gradual improvements of performance during extended practice. More general, participants are able to engage in deliberate practice to attain specific performance goals by problem solving and experimentation (for verbal descriptions by world-class golfers and musicians, see Ericsson, 2001, 2002). These performers systematically search for the perceptual and internal stimuli that allow them to coordinate and control their performance by using learning methods similar to those proposed in ecological psychology and dynamical systems theory (Beek et al., chapter 13).

In sports such as swimming, skiing, and tennis, athletes should therefore be able to attain some improvements in their speed and control by using similar types of solitary deliberate practice without the necessity for supervision by coaches (see Salmela and Moraes, chapter 11). However, most sports differ from the relatively predictable nature of typing. Future game situations are far more difficult to anticipate for athletes to actually prepare any advance selection of actions. How those skills that represent game situations can be improved is discussed in the next section.

Improvement in the Selection of Actions in Tactical Situations

In many types of sports, athletes rapidly select or generate actions in game situations where they confront one or more opponents. Expert performers gain their advantage, at least in part, from being more capable of foreseeing consequences of their actions and their opponents' actions (see Tenenbaum, chapter 8; Williams & Ward, chapter 9). For performers to actually improve their ability to anticipate and plan, it is necessary for them to set up practice tasks where their planning and selected actions can be evaluated against the actions of better performers (or ideally the best experts) in the same situations.

How is it even possible to know what the best actions are in a given game situation? In chess, aspiring expert performers typically solve this problem by studying published games between the best chess players in the world. These players re-create and play the games one move at a time to determine if their selected move matches the corresponding move as originally selected by the master. If the chess master's move differed from their own selection, then it would imply that their planning and evaluation must have overlooked some aspect of the position. By more careful and extended analysis, the chess expert is generally able to discover the reasons for the chess master's move. Serious chess players spend as much as four hours every day engaged in this type of solitary study (Charness, Krampe, & Mayr, 1996; Ericsson et al., 1993). Players can increase the quality of their move selections by simply spending a longer time than would be available during a real chess game to analyze carefully different consequences of possible moves for a chess position. With sufficient time for planning, a weaker player can match the move selections of a better player who has to make their moves rapidly under the typical time pressure of matches in chess tournaments. With more chess study, players can refine their representations and access or generate the same information faster. Chess masters can typically recognize an appropriate move immediately whereas it takes a competent club player about 15 minutes to consistently uncover the same move by successive planning and evaluation.

Similar evidence (from studies of baseball and tennis) supports that expertise in sport is linked to more refined representations of game situations (see McPherson and Kernodle, chapter 6). As the athletes acquire better control and become able to execute several alternative actions, they develop better descriptions of the current game situation to improve their selections of their actions. During practice, coaches and teammates direct players to relevant factors for a given game situation and then give them feedback on their selected action. At higher levels of performance, coaches and elite athletes study videorecorded games of sport performances, where they can remove the real-time constraints of performance during regular games. By analyzing the game situations, they can identify the best actions available and perhaps determine how these opportunities could have been anticipated in real time. In chapter 9, Williams and Ward discuss how these perceptual skills and their associated representations can be effectively developed in training devices and simulators that capture the essential perceptual and cognitive factors of game situations.

Summary

The expert performance approach rejects the commonly held view that improvements in an expert's performance happen automatically in response to extended experience as long as the aspiring experts have the necessary innate talent. This approach instead proposes that these improvements actually correspond to changes both in the cognitive mechanisms that mediate how the brain and nervous system control performance and in the degree of adaptation of the body's physiological systems. This approach also argues that these changes are induced by practice activities that are specifically designed to modify the current mechanisms so that performance can be incrementally improved, as is illustrated in figure 3.4. This framework attempts to integrate our knowledge of the biochemical consequences of activity (environment) and how those consequences can lead to the expression of dormant genes that reside in the cells' DNA of not just a select group of talented athletes but rather of all healthy people (genetics). Hence, the requirement of select individual differences in genetic endowment (the pool of all available genes of someone's DNA) for the development of elite performance is assumed to be quite limited, perhaps even restricted to a small number of physical characteristics, such as height and body size. This framework therefore attempts to explain the large individual differences in performance in sport in terms of consequences of individual differences in sustained activity and deliberate practice.

The general rule (or perhaps even the law) of *least effort* theorizes that the human body and brain have been designed to find means to carry out activities at the minimum cost to the metabolism. Consequently, when physiological systems, including the nervous system, are significantly strained by new or altered activities, these systems produce biochemical signals that initiate processes that lead to physiological adaptation and mediation of simpler cognitive processes that reduce the metabolic cost. This phenomenon is evident in most types of habitual everyday activities, such as driving a car, typing, or strenuous physical work, in which people tend to automate their behavior to minimize the effort required for execution of the desired performance. After participants have engaged in the same activities on a regular schedule for a sufficiently long time that the physiological and cognitive adaptations have been completed, then further maintained engagement in this activity will not lead to any additional improvements and the performance will remain at the same level.

The central claim of the expert-performance framework is that further improvement of performance requires increased challenges and the engagement in selected activities specifically designed to improve one's current performance—or in other words, *deliberate practice*. The future expert performers must always search for aspects of their performance that they can improve. They and their coaches then need to identify the deliberate-practice activities that will most successfully improve specific, targeted aspects of their performance, without decreasing other aspects of their performance.

Once we conceive of expert performance as mediated by complex integrated systems of representations for the execution, monitoring, planning, and analyses of performance, it becomes clear that the acquisition of expert performance requires an orderly and deliberate approach. Deliberate practice is therefore designed to improve specific aspects of performance in a manner that assures participants that attained changes can be successfully integrated into representative performance. Hence, practice aimed at improving integrated performance cannot be performed mindlessly nor independent of the representative context for the target performance during competitions.

Successful development of elite performance requires more than the extended engagement in the typical domain-related activities. Elite athletes are found to shape the cognitive and physiological mechanisms that mediate their performance by engaging in deliberate practice (see figure 3.4). The modification of complex cognitive mechanisms during deliberate practice requires problem solving and full concentration. Shaping physiological mechanisms likewise requires the challenging of the associated systems by exerted effort. In fact, research on aerobic fitness shows that to merely *maintain* one's fitness level, athletes have to engage in the same high intensity of exercise with dramatically elevated heart rate to keep their bodies' current physiological adaptations. However, once an adaptation is attained, it is possible to reduce the duration of the weekly training time from the level originally required to attaining it. The core challenge of deliberate practice then is for performers to maintain effort at improvement for as long as they wish to improve performance beyond their current level, by modifying the physiological mechanisms that mediate their performance. With such an approach, as each individual's level of performance increases, the demand for further effort is not reduced—if anything, the demand for effort is actually *increased.*

The specification of the processes that mediate the changes induced by deliberate practice clarifies some issues in sport and training. Some athletes seem to believe that the willingness to exert effort is the key factor for success. These athletes attempt to increase the duration of their practice without concern for maintaining high levels of concentration and are thus unable to preserve the quality of their performance. It appears likely that "practice makes permanent" and that these athletes will not improve their performance on the target event; however, they will become increasingly able to sustain a lower level of performance for longer periods of time. Other athletes try to push themselves too hard, without monitoring their level of concentration and control, thus making themselves vulnerable to accidents and injuries as a result of overuse. Still other athletes push themselves too hard, well beyond sustainable daily levels of practice, which leads to eventual exhaustion and burnout. Only by better understanding the mechanisms that mediate the process of learning and physiological adaptation will coaches and teachers be able to guide athletes to acquire expert levels of performance safely and effectively. Expert performers simply need help to negotiate the many constraints for daily deliberate practice and to respect the essential need for intermittent rest and daily recuperation.

More general, the framework also challenges researchers to specify the particular causal mechanisms that explain correlations between perceived characteristics of athletes and the level of their attained performance. Compelling evidence now exists that many abilities of the elite performers are not signs of innate talent, but rather, they are the results of extended practice, sometimes amplified by early starts of practice during childhood. Similarly, it is quite possible that when coaches perceive a relation between high levels of motivation and attained performance, their ratings of motivation may really reflect the athletes' willingness to engage in deliberate practice with higher quantity and quality. Other personality characteristics, such as self-confidence and anxiety, might at least in part be viewed not as causes of performance but rather as consequences of success or failure during past competitions and practice sessions that were designed to improve aspects of performance.

In conclusion, I am impressed by significant advances in the scientific study of the extended development of elite levels of performance in sport that are reflected in the chapters in this volume. There used to be a time when coaches and teachers were relatively passive consumers of new research ideas from laboratory studies of skill acquisition and eagerly applying them to training practices. Now the tide is starting to turn, and the insights of coaches and elite athletes on advanced skill acquisition and deliberate practice are stimulating laboratory researchers who are interested in the remarkable plasticity of perceptual-motor performance and achievement potential of all healthy children and adults.

EXPERTS' COMMENTS

■ Question

In this chapter, Ericsson and colleagues (1993, 1996) suggest that the primary determinant of high-level performance is how much deliberate practice the athletes have engaged in throughout their athletic careers. What role do you feel practice plays in the development of expert athletes?

■ Coach's Perspective: Nick Cipriano

As athletic coaches around the world learn of Ericsson, Krampe, and Tesch-Römer's (1993) theory of deliberate practice, I am inclined to believe that many will embrace it with much enthusiasm because it reinforces what coaches have been advocating for years; namely, that the training process coupled with a focused attitude is fundamentally important to achieving success. From a coach's perspective, I believe is it likely that deliberate practice may prove more important than talent in the development of expertise. The

Ericsson et al. (1993) theory of deliberate practice is intuitively attractive because it validates the endless number of hours coaches spend teaching skills and tactics to eager young athletes who appear "not to have what it takes" in the formative stages of athletic development. Although coaches respect and understand the role that talent plays in expertise development, they also understand that deliberate practice produces a steady rate of improvement, which will prove to be more important than talent in propelling the athlete beyond any inevitable performance plateaus. In addition, deliberate practice will play a vital role in getting the athlete to resume training after suffering a serious injury or after a disappointing performance at an important competition.

■ *Player's Perspective: Therese Brisson*

Ericsson and colleagues (1993, 1996) suggest that the primary determinant of expert performance is how much deliberate practice the athlete has engaged in throughout an athletic career. This certainly fits with my own experience as a high-performance athlete. It seems to take about 10 years, or 10,000 hours of practice, to reach the level of performance needed to excel on the international stage. Over the past few years, I have observed a trend in which younger players are selected for our national team. I attribute this to the fact that girls are now introduced to hockey much earlier, because playing hockey has become more socially acceptable for girls in Canada. For example, the oldest player on our team at the 1998 Olympics was 39 years old. She started playing hockey at 18 years old, when she began university. In 1994, the average age of the team was around 27 years old, with most players finding it difficult to make the team before the age of 23. This was because most girls did not start playing hockey until around 12 years of age in the early 1980s. Almost 10 years later, the average age of the national team has dropped by almost 3 years, and it is common to see players make the team for the first time between the ages of 18 and 20 years. This fits with the 10-year rule because in the early 1990s and today, it is common to see girls begin playing hockey at 7 or 8 years of age.

In high-performance athlete circles, we recognize three stages in an athlete's career: training to train, training to compete, and training to win. The first phase takes 4 to 5 years; the focus is on developing general athletic ability, general strength and conditioning, and a repertoire of skills, techniques, and tactics. At this stage athletes learn how to train, and there is very little competition. During the second phase, the focus is on refining skills, building specific strength and conditioning, and adjusting tactics for competition; toward the end of the phase athletes are introduced to competitive strategies and international competition. This phase can take another 4 to 5 years. In the final phase, the emphasis is on competing internationally, adjusting competitive strategies, refining mental and decision-making skills, and sport-specific training. One of the most unfortunate trends with hockey in Canada over the past 10 years is that young children are introduced to competition at very early ages, around 7 years of age. Elite programming can begin as early as 9 years of age. A team of 10-year-olds in the Toronto area played more than 100 games in a season! Children spend more time playing games and less time practicing. The trend has had a negative impact on skill development. In a typical hockey game, a child will handle the puck for less than 30 seconds. However, the same child can handle the puck more than 30 minutes in a 60-minute practice. Which situation do you think is the best for skill development? Measures are now taken to increase the practice-to-game ratio in youth hockey, but change will be a slow process.

Practice makes perfect, or does it? Certainly, I would agree with Ericsson that the practice must be focused on improving performance. In general, I think that a lot of practice time is wasted on activities that do not transfer very well to game situations. For example, we routinely practice breaking the puck out of our zone with no forechecking pressure, and we practice the power play with no defenders. This is where the tactics usually break down—while athletes are under pressure. Introducing tactics in this manner is fine, but simulation of the competitive pressures is essential. So I would say that *perfect* practice makes perfect.

Finally, one of the elements of the deliberate practice theory that has not been my experience is that the practice itself is not inherently enjoyable. I have played hockey for almost 25 years, and although there have been good times and bad, I have always enjoyed practicing and looked forward to going to the rink.

Part III

Developing and Retaining Sport Expertise

B Y FAR, THIS IS THE AREA that has garnered the most research in sport. This section of the book provides answers to many of the most pressing questions that arise with regard to the training of high-level performers. What follows are examples of the kinds of questions we hope to address in this section of the book (with the respective chapters for each).

- Is it better for aspiring young athletes to focus on one sport or to experience many sports before they concentrate their training on just one? Côté, Baker, and Abernethy (chapter 4) provide interesting data to suggest that varied sport experiences may be of benefit.

- How do the best coaches teach, critique, support, and motivate athletes? How much and what combination of training techniques should athletes engage in for various sports? Deakin and Cobley (chapter 5) provide intriguing and unexpected findings with regard to how the best athletes practice and what role the coaches play.

- How does one's motor skill development interact with the development of strategies and tactics in a sport? McPherson and Kernodle (chapter 6) examine how motor skills develop in conjunction with strategy and tactical skills in tennis.

- Do coaches, sport referees, and judges exhibit domain-specific expertise in the same way athletes do? Ste-Marie (chapter 7) makes the case that the development of skill in referees and judges is similar to the development of skill in athletes and that they too must circumvent the normal information-processing limits to consistently perform at a high level.

- What aspects of performance (anticipation, perceptual accuracy, decision speed, attentional focus, response selection, response consistency, strategy, etc.) best reflect expert behaviors in a particular sport? Why is it that athletes seem to have all the time in the world to respond and do not seem to be limited by the speed of the game? Tenenbaum presents a model that suggests how the best athletes make decisions and avoid the normal pitfalls associated with physiological fatigue and competitive pressures (chapter 8).

- Can we improve perceptual accuracy or decision speed through the use of perceptual- and decision-training programs? How best can we assess the value of these training programs and whether the learning they impart actually transfers to real-world game situations? If perceptual- and decision-training programs are proven useful, then at what age and skill levels could athletes potentially benefit from them and what proportion of overall practice time should be devoted to them? Each of these questions are of practical interest to coaches and athletes. Williams and Ward (chapter 9) provide extensive background on perceptual training, and they illustrate details on how to assess the efficacy of training. An important addition to this chapter is their description of the implementation of perceptual-training programs for soccer players of varying ages and skills.

■ How much and what sort of training activities are best for Master athletes, who hope to retain their former high levels of performance? Starkes, Weir, and Young (chapter 10) provide an optimistic view of what can be retained with continued practice. This is a must-read chapter for older athletes who continue to train.

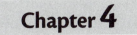

Chapter 4

From Play to Practice

▪ ▪ ▪ ▪ ▪

A Developmental Framework for the Acquisition of Expertise in Team Sports

Jean Côté • Joseph Baker
Bruce Abernethy

The objective of this chapter is to highlight changes in athletes' behaviors and environment that promote the optimal development of sport skills and the maintenance of motivation at each level of growth. This developmental approach to expertise is discussed with respect to the following:

- Stages of sport development
- General categories of activities that athletes can engage in throughout the course of their development
- Empirical findings that regard changes in the type of activities that expert athletes engage in at different stages of their development
- Changes in the social influences of athletes at different stages of their involvement in sport

Stages in Sport Development and Commitment

In their pioneering research, Bloom and colleagues (1985) interviewed 120 participants who were at the top of their respective professions in science, art, and athletics. Their study identified similar phases of learning for all domains of expertise: the early years, the middle years, and the later years. In a review of these phases of learning, Sosniak (1985) suggested that although time engagement in the actual domain of expertise was a crucial factor to learning for those involved in the study, it alone was not sufficient to ensure high levels of performance in the domain. Sosniak stated: "What a learner does, how he or she does it, and how things change as the years pass, are certainly more important variables than the absolute amount of time spent at an activity" (p. 409).

The sport development of two athletes can vary because of different learning opportunities, the instructional methods experienced, and the emotional environment in which learning takes place. Differences in unique environmental experiences during childhood may also lead to differences among elite and less elite athletes in motivation to practice, in the type of skills acquired, and in how and when exceptional abilities are developed. Issues of motivation and learning become important when one tries to understand the types of experience athletes should have and what should be taught at various stages of participation in sport. In the development of expertise, sensitive periods appear to exist where important decisions about participation have to be made, which include a reduction of playing activities and an increase of more serious training activities (Kalinowski, 1985; Monsaas, 1985). These periods of transition seem to concur with certain developmental factors that influence the acquisition of expertise during childhood and adolescence.

Monsaas (1985) and Kalinowski (1985) described the development of expertise from early childhood to adulthood using a sample of tennis players and swimmers (respectively). Data from the tennis players showed that during the early years, only 4 of the 18 players focused solely on tennis. The 14 players who did not specialize exclusively on tennis at an early age participated in a number of other sports, including football, basketball, baseball, soccer, and track. Monsaas (1985) stated that "in these early years only a few of the tennis players played tennis in the winter" (p. 223). Although Monsaas highlighted a great deal of variation in the amount of time that the players had spent on tennis during the early years, the players did experience a gradual increase in the amount of practice until the end of this phase of learning.

The next stage of tennis development, the middle years, are from approximately age 13 through the end of high school. Monsaas highlighted three major changes that characterize the transition from the early years to the middle years. First, the young athletes "began to view themselves as tennis players" (p. 236). Second, the players needed a new type of coaching that put more emphasis on technique and strategy. Finally, the transition from the early to the middle years was marked by an increase in time invested in tennis practice. The decision to play tennis full-time marked the transition from the middle to the later years, and this decision was typically made during college. Additionally, the later years were characterized by another important increase in the number of hours spent in tennis practice.

The development of the swimmers, although chronologically different from the tennis players, was also marked by an initial involvement that focused on interest, excitement, and inherent enjoyment through playing activities (Kalinowski, 1985). Kalinowski described the early years of the 21 swimmers in the following terms:

> These are crucial years, even more crucial than those that follow, because it is during this period that our subjects became interested and caught up in the sport of swimming. In time that interest became self-motivating. Had there been no excitement during the early years, and no sense that the young swimmer was very successful, there would never have been a middle or later period. (p. 141)

The early years lasted about two and a half years for half of the swimmers whereas it covered a longer period of time for the other half of the sample (Kalinowski, 1985). Between the ages of four and five, all the swimmers had started swimming. Until at least age seven, lessons included various types of games that were primarily designed to provide excitement and fun. At age seven or eight, about half of the sample moved directly from summer programs to more competitive and demanding year-round swimming programs while the other half remained in the less intense summer programs. Involvement in year-round swimming programs marked the beginning of the middle years and specialization on the sport of swimming. The transition from the middle years to the later years was then characterized by an increase in intensity and in time committed to swimming. Kalinowski did not suggest an age that generally marked the transition from the middle years to the later years.

In sum, although there were differences in chronological age as to when the tennis players and swimmers reached the middle and later years of their development, most of the athletes studied by Kalinowski (1985) and Monsaas (1985) started their involvement in sport by "trying out" different sports in a playful and fun environment. As the athlete moved from the early years to the middle and later years, this type of environment gradually changed and soon included specialization in the main sport with more practice time. Further, throughout their development, the athletes were provided with stimulating educational environments at home and with coaches who guided the improvement of their performance. Perhaps the most important finding concerned how athlete involvement and supporting conditions such as parental involvement changed as the athletes progressed in sport.

Côté (1999) extended Bloom's (1985) research through qualitative interviews with elite junior athletes in rowing and tennis. Similar to Bloom, he identified three stages of development (specific to sport) from childhood to late adolescence; namely, the sampling years (ages 6-12), the specializing years (ages 13-15), and the investment years (age 16+). In the sampling years, parents were responsible for initially getting their children involved in sport. Children were given the chance to sample a range of different sports and develop fundamental motor skills, such as running, jumping, and throwing. The main purpose was to experience fun and excitement through sport. In the specializing years, the child focused on one or two specific sporting activities. While fun and excitement remained central elements of the sporting experience, sport-specific development emerged as an important characteristic of the child's sport involvement. Critical incidents that made a child pursue one activity over others included positive experiences with a coach, encouragement from an older sibling, success, and simple enjoyment of the activity. The specializing years marked a transition in which athletes gradually decreased their involvement in various extracurricular activities and focused on one or two specific sporting activities. Finally, the child moved into the investment years, during which the child became committed to achieving an elite level of performance in a single activity. The strategic, competitive, and skill development characteristics of sport emerged as being the most important elements of the investment years. Côté (Côté, 1999; Côté & Hay, 2002) differentiated the notion of play in the development of sport expertise and suggested the concept of "deliberate play." Transitions between the sampling, specializing, and investment years were then operationalized by significant changes in athletes' engagement in deliberate play, deliberate practice, and other sporting activities.

Although the sampling, specializing, and investment years are similar to Bloom's (1985) three phases of learning (the early years, the middle years, and the later years), they are also different on two important aspects. First, the stages of sport participation are specific to sport and are anchored in the theoretical concepts of deliberate play and deliberate practice. The sampling, specializing, and investment years are therefore differentiated by and based on the amount of a participant's deliberate practice and deliberate play. Côté and Hay (2002) suggested that the sampling years are characterized by a low frequency of deliberate practice and a high frequency of deliberate play; the specializing years are marked by similar amounts of each; and the investment years are characterized by a high frequency of deliberate practice and a low frequency of deliberate play. The second difference between the two models is that the sampling, specializing, and investment years are identified by an age range that is consistent with general theories of child development, such as those identified by Piaget (1962) and Vygotsky (1978). In sum, the stages of sport participation are consistent with Bloom's original work, but they add sport-specific dimensions that can be tested for their scientific validity.

From Play to Practice: Definition of Terms

In a comprehensive review of studies regarding learning and skill acquisition, Ericsson, Krampe and Tesch-Römer (1993) concluded that the most effective learning occurs through involvement in a highly structured activity defined as *deliberate practice*. According to Ericsson et al., engagement in deliberate practice requires effort, generates no immediate rewards, and is motivated by the goal of improving performance rather than inherent enjoyment. Ericsson et al. demonstrated that expert performance in music was the product of extensive deliberate practice rather than being the result of innate abilities. They suggested that to achieve expert performance, deliberate practice has to be sustained over a period of at least 10 years.

Aspects of the Ericsson et al. (1993) theory of deliberate practice have been verified in the sport domain (Helsen, Starkes, & Hodges, 1998; Hodge & Deakin, 1998; Hodges & Starkes, 1996; Starkes, Deakin, Allard, Hodges, & Hayes, 1996). However, developmental analyses of children's involvement in sport have not yet determined what makes certain children engage in deliberate practice whereas other children turn away from the effort and persistence that is inherent to these activities. Côté (1999) has proposed that the structure of deliberate practice and playful activities changes as a function of the child's age. Further, the optimal learning and motivational activities in the later years are probably different than the activities associated with the best learning and motivational environment in the early years of an athlete's development in sport.

In fact, in attempts to define play, researchers have come up with criteria that differ considerably from the criteria of deliberate practice. Smith, Takhvar, Gore, and Vollstedt (1986) reviewed different definitions of play and suggested the following five criteria. First, intrinsic motivation: Play behavior is done for its own sake and not brought about by basic bodily needs or by external rules or social demands. Second, positive affect: The behavior is pleasurable and enjoyable to the child. Third, nonliteral: The behavior is not carried out seriously, but it does have an "as if" or pretend quality. Four, means/ends: The child is more interested in the performance of the behavior itself than in the results or outcome of the behavior. Five, flexibility: The behavior shows some amount of variation in form or context.

Although studies in sport may support the fact that deliberate practice activities can result in pleasurable or enjoyable affect (Starkes, 2000), deliberate practice activities are generally defined as being extrinsically motivated, being literal, focusing on outcomes rather than processes, and having somewhat rigid rules. Developmental psychologists and educators (Piaget, 1962; Wiersma, 2000) would argue that involving young children in such structured activities could have detrimental effects on learning and motivation. Just as Piaget (1962) suggested continuity between children's play and work, we suggest continuity between playing sport and participating in deliberate sport-specific practice activities.

Côté and Hay (2002) discussed the importance of athletes' playing games with rules during their early development. This type of play was described as *deliberate play,* a term that was chosen to contrast with three types of activities: the free-play activities of infancy and early childhood (Denzin, 1975; Piaget, 1962); the "structured practice" activities typical of organized sport; and deliberate practice activities (Ericsson, 2001; Ericsson et al., 1993). Contrary to the practice activities that are generally designed to improve performance, deliberate play activities are designed to maximize inherent enjoyment. Deliberate play activities are regulated by rules adapted from standardized sports rules, and they are set up and monitored by the children or by an adult involved in the activity. The concepts of free play, deliberate play, structured practice, and deliberate practice may be placed on a continuum of activities that are characterized by different dimensions (table 4.1).

The dimensions most likely to differentiate between free play, deliberate play, structured practice, and deliberate practice include the following: the goal of the activity, the perspective taken while engaged in the activity, the structure of the activity, the monitoring during

■ **Table 4.1**

Comparison of Free Play, Deliberate Play, Structured Practice, and Deliberate Practice Activities

Dimensions	Free play	Deliberate play	Structured practice	Deliberate practice
Goal	Fun	Fun	Improve performance	Improve performance
Perspective	Process (means)	Process-experimentation	Outcome (ends)	Outcome (ends)
Monitored	Not monitored	Loosely monitored	Monitored	Carefully monitored
Correction	No correction	No focus on immediate correction	Focus on correction (often through discovery learning)	Focus on immediate correction
Gratification	Immediate	Immediate	Immediate and delayed	Delayed
Sources of enjoyment	Inherent	Predominantly inherent	Predominantly extrinsic	Extrinsic

the activity, corrections made during the activity, the immediacy of gratification, and the sources of enjoyment. The dimensions qualifying deliberate practice activities were derived from the original study of deliberate practice (Ericsson et al., 1993) and studies conducted in sport (Helsen et al., 1998; Hodge & Deakin, 1998; Hodges & Starkes, 1996; Starkes et al. 1996).

Between the Ericsson et al. original study and the studies conducted in sport, one source of discrepancy relates to the concept of enjoyment. In the original study of deliberate practice, Ericsson et al. (1993) asked subjects to ignore the consequences of the activity and to focus on the inherent enjoyment of the activity itself. They then used interview questions to document the subjects' experiences. The questionnaires that were used in the sport research instructed participants to evaluate "the enjoyment derived from the actual activity" (Helsen et al., 1998, p. 18). This type of instruction might measure a different construct: Participants might confuse the enjoyment of the results of the activity with the enjoyment of the activity itself (Ericsson, 1996). Regardless, neither instruction would have allowed an external observer to assess an athlete's level of enjoyment, since no observable indicators of enjoyment were used to measure the concept (Côté, Ericsson, & Beamer, 2001). Despite the overall findings of the sport studies (Helsen et al., 1998; Hodge & Deakin, 1998; Hodges & Starkes, 1996; Starkes et al. 1996), we contend that play activities are more inherently enjoyable than deliberate practice activities—a view consistent with Ericsson and colleagues' original definition of deliberate practice (Ericsson, 1996; Ericsson et al., 1993).

Sport Involvement of Expert Athletes Throughout Their Development

To date, sport studies using the Ericsson et al. (1993) theoretical framework have focused on experts' descriptions of various practice activities and the ratings of these activities in terms of enjoyment, relevance, effort, and concentration. Few studies in sport, however, have been conducted with the purpose of tracing the development of expertise by assessing experts' performance at various stages of sport participation and the variables that could have affected their performance and motivation. A new methodology (Côté et al., 2001) has recently been developed to specifically assess the types of play and practice activities that are necessary to achieve expertise and the additional environmental conditions that are critical to the attainment of expertise throughout development. This methodology (or an adaptation of it) has been used with elite Australian team sport athletes (Abernethy, Côté, & Baker, 2002; Baker, Côté, & Abernethy, in press a, in press b) and Canadian ice hockey players (Soberlak & Côté, in press). It has provided reliable and valid longitudinal findings with important implications for the design of practice and the structuring of junior sport development systems.

Abernethy, Côté, and Baker (2002) used the new interview technique (Côté et al., 2001) to study a group of 15 Australian national team athletes (3 female netball players, 4 male field hockey players, 4 female field hockey players, and 4 male basketball players) and a comparative sample of nonexpert decision makers drawn from the same sports. Both groups completed a structured interview that was designed to elicit information regarding their sporting development from its initiation to the present day. In addition, researchers asked each subject qualitative questions regarding psychosocial events that marked each athlete's development. Collectively, the quantitative and qualitative questions focused on athletes' psychosocial development, involvement in various activities, and the performance milestones that occurred throughout their progress toward sport expertise.

The developmental changes that marked the careers of the expert players are in agreement with the sampling, specializing, and investment years as distinct stages of sport participation. An important transition point occurred at approximately age 13 when expert athletes began secondary school, reduced their involvement in other sports, and began to compete at the state or provincial level in their primary sport. Another transition point occurred at approximately age 16, when athletes made the decision to become elite athletes and consequently invested all their leisure time into training.

Figure 4.1 outlines important training factors that change throughout the development of expert athletes, including the number of sporting activities they are involved in and the number of hours invested in both deliberate practice and deliberate play.

As well, social influences such as the roles of coaches, parents, and peers change as the child progresses from the sampling to the investment years. These changes in training factors and social influences are discussed in the next section.

Number of Sporting Activities

Figure 4.2 outlines the number of activities expert and nonexpert Australian athletes (Baker et al., in press a) were involved in as a function of their age. From age 5 to 12, both experts and nonexperts increased

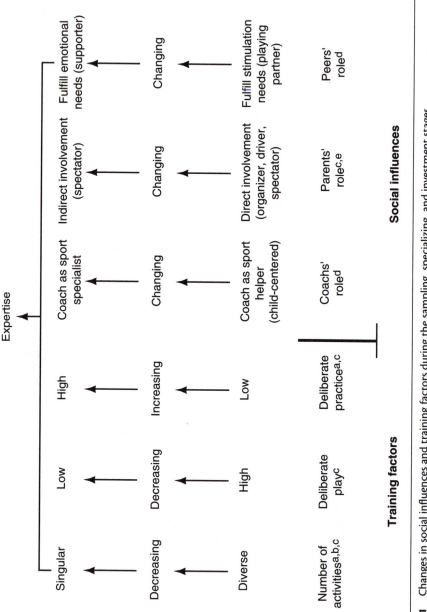

Figure 4.1 Changes in social influences and training factors during the sampling, specializing, and investment stages.

a = Baker, Côté, & Abernethy, in press a; b = Baker, Côté, & Abernethy, in press b; c = Soberlak 2001; d = Abernethy, Côté, & Baker 1999; e = Côté, 1999.

their participation in extracurricular activities; however for the expert athletes, this is followed by a rapid decrease in other activities from approximately age 13 onward, which would mark their entry into the specializing years. A comparable reduction of involvement in various activities after age 13 does not occur for the nonexpert athletes. The reduction in the number of activities in which expert athletes were involved continues until approximately age 17, the beginning of the investment years. After age 17, the expert decision makers were involved in an average of three sporting activities. An examination of these activities suggests that the athletes stayed involved in other sports for relaxation (e.g., golf) or for cross-training during the off-season (e.g., soccer). Data from the nonexpert athletes suggest that they never experienced the pronounced specializing and investment as experienced by the experts.

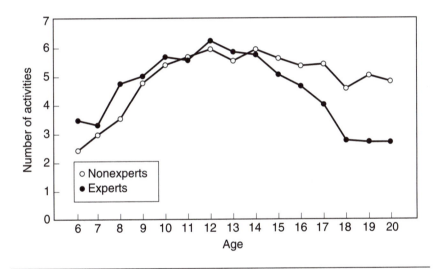

Figure 4.2   Expert and nonexpert involvement in other activities.

During the qualitative interviews, the athletes were asked to regroup the years for which their training remained consistent, and they were also asked to identify specific years at which their training changed in terms of quality and quantity. The periods of sport participation identified by the expert athletes, as illustrated in the following quotations, are consistent with the previously presented data and with the distinction among the sampling, specializing, and investment years made by Côté (Côté , 1999; Côté & Hay, 2002).

I had had different activities in my life (referring to the ages 6-12) at that time. I was still playing squash and still playing footy and doing other stuff as well. I had no idea I would focus on basketball at that stage. Between 12 and 16 . . . basketball was my main sport, I had cancelled out the other sports. But I wasn't 100% focused on basketball at that time. I still had my school and other stuff but it was definitely my number one sport. Pretty much basketball was everything from 16 on. It was pretty much all that I was concentrating on.

—Male basketball player

At around age 13, I was mostly playing and training once a week. From age 14-17 I did more training in terms of more times a week. I was training with the NSW [state] team and stuff like that. I didn't do much in terms of weights, sprints or endurance. The practice was more intense and regular. Then 18-19 I got the shock of my life when I started doing weights, sprints and endurance. At age 20- 23 I really worked hard for endurance training.

—Female netball player

Baker et al. (in press a) found a significant negative correlation ($r = -.54, p < .05$) between athletes' involvement in additional sporting activities and the amount of sport-specific training needed to achieve expertise. More specific, as the number of additional sporting activities that athletes were involved in increased, the number of hours of sport-specific training before national team selection decreased. This relationship suggests that the diverse experiences of the sampling years may be of functional significance for the development of expert decision making.

The retrospective data reviewed in this section on sport-specific training of elite athletes in team sports suggest that early specialized, single-sport training is not necessarily a prerequisite for the development of expertise in that sport. Indeed, it may actually be wise to delay sport specialization to maximize choice for the child and thus enhance the range of motoric experiences the child can ultimately bring to the principal sport of interest.

Hours of Deliberate Practice

Considerable evidence supports the monotonic relationship between accumulated amounts of deliberate practice and performance attained in team sport (Helsen et al., 1998; Helsen, Hodges, Van Winckel, &

Starkes, 2000). Ericsson et al. (1993) suggested that "the higher level of attained elite performance, the earlier the age of first exposure as well as the age of starting deliberate practice" (p. 389). Although findings from various studies showed that early exposure to sport is a strong predictor of performance, it remains to be confirmed whether the early exposure consisted mainly of deliberate practice activities. By tracing the development of expert performers in sport, Côté (1999) and Côté and Hay (2002) have emphasized the importance of deliberate play (as opposed to deliberate practice) in the early years of elite athletes—a view consistent with studies that investigated the early years of elite performers (Bloom, 1985; Carlson, 1988).

Helsen et al. (2000) showed that at about 10 years into their career, international field hockey players and soccer players greatly increased the amount of time spent in team practice. Similarly, Baker et al. (in press a) showed that expert Australian team sport athletes accumulated similar hours of sport-specific training versus nonexperts until approximately 10 years of involvement in their sport at around age 15, or the beginning of the investment years. After age 15, the rate of sport-specific practice accumulation by experts escalated dramatically beyond that accumulated by nonexperts. Nevertheless, Baker et al. found that the number of hours of reported sport-specific training by their expert athletes (being some 4,000 hours, on average) was far short of the 10,000 hours of deliberate practice reported for expert musicians by Ericsson et al. (1993). Further, the range of accumulated hours reported by the Australian expert athletes was highly variable, which suggests that additional factors (to the total hours of accumulated sport-specific practice) do indeed influence one's attainment of expertise in the team sport domain.

Soberlak and Côté's (in press) study of professional ice hockey players is consistent with Baker and colleague's (in press a) study of Australian team sport athletes. Soberlak and Côté showed that the total accumulated hours of the ice hockey players' deliberate practice from the age of 6 to 20 was only 3,072 hours, of which an average of 459 hours was accumulated during the sampling years. Conversely, an average of 2,215 hours of deliberate practice occurred during the investment years. These findings support evidence from previous studies (Baker et al., in press a; Bloom, 1985; Côté, 1999; Helsen et al., 1998) that identify the investment years as a period of elite athletes' devotion to specialized training. In sum, the athletes' development of expertise in team sport and subsequent progression to high levels of performance may be attributable to something other than a singular focus on deliberate practice activities from an early age.

Hours of Deliberate Play

Soberlak and Côté's (in press) retrospective study of 20-year-old professional ice hockey players was the first study to quantify the number of hours spent in deliberate play activities throughout development. The number of hours per year that athletes engaged in deliberate play activities (e.g., street hockey, backyard ice rink, mini sticks), deliberate practice activities (e.g., organized practices, power skating, dryland/weight training), organized games, and other sports are shown in figure 4.3.

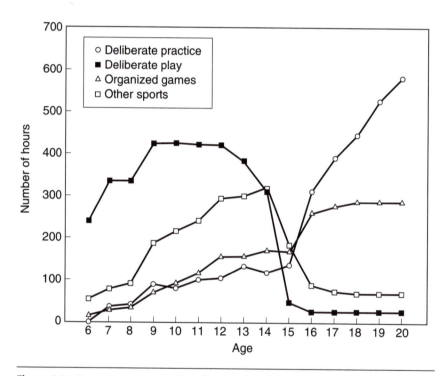

Figure 4.3   Hours per year spent in deliberate play, deliberate practice, organized games, and other sports.

As figure 4.3 reveals, athletes were involved in high amounts of deliberate play during the sampling years (ages 6-12). In contrast, the specializing years (ages 13-15) were characterized by a significant decrease in the athletes' involvement in deliberate play whereas in the investment years (ages 16+), athletes were involved in little deliberate play. Involvement in other sports followed a similar pattern to involvement in deliberate play activities. Conversely, involvement in deliberate practice activities and organized games started at a low level of involvement at age 6 but increased gradually from the sampling to the investment years.

A playful environment during the early years of a child's involvement in sport may explain the early learning and exceptional motivation of expert athletes because it appears to lead to subsequent learning and involvement in deliberate practice. Gould, Udry, Tuffey, and Loehr (1996) showed that early specialization and highly structured training in which control is passed to an outside agent (parent or coach) reduce intrinsically motivated behavior and can ultimately lead to more dropout and burnout among youths in sport. On the other hand, children are motivated to participate in deliberate play because of their own interest in the activity. This type of early involvement in sport may actually help children to gain a better appreciation of their ability and subsequently affect their decision to stay involved in sport (Brustad, Babkes, & Smith, 2001).

Developmental Aspects of Motivation

Self-determination theory and Vallerand's recent hierarchical model of motivation in sport (Deci & Ryan, 1985; Ryan & Deci, 2000; Vallerand, 2001) support the notion that early intrinsically motivating behaviors (deliberate play) will have a positive effect over time on overall motivation and ultimately one's willingness to engage in more externally controlled activities (deliberate practice). Ryan and Deci (2000) suggested that what is paramount in the development of highly motivated, self-determined experts is the following: the building of a solid foundation of intrinsic motivation, through involvement in activities that promote intrinsic regulation that provides participants with the opportunity to make autonomous decisions, develop competence, and feel connected to others. Involvement in a high amount of deliberate play activity during the sampling years can provide young athletes with the opportunity to engage in activities that are intrinsically regulated, which can subsequently help them to become more self-determined and committed in their future participation in sport.

Data from the qualitative interviews with Australian team sport athletes (Abernethy et al., 2002) support the notion that deliberate play is the most important activity to keep young children motivated and to help them learn basic sport skills.

> As a child we used to just get out and play against a wall, play various games involving ball. It could have been tennis balls, anything ball and bat oriented. I think as a netballer,

it was important to play a variety of games at an early age, because it did help with co-ordination. By the time I started playing netball I already had that base.

Female netball player

We used to play it [field hockey] down in the backyard quite a lot. Just for a bit of fun. Every afternoon we would get down in the backyard and play it. That is what was so fun about it. It was good playing against my brothers and sisters.

Female field hockey player

Although sports have become more organized and institutionalized in the last few years (De Knop, Engström, & Skirstad, 1996), expert team sport athletes' first experience in sport is still connected with the importance of playing and experimenting with new or different means of executing skills rather than attaining a goal. As illustrated in this section, the involvement of expert athletes in deliberate play activities allowed them to try new or different combinations of behaviors that eventually enabled them to reach their goal. The expert athletes' early involvement in deliberate play activities were preconditions to their motivation to pursue more specialized training and achieve exceptional performance.

Social Influences Throughout the Development of Expert Athletes

Children have three main sources of influence as they progress through their development in sport: coaches, parents, and peers. From the sampling years to the specializing years and on to the investment years, each group's role of influence changes. Some evolve into more complex roles; others fade into more supportive roles. Each group's influence throughout the stages is described as follows.

Role of Coaches in Developing Young Athletes

The important issue of how expert athletes spend their time during practice highlights the crucial role that coaches have in setting up optimal learning conditions (Côté, 2002; Côté, Salmela, Trudel, Baria, & Russell, 1995; Kalinowski, 1985; Salmela, 1996). Because of the changing cognitive, physical, and emotional needs of children at various stages of their sport participation, it is important that the role of coaches changes accordingly. In general, expert coaches have been shown to provide both physical (e.g., training facilities and equipment) and social resources to overcome the effort and motivational constraints associated with deliberate practice (Salmela, 1996). However, few studies have assessed how coaches' roles change from athletes' early sport participation to athletes' achievement of elite performance. Kalinowski (1985) and Monsaas (1985) describe coaches' roles in the early years as being kind, cheerful, and caring. In the later years, coaches were described as being more qualified in the sport and respected for their knowledge. Monsaas (1985) made the following statement about the first coaches of world-class tennis players:

> While these were not exceptional coaches, they tended to be very good with young children. They were regarded by the tennis players as extremely nice people who sometimes took on the role of a father figure. (p. 225)

In qualitative interviews, Australian expert team sport athletes (Abernethy et al., 2002) discussed the types of coaches they had in their first few years of involvement in sport. When the athletes were between the ages of 6 and 12, coaches' intervention style and the teaching content was straightforward—they let children play and focused just on their basic skill development.

> My first coach, she was just a nice lady, we used to have a lot of fun.
>
> Female netball player

> [When I started] I think I had some good coaching. They weren't necessarily what people call brilliant coaches, but they were enthusiastic and I think that was more important than anything.
>
> Female field hockey player

From a coaching perspective, involving children in deliberate play activities without imposing a rigid structure on their experience during the sampling years may have a unique and vital role in the child's development in sport. Deliberate play allows the child to experiment with various forms of movement in a stress-free environment that could be most conducive to learning. Deliberate play permits the development of social attitudes, encourages the child to be with others, and gives a child specific goals to work toward. Through play, the child grows, and the growth acts as a stimulus to play-change and later involvement in more structured deliberate practice activities.

Abernethy et al. (2002) noted that athletes started to develop a closer and more professional relationship with their coach at approximately age 13.

> Knowledge of the game, good coaches have a passion for it. They impart that passion on players. Because of the way they feel about the game they motivate people around them . . . [a coach at this level] has sound knowledge of the game, puts in a lot of hours, really tries to get the best out of players, and trains them at the highest intensity.
>
> Female hockey player

In sum, athletes' descriptions of their coaches' intervention in the first stage of their career focused on opportunities to move, to be engaged in motor activities, and to learn fundamental movement skills that eventually became the foundation for learning more complex sport skills later in their development.

Athletes started to develop a closer relationship with their coaches at approximately age 13. At the same time, coaches became more technical and "serious" regarding their athletes' involvement in practice and training. Such a transition in the coach's role—from being identified as "sport-helper" and "child-centered" during the sampling years to "sport specialist" during the investment years—may strengthen athletes' commitment to increasing the quantity and intensity of their training and to pursuing their sport to a higher level.

Role of Parents in Developing Young Athletes

Bloom (1985) highlighted the major influence of the family at the different stages of children's talent development in science, art, and athletics. They reported that in the early years of a child's involvement in an activity, parents tended to be supportive, which allowed their children freedom to decide whether to practice formally or not. This stage was followed by a period of dedication for both the performers and the parents. Finally, the later years were characterized by the participant's full-time commitment to improving performance, and the parents' role was more restricted, consisting mainly of financial support. Bloom's study thus provided a developmental perspective on the influence of family on talent development.

More recent, Côté (1999) studied the family environment of elite junior athletes throughout their development. The role of the parents changed from a leadership role in the sampling years to a follower/ supporter role in the investment years. During the sampling years, the parental belief that sport is an important factor in a child's overall development resulted in the parents' assuming a leadership role and encouraging their children to be involved in various types of enjoyable sporting activities. During the specializing years, parents became committed supporters of their child-athlete's decision to be involved in a limited number of sports. In all the families studied, parents did not put any kind of pressure on the children regarding what type of sport they should specialize in. This role of follower and supporter became more apparent in the investment years when parents made sacrifices in their personal lives and in their family's lives to allow their child-athlete to have optimal training conditions. During the investment years, parents responded to the various demands and expectations put on their child-athlete by fostering an optimal learning environment, rather than creating new demands or pressure.

As a follow-up of Côté's study, Soberlak (2001) used a structured interview technique to assess how the formal roles of parents of three professional ice hockey players changed as the athletes progressed from the sampling to the investment years. During the sampling years, parents' involvement consisted of the following: coaching their child; helping to structure their child's deliberate play activities (building a backyard rink); involvement without actual input on activities (driving the child to the practice site); observing and giving feedback; and participating with their child as a playing/training partner. During the specializing years, parents stopped coaching their children, and instead of helping them structure their deliberate play activities, they started helping them structure their deliberate practice activities. Parents' involvement during the specializing years can be summarized as facilitating their child's deliberate practice activities (setting up a weight room at home); becoming involved with them and their activities without giving them actual input; observing and giving feedback; and participating with their child as a playing/training partner. Finally, during the investment years, parents' involvement consisted of helping to structure the child's deliberate practice activities as well as observe and give feedback.

A common characteristic of the Côté (1999), Bloom (1985), and Soberlak (2001) studies is how the role of the parents changes from the sampling through to the investment years. Generally, parents have a direct involvement in their child's sporting activities during the sampling years, which consists mainly of coaching and playing/training with their child. The direct involvement becomes indirect, however, when the child moves from the sampling to the investment years. During the investment years, the role of the parents consists mainly of being a spectator at games and providing opportunities at home for their child to be involved in deliberate practice activities, such as by supplying a weight room.

Role of Peers in Developing Young Athletes

Reviews of the youth sport motivation literature have consistently listed peers as one of the main reasons why children participate in sport (e.g., Brustad et al., 2001; Weiss & Petlichkoff, 1989). Despite the well-known importance of peers in children's sport socialization, few studies have been conducted to examine the influence that peers have on an athlete's performance in sport.

In their study of 15 Australian elite team sport athletes, Abernethy et al. (2002) found that in the early stage of the expert athletes' career, all mentioned having a group of friends who were involved in sport. Interacting with friends who have interest in sport allows the expert athletes to "play" sport whenever free time was available. When they were with their friends, expert athletes described playing sports as their main activity:

> I suppose the fact that my friends all loved sport really helped. We were all so energetic when we were young. We would all get together and go round to our house and go and have a kick of a football or something. So I suppose that was really good because I grew up loving all different sports. And maybe that helped me get a bit of natural ability as well.
>
> Female hockey player

During the investment years, the expert athletes discussed the importance of having friends outside of sport as well as athlete-friends.

> The fact that you can go to friends outside of sport and just talk about anything [is important]. With a friend in sport, you have that common link, which is a pretty big common link. Whereas a friend outside of sport appreciates the fact of what you are doing in sport, but there is also an outlet to talk about other things.
>
> Male field hockey player

Overall, expert athletes were mainly influenced by peers who were involved in sport during childhood and adolescence. This type of relationship allowed them to spend a considerable amount of their free time playing sport. When sport became more serious at approximately age 16, the athletes mentioned that it was beneficial to have friends outside of sport as well as athlete-friends. This type of peer interaction during the later stage of an athlete's involvement in sport may fulfill relationship needs that are driven by more complex emotional issues. As athletes move from the sampling to the investment years, they establish a network of peer relationships that satisfy their more complex adult needs. During the sampling years, the origin of interaction with peers is driven by the young athlete's need for stimulation through deliberate play. As athletes progress to the investment years, peer relationships grow more intense and fulfill motivational and emotional needs that may facilitate involvement in deliberate practice activities. Continued research on the important issue of peer relationships is necessary to more fully understand the social influences that affect the development of expertise.

Summary

Ericsson and colleague's (1993) study of musicians, and subsequent studies of deliberate practice in sport (Helsen, et al., 1998; Hodges & Starkes, 1996; Starkes et al. 1996; Hodge & Deakin, 1998), strongly support the contention that deliberate practice is a major determinant of expertise. These studies, however, offer few insights as to why certain athletes chose to invest in deliberate practice whereas others do not. The major objective of this chapter was to highlight developmental changes associated with deliberate practice and the achievement of expertise in team sports. By taking a developmental approach, one that describes common changes in experts' behaviors and social influences from childhood to adulthood, we sought to generate a timeline that described when important observable, predictable, and measurable changes in sport practice and performance occur. A comprehensive understanding of the development of expertise in sport requires that we describe changes in behaviors and social influences at various stages of an athlete's involvement in sport.

As many others have noted (e.g., Brustad et al., 2001; Weiss, 1995), it is important not to see young athletes in sport as miniature adults with small-scale skills, attitudes, and abilities. A true developmental approach to expertise promotes the search for optimal approaches to the development of sport skills that are appropriate to each stage of growth. Because preadolescent athletes have not yet learned how to engage in task persistence, how to delay gratification, or how to be self-controlled, the focus of training for athletes of this age should be on learning basic cognitive and motor skills through deliberate play activities. By the time athletes reach adolescence, they will have acquired fundamental movement skills through deliberate play and will have developed mature cognitive skills. At this point, an appropriate shift in training would include more complex kinds of learning and deliberate practice activities. The roles of coaches, parents, and peers also follow predictable changes throughout the development of expertise that help athletes make the transition from playlike activities to more serious types of training.

The model presented in this chapter, which highlights the changing environment of athletes who achieved a high level of performance in sport, has many implications for the design of sport programs. The choice of learning objectives, curriculum sequence, and teaching methods will need to vary greatly for athletes of different ages. Early sport diversification, high amounts of deliberate play, child-centered coaches and parents, and being around peers who are involved in sport all appear to be essential characteristics of environments for young children that encourage their later investment in deliberate practice activities.

EXPERTS' COMMENTS

Question

In this chapter, Côté, Baker, and Abernethy suggest that there may be an advantage for young children to pursue a number of sports at a young age before they decide to concentrate on their primary sport. What do you suggest?

Coach's Perspective: Nick Cipriano

The research literature in wrestling supports a multilateral approach to an athlete's sport participation before one specializes in wrestling training. Researchers believe that participation in a variety of sports enhances general athleticism and better prepares the young athlete for the rigors of wrestling training. In North America, the age of specialization for wrestling is pegged at between 13 and 14 years of age, which coincides with the start of high school. All potential wrestlers have ample opportunity to sample other sports before they focus on wrestling training. A growing body of anecdotal evidence, however, strongly suggests that the most successful wrestlers in the world are introduced to formalized wrestling training earlier in life, anywhere from age 10 and onward. Even for such early starters, all are involved in a variety of sports activities that serve to supplement wrestling training.

The road to developing expertise in sport is indeed a lengthy one. The position advanced by Ericsson, Krampe, and Tesch-Römer (1993)—that it may require a minimum 10 years/10,000 hours of practice to attain expertise status—is certainly a position I support, based on my knowledge of training patterns in elite athletes. Within the continuum of expertise development in sport, the role of the coach is to accelerate the learning process and to shorten the duration of the journey to expertise. The 10 years/10,000 hours of practice is a benchmark that in my experience holds firm across various sport domains, and it is certainly one that applies to freestyle wrestling. Regardless of the activity, though, it appears that a 10-year period is the minimum time requirement for athletes to do the following: learn and perfect the technical-tactical skills of any sport; gain experience for high-level competition; develop volitional qualities that will sustain a prolonged effort; and cultivate biological adaptations that meet the physical demands of the sport. Each component is orchestrated over a prolonged period, and through repeated practice, simulation, and competition, the athlete will develop the tools necessary to achieve and sustain expert performance.

A freestyle wrestler typically engages in three distinct phases of training en route to becoming an expert. The first phase starts at the age of 13 to 14 years, which coincides with the start of high school. Although many wrestlers are exposed to wrestling before high school, relatively few engage in a training program that offers sufficient structure to serve a meaningful purpose. The four years of high school training serve as the formative years for skill development, and they are a critical time for the coach to cultivate the volitional qualities that will facilitate the athlete's making a long-term commitment to a training program.

On completing high school, the wrestler either continues to practice with a community-based club or becomes a member of a college program. The second phase is four to five years long and is characteristic of physical development, technical-tactical skill perfection, and the gaining of experience in high-level competition. The wrestler spends upward of 20 to 25 hours a week training, which is broken down into approximately 10 to 12 hours of specific training, 6 to 8 hours of supplemental training, 2 to 3 hours of video analysis, and 2 to 4 hours of recovery and regenerative exercises. At the end of the second phase, wrestlers start a specialized phase of training that focuses on high-level competition, technical-tactical perfection, and physical refinement. The third phase is generally between three and five years in duration, with superior performances emerging anywhere between the first and fifth year. In most cases, if a strong international performance has not been achieved within the first three years of the third phase (23-26 years of age), it is likely that the wrestler will not develop into an international-level performer.

With some noted exceptions (e.g., women's gymnastics), the developmental process for athletes in other sports is similar to that of the wrestler. All will engage in specialized training somewhere between 10 and 14 years of age, and over a 10-year period, they will develop specific technical-tactical skills, acquire appropriate competition experience, and in concert with physical maturation, emerge as international-level athletes.

■ Player's Perspective: Therese Brisson

I could not agree more with Côté, Baker, and Abernethy's point of view. My generation of athletes did all the sports—soccer, swimming, baseball, hockey, basketball, track and field, badminton, you name it. We had a variety of motor experiences, each of which had elements that transferred to other situations. We were good athletes first and specialists second, much later in life. I am very concerned about the trend in Canada toward specialization at an earlier age, especially in hockey, the sport I am involved with. Dr. Steve Norris, a highly regarded physiologist at the University of Calgary who works with many of Canada's top athletes, says that the younger athletes today are great hockey players, skiers, swimmers, and so on, but they are not very good athletes. In fact, he points out that the best athletes in high-performance programs are actually the older athletes. Therefore, one objective of the training programs Dr. Norris designs today has been to improve what he calls *general athletic ability*. A key element of the women's hockey team preparations for the 2002 Winter Olympic Games was a month-long summer camp at which the focus was on improving general athletic ability. We did a lot of skipping, jumping, quick foot movement, soccer, basketball, cycling, rock climbing, swimming, yoga, and running, but very little hockey. The objective of the camp was to be better athletes, and I think this camp was one of the keys to our success. However, the most effective time for this activity is much earlier in an athletic career.

Despite my support for the generalist approach, I think that windows of opportunity for learning motor skills do exist. In his book *Why Michael Couldn't Hit*, Klawans (1996) eloquently explains the inability of Michael Jordan, an undisputed expert basketball player, to make the transition to baseball. Klawans' explanation is that Jordan was not exposed early enough to the perceptual demands of hitting a baseball pitched at major league speeds. Jordan had passed the window of opportunity for developing this skill, and he never was able to hit consistently, even in the minors. Klawans presented evidence in expert violinists to further support this window of opportunity idea. PET scanning showed that children who learned to play the violin before 13 years of age activated completely different areas of the brain than those who learned after the age of 13. It seems that after age 13, the window of opportunity for developing expertise at violin playing closes.

I have noticed the effect of windows of opportunity in my own sport. For example, my first experiences in skating occurred when I was around 2 years old. At 6 years, I began playing ringette, a sport that is like floor hockey on ice. I didn't start to play organized hockey and practice puck handling until I was 12. No matter how much I practice, I will never have the puck-handling skills of some of my younger teammates, many of whom started handling a puck at 6 years of age. I think I had passed the window of opportunity for expert puck handling! However, my skating skills are much better than those of most of my peers. I think this is because ringette allowed me to concentrate on skating skills at a young age, because it does not present the demands of puck handling. Furthermore, from the ages of 14 to 20, I spent around 20 hours per week on the ice in the winter, playing, practicing, coaching, instructing, and refereeing both ringette and hockey. I think that skating in these varying contexts led to the development of superior skating skills and was the foundation for my development as an athlete. Despite extended practice, some of my teammates have improved weaker skating skills but can't seem to reach the same level of skating skill as those who did ringette or figure skating as a younger child. The best approach to developing sport expertise is to expose children to a large variety of motor skills and experience early on (6 to 14 years) so that children will not miss windows of opportunity and leave specialization for later on (15 years and older).

Chapter 5

A Search for Deliberate Practice

■ ■ ■ ■ ■

An Examination of the Practice Environments in Figure Skating and Volleyball

Janice M. Deakin
Stephen Cobley

A critical question in the study of expert performance is how much of the performer's skill is the product of learning. Discussion over the relative contributions of talent and practice to the development of expert performance shows no signs of abatement. Recently, Howe, Davidson and Slaboda (1998) have refocused the classic nature-versus-nurture debate in a review that considers the role of one's talent in the development of music expertise. In the absence of evidence for underlying factors of talent in music, these authors suggest that "differences in early experiences, preferences, opportunities, habits, training, and practice are the real determinants of excellence" (p. 399).

Ericsson, Krampe, and Tesch-Römer (1993) argued that expertise is directly related to the time spent in deliberate practice and that as a consequence, expertise attributes no role to underlying talent in the development of expert performance. By examining the activities that constitute the daily practice routines of expert musicians, Ericsson et al. (1993) reasoned that one could explain differences in the musicians' level of attained skill within the context of differential amounts of time being devoted to different activities. Their theory of deliberate practice suggests that it is not strictly the number of hours of practice that are paramount for the development of expertise, but rather the actual structure and content of those practice hours. Specifically, practice activities were considered to be deliberate practice if they were structured to improve current performance, if they were highly relevant to the particular domain, if they were substantial enough to require concerted effort to complete, and if they were not inherently enjoyable. Ericsson et al. (1993) reported that practicing alone was the only activity that conformed to these four tenets of deliberate practice for violinists and pianists. When the hours spent in practice alone were collected by retrospective recall, substantial differences existed among musicians who differed in skill, with the highest skilled individuals having practiced for many more hours than musicians of lesser skill. Thus, Ericsson et al. proposed that a monotonic relationship existed between expert performance and deliberate practice, such that more hours of deliberate practice translated directly into improvements in performance.

Deliberate Practice in Sport

Defining a central role for the influence of deliberate practice on the development of expert performance has led a number of investigators to examine the theory of deliberate practice in a sport context. Sports that have been studied with regard to this theory have included the following: figure skating (Starkes Deakin, Allard, Hodges, & Hayes, 1996); wrestling (Hodges & Starkes, 1996; Starkes et al., 1996); soccer and field hockey (Helsen, Starkes, & Hodges, 1998); and martial arts (Hodge & Deakin, 1998).

Starkes et al. (1996) investigated the role of deliberate practice in the development of expertise in wrestling and figure skating. The wrestling research considered four groups who differed in skill, from club level to international level. The figure skating research consisted of athletes on the national and junior national teams. To determine which activities constituted deliberate practice, researchers divided activities into four categories: practice alone, practice with others, activities related to wrestling/figure skating, and everyday activities not related to wrestling/figure skating. Within each category, the athletes estimated the number of hours per week that they spent in each of the various practice activities. They were asked to recall how many hours they had engaged in those activities at the start of their career and every three years since. The athletes rated the activities identified in the four categories according to their relevance to performance improvement, effort required (physical work), concentration required (mental work), and enjoyment experienced. Athletes also kept a week-long diary to examine the reliability of recall.

In contrast to Ericsson et al. (1993), no activities were rated as being both highly relevant and significantly lower than the grand mean for enjoyment. In fact, activities such as working with a coach, performing mat work (for the wrestlers), and doing on-ice training (for the skaters) rated significantly higher than the grand mean for both relevance and enjoyment. These findings have since been corroborated by research in the team sports of soccer and field hockey (Helsen, Starkes, & Hodges, 1998; Starkes, 2000) as well as in the martial arts (Hodge & Deakin, 1998), where team and group forms of practice were not only relevant, demanding, and enjoyable, but they also accounted for over half of the total time dedicated to practice. It would appear that no practice activities in any sport studied to date meet the conditions of high ratings for relevance and effort, with low ratings for enjoyment. Would it therefore be fair to assume that the theory of deliberate practice is not applicable to the sport? Ericsson (1996) responded to this discrepancy in the sport research by suggesting that it is the inherently social nature of sport that affects athletes' response to the question of enjoyment. That is, the athletes' positive assessment of enjoyment is reflective of their involvement in the sport, and it is not specific to the elements of practice itself. With specific reference to the wrestlers, he noted that "in spite of their enjoyment of some practice activities they still found [everyday activities like] sleep and leisure activities even more enjoyable" (Starkes, 2000, p. 445). According to Ericsson (1996), the fundamental assumptions of the deliberate practice model have not been violated by the findings from the work on sport.

That being said, when researchers attempt to compare the amount of time that participants spend in deliberate practice across domains, a particular difficulty arises that is due to the fact that researchers quantify deliberate practice differently. That is, practicing alone was the only activity to meet the criteria of deliberate practice for Ericsson et al.'s (1993) musicians, whereas "practice alone" in figure skating, wrestling, and the martial arts included activities that would not be considered deliberate practice based on their ratings for relevance (Hodge & Deakin, 1998; Starkes et al., 1996). For example, "practice alone" in figure skating included weight training, flexibility training, lessons with a coach, and individual on-ice practice. Although there is remarkable consistency in the mean estimates of hours spent in practice each week (violinists, 29.8 hours; pianists, 26.7; skaters, 22.2; wrestlers, 19.1; martial artists, 27.6), it must be kept in mind that the estimates represent fundamentally distinct constituents of practice across the different domains.

Although similarity in the cumulative hours of practice across domains (Starkes, 2000) speaks to the relationship between accumulated

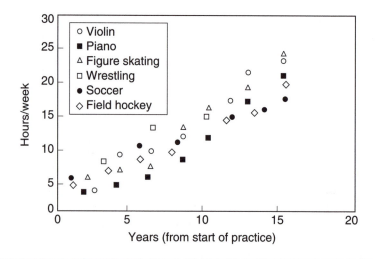

Figure 5.1 Cumulative hours of practice across domains from start of practice and each year thereafter.

Reprinted, by permission, from J. Starkes, 2000, "The road to expertise: Is practice the only determinant?" *International Journal of Sport Psychology*, 31: 431-451 practice and performance attained (figure 5.1), it does nothing to aid our understanding of the constituents of deliberate practice in sport domains. The inability to differentiate between experts and nonexperts on the basis of some component of practice suggests that either the relationship between actual practice activities and skill level needs further investigation or that the practice environment in sport is fundamentally different from that in music and chess (Charness, Krampe, & Mayr, 1996), such that all components of practice in the sport environment should be considered as deliberate practice.

The inference that all forms of practice in sport make an equal contribution to the development of expertise has neither intuitive appeal nor empirical support. Much research in the field of skill acquisition suggests that different content and different forms of practice have differential impact on the rate and level of learning. Further, empirical evidence (to be presented later in this chapter) suggests that a similar relationship exists between performance demands and preferred practice activities in both the music and sport domains. Specifically, it appears that in both domains, the activities most related to actual performance (practice the violin, mat work, on-ice training, games and tactics, sparring, technical skills) and the activities done with a mentor (violin lessons, work with coach) are the most highly rated practice activities on the dimensions of importance, relevance, concentration, and effort (Ericsson et al., 1993; Hodge & Deakin, 1998; Starkes et al., 1996). These findings, at the very least, suggest that expert performers and their mentors have identified specific elements of practice that are most essential to the attainment of performance goals or objectives. This clearly speaks against the notion of equal contribution of activities to the development of expertise in sport. In an effort to understand the relationships between practice activities and performance, we return to an examination of practice in figure skating.

Deliberate Practice in Figure Skating

We attempted to clarify the relationship between practice activities and skill in figure skating (Deakin, Starkes, & Allard, 1998) by identifying the precise activities that were considered to be most relevant to improving skating performance and by assessing the microstructure of actual on-ice practice sessions. To achieve the latter and to reduce the effects of variables such as different training centers, coaching staff, ice schedules, and off-ice training programs, we decided to select different groups of skaters from one skating school.

Identification of Relevant Practice Activities

Serving as participants were 20 members of the Canadian National Figure Skating Team. The mean age of the skaters was 17.25 years (±2.1). The average starting age was 5.2 years (±1.9), and they had been skating year-round since they were 9.0 years old (±1.9). The skaters completed a questionnaire that asked them to rate a variety of activities on a scale of low to high (0-10). The skaters rated the activities on the dimensions of their importance to improving and maintaining performance, to enjoyment, to the concentration required, and to the effort required. These ratings included how they felt at the present time and at the beginning of their competitive careers. The activities provided in the questionnaire were based on the results of our earlier work (Starkes et al., 1996), where on-ice practice, choreography, and lessons with a coach were rated as significantly higher than the grand mean for their relevance to performance and degree of enjoyment.

To determine which specific aspects of practice sessions and lessons constituted deliberate practice, the activities listed in the questionnaire were more specific than in our earlier work. For example, on-ice practice and lessons with a coach were separated into elements such as jumps and spins, program run-throughs, field moves, and connecting steps. Skaters were asked to rate these specific activities in terms of their enjoyment as well as the effort and concentration they required. The importance of on-ice warm-up was included in the questionnaire because coaches in general regularly emphasize the importance of warm-up as a means of preventing injury during training.

Rating of Practice Activities

The ratings of the practice activities' importance to improving and maintaining performance are provided in tables 5.1 and 5.2. Ratings for each activity's enjoyment and each activity's required effort and concentration (both at the time of the investigation and at the start of the skaters' competitive careers) were required to determine which, if any, activities met Ericsson's definition of deliberate practice. Activities that were rated significantly higher or lower than the grand mean are identified with a superscript.

To our knowledge, this study was the first to investigate whether there were differences in the relative importance of practice activities at two points in the careers of skaters. The ratings of all the activities increased from the start of the skaters' competitive careers to the present whereas the relative importance of the individual ratings was maintained over the course of their careers. Similarly, the skaters identified

■ Table 5.1
Skaters' Ratings of Practice Activities (Now)

Activity	Improve	Maintain	Effort	Concentration	Enjoyment
Grand mean	8.8	8.7	8.3	8.2	7.8
Individual activities					
Practice jumps and spins	9.1	9.4	8.5	8.8	8.7[H]
Practice field moves, connecting steps	8.5	8.4	7.0	7.3	8.0
Practice short program	9.3	9.5[H]	8.8	9.0	7.9
Practice long program	9.3	9.6[H]	9.0	9.3[H]	7.7
On-ice warm-up	7.7	7.5	6.3	5.3[L]	6.0
Lessons: choreography	9.3	8.8	8.0	8.6	8.4
Lessons: jumps and spins	9.6[H]	9.3	8.6	8.9	9.0[H]
Lessons: field moves, connecting steps	8.0	7.9	7.3	7.5	8.0
Lessons: short program	9.3	9.4	9.1	9.1	8.3
Lessons: long program	9.3	9.4	9.4[H]	9.0	8.1
Off-ice conditioning	9.2	9.3	9.1	7.5	8.3
Mental training	8.6	8.0	8.2	9.6	6.7
Group activities					
Off-ice conditioning	8.8	9.0	8.6	7.9	8.5
Stroking, ice theater	7.8	7.2	7.8	6.7	6.9
Mental training	6.9	6.2	7.9	8.3	5.7

H: significantly higher than the grand mean
L: significantly lower than the grand mean

the same practice activities as being important for improvement and maintenance at both points in their career. No such activities were rated as highly relevant and demanding of a high degree of concentration while at the same time not being inherently enjoyable. The evidence did support, however, the tenets for high concentration and high relevance: The activities that received the high ratings for improving or

■ **Table 5.2**
Skaters' Ratings of Practice Activities (Start of Competitive Career)

Activity	Improve	Maintain	Effort	Concentration	Enjoyment
Grand mean	6.6	6.4	6.6	6.4	6.0
Individual activities					
Practice jumps and spins	7.6	6.7	6.7	6.2	8.2[H]
Practice field moves, connecting steps	5.1	5.1	5.7	5.2	5.1
Practice short program	7.4	7.9	7.4	7.3	6.9
Practice long program	7.6	7.8	7.6	7.3	7.2[H]
On-ice warm-up	4.7	4.7	4.9	3.7	3.4[L]
Lessons: choreography	7.0	6.3	6.7	6.4	5.8
Lessons: jumps and spins	9.3[H]	8.8[H]	8.0	8.0[H]	8.7[H]
Lessons: field moves, connecting steps	6.1	5.8	6.4	6.5	6.0
Lessons: short program	7.9	8.6[H]	7.9	8.1[H]	7.2[H]
Lessons: long program	8.2[H]	8.7[H]	7.9	8.1[H]	7.2[H]
Off-ice conditioning	6.1	5.7	6.0	5.0	5.9
Mental training	4.4	3.7[L]	5.3	6.6	2.2[L]
Group activities					
Off-ice conditioning	4.6	4.7	5.6	5.1	4.4
Stroking, ice theater	6.0	5.3	7.0	6.7	5.2
Mental training	4.0	3.5[L]	4.8	5.6	3.3[L]

H: significantly higher than the grand mean
L: significantly lower than the grand mean

maintaining performance also received high ratings for concentration. This was confirmed by a Spearman rank-order correlation.

Table 5.3 illustrates the relationships between improvement, effort, concentration, and enjoyment for the present-time data. This strong positive relationship between relevance to improvement and concentration has been consistently observed across domains. For example, the work with Ericsson et al.'s (1993) violinists (.75), Starkes et al.'s (1996) skaters (.90), and Hodges and Starkes' (1996) wrestlers (.83) also reported a significant correlation between concentration (effort for musicians) and relevance. The fact that the rankings for enjoyment were not related to those on the dimension of effort or concentration suggests that the skaters were able to make an independent assessment of each dimension. Moreover, it supports the contention that the rankings for enjoyment were not simply an artifact of the rankings on the other dimensions.

■ Table 5.3
Spearman Rho Correlation for Skaters' Ratings

Present day	Improve	Effort	Concentration	Enjoyment
Improve				
Effort	.72*			
Concentration	.67*	.68*		
Enjoyment	.56*	.42	.38	

* p < .05

A second point of convergence between this investigation and other research on deliberate practice (conducted with musicians and athletes) concerns the nature of the activities considered most important for performance improvement. The ratings provided by the skaters in this study confirm that those activities that are directly related to an actual performance (namely, jumps, spins, and program run-throughs) were identified as being important for performance improvement.

Ratings that were related to maintaining performance were virtually identical to those for improvement. Similarly, skaters did not seem able to make differential attributions with respect to the two periods surveyed by the questionnaire. This lack of differences on both dimensions raises questions that are related to the construct validity of the questionnaire instrument for assessing retrospective importance. Rather than infer that differences do not exist in the relative importance of practice activities at different times in an athlete's development, we would prefer to suggest that the skaters were unable to differentiate between the constructs of improvement and maintenance. Similarly, we also suggest that skaters were unable to accurately recall what aspects of performance were most important to them at different points in their career. We do believe, however, that the retrospective recall methodology allowed skaters to infer the relative importance of practice activities in the past from their current importance to improvement. To the extent that methodological limitations may have obscured differences in ratings of importance, we remain uninformed as to the differential impact of specific practice activities on performance at different points in a skater's career. The use of other research techniques—such as cross-sectional methodologies or validation studies that use parents, coaches, or mentors—might provide insight into the relative importance of practice activities from a developmental perspective.

Microstructure of Practice in Figure Skating

The second study was designed to assess to what extent the components consistently rated important were represented in actual on-ice practice sessions. To investigate this question, we invited a subset of elite skaters from both the Canadian National and Junior National Figure Skating Team to participate. A total of 24 skaters, who were training at a nationally renowned skating school, met the criteria for inclusion in any one of three groups. The *elite group* comprised skaters who were on the National or Junior National Team and who had international competitive experience at the Senior level. The *competitive group* were skaters who were slated to compete in the upcoming season at the Juvenile or Pre-Novice level of provincial-level competition, and the *test group* were skaters who had proceeded through the testing levels and had no intention of competing.

The study involved the recording of on-ice activities, the administration of questionnaires, and the completion of a seven-day diary. Two figure-skating professionals observed and videotaped three on-ice practices for each subject. Practice length varied as a function of group such that the elite skaters had 60-minute practice sessions whereas the competitive and test skaters had combinations of 60-minute or 45-minute sessions, depending on the discipline being practiced (dance, free skating, figures). A log of practice activities, including jump attempts, spins, lessons, program run-throughs, and rest time, was recorded for each session. Interrater reliability of the observed practice activities was assessed, and it revealed that there were no differences between raters. The interrater reliability coefficient was 0.94.

Questionnaire data were collected to confirm the choice of practice activities emanating from the first study. The data included estimates of the number of times that the skaters attempted particular elements during a typical day during the summer seasons and competitive seasons (winter), as well as the amount of time during a typical week spent in a variety of activities, including skating-related activities, sleep, education, and nonskating-related activities. These skaters were also asked to rate the activities on a 10-point scale in terms of their importance to improving and maintaining performance levels at the present time and at the start of their careers.

What Skaters Rate As Important

Table 5.4 provides the details on the skaters' perceived impact of specific skating-related activities on improving performance. In general,

■ **Table 5.4**
Athletes' Perception of the Importance of Practice Activities to Improving Skating Performance

Activity	Improve	
	Now	**Start**
Grand mean	8.57	5.72
Individual activities		
Practice jumps and spins	9.46[H]	7.38
Practice field moves and connecting steps	8.09	4.82
Program run-throughs	9.48[H]	6.39
On-ice warm-up and stretching	5.95[L]	3.75
Private choreography lessons	9.25[H]	6.71
Private lessons on jumps and spins	9.38[H]	8.38[H]
Private lessons on field moves and connecting steps	7.46	5.00
Private lessons on program run-throughs	9.25[H]	6.96
Off-ice conditioning	7.76	6.57
Mental training	8.74	4.80
Group activities		
Off-ice conditioning	8.83	5.00
Stroking, ice theater	8.81	5.21
Mental training	8.38	3.50

H: significantly higher than the grand mean ($p < .05/13$)
L: significantly lower than the grand mean ($p < .05/13$)

the ratings substantiated the findings from the first study. Specifically, private instruction on choreography, jumps and spins, and program run-throughs were all rated above the mean for importance. We anticipated that activities related to injury prevention would receive high ratings, such as on-ice warm-up and stretching; however, skaters rated on-ice warm-up lower than the grand mean for importance to improving performance.

What Skaters Actually Do Versus What They Say They Do

For the purposes of this investigation, we were most interested in knowing whether the activities that skaters reported as being central to the development of expertise were in fact the ones that they actually undertook in practice. A comparison between reported importance and on-ice behavior revealed a number of interesting findings.

Practicing jumps and spins was rated higher than the grand mean for their importance to improving performance, and this rating was indeed reflected in on-ice activities. Despite the lack of group differences in the assessment of each practice activity's value, group differences did appear in the time-motion analyses. The elite and competitive skaters spent 68% and 59% of their sessions practicing jumps whereas the test group was engaged in those activities for only 48% of their on-ice time. These findings are consistent with Ericsson et al. (1993) in that the higher percentage of time spent in practicing jumps is reflected in the higher skill level of the elite and competitive skaters. The question of what activities were being performed across groups during the remaining practice time became much clearer when the amount of nonactive time (or rest time) was removed.

Role of Rest Time

We determined the rest time for each skater's three practice sessions and expressed it as a percentage of their total session length. We defined rest time as a measure of the skaters' unproductive time on the ice, which included talking with friends, standing at the boards, and leaving the ice surface. This measure did not include active recovery time from physical exertion. Rest time (by group) produced an inverse relationship with skill level. Specifically, the elite group spent an average of 14% of their total on-ice practice time on rest; the competitive group, 31%; and the test skaters, 46%.

The analysis of rest time indicated that the elite skaters utilized their on-ice time much more efficiently than either of the other groups. Not only did the elite group practice jumps and spins for a higher proportion of the on-ice session, but they also rested less and used the remaining 18% of their on-ice time to practice other elements of their programs, such as footwork and arm positions.

Any interpretation of skaters' reports of cumulative practice must be made cautiously. In spite of the ability to accurately recall scheduled hours of practice, the relationship between scheduled hours and actual hours of practice is not clear. Although the groups of skaters in this study had spent a similar number of years practicing, the actual active practice time would be in the order of 13 to 46% lower than the reported hours of scheduled practice. Therefore, the mean total number of accumulated practice hours for each group would be very different.

When we examined the relationship between what skaters say they practice and what they actually practice, we discovered a bias toward overestimation of the number and type of jumps each group actually performed in practice. Moreover, our examination revealed that all skaters spent considerably more time practicing jumps that existed within their repertoire and less time working on jumps that they were attempting to learn. It seems that although they may aspire to work on increasingly difficult elements, they opt instead to execute elements that require less effort on their part for successful completion. For example, the elite skaters estimated attempting 7 double jumps and 20 triple jumps per session whereas they actually attempted an average of 30 doubles and 6 triples. This difference amounts to a three- to four-fold discrepancy between what they *say* and what they *do*.

What do these findings indicate about the nature of practice in figure skating? First, although figure skaters identified no fewer than five individual activities as critical for improvement, it appears that most of their on-ice time is spent on only one of those activities. Second, the amount of time actually spent "practicing" during on-ice sessions is less than their estimates and is related to the skill level of the skater. Finally, during the time that the skaters are active, they spend far more time practicing elements that they have mastered and significantly less time attempting to acquire new elements. What is surprising about these findings is that in a constrained practice environment where coaches are present, skaters actively practice for between only 50 and 85% of the time available. Also, the expected relationship between perceived importance of a practice activity and the proportion of time spent actually practicing that activity was not substantiated. Without exception, skaters spent a disproportional amount of time practicing jumps and spins. In addition, they spent most of their time practicing what they knew, rather than what was new.

In figure skating, much of on-ice practice is self-regulated, with individual coaching occurring in some sessions and not others. In fact, skaters did not receive individual coaching for more than 25% of any 60-minute session. What is difficult to reconcile here is the difference between the attributions made by skaters as to the fundamental importance of individual instruction and the high proportion of practice time spent in the absence of both coaching and active practice. Perhaps like music, the role of the coach in figure skating is to prepare and present the elements that must be practiced between coaching sessions (Ericsson et al., 1993). Whether the skater chooses to practice those critical elements is under one's own control, given the nature of the on-ice practice sessions.

The flexibility in the control and selection of practice activities by the participant appears to be in sharp contrast to work in other sport domains, yet it is similar to that found in the domain of music. Therefore, we might expect that the relationship between hours spent in practice alone (defined in figure skating as on-ice practice) would be similar in figure skating and music, as would the number of cumulative hours of practice on this single activity. Recall, however, that the similarity in cumulative hours of practice across the two domains included (in figure skating) the individual "nonskating" activities *in addition* to the on-ice training. In this study, evaluation of the on-ice practice profiles of expert figure skaters suggests a stronger parallel to the practice patterns of expert musicians than to experts in other sports.

Expert figure skaters actively practiced a range of elements that were required for their competitive routines, but they, like athletes in every domain, spent a considerable amount of time repeating elements that were well within their repertoire. If repetition of acquired elements were not necessary for consistently superior performance, we would be far less likely to see professional golfers practicing putting or tennis players practicing ground strokes. Although the proportion of time allocated to the practice of new elements seems inadequate, at least for the expert figure skaters, we see a pattern of efficient use of practice time on a subset of elements that have been identified as essential for the attainment of expert stature within the domain. Similarly, little on-ice time was given by this group to activities that were not seen to be highly relevant to the development of expert performance. It would be interesting to address the question of the constituents of practice with those figure skaters who hold top-ten rankings in the world. It might well be expected that these very elite figure skaters would spend a higher proportion of on-ice practice working on elements that are at the limit of their current repertoire rather than on elements that are well within their capacity to perform consistently. Perhaps this measure of efficiency of on-ice practice is an important metric that can inform our understanding of the relationship between practice alone and the development of expertise.

Role of the Coach

Helsen, Starkes, and Hodges (1998, p. 14) have suggested that in team sports, the coaches control the content and duration of all practice activities per session, and as a result, they optimize practice time. Similarly, Allard, Starkes, and Deakin (1998) have closely examined the practice environment of wrestlers. They have concluded that unlike music or chess, where "the teacher designs practice activities that the individual can engage in between meetings with the teacher" (Ericsson et al., 1993, p. 368), the wrestling coach is always present to assign practice activities and ensure that they are carried out properly. They suggest that the time spent in a coached practice session is the essence of deliberate practice and therefore is the most relevant to the development of expert performance in sport. However, this definition of deliberate practice is clearly not in concurrence with the domain of figure skating, given the relatively small proportion of time that the skaters receive individual instruction.

Schultetus and Charness (1997) demonstrated the importance of the amount of coaching in skill for fencing. Using questionnaire data from 32 fencers, they reported that practice alone, fencing with others, and receiving coaching were related to the highest fencing rating achieved ($r = 0.526$). A breakdown of the practice estimates showed that practice alone ($r = 0.504$) and coaching ($r = 0.526$) provided the highest correlations with fencing rating. They reasoned that a coach structures practice time by assigning drills to sharpen technique, by giving feedback on technique, and by motivating the fencer. By completing these actions, the coach creates the framework within which deliberate practice can occur.

Recently, we have begun to study the role of an expert coach in the design, structure, and dynamics of practice cycles. Time-motion data have been collected in the sport of volleyball across a five-week period during the competitive season. Because matches were played each week, practices could be evaluated within the context of the number of days before the next competitive match. Practice plans and interviews with the coach were completed daily to cross-validate the sources of information (Cobley & Deakin, 2001). We were interested in many aspects of the coach's role within an individual practice session, including the amount of time the athletes were actively engaged in practice and the amount and type of instruction provided. In addition, but beyond the scope of this discussion, we wanted to investigate the possibility that a systematic relationship exists between the structure and content of practice and the competition-practice cycle.

A series of pre- and postpractice interviews were conducted with a nationally certified university coach over a five-week midseason period. All practices were videotaped for subsequent time-motion analyses. The skill level of the team was reflected in their top-ten national ranking over a two-year period.

Practices for this team lasted approximately 90 minutes per session. A typical practice devoted 15 to 20 minutes for warm-up activities. The remainder of the time was used for active practice in the form of team drills, many of which replicated game play. Athletes engaged in active practice for an average of 93% of total practice time. Participation in volleyball drills occupied 78% of the total practice time, with verbal instructions by the coach occurring 13% of that time. General instructions about the drill accounted for approximately one third of the total instruction time, with technical instruction taking an additional quarter of the time. The remaining time was equally distributed between team-specific tactical instruction and opponent-specific tactical instruction. Similar findings were reported by Allard et al. (1998) in their work on wrestling, where one third of each practice was spent in instruction, another third was spent in various forms of wrestling, and the final third was spent in warm-up activities and observation of other wrestlers.

The findings all speak to the central role of the coach in contextualizing the practice environment for their athletes in relation to upcoming opponents. Further confirmation for this conclusion comes from the interview data, where the volleyball coach stated that on-court practice time was precious and that it needed to be maximized. When probed on what "on-court practice time" actually meant in terms of the structure and organization of practice, the coach's response highlighted many of the tenants of deliberate practice: First, the athletes needed to be engaged. Second, the coach would create instructional opportunities to target skills or teamwork that would have a significant impact on the next match. Third, the opposition's plays would be run so that team members could work on their counterattack. Fourth, the intensity of practice would approximate that of match play. We suggest that implementation of this type of practice forms the basis for "priming" the athlete's information-processing system by constructing and demonstrating a number of possible response alternatives that each athlete could face in the upcoming competition. In the context of competitive sport, this model would be represented in the amount of time spent in team-specific and opponent-specific instruction, which (in our case study) amounts to approximately 50% of the total time spent in instruction.

It appears that in sports such as volleyball, soccer, field hockey, and wrestling, the coach creates, organizes, and controls the activities and athletes for the duration of the practice session. Time spent in coached practice would therefore constitute both deliberate practice and total practice time. This conclusion, however, does not bring us any closer to understanding the differential effects of various practice activities on performance. Given the central role of the coach in the development of practice, some insight into the question of the quality of practice might be gained by evaluating coaches, who themselves differ in level of skill and experience. We are only beginning to undertake work in this area. We expect that by employing a two-by-two matrix of expert and novice coaches and players, we will be able to investigate the interactions of skill level, practice activities, time in instruction, and time in active practice. Evidence from the pedagogical literature leads us to predict that coaches will spend more time in instruction with novice-level players and that instruction will be technical, or skill-based, in nature. We expect to see a general decline in time spent in instruction and an increase in the proportion of that time given to tactical instruction when observing skilled players and coaches. In the absence of previous work in the area, we anticipate that the extent to which novice-level coaches can supply tactical information and strategies will be limited by their own knowledge of these aspects of the game. Further, we expect to see intergroup differences in the ability to design and implement both practice techniques and systems that address tactical considerations for either their team or their opponent.

Perhaps not surprisingly, we have seen that for sports as diverse as figure skating and volleyball, the requirements of the expert performer, the characteristics of the practice environment, and the role of the coach vary greatly. Where time spent with a coach may well be the appropriate metric for deliberate practice in team sport, it is not applicable to the domain of figure skating. Examination of other factors related to the identification and retention of skaters in competitive figure skating may assist in our understanding of the factors that contribute to success in sport, where the execution of complex elements is central to positive performance outcomes.

Summary

We have presented data on the content and structure of practice with a view to understanding the relationship between practice activities and skill in figure skating. Consistent with past research, our data revealed that no skating-related activities attained high ratings for relevance, effort, and concentration while at the same time receiving low ratings for enjoyment. Although figure skaters identified no fewer than five activities that were considered central for improvement in the sport, analyses of the microstructure of the actual practice sessions revealed that the skaters spent a disproportionate amount of time on jumps and spins. Further, while practicing these two categories of activities, the skaters chose to complete elements that for the most part already existed within their repertoire, as opposed to new elements they were attempting to acquire. The amount of practice time actually spent practicing was proportional to skill level to the extent that expert skaters actively practiced for 85% of their on-ice sessions while the recreational skaters were active for only 55% of their on-ice time. Given the presence of coaching staff during on-ice sessions, we were surprised at the relatively ineffective use of ice time.

In contrast to the data on figure skaters, the data presented on an expert coach and the characteristics of practice sessions with volleyball players have illustrated how the coach creates, organizes, and controls the activities undertaken by the athletes for the duration of practice. The coach in this environment has a direct impact on the amount and intensity of deliberate practice undertaken by the athletes. Time in practice with a coach may well be the metric for deliberate practice in team sport where expert coaching is available. These findings highlight the role of the coach in the development of expertise for at least one category of sport activities. Investigating how the quality of practice is influenced by the level of expertise of coaches and athletes is one of the next steps in our evolving understanding of the interplay of coach, athletes, and expert performance.

EXPERTS' COMMENTS

■ Question

In this chapter, Deakin and Cobley present evidence from figure skating that even the best skaters (who are well aware of what needs to be practiced to improve) still spend a significant amount of practice time performing moves they already do well. As a coach, have you noted this phenomenon as well? Can coaches offset this tendency of athletes to practice already accomplished skills as opposed to the ones that may be of greatest benefit?

■ Coach's Perspective: Nick Cipriano

In my sport (wrestling), athletes spend a great deal of time on technical-tactical elements that they already perform well. Whether the time spent on such elements is indeed wasted time or whether it further facilitates improvement has never been addressed. However, in wrestling training, repetition and overlearning are the norm, and they have become an ingrained practice of every wrestler. From a coach's perspective, I believe the tendency is for coaches to focus on identifying weaknesses, then later conclude that if the weaknesses are strengthened, the athlete's performance will improve. In my experience, however, expert athletes have a tendency to view their performance from a more positive (strengths) perspective and less so from a weakness perspective. By way of example, when I review game film with athletes, I highlight mistakes made and suggest areas that need improvement. The athletes, however, often highlight the things that they performed well that led to a positive outcome or the things that the opponent performed well that led to a negative outcome. Remarkably, while I am focusing on the negative, the athlete is focusing on the positive. This observation leads me to believe that athletes may view their potential improvement through a positive perspective and thus aim for development by improving the things that they already do well, thereby camouflaging their weaknesses. My sense is that expert athletes spend much time on skills that they already perform well because it provides positive reinforcement, builds confidence, and is psychologically invigorating versus working on improving weaknesses, which requires much more effort and concentration. Additionally, they may perceive working on improving weaknesses as being too "worklike." As a coach, I attempt to deal with this phenomenon by reviewing game film with athletes and getting them to acknowledge the areas in need of improvement. I later structure training sessions and allocate specific time during the practice for the athletes to work on areas identified as weaknesses. I also often use sparring simulations to isolate an athlete's particular weakness that needs to be worked on. For example, for the wrestler who gets easily turned to his back with a gut-wrench action in par-terre wrestling, I develop a sparring situation that restricts the attack sequence to only a gut wrench.

In my experience, the individual who is crowned world champion or Olympic champion represents the perfect mixture of talent and deliberate practice. The role that talent plays in international-level sport can neither be underestimated nor ignored; world and Olympic champions are indeed talented. However, no one can deny that the achievement of a world or Olympic champion is largely founded on superior coaching from an early age; participation in an enriched training and competition program; a supportive social structure; and most important, a personal drive to be successful.

In my experience, international-level athletes can be categorized into two groups. The first group clearly consists of those who are international-level athletes but are lacking some basic quality that prevents them from achieving a top-level performance. Their inability to be the best is likely due to a combination of factors, including (but not limited to) a poorly developed work ethic, inferior technical skills, insufficient competition experience, and insufficient physiological development. Quite possibly, their initial level of talent may be so low that no amount of practice is going to make up for the shortfall. The second group of international-level athletes consists of the medal winners. All are highly talented for their chosen activity, and all engage in deliberate practice to the fullest. All too often, their final performance ranking is more a function of strategy, circumstances, and even good luck or bad luck (as opposed to deliberate practice or talent).

■ Player's Perspective: Therese Brisson

Deakin and Cobley show that even the best athletes in a given sport spend a significant amount of time performing moves they already do well despite being aware of their weakness. I have also observed this behavior in athletes, and I think there are a few reasons for this. First, it is quite natural to enjoy things one is good at and to spend more time on those things. It builds confidence and self-esteem. Second, and perhaps unique to team sports, is that a player is often selected for the strengths that she brings to the team, not her weaknesses. So it is important to focus on these strengths and be the best in this area. For example, one of my teammates is known for being a solid defender; she is reliable and stable. She rarely takes offensive risks or practices joining the attack because she knows that if she continues to excel defensively, she will always have a spot on the team. Finally, I think that coaching attitudes toward risk taking and errors can make a big difference in an athlete's performance. Coaches want complete players, athletes with good all-around skills. At the same time, they want consistent, reliable performance. To improve weaknesses you have to take risks, but coaches do not always welcome this. The real issue is one of timing: knowing when to take risks and when not to.

At some point in an athletic career, it may be appropriate to focus on strengths rather than weaknesses in practice. But it has been my experience that at some point, expert performers must undertake extensive periods of targeted improvement on their weaknesses. Athletes who are determined to turn their weaknesses into strengths are those who excel at an international level. For example, skating skills, physical conditioning, and solid defensive play in my own zone were my strengths around five years ago. However, my coach at the time told me one year, "I don't care what else you do; all I want to see from you is good, quick puck movement to the forwards, and initiate the attack." These simple instructions from the coach gave me the green light to focus all my attention and energies on a weaker aspect of my play, but one that the team really needed. The results were amazing, and I would say that at one point I led the team in breakaway passes. Good, quick passes out of the zone became a strong point in my game, and I think the team was much better for it.

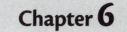

Chapter 6

Tactics, the Neglected Attribute of Expertise

■ ■ ■ ■ ■

Problem Representations and Performance Skills in Tennis

Sue L. McPherson
Michael W. Kernodle

Recently, Ericsson (1996b) proposed that those who attain expert levels of performance in a variety of domains are frequently characterized by two qualities: one, the desire to deliberately build knowledge and support processes when anticipating, evaluating, and reasoning alternative courses of action (i.e., higher-order processing during task performance) and two, the ability to resist relying on mechanisms of automaticity. Sport scientists have also considered support processes (or strategies) such as planning, self-monitoring, and anticipating during competition as important characteristics of elite sport performers. Yet, our understanding is limited about the knowledge and support processes used during sport competition (i.e., tactics) and their role in player development and expertise. For instance, motor behaviorists have studied the mediation processes of high-skilled and low-skilled players that underlie the anticipation of stimuli and motor skills in simulated sport contexts, yet the goal of such studies has been to develop theory about *motor learning* rather than *sport learning*. That is, these studies rarely assessed the players' decisions about shot selection in experimental contexts that would have allowed them the opportunity to reason about an opponent's tendencies, their weaknesses, or goals under the current circumstances. Further, Williams, Davids, & Williams (1999) noted that motor behaviorists continued to link elite players' well-developed perceptual strategies and decision-making capabilities to skilled performance, even though few had examined what specific information was used in the decision making and how the underlying knowledge bases were developed as a result of practice.

An exception has been the work of McPherson and French (and their colleagues), who have examined the development and interplay of players' knowledge bases and decision-making processes during strategic open-skill sport competition (French & McPherson, 1999, in press). To date, McPherson, French, and their colleagues have conducted several lines of longitudinal and cross-sectional sport-specific research at various levels of analysis. These studies examined players' knowledge bases and decision-making processes during simulated and actual competition. They also examined their performance behaviors during competition at several age and skill levels in basketball, volleyball, baseball, badminton, and tennis. Collectively, these studies indicated that knowledge bases and decision-making processes were necessary for the development of skillful performance. However, the relationship between variables differed across studies that supported the concept of sport-specific development. Also, the experts in these studies were highly skilled youth or adult players who had less than

10 years of both preparation and deliberate practice that is typical of elite performers (for review in all domains, see Ericsson, 1996a; for sport, see Starkes, Deakin, Allard, Hodges, & Hayes, 1996). Thus, sport-specific research that examines elite performers with 10 or more years of preparation is limited.

This chapter examines research in tennis, and it presents a new project that involves older, more elite players and adult male novices with more experience than those studied to date (McPherson, French, & Kernodle, 2001; Nielsen & McPherson, 2001). Tennis provides an exceptional testing ground for developmental theories of expertise in highly strategic sports. Players across ages play on standardized courts, use similar equipment, have equal opportunities to play the same positions and shots, and primarily abide by the same rules and regulations. In addition, players of varying ages and expertise levels may compete against each other (e.g., adult novices could play child experts). Further, the recording of players' observable and verbal behaviors during singles tennis competitions are easily manageable for scientists to collect, and they are unobtrusive to natural play. For example, natural pauses between points during singles competition can be used to collect players' verbal reports.

For this chapter, we first present issues unique to studying knowledge bases and performance skills in sport. Second, we examine knowledge-base theory and memory adaptations in cognitive skill development in sport. We illustrate this theory by presenting earlier work that compares problem representations and performance skills in male youth players and female adult players during competition at a variety of age and expertise levels. Third, we analyze research that compares problem representations and performance skills during competition in male adult professional players and male adult novice players. Finally, we discuss practical implications in terms of player development.

Issues Unique to Studying Knowledge Bases and Performance Skills in Sport

Before we address our findings and conclusions, it is necessary to briefly discuss the issues encountered when one studies knowledge bases and performance skills in sport. Specifically, in this section, we discuss the following:

- The difference between response selection and response execution in sport versus selection and execution in other domains

- Why verbal reports have proven value in the study of sport-specific expertise
- The role that two specific continuums will play in helping researchers analyze knowledge bases and performance skills in sport
- The evolution of an expert's knowledge base, specifically, the transformations of levels of processing
- The difference between action plan profiles and current event profiles in expert tennis players

Studying Sport Domains

Thomas, French, and Humphries (1986) influenced McPherson's work by presenting theoretical predictions concerning cognitive skill development in sport. They predicted that the type of cognitive processes sport performers utilize during competition would be linked to their knowledge base of the task. They defined *sport performance* as "a complex product of cognitive knowledge about the current situation and past events combined with a player's ability to produce the sport skill(s) required" (p. 259). Thus, knowledge of the game situation (current and past) and use of this knowledge during competition were predicted to influence players' performance, especially in strategic open-skill sports. They cautioned that linking previous findings derived from work by cognitive scientists in other domains (e.g., chess, computer language, medical reasoning) could be limited because sport-specific knowledge bases are unique in that both response selection and response execution have aspects of declarative and procedural knowledge. For example, during a tennis rally, what to do (declarative) and how to do it (procedural) would each represent the decision to hit a ground stroke crosscourt with topspin and the ability to carry out this motor skill. Thus, both response selection and execution can have procedures in highly strategic sports (see Abernethy, J.R. Thomas, & K.T. Thomas, 1993; McPherson, 1993, 1994). Therefore, the ability to select tactical shots may not always equate with the ability to carry out or execute these shots (cf. McPherson & J.R. Thomas, 1989). In light of these interactions between declarative and procedural knowledge in sport, J.R. Thomas et al. (1986) suggested that researchers who employ knowledge-base paradigms should develop observational instruments to differentiate players' response selection and response execution during actual competition.

Verbal Reports and Problem Representations

To this end, McPherson and J.R. Thomas (1989) developed an observational instrument to differentiate players' response selection and response execution performance skills during actual competition in tennis. They also developed a verbal report instrument to systematically assess the bases of players' decisions during simulated and actual competition (e.g., what information they attended to and how they used it). Before their study, motor behaviorists rarely used verbal report instruments to compare knowledge bases among athletes of varying age and expertise levels during actual or simulated sport performance. In contrast, cognitive scientists used verbal report instruments extensively to examine knowledge-base differences among high- and low-skilled performers in a variety of domains (e.g., text processing, physics, computer language, medical reasoning; see Anderson, 1987; Chi, Glaser, & Farr, 1988; Ericsson, 1996a). For example, studies that examined problem solving and task performance in adults and children have provided evidence that domain-specific knowledge, as opposed to general cognitive strategies, were responsible for higher-order processing and performance. In other words, performance was based on (respectively) factors such as type of knowledge and domain-related cognitive strategies rather than on variables such as labeling, rehearsal, and organization.

Ericsson and Simon (1993) provided evidence that verbal report data collected during or immediately following task performance allow investigators to monitor the contents of information accessed from long-term memory. In addition, they suggested that retrospective verbal reports (immediate recall) are most appropriate for assessing one's problem representations during motor performance tasks. Thus, in sport, players' utterances collected during actual or simulated tasks reveal information about their problem representations accessed during sport performance (McPherson, 1994).

Levels of Analysis in Sport Research

Quantitative analyses of players' verbal report data during competition have been essential in advancing knowledge-base theory regarding expertise in strategic open-skill sport domains. However, each sport (and every position within each sport) may require unique knowledge bases. In response to this complexity, McPherson (1994) created a framework to design and interpret research that examines knowledge bases and performance skills in sport. One continuum in the framework moves from response selection to response execution (depicted from left to right) according to the sport domain or the experimental context. For example, gymnastics and figure skating would be heavily represented in response execution whereas tennis and soccer would be heavily represented at both ends. The other continuum (depicted from top to bottom) moves from knowledge (knowing what to do) to action (doing it) according to the experimental context or the sport under investigation. Experimental contexts might consist of any of the following (moving from top to bottom): recall and situational tasks in static contexts, isolated tasks in modified game contexts, or actual tasks during competition. Again, the type of sport or experimental context influences whether response selection or execution is emphasized. For example, a serve in tennis would be located midway top to bottom but at the response execution side (the right side). However, suppose the athlete's task were to simply view a video of a tennis player who was serving and then determine the landing location of the ball. This experiment would be designed to assess decision accuracy; therefore, it would be located midway top to bottom but at the response selection side (the left side).

Development of Knowledge Bases in Sport

Recently, French and McPherson (in press) suggested that the knowledge base for sport includes all the traditional propositional networks of declarative knowledge for response selections and executions in addition to the procedures for such response selection and execution. According to French and McPherson, this knowledge base also includes other sport-specific memory adaptations and structures, such as action plan profiles, current event profiles, game situation prototypes, scripts for competition, and domain-related strategies that are stored in and accessible from long-term memory.

In high-strategy sports, McPherson (1994) proposed that as expertise increases via practice or competition, players' knowledge bases and domain-related strategies would undergo the following general transformations. First, plans based on varying levels of goals within a hierarchical goal structure would be replaced by condition-action rule decisions. Second, weak, inappropriate conditions and actions would be replaced by ones that were tactical, refined, and associated. Third, a global approach to sport situations with minimal processing of task-relevant events would be replaced by a tactical approach to sport situations with continual monitoring of important or relevant information (including past events and the current situation). Fourth, processing events in the environment or surface features of sport situations would be replaced by processing information at deeper, more tactical levels. Fifth, few monitoring and planning processes would be replaced by specialized monitoring and planning processes. Sixth, limited actions without specialized processes would be replaced by tactical actions that include specialized processes to enhance or modify actions. Finally, extensive years of high-level competitive play were predicted to be a necessary requirement to develop highly tactical problem representations.

Memory Adaptations

In tennis, McPherson (1999b) predicted that the knowledge bases and domain-related strategies of older more elite players would consist of two long-term memory (LTM) adaptations used during competition to mediate performance. These memory adaptations are called *action plan profiles* and *current event profiles,* and they were derived from earlier work that examined the utterances of female adult experts (university-level varsity) and novice tennis players during simulated situation interviews.

Action plan profiles are memory structures that are used to activate general rule-based action plan responses. Action plan profiles contain rule-governed prototypes stored in LTM, the objective of which is to match certain current conditions with appropriate visual/motor actions. These conditions drive the shot selection, and they are typically explicit environmental cues or general game strategies. Examples of the former include ball location and player locations, and examples of the latter include a player's being taught to move to the net on a short shot or use topspin on a second serve. Players who have achieved high levels of motor execution during competitive play may have action plan profiles that are tailored to their current skill levels, which include their style of play, patterns of possible actions, or desires—for example, some experts said they preferred net play. Because experts consistently generate similar tactical solutions to each situation in tennis, general action plan profiles are predicted to be more consistent among elite players in terms of solutions that result in the best possible tactics (cf. McPherson, 1999b). However, female experts demonstrated cognitive flexibility because they derived their solutions from a variety of sport-specific response selection processes and LTM condition profiles. These condition profiles are collectively termed *current event profiles.*

Current event profiles are memory structures that are used to merge active relevant information with past, current, and possible future events. They contain tactical scripts and situation prototypes in LTM. This information guides the building and modifying of pertinent concepts (past, current, or future) so that the players can monitor the competitive event and be ready for activation or updating when the need arises. The current event profile is built from past competition (or experiences before the immediate competition) and from specialized monitoring, encoding, and retrieval processes that are used to collect information throughout the current competition. For example, tennis experts may use these specialized encoding and retrieval processes to "fill in the blanks" when building a profile to assess their opponent's strengths, weaknesses, and tendencies (as well as their own). Building a script of game events may allow an expert easy access to and retrieval of important information to make decisions during competition (see Ericsson & Kintsch, 1995). McPherson predicted that elite players would use a variety of opportunities before and throughout a match to build their current event profile. These profiles may be used to compensate actions and make adjustments during time-constrained moments—for example, they could be used to anticipate an opponent's series of shots during a rally.

Problem Representations and Performance Skills in Youth and Adult Tennis

In tennis, McPherson examined problem representations and performance skills of novice and highly skilled players who ranged in age from 10 years old to adult. To investigate problem representations, researchers collected verbal reports during simulated situations (McPherson & J.R. Thomas, 1989; McPherson, 1999b) and between points during competition (McPherson & J.R. Thomas, 1989; McPherson, 1999a, 2000). The *situation interview* consisted of players' responding to questions about game situations (e.g., serve, backcourt and net situations) while viewing static diagrams of these situations (court diagrams of ball locations and player positions). The *immediate recall interview* between points consisted of the question, "What were you thinking about while you were playing that point?" In addition, adult players exclusively responded to an additional *planning interview* question between points: "What are you thinking about now?" Verbal reports were coded according to a model of protocol structure for sports that was modified for tennis. This model allowed quantitative analyses of verbal data according to each player's identified concept content (i.e., categories, features, or hierarchical levels) and associations (patterns of concepts), the purpose of which was to examine group differences in what knowledge was attended to and accessed by working memory.

Consistent with predictions, the adult experts' problem representations were found to be more advanced (i.e., tactical) than youth experts or novices (regardless of age) in terms of their action plans and current event profiles (McPherson, 1999a, 1999b, 2000). A comparison of the profiles of young and adult experts suggested that the profiles of the adult experts were built from smaller units of knowledge content and domain-related strategies and that they were derived from extensive years of high-level competition. The response selection memory model presented in figure 6.1 illustrates three levels of expertise (novice level youth and adults; intermediate level youth experts; advanced level university varsity adults) according to action plan and current event profile differences noted in female and youth players' problem representations. In each model, the upper box represents the game environment and consists of the continuous flow of game events during competition. These events include all possible environmental features and/or competition events (e.g., ball location, an opponent serving, a point lost, a rally) along with decision output labeled response selection behaviors. Response selection behaviors may be overt or non-observable decision outcomes. The lower box represents domain specific LTM and includes problem representations that may include action plan profiles, current

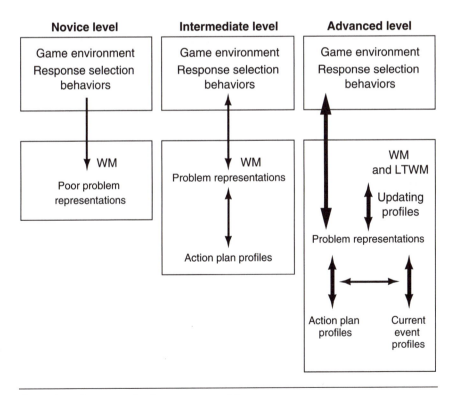

Figure 6. 1   Response selection memory model.

event profiles, working memory (WM), or long-term working memory (LTWM). Arrows represent activation of concepts from LTM, information input or retrieval pathways according to nearby labeled processes (e.g., WM, action plan profiles, updating profiles, etc.) and output (response selection behaviors). Also, the thickness of each arrow represents the depth and breadth of processing activities.

Immediate recall interviews indicated that the novices reacted to game events and at best generated goals regarding themselves ("Get it over," "Keep it in play"). Owing to their undeveloped representation of the task situation, the novices (especially the adult novices) applied a generalized WM strategy to monitor what happened to them or to their opponent; however, they were not able to interpret tactical features or develop action plans based on these events.

Youth experts, with fewer years of formal coaching and lower levels of competition than adult experts, primarily processed information to make decisions about their serves and shots (see the intermediate level in figure 6.1). Their problem representations were dominated by the action plan profile because they primarily attended to specific information (or conditions) about the current game context (their position, opponent's position, and ball location). Thus, youth experts attended to more relevant environmental features than did novices. In addition, retrieval into and out of WM was guided by the action plan profile. Thus, their domain-related strategies included their monitoring of current conditions and the success of their actions, as well as attaching verbal labels or cues to enhance motor executions.

Adult experts processed information about response selections along with other pertinent information about the current competition. Both action plan and current event profiles updated each other and influenced attended information, as is illustrated in the advanced level in figure 6.1. They monitored the success of their response selection processes (decision skills) as well as their motor executions. Thus, university-level varsity experts used current event and action plan profiles to make accurate response selections and regulate response executions during competition.

The skill-based differences in problem representations accessed during simulated situations were consistent with those retrieved by the players during actual competition. For example, youth and adult novices primarily generated concepts regarding execution goals ("Get it over the net"); limited conditions (e.g., limited diagnosis of the current game context); limited actions (e.g., few shots were planned); and no domain-related strategies. In contrast, experts (regardless of age) accessed information beyond what was presented in the scenarios. For example, they played out an imaginary game against an equal adversary to build profiles on information not available in the situation interview.

Overall, youth experts generated more extensive, tactical, and associated networks of condition-action rule decisions as compared with novices. However, they primarily accessed action plan profiles in response to game situations. Their concepts consisted of shots selected on the basis of their interpretation of the current environmental context, with a minimal analysis of conditions that regarded their opponent, game context, and so on. Finally, adult experts generated elaborate and sophisticated action plan and current event profiles that contained situation prototypes of possible game events. Further, their situation prototypes contained condition profiles—for example, profiles about their opponents, their serves, their weaknesses, and their tendencies during competition. These prototypes elicited domain-related strategies to monitor, interpret, and plan information to do the following: build or modify profiles, make decisions about possible action plans, and attach verbal labels or cues to movement parameters.

Players were scored during the games that were used to collect verbal reports. Scorers rated the tennis players' performance during competition according to the tennis performance coding system[1] to quantify each serve and shot (e.g., return of serve, volley, ground stroke). Analysis of performance skills indicated that level of expertise, rather than age, accounted for performance differences. Thus, youth experts exhibited more sophisticated selection and execution components than did adult novices. Both experts and novices were able to successfully control serves, but the serve attempts of the experts compared with the novices demonstrated higher relative frequency scores for strong serve selections and forceful serve executions. Similar to that of serve control, both groups successfully controlled shots at least 80% of the time; however, experts made higher percentages of strong shot selections and forceful shot executions. Over 80% of experts' serve and shot selections were considered tactical in the context of a given situation according to the player's position, the opponent's position, and position of the ball. In contrast, less than 50% of novices' serve and shot selections were considered tactical. Although youth experts' response selection performances appeared similar to adult experts, their problem representations were less developed.

In sum, adult experts' tactical response selections were consistent with their verbal data: They made tactical decisions based on sophisticated interpretations of conditions, and they planned for tactical actions. In contrast, novices made poor decisions, lacked sophisticated interpretations of conditions, and rarely planned actions.

Problem Representations and Performance Skills of Male Professional and Novice Players

The current project compared male adult professional players with novice tennis players[2] to examine differences in problem representations during immediate recall interviews and performance skills during actual competition. The professionals and novices played two sets of tennis (best three out of five games), and their verbal reports were analyzed for the first three games of the second set (16 immediate recall interviews were randomly selected; each interview was conducted between points). We were interested in the nature of professional players' problem representations accessed during competition because they were older, more elite, and had more years of experience than other tennis experts studied to date (17.3 years for professional male adults, 10.8 years for university-level varsity female adults, and 2.5 to 2.7 years for youth). Similarly, the male adult novices had more years of experience than others previously studied. Although years of tennis experience should not be equated with skill level, it has been noted that level of skill has had a positive linear relationship with amount of accumulated practice throughout several sport expertise studies (see Starkes, Deakin, Allard, Hodges, & Hayes, 1996).

Predictions Based on Previous Research

Consistent with previous research, professionals' responses to immediate recall interviews were predicted to exhibit highly evolved current event and action plan profiles. For example, professionals were predicted to access and interpret pertinent LTM conditions and form profiles as well as attend to specific aspects of the current context. In addition, professionals were predicted to utilize domain-related strategies throughout competition to encode, update, check, and modify conditions to either support their response selections or interpret pertinent game events. Although both groups were predicted to monitor the success of their motor executions, professionals were predicted to enhance their motor executions more often than novices by modifying conditions of application or by attaching verbal labels. In contrast, novices were predicted to access only rudimentary tennis knowledge. For example, novices were predicted to primarily utilize execution goals and rarely plan their actions or diagnose their opponent's actions. At best, they expected to exhibit some evidence of poorly developed action plan profiles by generating conditions about the current context (e.g., their court position).

Within the expert group, professionals were predicted to access more advanced problem representations than the university-level varsity players as a result of more years of higher-level competition and practice experiences. Similarly, professionals were also predicted to exhibit dramatically more advanced problem representations than youth experts. Among novices, adult males with more experience were predicted to access more appropriate knowledge (yet poorly developed problem representations) than youth or female adults. This prediction was based on earlier work that had demonstrated that youths with more task-specific practice (e.g., camp sessions, formal lessons) exhibited more appropriate tennis knowledge than did adults. Thus, novices' problem representations, regardless of age, were predicted to be less advanced than youth experts.

Performance skills of professionals were predicted to be more tactical in terms of measures of response selections and executions during competition as compared with novices. As noted in previous findings, both groups were predicted to control their serves and shots similarly since opponents were randomly selected within their respective group. Among experts, professionals were predicted to make tactical serve and shot selections more often than university-level varsity players. Among novices, male adults with more practice experiences than those studied to date were predicted to utilize more appropriate knowledge and exhibit higher levels of performance than youth or female adults.

Immediate Recall Problem Representations of Professionals and Novices During Competition

Immediate recall interview responses were scored for each player according to the model of protocol structure for tennis. Measures of content and structure were used to examine group differences in what knowledge was attended to and accessed by working memory during competition. Quantitative analyses were conducted on each player's identified concept content and structure—that is (respectively), total, variety, and sophistication or hierarchy of concepts for each major concept category; and occurrence of linked concepts. Mann-Whitney U tests were conducted on frequency scores to examine differences for each measure between male professionals and novices. (See McPherson et al. [2001] for frequency data of the concept content and structure for male professionals versus novices.) To illustrate the coding scheme, parentheses follow each sample verbal report and include the following: the identified concept (G = goal; C = condition; A = action;

D = do; R = regulatory); the subconcept category (excluding goals); the condition and action sophistication (0 = inappropriate or weak; 1 = appropriate but no features; 2 = appropriate and one feature; and 3 = appropriate and two or more features), and goal hierarchy (0 = skill regarding themselves; 1 = regarding themselves or opponent; and 2 = win attributes). (See McPherson [1999a, 1999b, 2000] for more details.)

Measures of goal concepts indicate that professionals and novices generated similar total, variety, and hierarchical levels because no significant differences were noted. However, novices were less variable than professionals. In addition, hierarchical levels of goals revealed that professionals and novices were primarily concerned with goals regarding themselves and executing the skill. Yet, consistent with our predictions, the novices' only responses to game situations were goals. For example, participant NI primarily generated goals during consecutive points: "I just have to keep making him make mistakes as I go through" (G, 1) and "I gotta keep putting the ball in play (G, 0) and making him make mistakes throughout the match (G, 1)." In contrast, professionals formed solutions in response to their goals. For example, player P7 stated: "Ok, so far my plan is working (C, their strength, 1), just let Dan make the mistakes here (G, 1), keep everything in play (G, 0), once he starts to fold a little bit (C, opponent's weakness, 1), I'm going to put some pressure on him (G, 1) and start coming in (C, position type, 1)."

Professionals generated significantly more total, varied, and sophisticated condition concepts as compared to novices, which supports predictions that experts access more extensive and well-developed condition profiles during competition than do novices. Further, novices exclusively generated weak conditions; in fact, two novices (N3 and N6) did not generate any conditions with features. As predicted, novices exhibited a limited diagnosis of game events and attended to less pertinent or inappropriate environmental features or game events. Typically, they attended to conditions related to some characteristic of their own play while ignoring their opponent, player position on the court, and so on. Thus, they seldom used encoding and retrieval strategies to interpret opponents' strengths, weaknesses, or tendencies as the competition progressed. If novices did attempt to interpret characteristics about their opponent, they displayed poor or weak interpretations. N6 illustrates novices' poor interpretations of conditions: "Don't take those first serves for granted" (C, their tendency, 1); "He can surprise me, I guess sometimes" (C, opponent's tendency, 1); "Looks like he is trying to concentrate and play much better" (C, opponent's tendency, 1); and "But, I think I am getting the hang of it" (C, their tendency, 1).

Professionals accessed and interpreted pertinent LTM conditions, formed profiles, and attended to specific aspects of the current context. Thus, they accessed and monitored condition concepts that were more extensive, varied, and sophisticated than did novices. For example, professionals encoded and updated conditions to make response selections or build condition profiles that concerned prior shots, tendencies, weaknesses, strengths, and so on. P10's utterances indicated that he continued to interpret and monitor an opponent's weakness and his subsequent shot selections: "I was thinking about trying to get the ball into his forehand (A, serve, 2), which I did (R, serve), he tends to hit the ball flatter (C, opponent's tendencies, 2)" and "Uh, I was thinking about getting the ball to his forehand (A, serve, 2), I did that (R, serve), got another cheap point (C, their strength, 1), I think his forehand is a little looser on the return of serve (C, opponent's weakness, 3)." They also formed tactical solutions regarding their shot, serve, and position type conditions. These tactical solutions were developed in response to pertinent interpretations of conditions (opponent's tendencies, game status, their prior shot) or goals (moving an opponent or executing a specific skill). Thus, as play progressed, professionals' condition profiles were updated, checked, and modified continually as they elaborated on conditions to interpret pertinent game events (their current event profile) or to support their response selections (their action plan profile).

Contrary to predictions, professionals and novices generated similar numbers of total, variety, and sophisticated action concepts during competition. Professionals represented shot selections or action plans as abstract tactical solutions (shot types based on opponent weaknesses and their tendencies) or goals (tactical yet general execution goals), thereby reducing the frequency of specific actions. Professionals were basing some actions on assessments of their opponent's strengths, tendencies, or weaknesses that had been monitored earlier in the match to form condition profiles of their opponent. At times, condition profiles about an opponent's tendencies or weakness were used to develop shot, serve, or position tactics. For example, P12 stated, "I got an easy first serve in (R, serve), it helped me get the point (C, game status, 1), I gotta stick to the backhand (C, serve type, 2), he's still chipping and charging (C, opponent's tendencies, 3)." Thus, conditions regarding serve, shot, or position types could be considered abstract action plans. Although some novices accessed more actions than predicted, their selections rarely included sophisticated conditions of application (why they selected a specific shot) or shot specifics (force, location). For example, utterances by N4 lacked shot specifics and conditions regarding their opponent: "Tried to just lob it over him (*A*, lob, 1) so he couldn't get it (*G*, 1)." Although some novices planned actions, they were rudimentary and usually reflected their desire to keep the ball in play.

Measures of regulatory concepts were not significant, yet professionals' and novices' use of regulatory concepts was indeed similar. However, novices labeled their errors poorly and did not interpret why their executions were successful or not. For example, novice N4 stated, "Hit it way too hard (*R*, ground stroke) and I'm starting to get tired (*C*, their weakness, 1)" and "Just try to return it hard (*A*, ground stroke, 1) and uh, nailed the fence and didn't even hit anywhere close to the court (*R*, ground stroke)." In contrast, professionals monitored the success of their actions in terms of execution outcomes as well as the quality of their decisions and the conditions that produced the action (response selection processes). For example, P3 noted that his failed execution resulted from his poor decision: ". . . shot that I missed (*R*, ground stroke) so I was just confused you know during the point (*C*, their prior shot, 1) but I wanted to go across or down the line (*A*, ground stroke, 3) . . ." In addition, professionals continually monitored the success of their motor executions as part of their response selection processes during competition. For example, P7 stated, "I missed the first serve (*R*, serve) so I need to get the second serve in with a lot of spin (*A*, serve, 3) to keep him on his toes (*G*, 1), I did that (*R*, serve) and pushed him back a little bit (*C*, opponent's position, 2) which I came in (*A*, position move, 1) and did a good volley (*R*, volley)."

Contrary to predictions, novices generated significantly more "do-concepts" than did professionals during competition (and a wider variety of them as well). All male novices, with the exception of one, generated do-concepts. Although they generated do-concepts, most lacked details about how to perform tennis motor skills. For instance, N4: "He just hit a serve (*C*, opponent's prior shot, 0) and I didn't hit it (*R*, return of serve), I didn't follow through (*D*, return of serve)" and "I didn't hold my racket right (*D*, ground stroke) and it went straight in the net (*R*, ground stroke)." Overall, novices generated do-concepts to explain why a motor execution failed rather than to attach verbal labels as possible solutions for enhancing their motor skills. In addition, novices rarely used do-concepts in their action plans. If they did, they were rudimentary. For example, N4 and N6 stated respectively: "I was trying to slow down my serve (*D*, serve) to get it in (*G*, 0)" and "Move your feet, move your feet and keep doing that (*D*, position move)." Overall, novices' utterances were rudimentary, and they primarily reflected the processing of game events in the moment. In contrast, only one male professional (P8) generated a do-concept.

In general, professionals monitored the success of their actions to update their condition profiles rather than to assign verbal labels to enhance their response selections. This finding is consistent with recent predictions in tennis (McPherson, 2000) because do-concepts may be used with more discretion as higher levels of expertise emerge. For example, tennis players with high levels of motor skills may deem an execution error as temporary and not consider the assigning of verbal labels as beneficial to their performance. Novices were similar to professionals in that both monitored the success of their motor executions similarly, yet unlike professionals, novices rarely modified conditions of application (e.g., select an alternative shot or modify their shot type). More important, novices used verbal labels to explain, rather than enhance, their failed motor executions. Further, such explanations were poor. Thus, unlike professionals, novices' actions were rarely linked to pertinent events (current or past), sophisticated situation prototypes, or domain-related strategies.

Measures of concept structure were significantly different between groups. Professionals generated more triple concepts (i.e., any combination of goal, condition, or action concepts) than did novices whereas novices generated more single concepts than did experts. Collectively, concept association and content findings suggest professionals accessed more varied, sophisticated, and interrelated concepts than did novices. These findings are evident in the sample verbal reports presented earlier.

Performance Skills of Professionals and Novices During Competition

Performance skills of these players were scored during the games that were used to collect verbal reports (for analysis of the entire competition, see Nielsen & McPherson, 2001). Each player's serve and shot attempts (return of serve, volley, ground strokes) were scored during competition (via videotaping) according to three performance components: the player's position, the opponent's position, and the ball location. Each component measured the tactical nature of the attempted shot based on the context of the game situation. Relative frequency scores for the optimal category of each performance component were derived according to the number of opportunities to respond in each corresponding category. These categories, presented earlier, were as follows: successful serve control, strong serve selections, forceful serve executions, successful shot control, strong shot selections, and forceful shot executions. Mann-Whitney U tests were conducted on relative

■ Table 6.1

Descriptive Statistics and Mean Rank Scores for Male Adult Components of Performance Levels During Singles Tennis Competition in Which Verbal Reports Were Collected

Variables	Professionals		Novices	
	Mean (SD)	Mean rank	Mean (SD)	Mean rank
Strong serve selections[a]	96.5 (8.6)	9.2	64.7 (21.5)	3.8
Forceful serve executions[a]	70.3 (18.0)	9.5	28.2 (10.0)	3.5
Successful shot control	100.0 (0.0)	8.0	95.5 (5.4)	5.0
Strong shot selections[b]	95.1 (5.5)	8.8	65.0 (22.0)	4.3
Forceful shot executions[c]	64.5 (8.3)	8.5	42.0 (29.4)	4.5

All players exhibited successful control serves. U values ($n_1 = 6$, $n_2 = 6$) of variables for expertise contrasts: 2 = .005([a]); 5 = .025([b]); and 7 = .05([c]).

frequency scores to examine professional and novice differences for performance components (table 6.1).

Consistent with predictions, both groups were similar for successful serve control. However, significant effects were noted for serve selection and execution as well as shot selection and execution. (Note: A *shot* is any shot other than a serve.) In other words, the professionals clearly outperformed novices. These findings were consistent with the verbal data because novices lacked action plan profiles. Collectively, novices' poor response selection and execution behaviors can be linked to several cognitive or motor factors, such as failure to consistently make tactical shot selections, weak knowledge concerning shot selections (e.g., intentions to keep the ball in play or just hit it over the net), and poor motor skill levels (or lack of confidence)—all of which influenced their attempts and abilities to carry out tactical response selections.

In contrast, the professionals were scored as having selected tactical (strong) serves for each serve attempt. Although professionals carried out forceful serve executions 70% of the time, their variability was high, which may have been due to the level of difficulty of the serve selected. For example, according to professionals' verbal data, more difficult serves were often attempted on the first serve as opposed to the second serve; otherwise, it varied according to the game status or their opponent's tendencies. Additionally, serve tactics among players varied according to their style of play or preferences (e.g., baseline versus serve and volley). Similarly, levels of tactical skill that concerned shot selections and executions were higher for professionals than they were for novices. Also, performance data indicated that professionals did not always attempt tactical shot selections or actually succeed in performing a forceful execution. Although professionals demonstrated consistency in selecting strong shots and carrying out forceful shot executions, shot selections were more successful than executions (95.5% versus 65%). This finding indicates that professionals continue to make tactical shot selections regardless of their ability to carry out such decisions. These trends were reinforced by the professionals' verbal data in that they used both action plan and current event profiles to select and monitor their shots. Although failed motor executions were frustrating to professionals at times, they remained on task, using this information to update the workability of a particular shot. For example, some professionals indicated they would continue to select a particular shot because it was a good choice, or they would elect to modify their patterns of shots to select a different shot.

Questions for Future Research

It sometimes seems that the more research that we do, the more questions that appear. In reviewing our data, we can make some conclusive suggestions for practical implementation, yet there is certainly a call for more data and research. However, in spite of the questions that this research has yielded, we will discuss these issues in the following sections:

- How our work compares with previous research
- The roles of action plan profiles and current event profiles in the development of expertise
- The implications for player development
- Real-world suggestions for designing instruction in tennis

How Did the Current Findings Compare With Earlier Work That Examined Female Adults and Male Youth Experts and Novices?

Among novices, male adults' verbal data during competition indicated that they generated more associated concepts than youth or female adults, yet their content remained undeveloped. Male adult novices also consistently generated more total goals and goals at the lowest possible hierarchy than did youth or female adults. In addition, male adult novices generated more and varied action concepts than youth novices whereas youth novices generated more action concepts than female adult novices did. However, male adult novices were highly variable (two participants did not generate any actions at all), and all adult novices generated more and varied conditions as compared with the youth novices. Among adult novices, males were more variable than females, yet the quality of conditions were similar among all novices. Their conditions were rudimentary; the conditions were primarily related to events about their play and rarely related to factors about their opponent or the current game context. However, some male adult novices' utterances during competition suggested that they were at times capable of generating rudimentary action plans and domain-related strategies—for example, monitoring their motor executions, attaching verbal labels to their failed motor executions, monitoring an opponent's behavior, generating shot types. These findings are consistent with player characteristics because adult males had more years of experience and higher skill ratings among the novice groups. Performance data indicated that male adult novices exhibited low percentages of tactical selections and forcing executions. These percentages were higher than youth or female adult novices; however, all novices were highly erratic in selecting and carrying out tactical serves and shots. Overall, male adult novices exhibited higher levels of performance skills and problem representations than youth or female adult novices, yet performance skill levels were much lower for all novice groups when compared with the experts.

Among experts, verbal data during competition indicated that youth experts generated less associated, yet more sophisticated, concepts than did male adult novices. Most important, verbal data indicated that professional players generated more extensive, varied, sophisticated, and associated tactical concepts for planning patterns of actions for building and updating conditions than did university-level varsity players (adult female experts) and youth experts. Surprisingly, professionals generated goals as often as male adult novices did and more often than did youth experts and university-level varsity players, which suggests that goals remain an important aspect of elite players' problem representations during competition. Further, professional and university-level varsity players utilized current event profiles in addition to action plan profiles during competition. Although youth experts attended to some aspects of the current context, they made few attempts to diagnose or build condition profiles and they rarely elaborated on conditions that produced their action. Further, youth experts exhibited less developed action plan profiles than did university-level varsity or professional players in terms of conditions of application and monitoring of motor executions (regulation strategies).

Also, youth experts used domain-related strategies to correct motor execution errors (do-strategies) as often as varsity players did. However, their errors were analyzed poorly compared to adult experts. Among adult experts, professional players monitored their actions more often than varsity players. In addition, adult experts monitored the success of their actions in terms of execution outcomes and the quality of their decisions or the conditions that produced the action (response selection processes). When monitoring motor executions, professional players used this information to modify their conditions of application whereas varsity players used this information to modify their conditions of application as well as their verbal labels to enhance their motor executions. Thus, elite players may not consider the assigning of verbal labels to enhance or correct motor executions during competition as beneficial to their performance (cf. McPherson, 2000). Finally, adult experts exhibited cognitive flexibility in the nature of their problem representations that were accessed during competition as a result of the breadth and depth of their situation profiles. Performance data indicated that professional players exhibited higher levels of response selection and execution scores during competition than did high-skilled youth and varsity players. Collectively, professional players' response selection performances were consistent with their problem representations because both were highly tactical and more sophisticated than varsity or high-skilled youth players.

How Do Action Plan and Current Event Profiles Develop With Expertise?

As predicted, male adult novices accessed undeveloped action plan profiles and domain-related strategies. However, contrary to predictions, some male adult novices during competition sporadically employed rudimentary sport-specific processes to monitor game events (e.g., failed motor executions), and they also attached verbal labels to enhance or correct motor executions. Overall, male adult novices lacked specialized encoding and retrieval strategies because they saw no need to update conditions (or actions), to plan actions, and to monitor pertinent events. Surprisingly, even though they had more experience and higher rankings as compared with youth and female novices, their problem representations were similar in that they generated goals as their plans rather than their actions. These findings suggest that in highly strategic open-skill sports, response selection processes may require direct instruction and they may take just as long to develop as motor skills. Thus, male adult novices were consistent with novices studied to date in that they approached the problem as a more global sport situation with minimal processing of task-relevant events. We speculate that without direct tennis instruction that is designed to build response selection knowledge, these novices (regardless of more years of experience) will fail to build action plan and current event profiles and will continue to exhibit poor response selection skills. In contrast, professionals exhibited higher-order processing as they processed deeper, more abstract tactical concepts.

During competition, professionals accessed highly evolved problem representations that contained well-developed action plan and current event profiles. Professionals employed sophisticated domain-related strategies to accomplish the following: plan actions based on elaborate and sophisticated action plan and current event profiles; monitor pertinent current and future events and the applicability of procedures; encode and retrieve current and past events for diagnosing and updating their condition profiles in response to changing conditions during competition. Verbal data among experts concurred with previous postulates made by French and McPherson (1999, in press) that suggest these profiles are built from smaller units of knowledge and domain-related strategies. For example, large differences were noted for condition profiles because professional players generated more associated, elaborate, and sophisticated current event profiles (or condition concepts) during competition than did university-level varsity players.

In addition, we predict that as levels of competition increase, certain aspects of expertise will not be monotonic as a result of different rates of development of performance skills and problem representations. For example, we found that some professionals either did a better job at modifying conditions of application for their serve game or had stronger baseline performance skills than others. Professionals also displayed cognitive flexibility because they derived their solutions from a variety of sport-specific response selection processes and LTM condition profiles. Therefore, individual differences among players at certain competitive levels may be due to variability in their problem representations (cognitive flexibility) or their performance skills (play preferences).

Collectively, the current research that examines professional players' problem representations and performance skills during competition suggests that tactical knowledge is an important attribute of expertise. Can a player achieve success with a limited current event profile? Yes! If this player has high levels of motor skills and well-developed action plan profiles, the athlete can then experience success when matched against a player of equal motor skill ability. However, the ability to make tactical decisions during competition may become more difficult to achieve because players at higher levels of competitive play approach similar levels of execution skills and physical ability (e.g., endurance). Therefore, the development of sophisticated processes for response selection (via specialized memory adaptations) may be a necessary requirement for achieving tennis expertise (French & McPherson, 1999, in press). The current study supports this postulate because verbal data suggest that players who compete at professional levels have better-developed action plan and current event profiles than do players who compete at lower levels. However, the professional players at best represented near-elite rather than elite tennis players (e.g., grand slam champions); therefore, the nature of memory adaptations in elite players remains to be resolved. Also, more research is needed to examine players at a variety of ages according to gender and competitive levels because the generalizability of the current findings is limited to tennis players with similar characteristics.

Although the tennis studies presented in this chapter were comprehensive, we feel a variety of tools and levels of analysis (see McPherson, 1994) should be utilized in the design of field and laboratory sport expertise research to fully examine the interplay among players' cognitive and motor skills during competition. For example, university-level varsity players (experts) reported more extensive problem representations concerning alternative actions and possible conditions when presented with static game situations (see McPherson, 1999b) as compared with their problem representations generated during competition. In addition, when novices were presented with situation interviews, they generated weak problem representations, which were consistent with their verbal reports during competition. Further, laboratory (or modified field studies) should simulate more real-world competitive contexts to allow players opportunities to engage in the type of information processing that they use during competition (e.g., to build current event profiles).

Analyses of performance skills during actual competition revealed that response selection and execution variables contribute to expertise at all levels in singles tennis. Overall, performance findings can be attributed to a higher level of tactical and motor skill development as a result of more practice experiences of males within their respective levels of expertise. These results are consistent with findings in other domains (see Ericsson, 1996b) in that at least 10 years (or 10,000 hours) of intense preparation is required to reach exceptional levels of performance. However, whether players' behaviors during competition reflect natural progressions or other factors—such as type of instructional environment, type of experiences, or practices outside of class—remains to be resolved. Therefore, future research should systematically document players' former experiences and current practices (see Deakin and Cobley, chapter 5) to fully examine the relationship of these experiences to knowledge and skill development. In addition, a sport such as tennis offers excellent settings to conduct longitudinal and cross-sectional research as compared with other sports (such as local basketball or baseball programs in school or recreational settings) because highly skilled youth (nationally ranked players) typically participate in player development programs for several years.

Analyses of verbal data revealed that adult experts' exceptional response selection skills are linked to their highly developed sport-specific long-term memory structures (i.e., current event and action plan profiles). Although tennis players studied thus far represent only a few points along a continuum of expertise (e.g., nationally ranked juniors or world-class tennis players were not studied), we feel the current findings present a strong case that tactics are an important factor of expertise, especially in highly strategic open-skill sports like tennis. Thus, the following are major research questions we consider pertinent to understanding how to facilitate the development of knowledge bases and learning of response selection processes in highly strategic sports.

- How do current event profiles and response selection processes develop among players of varying ages and expertise levels?
- What type of practice develops action plan and current event profiles and thus leads to high levels of response selection skills during competition?
- What type of game strategies and player tactics are appropriate for players of varying ages and competitive levels?

What Are the Implications for Player Development?

To date, authors of instructional texts (e.g., motor behavior, pedagogy, or sport-skills texts) and directors of player development programs (e.g., USTA) have done a better job at designing instruction that promotes players' action plan profiles rather than players' current event profiles. For example, ideas about how we might practice or teach skills that are related to current event profiles are (to our knowledge) limited (e.g., see French & McPherson, 1999, in press; K.T. Thomas & J.R. Thomas, 1994). With regard to current event profile training in tennis, we make a similar argument to one made by Starkes (chapter 10) regarding the perceptual training work in our field (sport) compared to other fields (e.g., medicine, aviation). That is, motor behaviorists who are interested in enhancing sport expertise may have undermined the application of innovative perceptual training techniques by waiting for absolute proof of its transferability. Likewise, despite absolute proof, we feel our recommendations for knowledge-base training are congruent with our experiences as instructors, coaches, and tennis players. However, in tennis, it appears that we may have an advantage in implementing new practices because leaders in tennis organizations have recently questioned the effectiveness of player development programs that rely heavily on technique or motor skill practice to transfer players to high-level performance.

What we believe offers promising solutions is to suggest that we first resolve issues that concern how we might practice or teach skills related to current event profiles. We feel that the best solution may be to combine instructional strategies that are designed to build current event profiles with those currently used to build action plan profiles and motor skills, thereby enhancing existing player development programs. We believe the framework presented earlier in this chapter provides a useful guide to design practices to build and assess several factors related to performance enhancement (see McPherson, 1994). Still, a great deal of collaboration among coaches, sport scientists, and players will be required to design programs that promote higher levels of performance.

What Does Expertise Research That Examines Performance Skills and Tactics in Tennis Suggest About Designing Instruction?

Each player, regardless of age or expertise level, made more appropriate response selections than they were able to carry out. Performance measures indicated that even for players at elite levels, forceful executions were difficult to achieve consistently. These findings are pertinent to player development because players, if not encouraged to do otherwise, may abandon more sophisticated tactics for less sophisticated tactics to achieve successful outcomes (i.e., motor executions). Therefore, we recommend that instructors provide feedback that assesses players' control and response selection skills according to the context of their game situations. This feedback could be provided during bouts of tactical skill practices and actual competition (videotape their matches). In addition, players should be taught to analyze their own (and others') tactical behaviors during performance and how to practice for improvement. Drill situations should also be designed so that players are allowed to make choices regarding their shot selections and so that players are asked why they selected their responses (or taught why their choices were poor or wise). Also, tactical skill must be rewarded. For example, scoring systems could be altered so that tactical serve or shot selections that do not result in successful executions are rewarded.

Again, it is important to note that response selection components provide a limited assessment of players' tactical knowledge because quality of shot selections are judged according to aspects of the current game context, such as player/opponent positions and location of the ball. Therefore, practices should be designed to promote current event profiles. Players cannot talk a good game within static situations when they are not somehow trained to create adaptations in memory structures that facilitate performance during competition (French & McPherson, in press). We believe that having players verbalize their thoughts is a good way to assess players' knowledge-base development and problem representations regarding tennis situations. For example, players can verbalize their thoughts during static game situations or while watching videotapes of competition. Plus, we've found that players' problem representations that were accessed during simulated tennis situations are reliable indicators of the type of problem representations players will access during competition. However, interviews at breaks during competition (between points or games) can best detect players' domain-related strategies accessed during competition.

Thus, we advocate that players periodically record their thoughts during competition. This will make them aware of their problem representations and decision skills utilized during competition. Also, coaches and players could listen to these recordings together to collaborate on ways to enhance players' problem representations.

In addition, we encourage that coaches periodically assess their players' performance skills (via videotaping) during tournament competition and make their critiques available to players as soon as possible. Also, following tournament competition, a player could participate in or be responsible for assessing one's personal performance skills and tactics. Further, while viewing the tape together, the coach could assess a player's action plan and current event profiles as accessed in the present ("What should you be doing here?") or during the competition ("Can you remember what you were thinking before serving this point?"). Finally, both player and coach could develop ways to improve and enhance performance and tactical skills via specific types of deliberate practice. Of course, the level of allocation and type of delivery of the previously mentioned instructional strategies must be modified according to each player's level of competition, motivation, and ambition. Research that has employed some of the previously mentioned instructional strategies has already shown promising results for adults at beginner levels of competition across a semester of instruction (McPherson & French, 1991; McPherson, 1994). In fact, these studies and others provide evidence that the focus of practice and instruction affects what aspects of performance (including problem representations) are acquired (see French & McPherson, 1999, in press). Finally, studying the effectiveness of the previously mentioned training strategies in conjunction with others (see Janelle & Hillman, chapter 2; Williams & Ward, chapter 9) offers exciting adventures for researchers and coaches who are interested in enhancing player development in highly strategic open-skill sports.

Summary

Researchers examining players' problem representations and decision-making processes during high strategy open-skill sport competition have made recent advances in knowledge-base theory. However, research in this area presents unique issues as both tactical and motor executions have aspects of declarative (knowing what to do) and procedural (doing it) knowledge. To clarify issues regarding sport-specific knowledge bases and performance skills, a framework (or continuum) was presented that we feel is useful in designing and interpreting experiments. In regards to procedural skills, a tennis performance coding system was presented to illustrate how assessing players' accuracy of response selection and response execution skills during competition provides important information about the development of players' serve and shot selection skills. Also, a model of protocol structure for sport was presented to demonstrate how players' verbal reports generated during simulated and actual sport performance can be used to systematically analyze tactical skill. Using previous research in tennis, we demonstrated that verbal report data collected during task performance provide vital information concerning the nature of players' problem representations and decision skills. In addition, a memory model was introduced to illustrate expertise differences in levels of processing during sport competition. This model depicts two specialized memory adaptations termed action plan and current event profiles. Action plan profiles are rule-governed prototypes stored in long-term memory used to match certain current conditions with appropriate visual and/or motor actions. Current event profiles are tactical scripts that guide constant building and modifying of pertinent concepts (past, current, and/or future) to monitor during the competitive event. This theory postulates that during competition advanced-level players will use well-developed current event and action plan profiles to make accurate response selections and regulate response executions; intermediate-level players will use primarily action plan profiles and at best access rudimentary current event profiles to make response selections and regulate response executions; and novice-level players will use rudimentary goals or at best access rudimentary action plan profiles to make response selections. To substantiate these postulates, we presented recent tennis research that examined adult male novices' and professionals' performance skills and problem representations during competition. Also, these new findings were used to illustrate the development of action plan and current event LTM profiles with expertise as these players were more advanced within their respective groups than those studied to date. Importantly, we concluded that tactical skills in high strategy sports will require direct instruction and may take as long to develop as motor skills. Several research directions and instructional strategies regarding player development were presented.

EXPERTS' COMMENTS

■ Question

In this chapter, McPherson and Kernodle suggest that professional tennis players not only develop an action plan profile for a particular competition but are able to diagnose the ongoing match and adjust tactics accordingly. They speculate that without instruction, athletes have few available responses to select from and never develop the diagnostic skills to employ a current event profile of a match. Do you feel this is also the case in wrestling? As a coach, how does one instill these diagnostic and current-event updating skills?

■ Coach's Perspective: Nick Cipriano

In freestyle wrestling, each competitor develops a general competition strategy that is largely based on perceived personal strengths and a preferred style of play. For example, the wrestler who believes that physical conditioning is a personal strength will establish a match strategy that utilizes fitness as a basis for executing specific tactics. Likewise, wrestlers who believe that their par-terre technical skills are particularly strong will employ a strategy that focuses on getting the opponent called for passivity, thus creating the opportunity to wrestle in the par-terre position. The strategy and tactics that wrestlers employ in competition are conceived in the practice environment, but they are often perfected in competition under stressful conditions. Through experience, wrestlers learn to better track match developments, and they slowly learn to adjust strategy and tactics accordingly. In my experience, I have found that highly accomplished wrestlers (as compared with novice wrestlers) can recall explicit details of their matches. I believe their recall ability is directly linked to their ability to process and interpret match developments, not only more readily, but also much more accurately. In my judgment, the coach facilitates development of this important psychological skill by integrating technical training with psychological training and by constantly reminding the wrestler during sparring sessions to monitor developments and adjust tactics accordingly. One specific strategy I use involves encouraging wrestlers to maintain a broad focus of attention during sparring and to visualize the actions of their opponent from a third-person perspective (as if watching the sparring from the sidelines). Being able to assess match developments from an external perspective allows a more accurate interpretation of strategic and tactical adjustments that must be made.

As coach, I have found that as wrestlers gain competition experience, they are less reliant on verbal feedback from the coach before initiating tactical adjustments. Experience and training take them from a state of dependency to a state of self-reliance in making tactical adjustments. In the early stages, novice wrestlers can successfully adjust tactics with verbal feedback, but when initiating strategic or tactical changes in the absence of feedback, they often make tactical errors that result in negative outcomes. Although developing self-reliance is the ultimate goal, analytical ability is largely a learned skill and developed through training. By incorporating competition simulations, visualization, and deliberate practice of common occurrences in actual competitions, athletes can improve their analytic ability. In my experience, the highly skilled experienced wrestler is able to make strategic-tactical adjustments with minimal input from the coach whereas most others rely on the coach to provide technical information that is used to adjust strategy and tactics during the course of a contest.

■ *Player's Perspective: Therese Brisson*

McPherson and Kernodle suggest that professional tennis players are able to develop action plan profiles and diagnose the ongoing match and adjust tactics accordingly. They speculate that, without instruction, athletes have few available responses to select from and never develop the diagnostic skills to employ a current event profile of a match. I have noticed that very skilled athletes also seem to get themselves out of difficult situations and recover from errors better than less skilled athletes. Athletes undertake tactical decisions depending on many factors, which include their own strengths and weaknesses, their opponents' tendencies, and the game situation. Coaches who act as high-level consultants rather than controllers have the most positive and lasting influence on the tactical element of an athlete's development. They provide direction and guidance and suggest strategies for improvement, but they don't control their athletes. The responsibility for training and performance is where it should be, with the athlete. It has been my experience that in the initial stages of development, athletes may need direction from coaches on tactics and adjustments. With experience, however, athletes become less dependent on direction from coaches, and they become self-reliant. Very skilled athletes use various techniques to develop this ability. For example, when I make an error on the ice, I replay the situation in my head but with the correct response when I get to the bench. This allows me to rehearse appropriate responses to a given situation on the ice.

[1]Control components examined each player's ability to attempt a serve or shot, such as return of serve, volley, ground stroke, and so on. Each attempt was coded as *successful* or *unsuccessful*. Successful control behaviors were defined as good court position, toss skills, ball contact, or footwork that enabled selection of an action. Unsuccessful control behaviors were defined as poor court position, toss skills, ball contact, or footwork, which did not allow the player to select an action. Selection components examined each player's decision making regarding serve and shot selections. Each selection was coded as a *strong* or *weak* behavior. Strong serve or shot selections were defined as appropriate or strong decisions (offensive or defensive) in the context of a given situation—that is, according to the player's position, the opponent's position, and the position of the ball. Weak serve or shot selections were defined as inappropriate or poor decisions in the context of a given situation. Execution components for serves were coded as *forceful, nonforceful, netted,* and *long* or *wide.* Forceful serve executions were successful and placed pressure on the opponent as a result of placement, speed, spin, or depth. Nonforceful

serve executions were successful but placed little pressure on the opponent. Both netted and long or wide serve executions were unsuccessful attempts as defined according to their outcome. Execution components for shots were coded as *forceful, nonforceful, forced error,* and *unforced error.* Forceful shot executions were successful and placed pressure on the opponent as a result of placement, speed, spin, or depth. Nonforceful shot executions were successful yet placed little pressure on the opponent. Forced error shot executions were not successful and resulted in a point lost as a result of an opponent's good shot. Unforced error shot executions were not successful and consisted of a point lost, owing to the player's mistake rather than the opponent's good shot.

[2] Professionals held national rankings and had National Tennis Rating Program (NTRP) ratings of 5.5 to 6.5 (see United States Tennis Association, 2001). They are former university players, and they reported playing an average of five professional tennis events each year at the time of data collection. One professional was formerly a member of his country's Davis Cup team whereas others were winners of at least nine tennis tournaments each (within the last 10 years). Male novices were low-skilled male players without tournament experience and had NTRP ratings from 2.5 to 3.5.

Chapter 7

Expertise in Sport Judges and Referees

■ ■ ■ ■ ■

Circumventing
Information-Processing Limitations

Diane Ste-Marie

Expertise has been studied within many domains and with a variety of approaches (refer to books by Ericsson, 1996; Starkes & Allard, 1993). Chase and Simon (1973) and DeGroot (1965) led the field by studying chess players, but the field soon broadened to include the study of other domains, such as music (Ericsson, Krampe, & Tesch-Römer, 1993), physics (Anzai, 1991), and sport (Allard & Starkes, 1991). Within the sport domain, researchers have investigated a broad spectrum of sports, including soccer (Helsen, Hodges, Van Winckel, & Starkes, 2000; Williams & Davids, 1995), snooker, (Abernethy, Neal, & Konig, 1994), and basketball (Starkes, Allard, Lindley, & O'Reilly, 1994), just to name a few. Recent research in tennis (McPherson & Kernodle, chapter 6) and golf (Beilock, Wierenga, & Carr, chapter 12) is presented in this book as well. A common denominator among these studies is that they have all examined athletes in a particular sport. Through this research, the expert athlete has been shown to have the following: superior recognition and recall of structured information; better anticipation skills through the use of advance information; more effective visual search strategies; and superior knowledge of interrelationships among relevant context variables (for recent reviews, see Abernethy, 2001; Williams, 2001; Starkes, Helsen, & Jack, 2001; Tenenbaum & Bar-Eli, 1993; 1995).

Beyond the research with athletes, scant attention has been devoted to other influential members of the sporting domain. Although research has been conducted on coaches (e.g., Côté, Salmela, Trudel, Baria, & Russel, 1995; Salmela, Draper, & Laplante, 1993) and instructors (e.g., Ilmwold & Hoffman, 1983), the work is limited and sport evaluators remain an understudied population. The role of the sport evaluator itself can vary depending on the sport. Some sports are evaluated on more subjective dimensions and thus need an evaluation committee (i.e., panel of judges) to determine the winner. Gymnastics, figure skating, and diving are common examples, as are other less obvious sports such as boxing, karate, and taekwondo. Referees also play a sport evaluation role in objective team-based sports. Even though the "highest points" determine the winner, referees are involved to ensure that rules of play are properly followed. Their impact on the development or outcome of a game can be significant. For example, the 1990 World Cup in soccer was won by a German player who scored the only penalty kick awarded during that match (Plessner & Betsch, 2001). In this light, it may serve the sporting community well to understand expertise in these two sport evaluation roles. Similar to the logic used with athletes (Williams & Grant, 1999), the mechanisms that differentiate experts and novices may assist us in developing training strategies to hasten the judge's or referee's journey to expertise. Furthermore, expert judges and referees who are responsible for sport evaluation expose athletes to the optimal conditions for competition. Thus, the main objectives of this chapter are to review key findings that have emerged from expertise research that has focused on sport judges and referees, to structure these findings within a cohesive framework, and finally, to recommend future areas of research in this field.

The basic structure of the chapter will follow the steps of what Ericsson and Smith (1991) refer to as the *expert performance approach*. The first step of this approach establishes the designated tasks that expose the characteristics linked to superior performance. Thus, I review the tasks that have been used by the various researchers who have investigated expertise in judges and referees. The second step of the expert performance approach involves conducting a detailed analysis that leads to strong inferences about the underlying cognitive structures that mediate superior performance. What serves as the framework for this second step is Salthouse's (1991) proposition of viewing expertise as the circumvention of human-processing limitations. The final step of the expertise approach delves into explanations about how experts acquire the inferred mediating mechanisms fundamental to their performance. In this regard, I highlight the importance of domain-specific experiences.

In the remainder of the chapter, I draw on relevant findings from the sport-athlete paradigms, and I make connections to similar research with judges and referees. What is important to consider, however, is that differences do exist across these varying roles in sport. For instance, athletes are involved much more in the perception-action link of sport performance, whereas judges and referees are tied more closely to the perception and decision-making aspects, without a strong need for an action component. Despite the differences that exist among these roles, certain similarities are also apparent. For example, all are responsible for the searching of relevant information from a moving display that results in decisions based not only on the perceptual information, but on stored factual and experiential knowledge.

With expertise research in general, a common criticism raised is that of borrowing paradigms that have proved successful in the past and assuming they can be automatically extrapolated to different domains (Starkes et al., 2001). In this context, I would argue that extrapolations from sport are valid. That is, certain common features in expertise designs of coaches and athletes can be transferred to the sport domains of judging and refereeing. Further, although it is recognized that expertise is task-specific, it is important to highlight that the expertise approach has sought to identify the common features that may occur in more than just one domain (Salthouse, 1991; Starkes et al., 2001). It is this latter approach to which this chapter is dedicated because common features for defining expertise in athletes are also identified for sport judges and referees.

Step One: Detailing the Tasks

Researchers investigating expertise in sport judges and referees have used a number of laboratory tasks to tap into the various dimensions of expertise (for a review, see table 7.1). These tasks can typically be described within two of the three basic knowledge categories—specifically, declarative and procedural knowledge (the third category is strategic knowledge). Declarative knowledge refers to the knowledge of rules and facts that pertain to the specific event in question, whereas procedural knowledge is commonly referred to as "how to" knowledge, which is seen in the actual performance of related tasks (Thomas & Thomas, 1994). A representative task for strategic knowledge has not been used within this population, which may be due to the likelihood that judges or referees of one sport tend not to judge or referee other sports. Consequently, studying the transference of basic rules or strategies across contexts may not have been of research interest. Nonetheless, understanding the contributions of strategic knowledge may be an avenue of future research.

With reference to tasks used to study referees, Deakin and Allard (1992)[1] used a battery of five tests with expert basketball referees. The battery consisted of a trivia test, rules test, hand signals test, recall of schematic plays, and a foul/violation detection test. The first four tests were of the paper and pencil design, testing participants' knowledge on the basic facts and rules that referees use in a game; thus, they can be described as declarative knowledge tasks. The detection test consisted of watching short segments of game play on video, determining whether a foul had occurred, and then identifying the actual infraction. The first part of this task assesses procedural knowledge because it relies on task performance of a related refereeing task. Having participants elaborate on the actual infraction returns us to accessing declarative knowledge because the participants relied on stored rule-based knowledge to perform the task.

The use of video footage has also been used by MacMahon and Ste-Marie (1999) with rugby referees. Similar to Deakin and Allard, MacMahon and Ste-Marie had rugby referees complete a procedural task. More specific, the referees were asked to make decisions about what

■ Table 7.1

Overview of Research on Expertise in Sport Judges and Referees

Authors: Sport/Participants	Technique	Basic findings
Bard, Fleury, Carrière, & Hallé (1980) • Gymnastics/Judges	Eye movement recording Error detection task	Experts fixate more on upper body* Experts have fewer fixations Experts make fewer mistakes
Deakin & Allard (1992) • Basketball/Referees, coaches, athletes	Foul detection task Declarative knowledge tasks	Experts superior at identifying type of foul* No difference for foul detection Superior knowledge for experts on rules/signals*
MacMahon & Ste-Marie (1999) • Rugby/Referees	Foul detection task Oral accounts of information	No differences between low-experienced and high-experienced referees Experts use more episodic and semantic information*
Plessner & Betsch (2001) • Gymnastics/Judges	Perceptual judgment task	Superior performance in discriminating joint angle deviance*
Ste-Marie & Lee (1991) • Gymnastics/Judges	Error detection task	Experts superior at detecting form errors*
Ste-Marie (1999) • Gymnastics/Judges	Error detection task Perceptual anticipation task Declarative knowledge tasks	Experts better at error detection Experts superior at predicting next element* Experts demonstrate superior declarative knowledge*
Ste-Marie (2000) • Gymnastics/Judges	Judges videotaped while judging at live competitions	Experts' direction of gaze is focused on gymnast for longer duration* Experts spend more time engaged in dual-task demands*

*Indicates that significant differences were found. When no asterisk is provided, only a trend was noted in the research.

call would be made on specific videotaped rugby plays. The referees were also asked to provide an oral account of the various sources of information used to make that decision. Within those explanations, reference to the rules and facts of the game as well as specific past experiences (episodic memory) were considered declarative knowledge, whereas information provided about where they looked to pick up relevant information was treated as procedural knowledge.

Both declarative and procedural knowledge have also been tested in gymnastics judging. Ste-Marie (1999) studied the declarative knowledge of gymnastics judges by asking them to provide information concerning the types of errors, written symbol code, and the level of difficulty associated with certain gymnastics skills presented on video. In addition, judges made predictive statements about gymnastic skills that were likely to follow a gymnastics sequence that had been stopped at a particular point on video.

Procedural knowledge has been examined through the use of video protocol, eye movement recording, and other perceptual judgment tasks. Further to the declarative tasks, Ste-Marie's (1999) video protocol also included judges' performing an error detection task on the specific gymnastics skill that had followed the stoppage point (after the predictions had been made). Ste-Marie and Lee (1991) also had gymnastics judges perform an error detection task, but those gymnastics skills were presented in isolation on short videoclips, rather than following a longer gymnastics sequence. Another perceptual-based task was done in a study by H. Plessner (personal communication, April 2001). Male gymnastics judges were presented with various cards that depicted the gymnastics skill of an iron cross on the men's rings event. Both experts and novices were asked to determine the joint angle deviation from that of a "perfect" iron cross.

Two other methods that were used to examine expert-novice differences in procedural knowledge have also used gymnastics judges. Bard, Fleury, Carrière, & Hallé (1980) used an eye-movement recording technique to investigate the visual search patterns of novice and expert gymnastics judges. Finally, Ste-Marie (2000) videotaped expert and novice judges while they were judging actual gymnastics competitions. Two main measures were later coded from the video data: direction of gaze and time spent engaged in dual-task demands (writing and watching the gymnast at the same time). All of these described tasks are procedural in nature because they tap into actual demands of the "performance" aspect of the domain.

In sum, both declarative and procedural knowledge tasks have been used in experiments to examine expert-novice differences in judges and referees; strategic knowledge has yet to be investigated. In the next section, I present the key findings from the tasks just described. These findings are structured within the framework used to support the argument that expert judges and referees have learned to circumvent the limitations that impede novices' performance.

Step Two: Expertise As the Circumvention of Limitations

As stated by Ericsson and Smith (1991), it is obvious that one can not directly observe the cognitive processes that result in superior performance, "but what can be observed concurrently with cognitive processes can be related to the underlying cognitive processes within the information-processing theory of cognition" (p. 19). Information-processing theory has often been used to model human performance, with an emphasis on how information from the environment proceeds through various cognitive, perceptual steps and thus culminates in a given decision or response (Haywood, 1993; Tenenbaum & Bar-Eli, 1993; for an alternative approach, see Beek, Jacobs, Daffertshofer, & Huys, chapter 13). Within such information-processing models, several steps have been characterized as having human performance limitations, such as attention and memory (Magill, 2001). A number of proposals have been advanced for how experts are able to overcome the limitations in attention and memory processes that seem to restrain the performance of most people who attempt to do the same task. Ericsson and Smith (1991), for example, proposed how extended practice can lead to adaptation of the basic physiological mechanisms and the acquisition of new qualitatively different cognitive mechanisms that mediate the superior performance of experts. In this chapter, I base my discussion on Salthouse's (1991) explicit description of how experts can acquire knowledge and skills to circumvent the capacity limitations that constrain the performance of novices.

Salthouse (1991) hypothesized seven processing limitations of nonexperts by pulling together research conducted in domains such as chess, music, and sport. Four of these processing limitations concerned the lack of knowledge in related aspects of the task—that is, the nonexperts did not know what to expect; what to do and when to do it; what information was relevant; and the interrelations among variables. In addition, nonexperts had three other processing limitations: difficulty in combining information; insensitivity to sensory/perceptual discriminations; and lack of production proficiency. In the sections to follow, I account for sport judges' and referees' expertise using four of the processing limitation categories identified by Salthouse. More specific, I argue that expert judges and referees do not encounter the same processing limitations as novices do because (a) they are more sensitive to sensory/perceptual discriminations, (b) they know what information is relevant, (c) they know what to expect, and (d) they know the interrelations among variables.

Another worthy point of mention is that not all processing limitations identified by Salthouse were applied to every activity domain referenced. Lack of production proficiency, for example, was linked only to music and sport performance, and not to chess. This distinction among the processing limitations relevant to a domain brings to light an important issue—that even though sport judges and referees are being treated within this chapter under the same framework, they too have their differences. MacMahon (1999) identified a number of characteristics that served to define the differences of these two sport evaluation roles, of which only three will be introduced here.

First, with respect to Poulton's (1957) closed- and open-skilled sport classification, subjectively judged sports can typically be classified as closed-skill sports in that the performance environment does not change nor do the expected execution of the movements. In contrast, referees are typically involved in open-skilled sports, where athletes respond in a dynamic environment with the play's development based on the immediate conditions available. Open-skilled sports also facilitate greater variability in terms of how the performers execute the movements. As such, differences emerge between the demands of the two roles. Gymnastics judges, for example, remain static in a particular spot for observation of the performances. They never change from one performance to the next. Referees, on the other hand, need to move around a playing field, constantly adjusting their position to get the best visual perspective possible. This difference should not only direct researchers in terms of the questions to pose, but it should also drive the protocol that is used to assess expertise. That is, although data gathered by video protocol for a judge may not be drastically different from the actual setting, using the same technique for referees may be more problematic.

As Abernethy, Thomas, and Thomas (1994) concluded, poor ecological validity within a paradigm may lead one to question whether the paradigm used contributes useful knowledge. As such, the testing of referees may be more valuable in settings that allow them to move freely within the play itself. Although not studied within an expertise context, two studies have used head-mounted video cameras on referees involved in actual game play (McLennan & Omodei, 1996, with rugby referees; and Oudejans et al., 2000, with assistant referees in soccer). Expertise studies that use similar equipment with referees would likely be fruitful in exposing other expert-novice differences. They would also make the task more ecologically valid in the sense of realistic stimuli and in terms of the movements required in the natural setting.

Another difference between the two sport evaluation roles concerns the nature of the decision being made. Within subjectively judged sports, judges typically analyze whether the motor skills that are performed match with a "perfect" template for the skill in question; thus, the quality of the movement becomes a key criteria. Conversely, referees are not concerned with the quality of execution. Rather, they focus on whether the movements fit within given boundaries (e.g., the hit is not too low) and whether players adhere to the rules of the game. An additional component to consider is that judges are external to the performance itself throughout the evaluation period, in the sense that there is no direct interaction between the athlete and the judges who are evaluating the performance. On the other hand, referees are directly involved in the play, continually blowing whistles to stop and resume play, speaking with the athletes, and making clear signals as to what their opinions were on a given play. These varying goals of analysis and interaction create different task demands that should be kept in consideration. Nonetheless, the similarities between these two roles do suggest that our understanding of expertise in one sphere can assist with the other and that common research suggestions may be worthwhile.

What exactly are those similarities between judges and referees in the sport evaluation context? First, it can be said that the responsibility of observing and interpreting perceptual events leads to comparable cognitive and perceptual processes. For example, within gymnastics, judges need to store information concerning the symbol code, level of difficulty, and deduction values for associated errors. Similarly, referees need to store information concerning the rules of the game, consequences of given behaviors, and the various hand signals attached to decisions made. This stored factual information will be retrieved, along with episodic memory (MacMahon & Ste-Marie, 1999), during the analysis of the complex movement patterns for identification of the movements or detection of errors and infractions. Working memory, as well as selective and divided attention capabilities, is also necessary in both roles. Both judges and referees evaluate under time-pressured situations, where incoming information is continual in that a performance is not one isolated event. Add to this variable the fact that social evaluation occurs as well—for example, from other judges on a panel or from fans in the audience. These factors often create an anxious environment for judges and referees.

Many of the described demands do challenge the limited capacities of attention, memory, and speed of processing that are characteristic of humans. Despite this, expert judges and referees are typically very accurate in their perceptions and subsequent decisions, and they perform better than novices in their domain. If one adopts the argument that this ability occurs because experts are less constrained by these limitations, it leads one to explicitly specify what the constraints on human information processing may be and how it is that experts go about circumventing them. I defend this argument in the following sections by addressing information related to four processing limitations.

Sensitivity to Perceptual Discriminations

Although Salthouse (1991) considered athletes and musicians in his introduction of this processing limitation category, it is a category that can also be considered with judges and referees. As discussed earlier, sport judges and referees are required to detect critical information in the movement patterns that unfold before them. In being able to accomplish this task, they have to be sensitive to subtle manipulations in the movement patterns that lead to decisions, such as an error deduction or call of an infraction. A number of studies have demonstrated superior detection or correct identification of pertinent information on the part of expert judges and referees. Deakin and Allard (1992), for example, showed that expert referees were significantly more accurate at identifying the type of foul or infraction in a basketball sequence than were coaches or players of the game. What is notable is that the performance level of the observers in just the detection of a foul was not different; rather, the differences were only at the level of proper identification of the foul. With judges, Ste-Marie and Lee (1991) found that expert gymnastics judges were better at detecting errors in a gymnastics performance than were novices. Similarly, Bard et al. (1980) reported that novice gymnastics judges made twice as many errors as expert judges when evaluating gymnasts' beam performances. Novices missed more errors that should have been detected, and they also falsely detected errors more than the experts.

A final set of results that demonstrate the differences in perceptual sensitivity is found in H. Plessner's (personal communication, April 2001) work with male gymnastics judges. In that study, expert gymnastics judges were better than novices at determining the amount of joint angle deviation from the "perfect" template of a men's iron cross on rings. Of more interest was that they also had the judges perform the same task under both full-attention and divided-attention conditions (i.e., judges performed a secondary task). Expert judges' performance on the task was not changed by the introduction of the secondary task, whereas novice judges were significantly affected. Such results suggest that the novices required more processing resources to do the task than the experts. This finding leads to the following questions: What are experts doing to enable these superior perceptual discriminations, and how do they do it with such ease? The next two sections link the response to these two questions to the experts' abilities to circumvent processing limitations.

Knowing What Information Is Relevant

Expertise research on athlete performance has definitively shown that experts attend more to relevant information than irrelevant information (see reviews by Abernethy, 2001; Starkes et al., 2001; Tenenbaum & Bar-Eli, 1993; 1995). This finding has been shown through a variety of techniques, such as through event and temporal occlusion, as well as through eye movement recoding data. The event occlusion technique is used to identify the specific information a person uses to make a given decision. The task is to make a decision via frames of film where parts of the scene are blacked out (occluded), thus eliminating specific visual cues. Abernethy and Russel's (1987) work with badminton players' making decisions about shuttle destination on serves showed that experts were only affected when relevant information was occluded, whereas novices were affected when relevant and even irrelevant information was occluded.

Eye movement recording techniques have also provided a wealth of information about athletes, both in natural settings like tennis (Singer et al., 1998) and in more laboratory-based settings that simulate sports, such as soccer (Williams, Davids, Burwitz, & Williams, 1994) and karate (Williams & Elliott, 1999). As Williams (2001) summarized, these studies demonstrate experts' superior eye movement patterns for seeking and detecting important sources of information, such as by focusing on more informative areas of the display or by using a "visual pivot" strategy, where fewer foveal fixations represent a more effective search strategy (Ripoll, Kerlirzin, Stein, & Reine, 1995).

Although eye movement recording has been used quite extensively with athletes, only one study has used this informative technique with gymnastics judges (Bard et al., 1980), and none have used it, to my knowledge, with referees. Both the judge and the referee, however, have similar task demands as that of the athlete. That is, they too have to quickly analyze the movement patterns performed by an athlete, which suggests that visual search patterns and the knowledge of relevant information are also pertinent. What is interesting is that Bard et al.'s data on judges do bear a striking resemblance of that found with athletes. In their analysis of visual search patterns of expert and novice gymnastics judges, expert judges had significantly more fixations on the upper part of a gymnast's body (a more central location), whereas novices concentrated on the more distal parts of the body, such as the legs and toes. Although not as significant, experts also had fewer fixations than did novices.

Taken together, these limited findings suggest that expert judges used a visual pivot strategy, where focus was on a central location, which allowed them to pick up other information via peripheral vision. In contrast, the novices' fixations to the distal parts of the body and their larger number of fixations reflected their less effective visual search strategy and their limited use of peripheral vision. Because novices make a greater number of saccades, they have more time intervals of inactive information processing. Thus, the argument is made that expert judges and referees adopt these more efficient and effective strategies because they know what information is relevant and can ignore irrelevant information accordingly. Given this information, it is also interesting to note that Abernethy (1993) has proposed that experts only take in the "minimal essential information" needed to determine various actions (see also Williams, 2001). Further, he argues that as individuals become more skilled, they are ever more attuned to the relevant information and, similar to Treisman and Gelade's (1980) feature integration theory, the information "pops out" of the visual display.

Through the knowledge of the relevant information, the selectivity of the visual search, and the attunement to the minimal information necessary, experts circumvent the total amount of information that comes into the system. In turn, this filtering allows the expert to better detect critical performance aspects that the novice may miss. An obvious shortfall in our current knowledge is that insufficient research has been done using eye movement recording techniques with judges and referees, and none has been done using temporal and visual occlusion techniques. It may be pertinent to do such studies because certain issues have been shown to alter the search behaviors employed by athletes, such as levels of anxiety (Williams & Elliott, 1999) and various constraints of the task (e.g., the number of actors involved; Williams et al., 1994). Our knowledge on the importance of these factors on judges' and referees' expertise will remain restricted until such experimentation is undertaken.

It is likely that task constraints would create differences among the participants. For instance, one difference is that referees typically deal with game situations in which there is more than one actor (e.g., rugby has 15 players on the playing field at one time), whereas judges often deal with only one actor (e.g., the gymnast, diver, or figure skater). Thus, generalizations concerning visual search patterns among these different conditions may be precarious at best. Even within one sport evaluator role, researchers would need to make such distinctions. For example, judges of synchronized swimming and figure skating may judge singles, pairs, or whole-team performances, highlighting the importance of recognizing the specific task constraints. Future research must seek to understand the varied dimensions that affect the visual search patterns used by judges and referees.

Knowing What to Expect

Closely tied to the idea of an evaluator's discerning the relevant information is that of using the relevant information to guide subsequent judgments. From the sport expertise research with athletes, it has been shown that highly skilled players, as compared with novices, are better able to use advance information to predict the outcome of visually presented information (e.g., Abernethy, 1991; Goulet, Bard, & Fleury, 1989; Tennenbaum, Levy-Kolker, Sade, Lieberman, & Lidor, 1996). Although similar advantages have also been seen in judges, the data are again limited to one study (Ste-Marie, 1999).

Ste-Marie (1999) demonstrated the use of advance information in gymnastics judging by showing that expert judges were significantly better at predicting an upcoming move than were novice judges. Moreover, Ste-Marie provided evidence that this predictive advantage was likely to be perception based, with experts better at interpreting biomechanical cues available from the gymnastics performance. These results fit with the earlier notion mentioned that experts are picking up the minimal essential information necessary to detect the coordination patterns of the movement patterns observed (Abernethy, 1993; Williams, 2001). The pickup of this minimal information and their ability to use it to anticipate upcoming movements effectively eliminate highly improbable events in the mind of the sport evaluator (Williams & Grant, 1999). This ability affects the sport evaluator in two important ways. First, experts experience a decrease in the number of knowledge structures that they activate (see also Tenenbaum et al., 1996). Second, as has been shown in the priming literature (e.g., Jacoby & Dallas, 1981), experts activate these knowledge structures faster than novices when the movement is actually executed. Thus, potential limits of information processing are bypassed because fewer knowledge structures are activated before the occurrence of the actual event. When the event does occur, primed activation of the knowledge structure results in faster access to necessary stored information.

These anticipatory skills, and the resultant decrease in information-processing demands, can also be used to explain the expert advantage for error detection found in gymnastics judges (Ste-Marie & Lee, 1991). When the actual skill is in line with the prediction, fewer processing resources are needed as a result of the primed activation of the knowledge structure. In other words, after a buildup of information, the evaluator can rely on a finite amount of domain-specific knowledge and can thus identify various aspects of the gymnastics skill, such as symbol code and level of difficulty, with less mental constraints. Consequently, more resources could be devoted to other task requirements, such as the detection of performance qualities. Indeed, Ste-Marie (1999) did show that when gymnastics judges had anticipated correctly an upcoming gymnastics skill, they were better in the error detection task than when they had anticipated incorrectly.

To date, little other research has been done to determine if these better anticipatory skills hold in other areas of sport evaluation, and future research on this issue is recommended. A note of caution, however, follows this recommendation and is in line with the observations raised earlier in this chapter about the ecological validity of the tasks. MacMahon (1999), for example, did try to gather information about anticipatory skills in rugby referees using a similar video protocol to that of Ste-Marie (1999). What unfolded was a bit surprising at first, but soon made sense when the natural setting was considered. More specific, the more experienced referees took longer than the less experienced referees to make their decisions (via voice reaction time data), and they were exceedingly reluctant to anticipate what a call would be when the video had been stopped in the midst of a rugby play. This reluctance, and the longer response times when a response was given, was postulated to be a product of the advantage law, wherein a rugby referee should not call an infraction if it is followed by an advantage gained by the opposing team. Thus, the measures and the laboratory setting constrained the researcher from truly testing the types of anticipatory skills that referees likely possess.

Knowing the Interrelations Among Variables

Up to this point, the emphasis has been on how expert judges and referees treat visually presented information more effectively. Another important area that has been shown to differentiate expert and novice athletes includes their more elaborate declarative knowledge base for their sport and their understanding of the different interrelations among the variables confronted (Abernethy et al., 1994; Vickers, 1986, 1988). French (2001), for example, has shown that highly skilled baseball players differ from less skilled players in their more generic baseball knowledge and processing of tactical information and that their decisions are directly related to the skills they can execute on the field. Consideration of how the experts interrelate the perceived information with other stored information is of great importance in understanding expertise in this domain.

MacMahon and Ste-Marie (1999) reported that rugby referees with greater experience used more episodic and semantic information to interpret the information to make their calls than did referees with less experience. Along similar lines, Deakin and Allard's (1992) results with basketball referees showed that referees knew significantly more about the rules of the game and the hand signals to be used in officiating than did the coaches or players. Results with judges parallel that of referees. Ste-Marie's (1999) research showed that expert gymnastics judges knew the symbol codes and the level of difficulty associated with gymnastics skills significantly better than did novice judges. In fact, Salmela (1978) had long ago mentioned that the best determinant of expert judges is their knowledge of the international federation code book.

In this code book, there are thousands of gymnastics skills, each associated with specific symbol codes and level of difficulty. Moreover, this level of difficulty changes via the level of difficulty of the gymnastics skill that precedes its execution. When judges are evaluating a routine, these symbol codes are to be written down concurrently with error deductions being noted and level of difficulty being monitored (so that a base score can be derived at the termination of the routine). The error deductions noted throughout the performance are then subtracted from the base score to arrive at the final given score.

Thus, it can be argued that when evaluating a given event, expert judges and referees are able to access the necessary information related to the visual processing and can be more accurate with that information than novices. This ease of access to information, from knowledge structures that are richer and more elaborate, shortcuts the processing limitations typically encountered when retrieving information necessary to make decisions or judgments. We also need to consider that the richness of the knowledge structures likely allow for greater "chunking" of information. Consequently, when information has to be maintained in working memory, such as would be the case for determining level of difficulty, a series of three gymnastics movements is likely to be represented as one chunk for experts, but as three individual items for a novice. Such a hypothesis has yet to be tested, however, and visual recall strategies or verbal reports may be useful techniques to address this issue. Whether such differences in "chunking" occurs would be important to discern because it would provide information about the parameters of the retrieval structures of judges.

In sum, much of the data obtained from the study of expert judges and referees fits well within the proposition that they have learned to circumvent processing limitations encountered by novices. Novices may in fact adopt behaviors, either purposefully or nonpurposefully, that effectively decrease the amount of information that needs to be processed. Ste-Marie (2000) did show that novice judges, as compared to expert judges, look down significantly more toward the paper on which they are required to record the skills performed by a gymnast, even while the gymnastic performance is ongoing. Moreover, this behavior did not occur because the novices were just spending more time writing because it was shown that both the expert and novice judges did the same amount of writing throughout the gymnastics performance. It was just that the experts were able to do the written component of their task while watching the gymnast, whereas novice judges were not able to engage in the dual-task demands as proficiently. Ste-Marie suggested that novice judges were perhaps coping with the "information overload" by taking their attention away from the gymnastics performance and focusing on other required demands, in essence alternating attention. In the next section, I attempt to address perhaps the most difficult step in the expertise approach—analyzing how experts acquired these four basic cognitive structures (i.e., knowing what to expect, knowing what to do and when to do it, knowing what information was relevant, and knowing the interrelations among variables).

Step Three: Accounting for Expertise

The final step involves accounting for how it is that expert judges have acquired the cognitive structures necessary to circumvent these processing limitations. In line with others (e.g., Ericsson, 1996; Starkes

& Allard, 1993), domain-specific experience is considered critical for the development of the knowledge of what is relevant and what is to be expected, as well as the interrelatedness of information and the sensitivity to perceptual discriminations. What is acquired through this experience, though, is a tougher issue. Although some researchers have emphasized memory function (Chase & Simon, 1973; Richman, Gobet, Staszewski, & Simon, 1996), others have specifically studied the ability to plan and reason (Charness, 1981) or the practice and learning mechanisms (Anderson, 1982). A common link within these proposals is that the authors suggest that a small number of mechanisms should be forwarded to account for the development of expertise. Moreover, the identified mechanisms should fit within the limits of human information-processing capabilities (Ericsson & Smith, 1991; Richman et al. 1996; Salthouse, 1991). The basic mechanisms that have surfaced in this chapter tie in well with perceptual and memory retrieval structures emphasized by Richman et al. (1996), as well as Chase and Simon (1973).

Another question that arises is, how specific does the experience need to be for the development of the related cognitive structures? Allard, Deakin, Parker, and Rodgers (1993) described research with figure skating and diving judges. They argued that experience as an athlete in the sport itself was not only useful, but also essential for a number of factors. What is interesting is that two of the factors included the knowledge of what to expect and of the interrelatedness of information. Deakin and Allard's (1992) research, however, has shown that declarative knowledge and superior performance on various tasks were functions of the role played in the sport. Although referees were best at stating the rules, knowing the signals, and naming both the fouls and violations, coaches actually did better on recall accuracy for structured game plays. Thus, being a coach or athlete did not actually develop the declarative knowledge essential to refereeing. These results led them to argue that the development of declarative knowledge was "not a byproduct of experience in the sport" (Allard et al., 1993, p. 106). Similar observations were made by Williams and Davids (1995). Williams and Davids (1995) also argued that declarative knowledge was a constituent of skill, rather than a by-product of overall experience within the sport. These discrepant conclusions about the types of experiences that transfer in a given domain suggest that further research is necessary to determine how one's knowledge base for judging and refereeing develops.

Other questions still exist, such as whether the acquired cognitive structures are mediated by a general type of knowledge that simply becomes more extensive (Salthouse, 1991) or whether knowledge structures develop that are in fact distinct. Ste-Marie's (1999) research with judges lends itself to the latter possibility, because the breadth and depth of the knowledge of the international code book was not correlated with experts' better perceptual anticipatory skills. Always to be considered, however, is that although domain-specific experience is often a highlighted factor of expertise, the attainment of expertise is not actually an automatic consequence of mere experience. Rather, structured and effortful training is necessary to acquire it (e.g., Ericsson & Lehmann, 1996). Further investigations concerning the relative contributions of experience and training on the development of knowledge structures are recommended for expertise researchers.

Applications in the Training of Judges and Referees

Investigations that concern the relative contributions of experience and training would create the necessary bridge to bring the findings into the applied setting of actual training for judges and referees with the purpose of enhancing skills. Although some guidelines have already been noted, such as visual training software, rather than investing in such endeavors as the training via visual hardware (for more detailed comments on this issue, see Abernethy, Wann, & Parks, 1998; Williams & Grant, 1999), more well-structured experiments that use suitable control groups and include adequate transfer tests need to be carried out. Starkes and Lindley (1994) noted in their research involving video simulation training that despite a better performance following the training on the video-based test, the training was not shown to enhance on-court performance. More encouraging results, however, were found by Taylor, Burwitz, and Davids (1998). In their study, video-based training did transfer to better badminton play when an on-court assessment was used. Studies of this nature have not yet moved into the research on expertise in judging and refereeing. When such research has been done, perhaps a similar positive transfer will be noted.

As forwarded by several researchers, facilitating expertise through general-skills training is ill-directed (Abernethy et al., 1994; Starkes et al., 1994); thus, recommendations for training need to be domain-specific, which will result in different training strategies for sport judges as compared with referees. Nonetheless, trainers could use common strategies as well, such as training novices to attend to important biomechanical information that is useful for anticipating future movement patterns. If novices can be trained in this way, their information-processing demands will be reduced and thus replaced by the simple processing of subsequent movement patterns (cf. Abernethy, 2001; Ste-Marie, 1999). A consistent finding is the advantage associated with a superior declarative knowledge base on the part of experts. Training that moves toward effortless retrieval of important information for decision making in this context leads one to consider learning strategies such as the spacing effect (Melton, 1967; Jacoby, 1978) and encoding specificity (Tulving & Thompson, 1973).

Summary

The principal issues presented in this chapter concerned our knowledge of expertise in judges and referees who are involved in various sport domains. Although much has been learned, the chapter highlights areas where significant gains still need to be made. Many other techniques have yet to be employed in the research of this subject, such as think-aloud protocols and event- or temporal-occlusion techniques. Of the tasks that have been used, more representation from other refereed and judged sports should follow. For example, most sport judging tasks have only been done with gymnastics judges. Increasing efforts need to be made to situate the judge or referee in the actual conditions that are encountered in the real-life task.

Pulling these types of tasks into the study of expertise in judges and referees will also allow us to further define the limitations that novice judges confront. Although four of the seven areas that were identified in Salthouse's (1991) work were presented here, three have yet to be investigated, because they too may apply to judges and referees. For example, expert-novice differences that concern knowledge of what to do and when to do it, as well as the ability to combine information, have not been investigated. Testable hypotheses concerning these factors should allow us to learn more about how experts outperform novices. In addition, for those four areas that were presented, the studies have been limited in the specific area, and untested propositions were often forwarded—for instance, the use of minimal information by experts; how visual search patterns may differ depending on the number of actors to evaluate; and the likelihood of experts' use of superior chunking performance. These issues point to the fact that much more research is needed in this field.

Finally, questions that all expertise researchers struggle with, regardless of the domain of study, include issues concerning what is acquired through domain-specific experience, how specific the experience needs to be to contribute to a particular domain, and whether the cognitive structures are mediated in a general or specific sense. What I find truly fascinating about these questions and the study of expertise, is that despite the diversity of fields studied, our research converges on common mechanisms and theoretical development. In this light, I encourage more expertise research that uses judges and referees in the sport domain. The study of this, or any, population will advance our understanding of the fundamental issues and bring us toward a clearer understanding of expertise.

EXPERTS' COMMENTS

■ Question

How important is it for a coach to have also been a competent athlete? Ste-Marie's research suggests that there may be some advantages afforded by a coach's or judge's having been an athlete in the sport.

■ Coach's Perspective: Nick Cipriano

Freestyle wrestling is a complex sport and requires thousands of different technical-tactical combinations that must be mastered en route to becoming an expert. Because the skills are executed in a dynamic state, coaching is especially important with regard to instruction and feedback. To this end, freestyle technical skills are initially taught as closed skills, with the hope that eventually the skill will be performed with less attention, which will therefore free up attention so that it may devoted to strategic issues. Once the wrestler is able to execute the skills, tactical training is initiated and the wrestler learns to execute the skills in a dynamic condition. Because this transition phase is of prime importance, the coach who has personal experience as a high-level competitor is best equipped to articulate the dynamics of each tactical sequence. Such individuals are generally more successful than coaches who have limited personal competitive experience, and their athletes generally display superior technical-tactical skills. For this reason, many developing countries often employ foreign coaches who are known for being highly technical and having much personal competition experience work with their young wrestlers, teaching them the technical-tactical sequences of the sport and orientating them toward competition.

■ Player's Perspective: Therese Brisson

Ste-Marie's research suggests that experience as a high performance athlete may offer some advantage to coaches and judges. In general, I agree with this view. I used to officiate in ringette, and I found that my experience as a player helped me determine how the game would unfold. I also knew where to look and where potential infractions might occur. Experience as an athlete allows selective processing, and in some cases, this can be very helpful. I have also found that instructors who have competed internationally are the most helpful. They have played the game at a high level and they understand the little things that can make a big difference. Identification of critical factors for success and the ability to communicate these are skills that help athletes get to the next level in their development. This is especially true for open-skill sports like ice hockey.

Another element of Ste-Marie's work that has always interested me is the way judges form memory representations while observing warm-up performances, and these representations influence judging. This is clearly at play in team selection scenarios and is something of which athletes are intuitively aware. During selection camps or while under observation by national team coaches, athletes minimize risk taking and engage in activity that will minimize errors. In this environment, athletes will do what they are comfortable and confident with. Athletes believe that coaches will form lasting impressions of them based on observation of a few errors during practice. This is not always the ideal environment for improving performance. The athlete who finds the confidence to experiment and undertake new challenges in this situation will truly excel in the long run. I think coaches can really make a difference in this area by balancing the time for training and selection and setting clear goals for each.

---

[1]To keep with the structure of the chapter (following the three-step expertise approach), only the tasks used in the various studies will be described at this point. The results of each study will be reviewed in steps two and three in this chapter.

Chapter 8

Expert Athletes

■ ■ ■ ■ ■

An Integrated Approach to Decision Making

Gershon Tenenbaum

Expert decision makers in sport, such a Michael Jordan in basket-ball and Wayne Gretzky in ice hockey, perform their best ma-neuvers under temporal and emotional pressure. Wayne passed the puck to his teammates in crucial periods of the game as if he were performing it naturally in practice. Michael was at his best when the game was tied and only a few seconds were left on the clock. When defended by a taller player, he altered his moves in such a way that al-most always gave him the advantage over his opponents. How exactly do expert athletes make decisions under regular and demanding con-ditions, and how can research explain and account for such a process?

After two to three decades of extensive research on expert behaviors and performance, sufficient evidence exists to establish a scheme of ex-pertise decision making. The aim of this chapter is to present research findings and integrate them into a comprehensive scheme. Included in our discussion will be the cognitive stages as well as the emotional and motivational states necessary for decision making in high-level sport. The scheme draws on works that were carried out on visual attention and anticipation, long-term working memory, expertise knowledge structure, emotional and arousal level, and self-efficacy related to athletic decision making and performance. Because the scheme is com-plex and draws on many areas of research, the chapter serves as an introduction to the scheme and illustrates the various areas of research endeavors it encompasses.

Sport-related decision making (DM; here also termed response se-lection) has been studied quite extensively in the last two decades. A collection of theoretical and applied articles on cognitive sport-related cognition was edited by Straub and Williams (1984). This publication was followed by three special issues of the *International Journal of Sport Psychology (IJSP)*, which were devoted to DM and expert performance in the motor domain. The first issue was edited by Ripoll (1991) and consisted of articles that introduced impressive experimental findings on the following: visual search strategies, semantic and sensorimotor visual functions, visually guided locomotion and anticipatory mecha-nism, time accuracy and decision time in high-speed ball games, and attention-orientation styles in motor tasks. The second issue, edited by Tenenbaum (1999), was devoted to the development of expertise in sport, and it debated the role of nature and nurture in its development. This issue outlined the cognitive components associated with expert DM and how these components develop. Some articles concentrated on the nature of the knowledge base required for making expert deci-sions. The third *IJSP* issue was edited by Temprado (1999). The articles in this issue introduced several works and concepts of motor learning, acquisition, and control, which all rely on the dynamical systems approach to simple and complex skill acquisition. Moran's (1996) book summarized the research and the theoretical concepts of attention and concentration in sport, and it showed how these components can be developed and controlled through the use of mental techniques. With the work that has been done in the sport and exercise domain as well as the research published in general and experimental psychology journals, these publications have outlined the relevance and applicability of different approaches to the study of DM and action in sport. In this chapter, the main cognitive components related to expert DM are reviewed, and they are used to establish an integrated conceptual framework to account for the processes involved in accessing DM.

At around the same time of the Straub and Williams book (1984), Bloom (1985) as well as Ericsson and colleagues (Ericsson, 1996; Ericsson & Charness, 1994; Ericsson & Lehmann, 1996) introduced their concepts on the nature and development of expert behaviors across many domains, such as music, medicine, dance, academia, and sport. Their concepts were accepted and examined extensively, in particular the role of "deliberate practice" on the development of high-level sport skills (see Starkes, 2000). The expert DM process was better clarified by the work of Ericsson and Kintsch (1995) on long-term working memory (LTWM) theory. The LTWM theory was originally developed to account for the extensive memory span achieved by subjects who underwent extensive systematic practice of memorizing digits. In this chapter, this theory is used to outline the link between the cues picked up by the visual system and the ones processed through the elaboration of long-term stored information.

Independent of this line of conceptual and scientific interest, several important advancements were made in social psychology that have a direct relevance to the quality of DM and its translation into a motor action. Bandura's (1997) social-cognitive approach to human behavior has stimulated extensive interest in the role that task-specific self-efficacy and perceived competency play in the control of human behaviors. His conceptualization and the experimental studies that followed it indicate that DM and action are very much determined by self-efficacious beliefs and that they should be taken into account when making and executing decisions in the sport environment. This concept is introduced here and incorporated within the scheme developed in this chapter. The concept of the "individual zone of optimal functioning" (IZOF) is also related to the concept of self-efficacy, and together they constitute an important part of the conceptual framework of accessing expert DM in sport.

Conceptual Framework

By definition, response selection in sport indicates adaptive behavior based upon the capacity to solve problems. From an information-processing perspective, motor behaviors in competitive situations consist of encoding the relevant environmental cues through the utilization of attention strategies, processing the information through an ongoing interaction between working memory and long-term memory, making an action-related decision, and executing the action while leaving room for refinements and modifications. The types of decisions associated with the information-processing stages are presented in figure 8.1.

The first decision an athlete makes is where to gaze to capture the most important features in the environmental display. Afterward, a selection decision is made that enables the athlete to eliminate irrelevant information and use the relevant information to enable anticipation of upcoming events. Anticipation consists of an ongoing elaboration between the incoming environmental information and the knowledge structure inherent in long-term memory. With expertise development, the long-term working memory is the mechanism that allows the athlete to better process the information, anticipate it, and take a course of action. The timing of the action and any possible alterations are additional decisions made when the conditions dictate.

The constraints of such a scheme in eliciting skilled motor actions is related to serial processing, which may appear too costly and inefficient under extreme temporal conditions. Under long duration (e.g., a basketball point guard dribbles the ball while scanning players' positions in the court), the athlete operates under a serial operational mode, which leads to a final action selection decision. Such a strategy is of low cost and high benefit. Under such a condition, time pressure allows athletes to perform planning and alterations based on anticipatory mechanisms, which are elaborated through long-term stored representations (i.e., knowledge base). However, under extremely short temporal conditions, when serial slow-paced processing is not accessible, the cognitive and motor systems operate faster, and they depend on knowledge structure and motor schema, which are accessed automatically without relying on conscious awareness (Tenenbaum & Bar-Eli, 1993, 1995).

In this chapter, I adopt a cognitive view on accessing decision making (DM) in sport. The open-sport environment is dynamic, and it relies on moves and maneuvers that vary in speed, distance, space, and complexity. Different strategies and mechanisms are therefore developed and adjusted to enable an athlete's response selection, execution, and alteration.

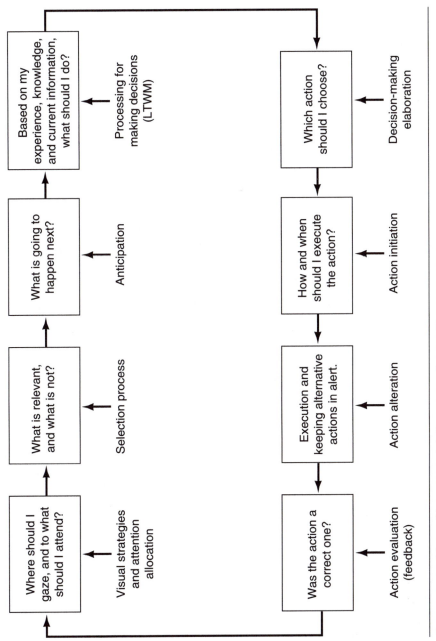

Figure 8.1 Decision-making types and their corresponding cognitive components.

The chronometric type of information processing and DM in sport considers anticipation of upcoming events as a process that precedes response selection and execution. Attention processes are determined by the visual strategies used to scan the environment to feed forward the information for further processing. Response selection and response execution depend on the interaction between the information selected and the long-term knowledge base of the athlete. Response-alteration is the final stage of processing, and it depends on both knowledge construction (number and strength of alternative responses activated in the brain) as well as its latency and activation level. The mechanisms and processes that lead to DM and its refinement are considered a great challenge to researchers and practitioners in the fields of motor learning, control, and development.

Next I present a review of the general and sport-specific literature that elaborates on the processing steps depicted in figure 8.1, where the features of expert DM are outlined and discussed. Finally, I introduce a multifaceted scheme that consists of a holistic view on DM, its antecedents, and its consequences.

Visual-Spatial Attention and Decision Making

Visual search is an applied process of locating objects in the visible field for further elaboration, mainly through selection and discrimination, to enable decision making (i.e., response selection) and implementation of motor actions. The process of visual attention is necessary for the elimination of spatial uncertainty (Prinz, 1977). In sport, visual attention is required to detect, recognize, recall, and select stimuli for higher-level processing when a decision is to be made and carried out in the form of a motor response. In closed-type motor actions, athletes attend to a limited number of internal and external cues. In open-type sports, the location of objects and subjects (as well as their intentions) is used as a crucial cue for further processing, making decisions, and carrying out the response selected to be executed.

Early studies on visual patterns in basketball (Bard & Fluery, 1976) showed that senior players made fewer fixations of longer duration than younger players when observing game display. Similar results were also reported by Bard, Fleury, Carrière, and Hallé (1980) for female judges of competitive gymnastics who had different levels of experience. Ripoll (1979) in table tennis, and Abernethy and Russell (1987) in cricket, reported similar findings on eye movement patterns (see figure 8.2). Recent findings (for a review, see Williams, Davids, & Williams, 1999), however, suggest that depending on the nature of the task and what is asked of them in the experimental setting, experts have more fixations of short duration in certain cases. Thus, one may assume that the leading strategy consists of fewer fixations for longer duration with some deviations per task requirement.

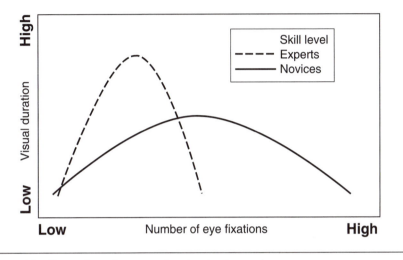

Figure 8.2   Comparison of expert and novice visual strategies.

Once a field is scanned by the visual system, two strategies can be used (Neisser, 1967): a target control strategy and a context control strategy. The target control strategy consists of detecting targets within the display until a target is detected, which is compatible with the mental representations in long-term memory. The context control strategy consists of a visual search carried out under the control of memory representations, which are not necessarily sensitive to individual objects, but rather to a greater number of items in the display. Under such a strategy, the observer is under a situational control when the stimulus is compatible with the representational memory of the context. We posit that with practice, as the number of representations and their logical connections increase, the players who apply mental operations in an open environment will shift from target control to context control so that they may (a) reduce the information-processing load (i.e., complexity), (b) increase the efficiency of the visual scan, and (c) simplify the long-term working memory (Ericsson & Kintsch, 1995) elaborations for response selection.

Research findings have shown that the strategy used for controlling the visual field alters during the course of skill development (Prinz,

1977). Without practice, people use target control strategy because the context is unfamiliar to them. With additional practice, memory representations become more sensitive to objects that together make up a considerable part of the display. The change from target to context control begins with training and accumulation of knowledge base (Beitel, 1980; Gentile, Higgins, Miller, & Rosen, 1975). The findings that pertain to the number of eye fixations and their duration substantiate the claim that experts use a context control to increase the benefits and reduce the costs associated with scanning a complex dynamic visual field. Though in other cases target control is more beneficial for decision making (Williams et al., 1999).

Examinations of visual search patterns used in preparing serve returns in squash, badminton, and tennis indicated that eye fixation depends on the search sequence (Abernethy, 1987b). Fixations on large features occur early in the sequence, then later the gaze is transferred to the racket. This change in direction of eye gaze is a strategy that probably decreases the situational uncertainty (Ripoll, 1988). Ripoll further argues that the difference associated with skill level is that experts direct eye gaze to a position in which many events can be perceived integratively during a single eye fixation (i.e., synthetic analysis), whereas novices gaze at events according to their chronological order (i.e., serial analytic assessment). Ripoll (1979) also showed that in situations of uncertainty, expert players employed strategies that optimally adopt the sensorimotor system to the extremely high constraint of the situation.

Based on many studies, an argument made by Cave and Bichot (1999) states that

> The visual system is powerful enough to classify and identify many visual objects in parallel, and that selection is necessary only in later stages, when visual information is used to guide responses. Under this view, selection operates not on a raw, unprocessed, spatially organized visual input, but on an abstractly organized symbolic representation of the objects identified in the visual input. . . . Location is just another property to use as an index in selecting from among these representations, and location affects selection only because it affects perceptual organization. (pp. 207-208)

Expert athletes had fewer fixations of longer duration than novice athletes (figure 8.2). The novice athletes seem therefore to use a target control strategy in which a spotlight beam passes over the entire display, focusing on relevant and irrelevant aspects alike. The experts seem to operate on a context control strategy, which consists of eye fixation to a single location, from which it is possible to capture events around the visual fixation point. Along with skill development, visual attention shifts from one location to another by chunking the essential stimuli in the visual field and processing them into a meaningful and integrated image, which with long-term memory elaboration elicits a motor response. This response is not always evaluated by how fast it is executed (i.e., response time, RT), but rather by its appropriateness to lead to an advantage over the opponent. Fast information processing may be an advantage under some circumstances, but it is a disadvantage if the selected response is not the correct one or is anticipated by the opponent.

Several studies have demonstrated the following: first, that a stimulus is identified more quickly when one has more time to focus attention at its location; second, that stimuli in the periphery are harder to identify, thus allowing more room to benefit one's attention (e.g., Eriksen & Murphy, 1987; Tsal & Lavie, 1993). This distinction, however, accounts for the advantage that expert athletes have in making decisions when they shift attention on the basis of context rather than targets (Ripoll, 1988). Once visual attention fixates on a certain spatial location, more attention is allocated to the events near this space. Features that occur more quickly are detected, which allow early anticipatory operations to select the appropriate response, and even alter it, if necessary. A target visual control strategy is limited in its capacity to allow sufficient time for both detection and response selection to be as efficient (as if they were being used in a context visual control strategy).

Studies in sport (for a review, see Tenenbaum & Bar-Eli, 1993, 1995) have indicated that accumulation of declarative and procedural knowledge (i.e., expertise) is associated with a shift in visual attention from target control to context control. If this were the case, then one should wonder what in the visual area (selected for attention focus) is more, less, or equally attended to? If novices operate under target control strategy and if their knowledge base is limited, then according to LTWM and studies in cognitive psychology (Cave & Bichot, 1999), only the target and its near area can be attended to. This supposition would lead to a limited response selection capacity and thus results in poor DM and errors. In contrast, visual context control does the following: It directs attention to cues within a larger area around the visual fixation point; it eliminates irrelevant cues from being elaborated within long-term memory; and it allows faster access and retrieval of an appropriate response. The relationship between the visual strategy, LTWM, and response selection is illustrated in figure 8.3.

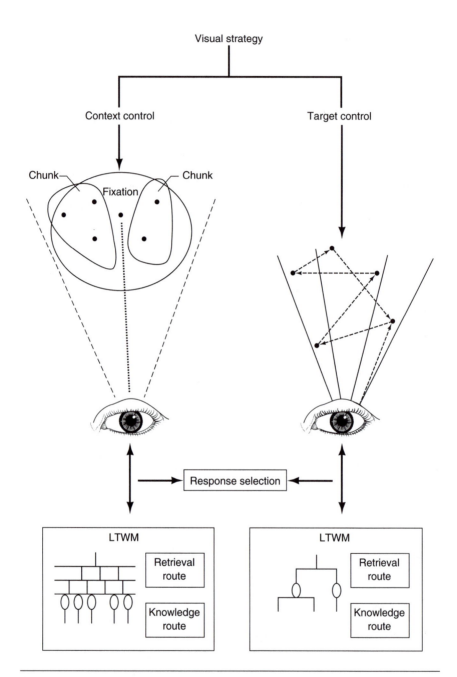

Figure 8.3 Visual strategy elaborations with LTWM and response selection.

The research on attention allocation (Downing, 1988; Downing & Pinker, 1985; Henderson & MacQuistan, 1993) indicates that attention is uniformly distributed within the targeted area, then it falls off gradually from the edge. Research has also focused on the capacity of people to allocate attention simultaneously to different locations within the visual field to optimize performance. In open-skill sports, where anticipatory mechanisms play a major role, expertise development is associated with allocating attention to several locations. The attention to one location depends on its relevance to the response selection optimization. Context visual control plays a major role in discrimination and selection processes, which in a later stage enhances the response selection process. Target control consists of serial-type processing and therefore is insufficient in locating other sources of information in the environment at the moment. However, expert performers use this strategy per task demands. The nature of attention alteration with experience, deliberate practice, and expertise development remains to be further studied.

Cave and Bichot (1999) were aware that RT and motor response selection were different entities. They claimed that although visual selection is important for action, it does not have to be implemented exclusively in the later stages of processing (in the areas of the brain that play a role in planning and performance). Visual attention effects can be seen in all brain areas; therefore, it is highly probable that it has a strong effect on motor response selection and action. In sport, it seems that each stage of development has its characteristics and computational limitations. In the early stage of skill development, attention resources are limited and operate serially so that the system is inefficient in its capacity to select responses from long-term memory. With expertise development, the visual system operates in a manner that allows easier retrieval routes to be accessed from long-term memory so that response selection is done with minimal effort. Such a system operates automatically, but it is also alert to environmental disturbances so that one can make adjustments, if necessary, in due time.

How Information Is Coded, Processed, and Retrieved

The visual system feeds forward information, which is further processed until a motor response is chosen and executed. For efficient information processing, two systems mutually operate: a perceptual anticipatory system and a long-term working memory (LTWM) system. Each of these systems is described in the following sections.

Perceptual Anticipation

Environmental feature detection and pattern recognition result in advanced anticipatory recognition, a characteristic that accounts for a substantial variation in DM behaviors of athletes who vary in skill level (Abernethy, 1987a). Repetition and competition experience guides the sensory system in a manner that enables quick access to knowledge structures (i.e., neural representations), which facilitates anticipation and predictions (Keele, 1982). Results of studies in various fast ball games indicate that advanced identification facilitates response selection processes, particularly under conditions of extreme uncertainty (Abernethy, 1987b). According to Abernethy, experts use shorter viewing times and therefore have more time to select their responses. Several studies (for a review, see Tenenbaum & Bar-Eli, 1993, 1995) indicate that players attend to similar advanced cues, whereas experts exhibit superior forecasting accuracy as to the final destination of a ball sequence. Novice, intermediate, and advanced players process information of early ball flight quite differently. That is, anticipation of the final move becomes more accurate, depending strongly on the player's prior knowledge of similar strokes. Tenenbaum, Sar-El, and Bar-Eli (2000), however, have shown an expert advantage over novices only in about 50% of the tennis strokes. Experts focused attention on several cues simultaneously at early stages of their opponent's action initiation, rather than on one cue, which is typical for younger and less qualified players. Of vital importance were the findings that intermediate players anticipated the final ball location similarly to expert players. Though only one study used athletes of intermediate skill level, the finding points toward the possibility that similar practice and competitive experience result in similar anticipatory capabilities in top- and intermediate-level athletes. It may be that differences in action execution are determined by variables other than just anticipatory capabilities.

Support for the claim that other variables may play a major role in response selection and response execution is found in Tenenbaum and Bar-Eli (1995). Under uncertain conditions (short exposure to event sequence, extreme temporal conditions), novices and tennis players of intermediate skill level were more confident in their predictive decisions than were experts. Shortly before, at, and after ball-racket contact, however, experts were substantially more confident in their anticipatory decisions. This distinction was apparent in all types of strokes where anticipatory decisions were made.

The differences in self-confidence in anticipatory decisions associated with expertise-level of athletes introduced additional dimensions that have been neglected in the study of expert behavior in sport. In the study by Tenenbaum et al. (1996), ball-racket contact is the stage at which final decisions and effort correction take place. Therefore, when anticipatory confidence in the final stages increases and a solution is determined, a qualified action is executed. Thus, superior anticipatory capability with high self-efficacy together produces high-quality action. A scheme that integrates anticipatory capacity with self-efficacy and skill level is presented in figure 8.4.

It is clear that in the last stages of anticipation, a superior knowledge about the final ball location accompanied with high self-efficacy results in superior response selection and execution.

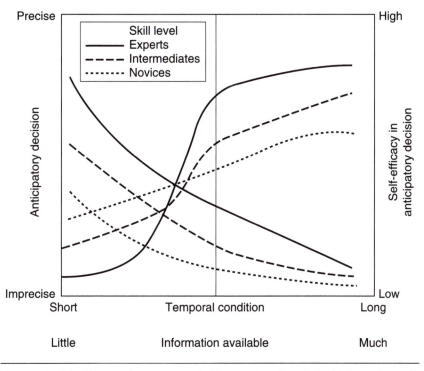

Figure 8.4   Self-efficacy and anticipatory decision as a function of visual information available to the athlete.

Response Selection and Response Alteration

The process of response selection is heavily dependent on factors that are external to athletes (e.g., moves initiated by athletes of the opposing team). The actions taken by others require alteration of response selection, even after the completion of the response initiation and execution phases. Thus, ability and flexibility in action alteration is believed to be a skill that develops with practice and experience, and it is more evident in expert performers.

The information-processing approach assumes that decision making consists of cue identification, which results in some kind of processing and therefore triggers a response selection. Thus, the onset of environmental stimuli is used for adjustment and preparation before action is carried out (i.e., before response execution; Holender, 1980). When precueing occurs, the selection process of essential cues is more efficient. Priming as an indicator of "readiness for a response" results in RT reduction, but it does not alter the postsignal processing demands (Alain, 1991). Evidence exists that athletes can apply automatically and voluntarily strategic types of signal detection. As expertise develops, a smooth shift between the two mechanisms enables the athlete to relate more selectively and efficiently to the dynamics and complexity of the open environment (Alain & Proteau, 1979; Nougier, Stein, & Bonnel, 1991). Furthermore, it has been reported that certain information sources in the sport environment are more important than others (i.e., priming); therefore, the type and intensity of priming are essential for response selection (Alain & Sarrazin, 1985). Accordingly, athletes choose the priming option that has the highest utility value—that is, that which will ensure the best chances of triggering the appropriate response in the shortest delays (Alain, 1991).

In open-skill dynamic environments, priming can be initiated by several cues at the same time, which makes the response selection harder. Furthermore, the intensity and longevity of these "priming cues" are of much relevance to the decision-making process (Alain, 1991). Nougier et al. (1991) argued that under highly uncertain conditions that are typical in sport, expert athletes are endowed with specific strategies that are useful for DM. Expert athletes, through implicit and explicit learning experiences, attend to all the signals that may trigger a response, rather than a limited number of signals, which in turn may lead to an error. Some evidence for this claim was found in volleyball players by Casteillo and Umilta (1992). Players shifted their attention faster than nonplayers did to valid cues, but not to invalid cues. This attention advantage, which accumulates over practice, enables expert athletes to efficiently elaborate on the essential cues in their environment and consequently choose a response and response alternatives.

Several studies (Coles, 1989) used Lateralized Response Potential (LRP) of brain activity in compatible and incompatible conditions to suggest that in open environmental conditions when athletes encounter an uncertain situation, they are likely to initially entertain less appropriate solutions before they choose the optimal one. They do so through a process of discrete decisions, rather than through a process of one drawn-out decision. Not only can two responses be simultaneously activated, they can also compete against each other (Coles, Gratton, Bashore, Eriksen, & Donchin, 1985; Eriksen, Coles, Morris, & O'Hara, 1985). However, based on the findings in sport and other domains, my argument here is that the enhanced knowledge base and structure of experts enable them to apply more frequently a continual-type of processing. This strategy enables them to make faster responses, and at the same time, it increases their readiness to make changes if necessary.

The skill of rapid response alteration may be related to the shift between automatic and voluntary attention control (Nougier et al., 1991). Peripheral cues may capture attention automatically, whereas central cues initiate voluntary attention movement. It is probably the difference in voluntary orientation of attention that enables the experts to arrive at superior DM.

Expertise and Long-Term Working Memory

Since the seminal work of De Groot (1965) and Chase and Simon (1973) on expertise in chess players, similar recall paradigms were used in a variety of sports that were aimed at investigating how expert athletes encode, process, and retrieve meaningful specific information as compared with nonexpert athletes (Allard & Burnett, 1985; Borgeaud & Abernethy, 1987; Tenenbaum, Levy-Kolker, Bar-Eli, & Weinberg, 1994). Similar to the results on expertise in chess, the differences in recall capabilities in sport typically emerged in structured positions, but not when the display was randomly arranged. The advantage that experts exhibited when game patterns were studied disappeared once the logical arrangement of the environment was randomized.

In the chess domain, Chase and Simon (1973) argued that the expertise advantage was due to the fact that expert players can "chunk" familiar game patterns and that these chunks are larger and richer in details than those used by lesser skilled players. Others argued for skill-level differences in encoding and retrieval mechanisms (Millslagle, 1988). Today, expert memory advantage is accounted for by a more comprehensive theory, namely that of long-term working memory (LTWM) (Ericsson & Kintsch, 1995).

The constraint of a limited capacity working memory system (Baddeley, 1986) seems to be irrelevant in expert memory performance.

Skilled performers appear to be largely unaffected by interruptions that regularly have debilitating effects on standard working memory tasks. Concurrent activity also seems to produce little interference. Furthermore, experts appear to process and store much more information than novices do in their domain. Ericsson and Kintsch (1995) have suggested that with domain-specific practice, people can utilize long-term memory (LTM) as a means of extending short-term working memory. The LTM contribution occurs through the creation of domain-specific retrieval structures that can be used to enhance storage and maintain items in a more accessible and less interference-prone state.

Though the LTWM theory accounts for differences among different skill-level experts in short-term memory retention-type tasks, it suggests a reliable conceptual framework that consists of a hierarchical knowledge base. This knowledge base enables efficient retrieval of task-specific memory traces. In memory tasks, the response is based on retrieval of identical information that is shown to the athletes before examination. In decision-making tasks, the same memory traces enable the actor to use the feed-forward information to retrieve a decision that is passed on to the motor system. It also enables performers to stay alert to alternative responses.

In a recent study (Tenenbaum, Tehan, Stewart, & Christensen, 1999), researchers examined the effect of expertise and age on memory for gymnastics floor routine sequences. Sequences typically had between 10 and 12 gymnastics elements. The young gymnasts with little expertise performed poorly. They tended to recall only a few elements in the routine, of which only one could be recalled in its correct position. Recalling "missing" elements from the middle of the sequence was almost impossible. In contrast, the older experts outperformed all their counterparts. Their absolute and serial position recall was best. This group of gymnasts had good memory for serial position, regardless of the original order in which the gymnastics elements were presented. They also recalled two missing elements that were not presented to them in subsequent trials.

Knowledge base forms the associative-based retrieval route that Ericsson and Kintsch (1995) proposed. Thus, evidence supports the contention that even young children can produce sophisticated organizational and retrieval structures in their domain of interest. The young expert gymnasts in Tenenbaum et al.'s (1999) study used high-level and well-organized domain-specific knowledge structures as effective retrieval routes. Their ability to recall the missing items is consistent with the notion that they could access the long-term memory of the floor routine. Only an associated route was applied in this case. Thus, when expertise is attained, more relevant information is fed forward to LTM, and faster and better response selection is made.

The recall results of the older and less skilled gymnasts reflect developmental differences in the use of retrieval strategies. Older novice gymnasts were able to form rudimentary retrieval structures based upon general memory strategies (Tenenbaum et al., 1999). If we are to assume that these gymnasts lacked an extensive knowledge base, they probably relied on the general cues route of Ericsson and Kintsch's (1995) scheme in which general memory processes are involved in producing a useable retrieval structure. In contrast, older experts' superiority is attributed to both general and domain-specific retrieval structures. Within this framework, experienced experts demonstrated an ability to do the following: pick up the relevant information in the playing environment, use their knowledge structure for fast elaboration on these cues, and select a response that (coupled with high self-efficacy) results in a successful performance outcome.

Arousal, Being in the "Zone," and Self-Efficacy

Perceptual anticipation and response selection, unfortunately, do not function in a vacuum. That is, despite an athlete's level of expertise, other factors influence the degree to which one interprets perceptual information and chooses the appropriate executions. In the following sections, I examine three such variables:

- An athlete's state of arousal; specifically, how arousal affects perceptual mechanisms
- The individual zone of optimal functioning (IZOF), or in other words, the way an athlete utilizes emotions to facilitate optimal performance
- Self-efficacy, or "I think I can; therefore, I can"

Arousal, Attention, and Vigilance

Athletes make decisions while physically and emotionally aroused. Most of the research related to cognitive operations in general, and to sport operations in particular, has failed to consider these variables and take them into account. When stress is evoked, athletes alter and adapt their attention processes. Under low levels of arousal, athletes process all cues equally, whether the cues are relevant or irrelevant, which results in a lack of selectivity. Under moderate arousal, athletes' selection processes result in attending only to the relevant cues, thus reducing the degrees of freedom in the environment and simplifying the processing of information. Elevated arousal levels narrow attention's width, and this mechanism excludes some relevant information from being fed forward for processing (Cox, 1985; Landers, Wang, & Courtet, 1985; Wickens, 1984). Abernethy (1993) related expertise to the monitoring process of arousal. He stated that "superior self-monitoring, which has been advanced as a characteristic of expertise across a range of cognitive and motor tasks . . . may also manifest itself in superior arousal control by experts" (p. 134). He further claims that practice and exposure to stressful competitive stimulations develop greater tolerance to variations in arousal level and thus result in superior attention processes, which ultimately lead to superior decision making and response selection.

Sustaining alertness (i.e., vigilance) is another important feature, which should be taken into account when athletes make decisions while being engaged in physical and mental effort. Relying on signal detection theory, Abernethy (1993) claimed that overaroused or anxious athletes are more likely to select and make responses when they are not required (i.e., false alarms) and that low-arousal athletes produce both false alarm and correct responses. Thus, optimal arousal results in minimized "false alarm" responses and increases correct responses. Sustaining alertness (i.e., concentration) is often a hard task, and fatigue and sleep deprivation exacerbate the decrement in vigilance. "If one assumes any kind of similarity between the laboratory findings and alertness decrements in sport performance, it is clear that human performance limitations on the sustainment of alertness are likely to be a major constraint to performance in many sport tasks" (Abernethy, 1993, p. 137). Abernethy further claims that observations and anecdotal testimonies provide evidence that successful performances were associated with alertness preservation (i.e., high concentration) over a relatively long period of time. Sustaining concentration was achieved by a minimization of fatigue level via technique efficiency, physical fitness, task-related strategies, as well as conscious control over one's activation level.

The Individual Zone of Optimal Functioning (IZOF)

The IZOF scheme (Hanin, 2000) postulates how athletes regulate themselves psychologically to experience emotions in a way that is most suitable for their optimal performance. Once emotion-related performances are observed, the emotion zone under which optimal performance occurred can be determined within a given range and error. The IZOF is therefore defined as the

> optimal emotions . . . most relevant and appropriate for a particular athlete under specific conditions. . . . Optimal performance state includes both positive and negative emotions reflecting idiosyncratic strategies and skills an individual athlete might use in recruiting and utilizing resources (Hanin, 2000, p. 67).

Hanin (2000) further developed the concept as being multidimensional in form, time, and context, as well as with regard to the content of emotions experienced and their effect on performance. The scheme relates to emotional function where optimal functioning refers to specific recruitment of resources that generate energy in the level that results in optimal performance. In contrast, dysfunctionality results in failure to recruit the resources needed for optimal functioning, which results in poor performances. Today, the IZOF incorporates functionally optimal and dysfunctional patterns of pleasant and unpleasant emotion in elite athletes representing various sports (Hanin, 2000, p. 69). However, the IZOF has never been tested within the context of DM, response selection, and response execution context.

Self-Efficacy and Decision Making

When an athlete is engaged in physically demanding tasks, persistence and performance outcomes are very much determined by the perceived competence and self-efficacy one holds in relation to the specific task. The social-cognitive approach, in particular the theory of self-efficacy (Bandura, 1997), emphasizes the role that these task-specific states have on perceiving, coping, and performing tasks that evoke physical exertion and emotional distress.

Self-efficacy refers to beliefs in one's power to produce a given level of attainment. It is considered to be a cognitive state that has a direct impact on how well one performs his or her actions; thus, it is both a state and a coping strategy that either facilitates or inhibits one's abilities. Self-efficacy in the current context is delimited into two aspects: self-efficacy in selecting the appropriate response out of a given number of response alternatives and self-efficacy in one's ability to execute the selected response correctly and precisely.

Results of one study that incorporated self-efficacy in the anticipatory decisions in novice, intermediate, and expert tennis players (Tenenbaum, Levi-Kolker, Sade, Lieberman, & Lidor, 1996) indicated that decision-making processes and response executions (i.e., performance) are strongly associated with the level of self-efficacy one holds in these particular tasks. Experts may not always differ from the less skilled in their cognitive processes, but their DM process is performed with higher self-efficacy, which in turn results in a more efficient and skilled performance.

A Multifaceted Scheme of DM in Sport

A schematic summary that incorporates the necessary conditions for DM is illustrated in figure 8.5. The scheme consists of several mechanisms that operate sequentially in novice athletes, but in parallel in expert athletes. Visual-spatial attention, in the form of target or context control, is used for the selection of essential information that is fed forward for further processing. The collaboration between WM and LTM is continuous and does not cease when a response is selected and executed. Thus, the effectiveness of the process depends heavily on the richness, the variety, and the mechanisms that allow athletes to switch from one mode of attention to another at a given time (Fisher, 1984). Expert DM consists of the integration of visual-attention mechanisms, anticipatory mechanisms, and their elaboration with long-term rooted representations (i.e., knowledge structure), which allow an efficient and fast processing of information as well as response selection, alteration, and execution.

Each of the cognitive components presented in figure 8.5 was discussed in detail in this article. A brief overview of the main features required for expert DM is sufficient for elaborations of the multifaceted scheme of DM in an open-skill environment. Being a dynamic environment within which objects constantly and simultaneously move and change location, a context control of visual-spatial attention operates so that all the relevant features can be selected and forwarded for further elaboration and processing. This strategy enables the athlete to shift attention voluntarily from a wide mode to a narrow mode, and vice versa, while searching to establish an advantage over the opponent. If the targets in the environment were searched serially, eye movements become more frequent, and more irrelevant information is fed forward and processed. Such an inefficient mechanism results in slow information processing. Late response selection also leads to increases in the probability of errors. It should be noted that while visual attention is operating, the information is fed forward simultaneously for higher-level processing so that decisions can be made if time allows. A key feature in expert behavior is the collaboration between the information gathered by the visual system and the long-term storage through LTWM. Experts use a context controlled visual strategy to do

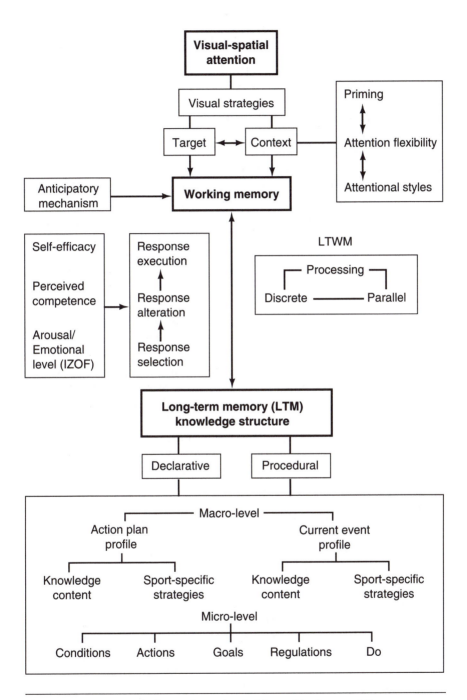

Figure 8.5 A conceptual scheme of accessing decision making in open-skill sport.

the following: to reduce environmental complexity, to increase the efficiency of the visual scan, and to simplify the LTWM process needed for response selection and execution.

More energy was allocated to the regions around the visual fixation center. Processing "cost" was attributed to the distance between cueing and imperative stimuli, as well as locating sides with respect to the horizontal axis and the vertical axis. Spatial location of attention facilitates visual selection processing: The closer the objects are to the fixation point ("cost"), the faster they are processed ("benefit"). However, when faraway locations were cued, the "cost" associated with faraway locations disappeared. It seems as if expert athletes rely on their extensive and enhanced knowledge structure in their selection of visual information so that all the relevant cues can be easily captured, regardless of the distance of the objects from the fixation point. The expert selection process operates on abstractly organized symbolic representations of the objects and by moves identified in the visual array. Novice players, however, operate on the raw and unprocessed spatially organized visual input, which in turn makes the search inefficient and limits the elicitation of the appropriate response selection. It is argued that visual selection operates serially by novice athletes because they shift attention to different locations with respect to objects. In experts, however, spatial selections are driven by symbolic representations, which are visually organized in the field. Once a visual location fixation is determined, it is powerful enough to perform perceptual grouping at the same time. In contrast, when target control guides the mental operation, perceptual grouping is entirely blocked.

The elaborations between the visual perception and representations in long-term memory (LTM) allow the athlete to speculate about the upcoming events before these events occur (i.e., anticipation). A context control visual strategy allows the expert athlete to pay attention to both close and faraway cues that facilitate anticipation of upcoming events. Once a target control visual strategy is used, the attention shift decreases the brain activity in the pool of neurons. At the same time, the receptive fields cover the location previously selected while increasing the neurons' activity in the new field of attention allocation (Cave & Bichot, 1999). In this way, information is not kept in working memory to facilitate a response selection from LTM. Novice players operate under such strategies until they learn to shift their attention to context control so that cues are captured simultaneously within the entire visual field. Doing so allows selected information to be fed forward to elaborations for response selection. The attention to one or many cues promotes anticipation and allows more time for elaborations. This process then results in decreased uncertainty and increased accuracy as well as appropriate responses to be executed with high self-efficacy. It is also important to note that a target control visual strategy leads attention to be focused on small areas in the visual field, whereas context control enlarges this area and therefore enables one to make greater and more meaningful chunks of the field. This additional advantage results in advanced anticipatory capabilities of expert athletes.

Anticipatory capability, according to the scheme, depends on the efficiency of the elaborations between working and long-term memory. For this elaboration to be fast and reliable, an extended knowledge base is required that contains both declarative and procedural networks. In addition to more efficient and holistic visual strategies, expert DM relies on shorter viewing time, which in turn extends the time required for response selection (Abernethy, 1987a). The reliable and fast elaboration between working memory and long-term working memory (LTWM), as mentioned previously, is knowledge-base dependent. Recently, French and McPherson (1999, p. 179) "view the knowledge base for sport to include all the traditional prepositional networks for conceptual knowledge (both tactical and skill related) and procedures for response-selection and execution. In addition, the knowledge base also includes other sport specific memory adaptations and structures such as action plan profiles, current events profiles, game situation prototypes, scripts for competition, and sport specific strategies that are stored and accessible from long term memory."

French and McPherson (1999) conceptualized the knowledge structure of open-skill ball games in two levels, a micro- and a macro-level. A micro-level refers to what knowledge is attended to during performance and accessed to the level of working memory. This knowledge (i.e., information) depends on the visual strategies used by the athletes to enhance their anticipatory capabilities at each moment. The macro-level knowledge refers to the action plan profile (i.e., procedural knowledge) and the current event profile. Each of these two macro-knowledge dimensions has "knowledge content" and "sport-specific strategies" components.

The LTWM concept presented by Ericsson and Kintsch (1995) was designed to account for the superior memory in expert performers after relatively short exposure to meaningful training situations. In the current scheme, LTWM is extended to account also for the superiority that expert athletes exhibit in response selection, response alteration, and response execution. LTWM consists of knowledge structure as one source of retrieval cue; therefore, it is apparent that the same processes that operate to elicit cues as forwarded by WM would operate for selecting the appropriate response when activating the macro- and micro-routes in LTM. Domain-specific retrieval structures that enhance storage and keep items more accessible and less in an interference-prone state also enable access to actions and alternative actions that are prioritized with respect to their appropriateness at every moment.

Finally, to allow for efficient DM processes, athletes should regulate their arousal and emotional level to optimize the visual attention search to smoothly feed forward the relevant information for higher-level processing via LTWM. Self-efficacy (Bandura, 1997) and staying in the "zone" (Hanin, 2000) are of vital importance in optimization of response selection operations. To consistently make correct decisions and minimize error rate, athletes should possess both cognitive and emotional qualities.

Future research should be devoted to the study of decision making in real-life situations under conditions of optimal and less-than-optimal functioning. Emotions and cognitions should be measured simultaneously to determine the various "zones of operations" along with cognitive processes such as attention, anticipation, and LTWM. Self-efficacy in executing the decisions also should be accounted for. Such an endeavor will be sounder when operationalized in real-life situations.

Summary

In this chapter, I've outlined the cognitive processes underlying decision making in sport. Though the decision process is multifaceted, it is operationalized fast, smoothly, and efficiently once the cognitive skills are acquired through extensive practice and competitive experiences. The knowledge structure accumulated through many hours of specific and concentrated practices enables the athlete to use visual strategies, which enhance anticipation of upcoming events. Enhanced anticipatory capability allows the athlete to select a response in due time, while maintaining other responses on alert for possible selection once the environment demands it. The knowledge structure also enables an efficient collaboration between working and long-term memory, which minimizes error conductance and maximizes response utility. Self-efficacy and optimal emotional intensity and functionality are needed to secure efficient information processing and consequently response selection and action execution. The integrated conceptual scheme presented in this chapter needs careful examination in real-life situations.

EXPERTS' COMMENTS

■ Question

To become an expert athlete, one has to maintain motivation to practice and compete over long periods of time. Are the best athletes inherently more self-motivated? What role do coaches play in the motivation cycle? How does arousal affect an athlete's decision-making process?

■ Coach's Perspective: Nick Cipriano

No one really believes that the road to the Olympics is indeed paved with blood, sweat, and tears. Most knowledgeable people would agree, however, that earning the privilege of competing at the Olympic Games requires a singularity of focus, and it also requires making sacrifices that (to people who are not athletically orientated) are exceptional. Although every young athlete dreams of being either an Olympian or a professional athlete, few will ever develop the motivational stamina to facilitate their dreams' coming to fruition. In my role as wrestling coach at McMaster University, I meet many motivated young wrestlers at the start of each new academic year, and all aspire to improve their standard of play. Before their arrival, all have practiced the sport for several years (anywhere up to six years), and they all typically demonstrate a moderate-to-good level of skill development. Equally important, most understand the rigors of the sport and have a solid grasp of their strengths, weaknesses, and the challenges that await them. Because there are no financial incentives given to them for being on the university team, nor are any academic concessions made, their participation and membership on the team are strictly voluntary. Also, because they are free to cease their participation at any time without consequences, I can safely assume that the wrestlers who remain with the team are indeed inherently motivated and intrinsically directed. To those individuals, I offer a training program that will challenge them and provide them with every opportunity possible for personal growth, development, and the achievement of their athletic dreams.

Unfortunately, within six to eight weeks of the start of training, it becomes abundantly clear as to those athletes who are able to endure the rigors of daily wrestling practice and those who will soon opt for less demanding activity. The wrestlers who continue to practice, in my experience, are the ones who demonstrate the highest need to win at everything, be it sparring, playing soccer, running, swimming, or any other activity we engage in for supplemental training. Moreover, they are the ones who will typically arrive early for practice and who will stay late after practice to review technical-tactical elements. They are also the ones who easily seek help from their more skilled teammates. In every respect, they are hungry to improve, and they possess an intense desire to succeed. For wrestlers who demonstrate most, or all of these characteristics, it is my responsibility as a coach to ensure that their level of motivation for practice and competition is maintained at a high level. I accomplish this by meeting with the athlete on a regular basis, reviewing performance goals, making appropriate training adjustments, adjusting a competition schedule, and generally facilitating their continued focus toward practice and improvement. Another important role I play is that I provide reinforcement and reassurance to the athlete when an unexpected setback occurs, be it an injury or a disappointing performance. My role as coach in developing the athlete's motivational stamina is getting the athlete to understand that setbacks and some poor performances are inevitable components of the athletic developmental process. Persevering through setbacks is part of the process. It is but one way of fostering the development of motivational stamina to present within a framework that setbacks provide opportunities for reevaluation of the training program and further defining personal goals.

In summary, there can be no denying that the best athletes are indeed more inherently motivated. My personal sense is that the best athletes are driven to achieve a higher performance standard, and they easily prioritize their life activities around a singular goal. Adopting an uncompromising attitude and refusing to acknowledge failure as a possibility, the athlete develops the motivational stamina to endure a difficult and long journey to becoming the best in the sport. Throughout this process, the coach plays a critical role by providing subtle reminders that the journey is worthwhile, even if the outcome is not guaranteed.

Player's Perspective: Therese Brisson

Team-sport athletes, who function in open-skill environments that are constantly changing, need strategies for dealing with the problem of perceptual narrowing with elevated levels of arousal. Defenders in ice hockey, for example, are presented with a unique challenge in that they must handle the puck in the most high-risk area on the ice (in our own zone in front of our net) under pressure from opponents. Good, quick decision making is the key to expert performance.

As a defender, one problem I have experienced is that with very high levels of arousal, I missed some of the most sensible options available to me and made bad decisions with the puck. I call this the "fast feet, slow head syndrome." The other problem that can occur at very low arousal levels is that too many options seem to be available. Here is an example of the thinking: I pick up the puck in my zone and I see a winger on my side of the ice open. But no, if I carry the puck around the net, I can get it to the far winger. And when there, I see that if I carry the puck a little more, I can pass it to the center who is far up the ice and closer to my opponent's net. Of course by this time, I have lost the puck and I am chasing my opponent back to my own net!

There is no time in hockey to evaluate all options and pick the best one. You have to choose the first, best one. The optimal level of arousal for doing this is different for all athletes. I am a high energy, get-it-done kind of person; therefore, part of my routine involves relaxing, imagery rehearsal of decision making the afternoon before a game, and not thinking too much about the game in the last 4 to 5 hours before game time. However, I know other athletes who need to energize themselves before games with loud music and lots of activity to increase their energy levels.

Optimal levels of arousal also depend on the task itself. The simpler the task in terms of options, and the larger the muscle groups involved, the higher the optimal energy level. For this reason, I think one of the most difficult events in Olympic sport is the biathlon. These athletes work at their maximum capacity during the cross-country skiing loop, and then they must bring down their arousal level considerably in order to hit the targets in the rifle shooting part of the event. The arousal control they have is truly amazing. What they do is similar to the following: Do a vigorous warm-up, get your heart rate to a maximum, do a few weightlifting screams, and then try to thread a needle. It's not easy.

Sleep deprivation has adverse affects on attention and concentration and is an important factor in international competition where athletes travel long distances to different time zones. For example, our team had a long journey from Calgary to Stockholm via Toronto and Frankfurt. After 18 hours of travel, we arrived at our destination, unpacked, had lunch, and went to practice. We were pretty tired, so after about 40 minutes of practice, the coach had us scrimmage, but we had to shoot the wrong way just for fun. (I shoot right, but had to use a left stick.) I discovered that I couldn't even skate while holding the stick the wrong way.

At our first event in Finland a few years before that, we played so poorly in our first game that the coach had the team skate lines between periods to wake us up. After traveling to Finland from Calgary, 3:00 to 4:00 A.M. was when everyone awakened and couldn't get back to sleep, leading to endless nights of card playing, and very little rest. The problems on the ice were not physical, but mental. We were skating, passing, and shooting well, and we didn't feel tired. The problem, however, was with bad decision making. The lack of sleep affected our attention, concentration, and ultimately our performance.

Strategies for dealing with international travel and jet lag are crucial for elite athletes because the adverse affects of sleep deprivation on concentration and attention can undo years of training and competition. An important element of our current junior national team program is to expose athletes to international travel, so that by the time these athletes make it to the senior team, they have had experience coping with the unique demands of international travel.

Finally, another interesting factor to consider is the role of motivation on performance and development of sport expertise. It has been my experience that the best athletes are inherently more self-motivated. The world of sport is replete with athletes who have a lot of talent, but no motivation to train, improve, and perform. We see many examples of this in all levels of hockey in Canada. Of course, coaches use many techniques to motivate athletes, but my own view is that this is only a short-term intervention, which has little effect on the long-term development of athletes. Remember, it takes about 10 years to develop expertise in sport! I would advise coaches not to rely on motivation techniques as a long-term approach to athlete development. Rather, it is a short-term tool that can get an athlete through a particularly challenging training or competitive situation. As an athlete, I would much rather have a less skilled but more motivated and committed teammate than a very skilled unmotivated one. You can always count on the self-motivated athlete to give attention to detail, train hard, and deliver a consistent improvement and performance.

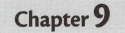

Chapter 9

Perceptual Expertise

■ ■ ■ ■ ■

Development in Sport

A. Mark Williams
Paul Ward

Aconsiderable knowledge base now exists regarding the nature of perceptual expertise in sport. Testimony to this expansive literature is the number of recent books (e.g., Williams, Davids, & Williams, 1999; Davids, Savelsbergh, Bennett, & van der Kamp, 2002) and special issues of journals (e.g., see Tenenbaum, 1999; Williams, 2002) that are devoted to this theme. This interest in perceptual expertise is related to the growth in expertise research in general (e.g., see Ericsson, 1996; Starkes & Allard, 1993; Williams & Reilly, 2000) and to increasing awareness that skilled perception is one variable that precedes and determines appropriate action in sport. Although researchers have learned much about the nature of perceptual expertise in sport, knowledge is sparse about whether or how perceptual skills may be developed through instruction and practice. This deficiency is surprising, and rather disappointing, given the potential contribution that this area of study could make to performance enhancement in sport. It is widely accepted that perceptual skill accrues as a result of task-specific practice, rather than through maturation or growth (Abernethy, 1988; Ward & Williams, in press), but the crucial question is whether the acquisition of such skills can be facilitated via appropriate training and instruction.

The intention in this chapter is to provide a critical review of contemporary research on the development of perceptual skill in sport. The chapter is divided into three distinct sections. Initially, we briefly highlight the nature of perceptual expertise in sport with reference to recent research and theory. Next, we provide a critical review of the research that has examined whether perceptual skill can be developed through training and instruction. We summarize contemporary research and include recent empirical work from our own laboratory. In the final section, we address several practical issues and questions relating to the design, implementation, and evaluation of perceptual-training programs. Although several of the questions posed may not relate directly to the theoretical background provided in the opening sections, they nevertheless highlight important considerations for those who attempt to implement perceptual-training programs. We do attempt, however, to answer these questions with reference to existing research and theory. We certainly hope that the ensuing discussion will act as a catalyst to encourage new and innovative work in this area. We begin with a brief review of some of the key findings that relate to perceptual skill in sport.

Perceptual Skill in Sport: Some Key Findings

Anecdotal evidence and lay opinion suggest that experts are endowed with "superior vision," or a "great eye." Although such claims have historically received support from vision scientists and optometrists, virtually no empirical evidence substantiates such a presumption (for recent reviews, see Abernethy, Wann, & Parks, 1998; Loran & MacEwen, 1995; Williams et al., 1999). For example, Ward, Williams, and Loran (2000) tested the general visual function of elite and sub-elite soccer players between the ages 8 and 18 years using standardized measures of static and dynamic visual acuity, stereoscopic depth, and peripheral awareness. Improvements in visual function were observed with age; however, meaningful skill effects were not. The elite soccer players did not demonstrate superior levels of visual function when compared with their subelite counterparts, and neither group of players recorded above-average levels of visual function. It appears that having supernatural levels of visual function is not a prerequisite for high-level sport performance. To the contrary, the novice performer occasionally outperforms the expert on tests of visual function (e.g., see Helsen & Starkes, 1999a).

Since the limits to performance are not determined by the physical or optometric characteristics of the visual system, attempting to improve visual function above "normal" levels would appear to be of little potential benefit. Moreover, although some researchers have demonstrated that performance on various tests of visual function can be improved by prolonged periods of practice (e.g., Junyent & Fortó, 1995; Kluka, Love, Hammack, & Wesson, 1996), no empirical evidence exists to show that this improvement transfers to the sporting arena. Any improvement is likely to be due to either placebo effects or increased familiarity with the testing environment, rather than any meaningful training benefit (cf. Wood & Abernethy, 1997).

It is now accepted that the expert's perceptual superiority over the novice is due to enhanced sport-specific cognitive knowledge structures acquired through years of deliberate, purposeful practice (Ericsson, Krampe, & Tesch-Römer, 1993; Ericsson, 1996). The expert has a more refined, more accessible knowledge base than the novice does as a result of enhanced strategic processing of task-relevant information. Thus far, researchers have identified a range of perceptual and cognitive discriminators of expertise. The relative importance of these skills is determined, at least in part, by the unique constraints of each sporting domain. For example, when compared with their novice counterparts, experts demonstrate

- superior recall and recognition of sport-specific patterns of play (e.g., Allard, Graham, & Paarsalu, 1980; Starkes & Deakin, 1984; Williams & Davids, 1995);
- faster detection and recognition of objects, such as a ball within the visual field (e.g., Allard & Starkes, 1980; Millslagle, 1988);

- more efficient and appropriate visual search behaviors (e.g., Aber-nethy, 1990; Vickers, 1992; Williams, Davids, Burwitz, & Williams, 1994; Williams & Davids, 1998);
- an enhanced ability to effectively pick up advance (pre-event) visual cues, particularly from an opponent's postural orientation (Abernethy & Russell, 1984; Jones & Miles, 1978; Williams & Bur-witz, 1993);
- greater attunement to relative motion information when present-ed in the form of point light displays (e.g., Abernethy, Gill, Parks, & Packer, 2001; Ward, Williams, & Bennett, 2002);
- more accurate expectations of likely events based on the refined use of situational probabilities (Alain & Proteau, 1980; Ward & Williams, in press); and
- perceptual processes that are more robust to changes in emotional states, such as anxiety (Williams & Elliott, 1999).

This brief overview of the key findings from the literature on percep-tual expertise suggests that cognitive interventions that develop the knowledge bases underlying skilled perception have more practical utility in facilitating the acquisition of expert performance than clini-cally based visual skills training programs.

In the next section, we review recent research that has examined whether perceptual skill can be facilitated using such interventions.

Perceptual Skill in Sport: Can It Be Trained?

Scientists have employed a number of techniques to examine whether perceptual skills can be trained. The progression of these methods over the years has been largely due to technological advances (as opposed to theoretical). The methods employed have ranged from simple slide presentations to video simulations and field-based interventions. The majority of this work has attempted to train players to pick up postur-al cues more effectively as opposed to other potentially trainable skills, such as the recognition of patterns of play. A historical overview of the experimental designs and key findings is presented in table 9.1.

Video Simulation Techniques

The majority of studies have employed video-based simulations with varying degrees of instruction and feedback to try to enhance percep-tual skill in sport. The typical approach has been to produce video simulations that re-create the performer's customary view of the action—for example, the return of a serve in tennis or a soccer penalty kick. These film sequences are then presented to a training group in either real-time or slow motion, with the directive to focus attention on the most informative cues. The relationship between these key sources of information and the subsequent action requirements are highlighted, and feedback about the correct response is then provided (e.g., see Farrow, Chivers, Hardingham, & Sachse, 1998; Franks & Hanvey, 1997; McMorris & Hauxwell, 1997; Singer et al., 1994; Tayler, Burwitz, & Davids, 1994; Williams & Burwitz, 1993). Williams and Burwitz (1993) employed this type of approach to improve novice goalkeepers' anticipatory performance at soccer penalty kicks. A significant pre- to posttest improvement in performance was observed on a film-based anticipation test after only 90 minutes of video simulation training. Similarly, Farrow et al. (1998) observed a significant improvement in performance on a film-based anticipation test following four weeks of simulation training with a group of novice tennis players.

Williams and Grant (1999) recently provided a detailed and critical review of early research on perceptual training. In their summary, they cite a number of research studies to support the proposition that perceptual skill in sport can be trained using video simulation with appropriate instruction and feedback. Although they highlighted the potential of such training programs, they also identified various shortcomings and thus proposed suggestions for future study. For example, several researchers have failed to employ placebo (e.g., a group that reads or views other instructional material) and/or control groups (e.g., a group who receives no training or one that merely observes training film without receiving formal instruction) in addition to the conventional training group. The improvements in performance observed in these studies may be due to conformational bias or increased familiarity with the test environment as opposed to any meaningful treatment effect. In addition, suitable transfer tests have not been employed to examine whether training did actually facilitate performance in the real-world context (e.g., see Farrow et al., 1998; Franks & Hanvey, 1997; McMorris & Hauxwell, 1997; Williams & Burwitz, 1993). The design and implementation of some measure of transfer is essential to determine whether the improvements observed in the laboratory setting actually transfer back to the game situation.

Several researchers have attempted to address the issue of transfer, with varying degrees of support for the practical utility of sport-specific training programs (e.g., Singer et al., 1994; Starkes & Lindley, 1994; Scott, Scott, & Howe, 1998; Tayler et al., 1994; Williams, Ward, & Chapman, 2003). Starkes and Lindley (1994) used video and on-court tests to

■ Table 9.1

A Summary of the Key Studies on Training Perceptual Skill Presented in Chronological Order

Authors	Year	Sport	Participants	Groups Experimental	Control
Damron	1955	American football	High school players (52)	• 20-min sessions (18) • 2D or 3D tachistoscopic slide presentation • Verbal instruction	
Haskins	1965	Tennis	Experienced players (11): 4 pilot and 7 test	• Pilot: 1-session training program (n = 2); 2-session training program (n = 2) • Test: 2-session training program	
Londerlee	1967	American football	High school players (28)	• 10-min sessions (9), 20-min session (1) over 3 weeks • Film-based or flash-card training • Manual progressive temporal occlusion training • Low and high IQ groups	
Day	1980	Tennis: forehand drive	Advanced junior players (ages 12-16): 11 male and 10 female	• 10-week film-based training • Anticipation and occlusion training • Verbal instruction	
Burroughs	1984	Baseball	Exp 1: Collegiate players (23) Exp 2: Collegiate players (36)	Exp 1: • 60-min session (1) • Film-based simulation/occlusion training • Feedback after each pitch Exp 2: • 45-min sessions (4-6) • Real-time training and/or slow-motion training • Questions during, and feedback after, each pitch	Exp 1: • Completed the posttest only

Groups			
Placebo	**Labratory test**	**Transfer test**	**Conclusions**
	• Slide recognition test • Verbal response	• Simulated field-based recognition test • Verbal response	• No pretest measure • Superior performance by 2D training group on the lab test • Similar performance by 2D and 3D on field
	• Film-based test • Movement response/film analysis		• Significant improvement in response time on the posttest under both pilot and test conditions
		• Simulated field-based recognition test • Verbal response, timed using a stopwatch	• No pretest measure • Significantly quicker response times for film-based training compared with flash-card group • No difference in response accuracy • No differences between IQ groups
	• Film-based occlusion test • Pen and paper response	• On-court occlusion test • Pen and paper response	• Improvement in response accuracy on depth and lateral judgments during film-based test only.
	Exp 1: • Field-based occlusion test • Verbal response Exp 2: • Field-based occlusion test • Verbal response • Delayed 6-wk posttest for slow-motion group only		Exp 1: • No pretest measure • Significantly better performance by trained group on posttest Exp 2: • Improvement in response accuracy on first and delayed posttest by slow-motion group • Improvement in performance by real-time training group • No improvement by combined real-time/slow-motion training group

(continued)

				Groups	
Authors	**Year**	**Sport**	**Participants**	**Experimental**	**Control**
*Christina, Baressi, Shaffner	1990	American football	Experienced player (1)	• 4-week training program • Film-based simulation • Question and answer sessions • Feedback provided	
Williams, Burwitz	1993	Soccer: penalty kick	Novice players (10)	• 90 min of film simulation training • Key cues highlighted • Feedback every trial	
Singer, Cauraugh, Chen, Steinberg, Frehlich, Wang	1994	Tennis: serve and passing shots	Novice players (34)	• 20-min laboratory sessions (3) • Film-based simulation training • 20-min on-court sessions (6) • Key cues highlighted • Feedback every trial	• 20-min laboratory sessions (3) • Film-based simulation training • Feedback every trial • 20-min on-court physical quickness and agility sessions (6)
*Starkes, Lindley	1994	Basketball: "open play"	Novice players (18)	• 30-min training sessions (6) • Film-based simulation • Feedback provided	• Completed pre- and posttests only
Tayler, Burwitz, Davids	1994	Badminton: serve	Novice players (16)	• 60-min training session (1) • Film-based simulation • Key cues highlighted • Feedback provided	• 60-min training session (1) • Film-based simulation • Feedback every trial
*Grant, Williams	1996	Soccer: "open play"	Novice players (16)	• 2-hr training sessions (3) • Skills practices • Small-sided games • Key cues highlighted • Feedback provided	• 2-hr training sessions (3) • Skills practices • Small-sided games

Groups			
Placebo	**Labratory test**	**Transfer test**	**Conclusions**
	• Film-based test • Joystick response		• No change in response time as a result of training • Significant improvement in response accuracy
	• Film-based anticipation test • Pen and paper response		• Significant improvement observed on the posttest
	• Film-based anticipation tests • Verbal response	• On-court evaluation using Likert-type rating scale	• Significant improvement in performance on the anticipation tests for the experimental group only • No differences for either group pre- to posttest using the on-court assessment
	• Film-based test • Verbal response	• On-court evaluation involving "freeze" play situations	• Improvements in accuracy and response times for experimental group • No differences on transfer test
	• Film-based anticipation test • Movement response	• On-court assessment using video analysis	• Significant improvement in performance for the experimental group only on both the laboratory test and on-court evaluation
		• Simulated small-sided "freeze" play situations	• Significant pre- to posttest improvement in accuracy for the experimental group only

(continued)

				Groups	
Authors	**Year**	**Sport**	**Participants**	**Experimental**	**Control**
Adolphe, Vickers, Laplante	1997	Volleyball: service return	International players (9)	• 6-wk on-court training program • Focus on improving visual attention and ball tracking	
Franks, Hanvey	1997	Soccer: penalty kick	Experienced players (18)	• Key cues highlighted • Film-based simulation	• Observation of film-based simulation only
McMorris, Hauxwell	1997	Soccer: penalty kick	Novice players (30)	• Film-based simulation training (250 or 500 trials) • Written instructions to look for certain precontact cues	• Completed pre- and posttests only
Farrow, Chivers, Hardingham, Sachse	1998	Tennis: serve	Novice players (24)	• 15-min sessions (8) over 4 weeks • Film-based simulation training • Key cues highlighted • Feedback every trial	• Completed pre-and posttests only
Scott, Scott, Howe	1998	Tennis: serve	Intermediate players: 3 male and 3 female	• Multiple 10-min sessions • Variable speed film-based simulation training	
Abernethy, Wood, Parks	1999	Squash: strokes	Novice players: 15 male and 15 female	• 20-min sessions (4) of film-based simulation training and one 20-min motor practice over 4 weeks • Instruction on stroke kinematics and key cues • Event and temporal occlusion/slow-motion training and feedback • On-court motor practice	• 20-min on-court physical practice (1)

Groups			
Placebo	Labratory test	Transfer test	Conclusions
		• Recording of visual gaze and physical actions in dynamic on- court situations	• Significant improvements in visual tracking and stability of gaze before ball contact on the posttest • Improvements in service return accuracy scores over a 3-yr follow-up period
	• Film-based anticipation test • Press button response		• Significant increase in accuracy for the experimental group only
	• Film-based anticipation test • Pen and paper response		• Significant improvement in performance on the anticipation test for the experimental group only • No difference between experimental groups that viewed 250 or 500 practice trials
• 15-min sessions (8) over 4 weeks • Videotapes of professional matches • Questions about these matches	• Film-based anticipation test • Movement response		• Significant improvement in speed of response for experimental group only on the film-based anticipation test • No differences in response accuracy
		• On-court assessment via point system	• Significant improvement in serve-return performance
• 20-min training session (4) and 20-min motor practice (1) over 4 weeks • Coaching manuals and videotapes of professional matches	• Film-based temporal occlusion test • Press button response • Visual function tests		• Significant posttest improvement in predicting stroke direction and depth in experimental group only • No improvement in visual function

(continued)

■ **Table 9.1**
(continued)

				Groups	
Authors	**Year**	**Sport**	**Participants**	**Experimental**	**Control**
Williams, Ward, Knowles, Smeeton	2002	Tennis: ground strokes	Novice players (30)	• 45-min session of film-based simulation training and 45 min of on-court training • 2 groups: explicit instruction or guided discovery • Stroke kinematics and key cues highlighted • Slow-motion/temporal occlusion training and feedback • Perception-action coupling training on-court	• Completed pre- and posttests only
Williams, Ward, Chapman	2003	Field hockey: penalty flick	Novice goalkeepers (yet experienced outfield players) (24)	• 45-min session (1) • Film-based simulation training • Key cues highlighted • Progressive temporal occlusion training and feedback	• Completed pre- and posttests only

* Please note that these studies attempted to train decision making as opposed to perceptual skill.

assess pre- to posttest training differences in novice basketball players. A treatment group participated in six 30-minute training sessions involving video simulation, practice, and feedback, whereas a control group completed the pre- and posttests only. The trained group showed a significant pre- to posttest improvement on the film-based anticipation test as compared with the control group, but neither group improved their performance during the on-court test. The transfer test required participants to make judgments at the end of various play sequences that were realistically acted out on court. Although these findings suggest that the improvements observed on the posttest are specific to the laboratory setting, the authors highlight the difficulties that are involved when attempting to create realistic and sensitive measures of transfer (cf. Singer et al., 1994).

These difficulties were addressed by Williams et al. (2003) in a study involving the penalty flick in field hockey. Researchers employed both

Groups			
Placebo	Labratory test	Transfer test	Conclusions
• 45-min session (1) • Instructional video on stroke and match play	• Film-based anticipation test • Movement response	• On-court assessment using video analysis	• Significant improvement in response time on posttests by experimental groups only • Greater improvement on-court than in the laboratory • No difference in pre-post response accuracy scores
• 45-min session (1) • Instructional video on field hockey goal-keeping skills	• Film-based anticipation test using video analysis	• Field assessment using video analysis	• Significant pre-post improvements in response time by experimental group only on laboratory and transfer test

field- and laboratory-based measures of anticipatory performance. The laboratory-based anticipation test required participants to respond in an interceptive manner to a near "life-size" image of the player taking the hockey flick presented on film, whereas in the field-based test, the goalkeepers attempted to save actual penalty flicks from the same players presented on film. To facilitate the comparison of scores between the field and laboratory settings, split-screen digital-video analysis was employed to measure the initiation of movement relative to ball contact by the penalty taker, as well as to measure the response accuracy of the goalkeeper. An illustrative example of the split-screen video data is provided in figure 9.1.

A total of 24 novice hockey goalkeepers were divided into three groups. A training group was exposed to video simulation training whereby the key information cues underlying anticipation of the penalty flick were highlighted under normal viewing using a freeze-frame

Figure 9.1   An illustrative example of the split-screen video technique used for analysis by Williams et al. (2003) in their laboratory-based test of anticipation in the hockey penalty flick.

facility. Participants were then provided with an opportunity to practice under progressively shorter viewing conditions. The important information cues were derived from a review of the related literature and from an initial study where visual search and performance data were taken from a group of expert hockey goalkeepers. A control group merely completed the laboratory- and field-based anticipation tests, whereas a placebo group viewed an instructional video focusing on the technical skills involved in hockey goalkeeping.

The results are presented in table 9.2. Participants who underwent the training program significantly improved their performance beyond that of the control and placebo groups, on both the laboratory and field-based tests of anticipation. Significant pre- to posttest improvements were observed in response time for the training group only. Although these results highlight the benefits of such interventions, the training group's performance on the posttests was still below that of the expert group, which highlights the important role that continued, long-term practice plays in the acquisition of expertise (see Ericsson, 1996; Ericsson et al., 1993). Nevertheless, these findings provide strong evidence to support the use of video-based training programs as a method of enhancing perceptual skill in sport (see also Scott et al., 1998; Tayler et al., 1994).

■ Table 9.2
The Decision Time (DT) and Response Accuracy (RA) Data for Each Group on the Laboratory- and Field-Based Pre- and Posttests

Group		Laboratory test				Field test			
		Pretest		Posttest		Pretest		Posttest	
		DT (ms)	RA (%)	DT (ms)	RA (%)	DT (ms)	RA (%)	DT (ms)	RA (%)
Placebo	M	738.5	57.8	744.2	54.1	631.2	36.8	626.2	38.7
	SD	64.1	15.6	61.0	21.4	59.7	12.2	48.2	12.1
Control	M	808.5	65.9	778.8	68.0	670.6	35.6	672.7	38.7
	SD	22.7	13.9	33.3	17.2	45.0	6.7	61.6	10.6
Training	M	788.0	65.0	684.0	65.0	629.1	46.8	585.2	51.8
	SD	41.8	20.7	35.9	14.8	59.6	9.6	27.6	9.9

Data from Williams et al., 2003.

Field-Based Techniques

Although several researchers have coupled video simulation with on-court training (e.g., Day, 1980; Singer et al., 1994; Tayler et al., 1994), few *in vivo* (i.e., real-life) studies have ever been performed. In one such study, Grant and Williams (1996) used small-sided practice matches and drills, complemented with instructional feedback, to highlight the important sources of information that underlie game-reading skills in soccer. A matched group of novice soccer players participated in similar practice sessions, but they received no instruction or feedback regarding the most informative cues on which to focus their attention. The results showed that the training group was the only group to record significant pre- to posttest improvements in accuracy in response to "freeze-play" situations presented *in situ* (i.e., in the field setting).

In a study by Adolphe, Vickers, and Laplante (1997), elite volleyball players participated in a six-week in situ perceptual-training program designed to improve visual search behaviors and performance accuracy in passing to the setter area. The intervention included video feedback on gaze behavior with on-court sessions to improve ball detection, tracking, and forearm passing skills. Significant pre- to posttest improvements were found in tracking onset, tracking duration, and the ability to maintain a stable gaze on the contact point during step corrections. Researchers performed a three-year follow-up to examine the duration of the players' serve reception performance scores. The players who participated in the perceptual-training program showed much higher performance levels as compared with a matched group of players who had not undergone such training, although it could be argued that several other factors, such as improvements in technique, may also have contributed to the observed improvement. Further research is necessary to determine whether field-based interventions, particularly those employing "designer games" or a "games for understanding" approach (e.g., see Charlesworth, 1994; Steinberg, Chaffin, & Singer, 1998; Thorpe, 1996), are more effective in enhancing perceptual skill than video-based simulations.

Cognitive interventions that highlight the most informative cues and corresponding action requirements, whether by video simulations or instruction in situ, appear to have practical utility in facilitating perceptual skill in sport. First, experts consistently outperform novices on measures of perceptual and cognitive skill. Second, a reasonable number of studies show an improvement in performance on various video or film-based tests of anticipation following such interventions. Third, a handful of studies demonstrate that the improvements observed on laboratory tests of anticipation actually transfer to the performance setting. However, what is clearly evident following even a cursory glance at the literature is the relative lack of empirical research work on this topic, particularly when compared with the vast knowledge base that exists on expertise in general. Our intention, therefore, in the final section of this chapter, is to highlight several potential areas for further investigation.

Training Perceptual Skill in Sport: Some Unanswered Questions

In this section, we discuss a number of important practical questions regarding the design, implementation, and evaluation of effective training programs. We certainly hope that some of the questions we pose will stimulate further research endeavors and lead to more prescriptive guidance for coaches and practitioners involved in performance enhancement in sport.

Can Other Perceptual Skills Be Enhanced Through Training— Such As Pattern Recognition and Use of Situational Probabilities?

Hardly any research has focused on the training of perceptual skills, with the exception of advance cue utilization. The lack of research is disappointing, particularly when one considers that the ability to recognize patterns of play and to use situational probabilities are amongst the strongest predictors of perceptual skill in team-sport ball games (see Ward & Williams, in press; Williams & Davids, 1995). Some evidence suggests that pattern recognition skills can be improved through repeated exposure to a variety of related action sequences. Christina, Barresi, and Shaffner (1990) used video training to successfully develop pattern recognition and decision-making skills in American football, whereas Wilkinson (1992) reported long-term retention of pattern recognition skills in volleyball players following their perceptual training. A suggestion is that exposure to specific patterns of play results in the development of specialized receptors or detectors through a process called *imprinting* (Goldstone, 1998). These detectors supposedly develop and strengthen with exposure to the stimulus (or stimuli), which results in increased speed, accuracy, and general fluency with which stimuli are processed. In our laboratory, work is ongoing to determine whether repeated exposure to different types of offensive sequences in soccer via video simulation can facilitate the recognition of similar patterns of play. Laboratory-based recognition and recall tests coupled with various measures of transfer are being employed to evaluate the effectiveness of such training programs.

It appears that no published studies exist that concern the issue of whether knowledge of situational probabilities can be trained, despite its perceived importance in guiding the search for contextual information during anticipatory situations (see Williams et al., 1999; Williams, 2000). Video technology, perhaps coupled with quantitative match analysis data, may conceivably be put to good use in this regard. Many major sports teams and individual athletes now use video to review recent performances and to scout forthcoming opponents. Although this process is often informal and dependent on access to qualitative video sequences, players and coaches are now familiar with this type of intervention and may be amenable to a more structured form of practice. These structured training sessions may involve presentation of quantitative statistics that highlight the moves and actions typically performed by forthcoming opponents. For example, analysis may reveal that the opposition typically plays to a certain pattern or that attackers are consistent (i.e., predictable) in their movement patterns. Awareness of such points markedly improves players' abilities to make accurate predictions regarding their opponents' actions. This information can also be built on in training that uses specific coaching practices or drills.

Perhaps the main reason for the lack of research on the trainability of pattern recognition and situational probability skills is that little is known about the important perceptual invariants that underlie these skills. For example, with regard to pattern recognition skills, what are the essential information sources that define the pattern? Are all the players important, or is it merely a small cluster of players who give each pattern its unique signature? In the case of situational probabilities, what information should be conveyed to the learner? Which probabilities are important, and which ones should be ignored? Systematic programs of research are required to determine the key sources of information that underlie perceptual skill in each sport. A wide array of experimental techniques now exist to explore these issues, such as eye movement recording, temporal and event occlusion techniques, liquid crystal occlusion glasses, point light displays, and verbal reports (for a review, see Williams et al., 1999). A detailed understanding of the specific sources of information that determine perceptual skill in each sport is an essential cornerstone in the design and implementation of successful training programs (Williams & Grant, 1999).

How Should Information Be Conveyed to the Learner?

The traditional instructional approach, whether it refers to perceptual or motor skills, has been essentially prescriptive and highly directive in nature. Under this approach, coaches have typically provided detailed instruction and feedback as to correct athletes' behavior (e.g., Farrow et al., 1998; Williams & Burwitz, 1993). However, scientists have recently advocated a more hands-off, or less prescriptive, approach to instruction (e.g., see Davids, Williams, Button, & Court, 2001; Williams et al., 1999). The suggestion is that implicit instructional techniques may be more effective than explicit awareness strategies, particularly under conditions involving high uncertainty or stress (e.g., Hardy, Mullen, & Jones, 1996; Masters, 1992; Maxwell, Masters, & Eves, 2000). Athletes who learn skills via explicit strategies are more likely to break down under pressure because under duress, they reinvest themselves in controlled processing. Thus, they shift their attention away from external environmental cues and shift it toward internal monitoring of feelings, thoughts, and movements.

Magill (1998) argued that to train perceptual skill, visual attention should merely be directed toward information-rich areas of the display, as opposed to specific information cues. In this approach, knowledge is acquired implicitly, rather than via conscious or intentional processes. For example, when learning to anticipate an opponent's serve in tennis, players should not be directed to focus their gaze on specific information cues, such as the ball and racket orientation at impact. According to Magill, highly directed coaching does not allow players to learn how to search; however, completely random searching is likely to be time consuming and inefficient while leading to losses in self-confidence and motivation. Players should therefore be directed toward the contact zone so that they can discover the regularities between racket and ball orientation for each type of serve. A variety of ball and racket orientations are required to be viewed so that the learner can become progressively attuned to the invariant regulatory features.

Williams, Ward, Knowles, and Smeeton (2002) compared the effectiveness of *guided discovery* with the more traditional directed approach to perceptual training, using forehand and backhand drive shots in tennis. One group of novice tennis players was trained via conventional explicit instruction, whereby the key information cues were highlighted during separate 45-minute video simulation and on-court practice sessions. With the experimental group, researchers employed a more "problem focused" (or implicit) technique. In this latter approach, learners were merely directed toward potentially informative areas of the display, such as the trunk or hips, and they were encouraged to discover on their own meaningful relationships between various postural cues and shot outcomes. A placebo group observed a general instructional video on tennis, and a control group merely completed the pre- and posttests. In the laboratory, filmed images were presented on a large screen, players were required to respond as if they were intercepting tennis forehand and backhand shots. With the on-court transfer test, researchers filmed the players' anticipatory responses to a live model. The order of presentation of laboratory- and field-based tests was counterbalanced across groups. The experimental layout for laboratory- and field-based tests is highlighted in figure 9.2.

The two experimental groups significantly reduced their decision times on both the laboratory and on-court posttest relative to the placebo and control groups. There were no significant differences in response accuracy across groups or test sessions. More important, as far as the current discussion is concerned, no differences were observed between the two experimental groups. Both groups were significantly faster in responding as a result of training, and this improvement transferred to the field setting. The data are presented in figure 9.3. It appears that the guided discovery approach proposed by Magill (1998) and others (e.g., Davids et al., 2001; Williams et al., 1999) is at least as effective as more traditional, prescriptive approaches to instruction. It would be interesting to see if the improvements in perceptual skill are maintained over prolonged periods of time and whether the implicitly trained players' perceptual processes are more robust to changes in emotional states, as proposed by Masters and colleagues (e.g., Masters, 1992; Maxwell et al., 2000). Clearly, there is much scope for future research on this topic.

How Do We Create Effective Simulations for Training Purposes?

As evidenced in this review, the majority of perceptual-training studies have employed video simulation techniques. The advantages of using video technology in this way are that learning can occur at a self-regulated pace, in and out of season, when the athlete is injured or fatigued, and the equipment is relatively inexpensive and accessible. Video images can also be easily manipulated for training purposes by highlighting or occluding relevant or irrelevant sources of information. One question to ask, however, is whether video is the most effective training medium. Certainly, research suggests that video simulations

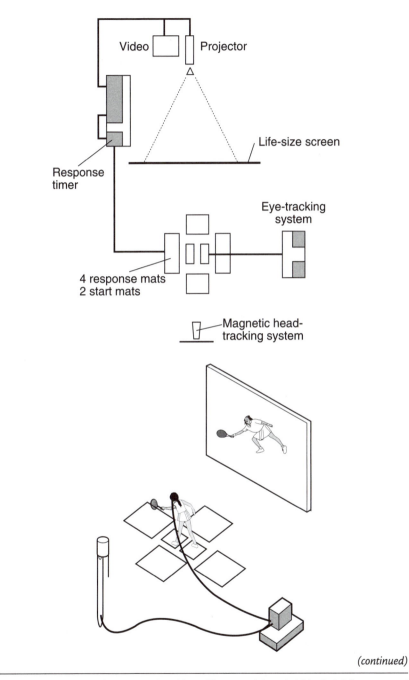

Video   Projector

Life-size screen

Response
timer

Eye-tracking
system

4 response mats
2 start mats

Magnetic head-
tracking system

a

(continued)

Figure 9.2 Experimental setup employed by Williams et al. (2002) *(a)* in their laboratory and *(b)* field-based tests of anticipation in tennis.

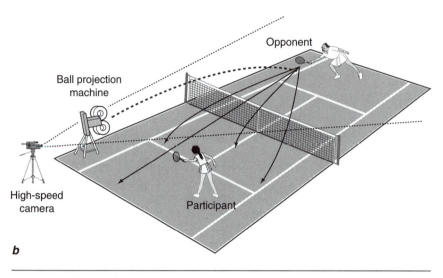

Figure 9.2   (continued)

are more effective than slide presentations (e.g., see Helsen & Starkes, 1999b; Starkes & Lindley, 1994). The jury is still out on the relative effectiveness of video- and field-based practices, but simulators and virtual reality environments may pave the way forward as potential training aids. Although simulators and virtual training environments are considered together for the purposes of this review, the main difference is that simulators establish a physically present environment and virtual reality creates a computer-generated environment (for a review, see Lee, Chamberlin, & Hodges, 2001). Another important question to ask, however, is whether these technological approaches are more effective in facilitating learning, particularly in view of the potential increase in cost and reduction in accessibility.

In virtual environments, the learner is placed into a situation that looks, feels, smells, and sounds to some degree like the real setting. The learners can move their head, eyes, and limbs to explore the multisensory, three-dimensional environment, and they can interact with objects and people (Psokta, 1995). Some systems involve head-mounted displays, whereas others employ desktop computers or projected images that involve one or more screens (see Loomis, Blascovich, & Beall, 1999; Romano & Brna, 2001; Wilson, 1997).

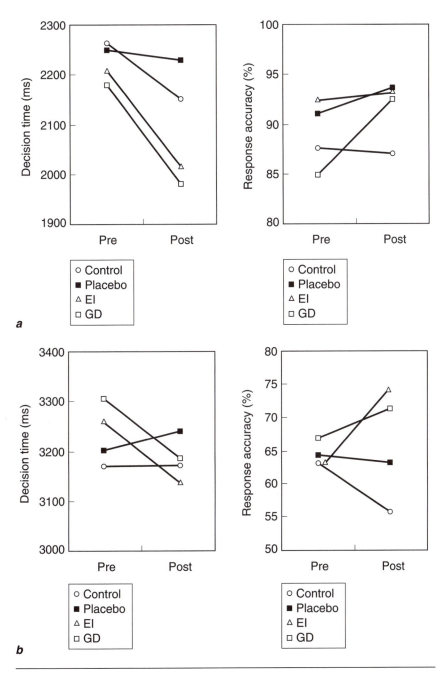

Figure 9.3 The decision time and response accuracy data for each group across the pre- and posttests in (a) laboratory and (b) field settings. (EI, explicit instruction; GD, guided discover)

Data from Williams et al., 2002.

Although head-mounted displays provide stereoscopic vision and a wide field-of-view, they are removed from the real world since only one user can be immersed in the environment at any time. Projector-based systems, however, are more immersive than those employing computer monitors. They can afford a wide view of the action, particularly if several systems are combined to create a "reality room" or "cave," and they allow several users to interact with the virtual environment, using devices such as a "data-glove" (see Avis, 2000). These systems afford a unique way to visualize and explore different performance settings as well as navigate and interact with virtual objects. For example, as the virtual outfielder in baseball moves to intercept the ball, the visual detail of the playing field moves around the participant and the ball "looms," providing depth and timing information, reinforced by haptic information as the virtual ball makes contact with the glove. Few researchers have examined the potential of virtual training environments in sport (for exceptions, see Andersson, 1993; Todorov, Shadmehr, & Bizzi, 1997), yet such systems have been used extensively in the training of surgeons (see Tendick et al., 2000) and pilots (see Allerton, 2000). Although there are problems to be resolved, such as the slow graphics update and difficulty in creating realistic tactile stimuli and three-dimensional sound production (for a more detailed discussion, see Abernethy et al., 1998; Avis, 2000), such technology is likely to play an increasing role in performance enhancement in sport. An excellent example of how such a simulation is already being employed in American football may be viewed at www-VRL.umich.edu/project/football/.

A potential advantage with simulators and virtual training environments over video is that they allow the learner to move in response to the evolving display. Several researchers have suggested that the close functional links between perceptual and physical (action) variables should be maintained during practice and performance (e.g., see Gibson, 1979; Michaels & Carello, 1981). The suggestion is that during training the performance environment should be preserved by presenting learners with visual, tactile, and auditory information and by requiring them to move in response to the action. Such training environments possess higher "fidelity" than those relying purely on the visual system (see Alessi, 1988). Although specificity of practice is regarded as one of the most important principles underlying skill acquisition (e.g., see Proteau, 1992), clearly, as evidenced in this review, learning can occur in the absence of multisensory input and physical response requirements. The questions that remain to be addressed are as follows: First, do simulations that involve several sensory modalities facilitate transfer and learning more proficiently than those that merely involve vision? Second, are simulations that require learners to physically respond to the action sequences more effective than those based merely on observation?

Milner and Goodale (e.g., 1995; Milner, 1998; Goodale & Milner, 1992) have argued that different neural pathways underlie perception and action. The ventral stream that runs from the striate cortex to the inferotemporal region is presumed to be crucial to the visual perception and identification of objects, whereas the dorsal stream that runs from the striate cortex to the posterior parietal lobe is responsible for the visual control of action. It may be that video simulations place much heavier demands on the ventral stream, whereas virtual environments, simulators, and field-based practices are able to effectively train both the ventral and dorsal roots (Williams & Grant, 1999). The implication is that training should be specific to the unique functional demands of each sport. For example, the training of pattern recognition skills in soccer may be achieved effectively using video-based training, since, in the real game setting, these skills may be somewhat detached from the ensuing response requirements (e.g., players can often decide to move away from, rather than toward the ball). In contrast, learning to anticipate and to play a forehand volley return in tennis may benefit from either training on the court or using a simulator or virtual environment. The argument is that the ability to identify an opponent's intended stroke and to successfully execute a return stroke in tennis is more tightly coupled, which requires an immediate response from the player than the soccer example presented. There is considerable scope for innovative and creative research to determine the potential applications of simulators and virtual training environments in performance enhancement (see Loomis et al., 1999).

What Is the Best Way to Assess Transfer From Laboratory to Field Settings?

The problem of how best to assess transfer is perhaps the biggest concern for those attempting to undertake research in this area, although, coincidentally, it may be the least important as far as coaches are concerned. This type of intervention may be justified from the practitioner's perspective, provided that the athlete gives consent and appears to demonstrate a positive change in performance. Clearly, for sport scientists, the need for empirical verification (i.e., evidence-based practice) is essential to avoid the trap that has besieged numerous opticians and sport vision specialists.

The problem may actually be solved through collaboration between scientists and practitioners. What may ultimately provide the best solution is a marriage between subjective measures based on coaches' opinions and objective measures based on video and quantitative match analyses. To improve objectivity, the opinions of coaches could be gleaned pre- and posttraining by developing behavioral assessment scales (e.g., French & Thomas, 1987; Oslin, Mitchell, & Griffin, 1998), whereas to improve reliability, a panel of expert coaches could be used to assess perceptual skill over a number of matches. The validity of these assessment scales could be substantiated by identifying behavioral indicators of perceptual skill with qualitative and quantitative video analysis (e.g., see Jordet, 2001). Several digital video analysis packages now exist on the market that provide detailed quantitative and qualitative evaluation of game performance (e.g., see Hughes & Franks, 1997). In addition, many sport participants and organizers keep seasonal records on various aspects of performance, such as service return accuracy in volleyball (e.g., see Adolphe et al., 1997). Although it may be difficult to directly apportion any improvements to any intervention, data obtained via seasonal records may help substantiate the validity of the training protocol. It may prove much easier to assess training improvements in more closed-skill situations, such as in the return of a serve in tennis or the penalty flick in field hockey. In these situations, improvements in technology enable many components of performance to be examined in situ using high-speed film analysis (e.g., see Williams et al., 2003).

How Should Practice Be Structured for Effective Perceptual Learning?

The question of how practice should be structured for effective learning has always been a topical area for debate in the motor skills literature (for detailed reviews, see Lee et al., 2001; Schimidt & Lee, 1998). The general consensus is that variability of practice and high-contextual interference practice conditions are beneficial for skill acquisition. In contrast, few researchers have examined whether similar principles apply in the learning of perceptual and cognitive skills (for a recent exception, taken from the ergonomics literature, see de Crock, van Merriënboer, & Paas, 1998). When designing perceptual-training programs, practitioners could include video sequences from several players as they perform a variety of different strokes or from one opponent who plays a certain type of shot. Although guidance as to the most effective practice schedule may be gained from literature that deals with motor skills, we need confirmation that the same principles apply to perceptual skill learning as well (Williams & Grant, 1999).

Furthermore, research is needed to examine the optimal frequency and duration of perceptual-training sessions. The average length of a session has ranged from 15 minutes to 2 hours, whereas the frequency has varied from a single session to a six-week training period (for a review, see Williams & Grant, 1999). Does perceptual training continue to improve with training and practice, or is there an optimal point beyond which the additional training benefits are minimal? It may be that the benefits of perceptual training are observed almost immediately and that extending practice beyond this initial stage has only limited benefits. For example, McMorris and Hauxwell (1997) demonstrated that perceptual performance did not improve any further when they doubled the number of practice trials on a soccer-based simulation. Longitudinal research studies are required to map changes in perceptual skill over time as a result of practice and instruction. Retention tests, however, should be employed to determine whether the typical improvement observed following perceptual training is relatively permanent or the result of transient changes in performance (Williams & Grant, 1999).

Another interesting issue is whether perceptual training can be enhanced through mental imagery. Recent work on the use of motor imagery as a training aid suggests that when a high degree of functional equivalence exists between motor execution and the imaged action, an improvement in motor performance is likely to occur (e.g., see Decety & Ingvar, 1990). The research evidence pertaining to perceptual skills is less clear. Neurophysiological research indicates that imagery activates similar areas of the visual cortex to those invoked during visual perception (Goebal, Linden, Lanfermann, Zanelle, & Singer, 1998; Kosslyn, Behrmann, & Jeannerod, 1995; for a review see Jeannerod, 1999). Imagery, however, can have both selective interference and facilitation effects on perceptual tasks or processes. Although common mechanisms (e.g., attention, working memory) are used and may compete during imagery and perceptual processes, imagery may also aid in selectively priming appropriate neural mechanisms in the visual system (Phillips & Christie, 1977; Finke, 1986). With regard to training perceptual skills in sport, it may be that imagery can be used in association with video simulation techniques to facilitate perceptual skill development. How imagery techniques should be implemented into perceptual-training programs may be an interesting area for future research.

Are There Key "Time Windows" for Acquiring Perceptual Skills?

Coaches often ask at what age should perceptual training commence and whether such instruction should occur early or late within the learning process. With regard to the former question, hardly any empirical evidence exists to guide current practice. However, there is research to suggest that perceptual skills improve with age and experience (e.g., see Abernethy, 1988) and that elite athletes can be differentiated from less elite counterparts as early as 8 to 10 years of age (e.g., see French & Thomas, 1987; Ward & Williams, in press).

McPherson and Thomas (1989) showed that 8- to 10-year-old tennis players' decision-making skills could be improved following specific instruction, whereas Grant and Williams (1996) reported similar observations using 12- to 14-year-old soccer players. In contrast, in a recent study Groom and Paull (2001) found no improvement in the anticipation skill following perceptual training in a group of 6-year-old soccer players. It is therefore very difficult to provide definitive guidelines to coaches regarding the chronological age at which such skills should be taught, and, indeed, such a strategy may not be advisable as a result of individual differences in cognitive development (McMorris, 1999). One suggestion is that players should be amenable to perceptual training by 12 years of age (e.g., Williams & Grant, 1999), but this guideline is based on intuition and the opinion of expert coaches, rather than empirical evidence.

French and McPherson (1999) argued that the development of tactical and strategic knowledge is closely related to motor skill development. They provide evidence to suggest that children may not develop task-specific cognitive or perceptual skills before physical mastery of the associated skills. According to this argument, the training of perceptual and decision-making skills should not progress until the learner has developed the necessary motor skills to implement an effective response. The content and focus of practice sessions are not only likely to regulate motor skill development but also produce different knowledge representations that affect how players read the game. One current controversy involves whether this type of instruction should be employed with experts (Andrews, 1988), intermediates (Helsen & Starkes, 1999b), or novices (Chamberlin & Coelho, 1993). Although the majority of training studies have employed novice participants, the answer to this question may depend on the nature and difficulty of the skills being taught as well as the type of simulation employed (for an interesting discussion, see Alessi, 1988). It seems desirable for the learner to have at least a basic understanding of the technical and strategic skills involved. Consequently, since novices are likely to be preoccupied with the basic skills, it may be that more strategic considerations, such as anticipation and decision making, should be left until intermediate stages of learning. Alternatively, at elite levels of performance, perceptual and cognitive skills are more likely to discriminate players than technical or physical characteristics (e.g., Williams & Reilly, 2000). Although the actual improvement in perceptual skill at this stage is likely to be small, the benefits may be more substantive.

Summary

A review of the literature indicates that psychological interventions that attempt to develop the knowledge bases that underlie skilled perception are likely to be more effective in developing perceptual skill than visual skills training programs. Video simulations appear to be particularly effective when coupled with appropriate instruction and feedback. Although such interventions have practical utility in enhancing sport performance, several questions remain unanswered. On a more positive note, however, there is much scope and opportunity for innovative research as highlighted in the final section of this chapter. If this area of study is to make a significant contribution to practice and instruction in sport, then scientists, practitioners, and coaches must work together to develop, implement, and evaluate appropriate training interventions.

EXPERTS' COMMENTS

■ *Question*

In this chapter, Williams and Ward suggest that perceptual training that uses structured videotape presentations with time and decision pressures may aid athletes in their game perception and decision making in tennis and soccer. Is perceptual training likely to be of benefit in wrestling and ice hockey? Why or why not?

■ *Coach's Perspective: Nick Cipriano*

My experience is limited regarding structured videotape presentations that include time and decision pressures. It is a practice that has received little to no exposure in training freestyle wrestlers. However, what is used extensively is videotape for purposes of learning technical-tactical actions, reviewing a personal performance, and scouting the opposition. I am inclined to believe that perceptual training is not likely to be beneficial for training freestyle wrestlers, primarily because the wrestlers are in such close proximity to one another during the matches that there are no visual cues present that serve to trigger either an action or reaction. Rather, the initiation of an active or reactive movement is often based on sensing a muscular contraction or noting a subtle facial gesture that may preempt an attack. With expert wrestlers, it would be virtually impossible to structure perceptual training for all potential situations that commonly occur in freestyle wrestling—one, because their purposeful tactical actions are so well camouflaged or intentionally transparent, and two, because their actions can be so diverse.

■ *Player's Perspective: Therese Brisson*

Williams and Ward suggest that perceptual training (using structured videotape presentations with time and decision pressures) may aid athletes in their game perception and decision making in tennis and soccer. One of the drawbacks of video use in the past is that it gives an athlete the third-person perspective rather than the perspective of the performer. New commercial applications for recording, coding, saving, and organizing digital video clips have made it much more practical and effective for use in sport situations. Video is currently used in many sports to teach skills and strategy, to understand opponents' tendencies, and to improve decision-making skills. It is used extensively in hockey in training, in preparation for competition, and during the competition itself. When working on power skating, one of our assistant coaches (a bit of a video nut) routinely brings his camera to give athletes immediate feedback about progress. Replay images played on the Jumbotron in major hockey venues in North America are a rich source of information for athletes. The replay can be viewed at the next stoppage in play, evaluated for errors, and then used to plan corrections. I have realized that I really miss this source of information when playing at smaller venues.

Imagery training is another approach that I have used with much success to improve decision making. Over the course of the 6-month training period leading up to the 1998 Winter Olympic Games, I developed and implemented an imagery training program. In my journal I recorded my notes and observations about the imagery training usually every day, sometimes every second day. My journal had three sections: physical training, diet, and nutrition supplementation; data bank of individual and team tactics and systems; and daily notes and observations on individual and team practice, progress, and performance. After the Olympics, I wanted to evaluate how useful the program was. I selected videotape recordings of important international competitions prior to the imagery training (six games), midway through the program (five games), and at the end of the program (six games at 1998 Olympic Games) to assess my on-ice performance (a total of 45 hours of videotape). Qualitative analysis of the videotape involved examining every shift I played and coding decisions I made as either being "correct" or an "error." Five categories of decisions that I could make during the course of the game were coded and examined: breaking out of the defensive zone under pressure, covering defensive zone, defending opponent's attack, attacking the offense, and supporting the puck carrier. Game statistics, efficiency statistics, depth chart rankings, and coaching evaluations were also used to evaluate my performance before, during, and after the imagery training program. The coded videotape data indicated that I improved my decision-making ability in all areas, reducing the number of errors per game in each of the categories: breaking out of defensive zone (4.5 to .75), covering defensive zone (3 to 1), defending opponent's attack (4 to 1), attacking the offense (4 to 2), and supporting the puck carrier (6 to .5). Better offensive and defensive statistics, higher national and international rankings, and better coaching evaluations also were evidence of my improvement. Important themes that emerged from a content analysis of the journal were a shift in focus from outcome to performance, positive thinking, organization of knowledge, a progressive shift in focus of the imagery training routine from the task outcome to programming movement patterns, to rehearsal of response selection, and finally to stimulus identification (perception) rehearsal. This represented a progressive shift in focus of the imagery to earlier stages in information processing over the 6-month period. I think this last finding has great practical application for developing imagery training routines and getting to what I call *perceptual practice*.

Chapter 10

Retaining Expertise

■ ■ ■ ■ ■

What Does It Take for Older Expert Athletes to Continue to Excel?

Janet L. Starkes • Patricia L. Weir
Bradley W. Young

At the 2001 Columbus Marathon, Ed Whitlock at age 69 ran the 26.2-mile race in 2:52:50, which translates to sub-seven-minute miles over the entire course. Although he placed 72nd out of 3,428 runners, he managed to set a world record for his age. To put this in context, the world record in 1908 was 2:55:19, and it was held by a young man named Johnny Hayes. Whitlock has been a runner since he was young, and he is physiologically impressive for his age. With 9.5% body fat and a $\dot{V}O_2$ max of 52.8 ml\kg\min, he is physiologically like an active 35-year-old. More noteworthy is the fact that he continues to train by running two-and-a-half to three hours per day, every day (McGowan, 2001). Although Whitlock's case is remarkable, he is not unique. Masters' athletics is on the rise, and age-related competition is now available worldwide in most sports. In track and field, for example, the World Association of Veteran Athletes (WAVA) sponsors world championships, and performance is prorated by age-related performance tables known as *WAVA tables*. Similar competition is available in sports as varied as soccer, wrestling, baseball, and swimming.

Whitlock's case presents questions for the sport expertise literature that are not readily answerable. For example, to stay competitive, does someone who has trained for a lifetime need to maintain the same level of training? What impact do increases or decreases in training volume have in Master athletes? Does continued physical training help stave off the inevitable physical and cognitive declines associated with aging? How does one maintain motivation to train over an entire lifetime? Do the components of practice or the relative amount and importance of certain components of practice change in aging experts? Finally, contrary to popular beliefs, is it possible to continue to improve performance with training later in life?

Virtually all of our knowledge about expertise has been obtained by observing participants and their training to peak performance. The age of peak performance in sport is generally between 20 and 30 years, although the precise ages often differ by sport. In swimming, for example, peak performance occurs around 20 years, whereas short-distance running is around 23 with long-distance running about 27 years (Ericsson, 1991).

Ericsson, Krampe, and Tesch-Römer (1993) conceptually charted a course for the acquisition of expertise in the domain of music that has since, to varying degrees, been replicated by research in the arts (Simonton, 1996), in chess (Charness, Krampe & Mayr, 1996), and in sport (Helsen, Starkes & Hodges, 1998; Hodge & Deakin, 1998; Hodges & Starkes, 1996). This framework posits that the degree of acquisition that a performer is able to realize is a function of past accumulation and concurrent amounts of deliberate practice. Furthermore, the development of high-level performance cannot be achieved in the absence of sociocultural resources or long-term motivated behavior.

Krampe and Ericsson (1996) attempted to extend the critical role of deliberate practice during the initial phase of performance acquisition to the maintenance of superior performance. They proposed that continued investment in goal-oriented deliberate practice selectively maintained the superior performance of older performers beyond the onset of "normal" age-related decline. Krampe and Ericsson explicitly addressed this hypothesis by conducting research with young and old experts, as well as young and old amateurs, in instrumental music. Pianists were tested on a battery of both general-processing and domain-specific tasks, and they were also asked to retrospectively recall the amount of deliberate practice in which they had engaged at different periods of their careers. Results for the general-processing tasks demonstrated age-related slowing for the older amateurs and older experts. For the domain-specific tasks, however, only the older amateurs demonstrated performance decrements in line with normal aging trends. Interestingly, age-related decline for the older experts was rather negligible for the domain-specific tasks. In fact, the older experts performed at levels nearly equal to their younger expert counterparts. The authors concluded that it was the amount of deliberate practice invested during the later phase of the older experts' careers that moderated the normal aging decline. On average, older experts maintained 10.8 hours per week of deliberate practice, and although this amount was less than the younger expert pianists' total (26.7 hr), they still invested more time in practice than the younger (1.9 hr) and older amateurs (1.2 hr). The authors coined the term *maintenance practice* to reflect the preservative role of such training, and they claimed that it was most pivotal when a performer was between the ages of 50 and 60 years.

With regard to the complex relationship between performance and practice structure beyond peak performance, it is important for us to examine age-related changes in performance over time. To that end, we look at the different pictures of aging as obtained from cross-sectional analyses versus longitudinal studies. Next, we turn to an examination of the ways in which older athletes may change the content and nature of their training practices to maximize skill retention.

Cross-Sectional and Longitudinal Analyses of Athletic Performance

Age trends in athletic performances have provided researchers with a valuable analytic tool by which to quantify the extent and rate of performance change. The literature has seen the use of two experimental designs: cross-sectional and longitudinal. Cross-sectional designs typically involve gathering information on a large number of participants within different age groups that are divided by a five-year span. In contrast, a longitudinal design follows the same group of individuals over a specific time frame so that intra-individual differences in performance can be noted. Although a longitudinal study is more time consuming, it typically involves a smaller number of participants. In terms of performance changes, researchers predict that cross-sectional trends will exhibit steeper performance declines with less curvilinearity than will longitudinal trends (Stones & Kozma, 1982, 1984; Starkes, Weir, Singh, Hodges, & Kerr, 1999; Weir, Kerr, Hodges, McKay, & Starkes, 2002). This prediction is based on the knowledge that cross-sectional records represent peak performance levels for the various age categories; thus, they do not reflect preasymptotic levels of competitive fitness. It is important to acknowledge that regardless of the type of design employed, performance changes often reflect the influence of factors other than strictly the passage of time. Stones and Kozma (1984) have identified four such factors: one, the level of training during the period immediately prior to competition; two, secular events that affect levels of participation; three, the effects of injury; and four, changes to the level of motivation.

Figure 10.1 shows hypothetical performance curves based on age. Figure 10.1a is a purely linear graph. It suggests that performance declines over age, but it does so at a stable rate across the lifespan. Figure 10.1b shows a more quadratic form. This graph suggests that the rate of decline in performance is relatively stable until age 60. Afterward, age losses are greater over the next 30-year period than at any time prior. Thus, linear results suggest a consistent decline with age, and quadratic results indicate a change in the rate of performance loss over age.

When one sees quadratic changes with aging, it unfortunately presents a somewhat more pessimistic view that as people get older, their performances decline at an ever increasing rate. In contrast, when one sees only linear changes, the view of aging is more optimistic. In the following sections, we show that data from cross-sectional studies are more likely to show quadratic changes with age than do longitudinal studies. Longitudinal studies suggest that the performance changes one sees with age are not all that dramatic. We also show that differences in the degree of linearity and quadracity of age on performance curves depend in part on gender, as well as the sport one chooses to examine.

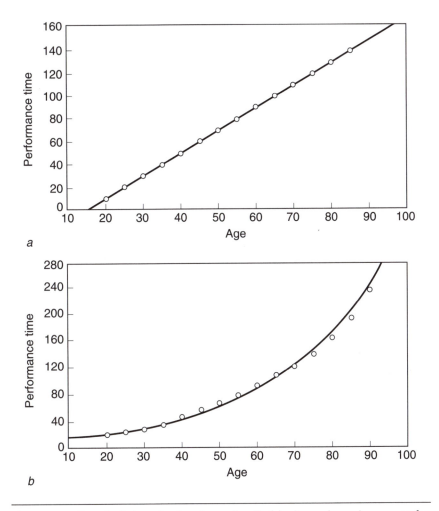

Figure 10.1 Hypothetical graphs that show primarily *(a)* a linear change in mean performance or *(b)* a quadratic change. The former indicates a stable decline in performance across age whereas the latter indicates a change in the rate of decline beginning around age 60.

Stones and Kozma (1982) examined changes in track-and-field performances using three different types of designs: cross-sectional, longitudinal, and secular. Cross-sectional data examined participants ranging in age from 40 to 74 years, arranged via five-year intervals. Longitudinal data were collected from all athletes for whom performances were recorded for a minimum of three years. Secular changes were quantified as the best performances per year from 1973 to 1979 for three age groups: 40 to 49 years, 50 to 59 years, and 60-plus years.

Performance changes were expressed as the percentage change per year. With this measure, positive values reflect performance deterioration whereas negative values reflect performance improvement. Overall, cross-sectional performance decline was significantly greater than that associated with any other type of trend (table 10.1). Performance improvements were noted for secular trend at the 50-to-59 and 60-plus cohort levels. Moderate performance declines were observed for the longitudinal trend and secular trend between 40 to 49 years.

■ **Table 10.1**
Mean Percentage Performance Change Across Events

Mean percentage overall		Secular cross-year		
Cross-sectional	Longitudinal	40–49 years	50–59 years	60+ years
1.58%	0.76%	0.32%	−2.1%	−2.4%

Positive values reflect performance deterioration; negative values reflect performance improvement.

This study on Master athletes was one of the first to quantify performance changes across different designs. In 1984, Stones and Kozma performed a more detailed analysis on the longitudinal data obtained for their 1982 study. The average duration of the longitudinal span across the 81 athletes was 5.3 years. Athletes were simply classified as being between 40 and 49 years old, or over 50. The focus of the analysis was to quantify the shape of the performance on age curves using polynomial regression. The linear coefficients were interpreted as estimates of the mean performance change over the longitudinal span, whereas the quadratic coefficients represented the rate of performance change with age. For the current data set, the linear trend was significant in indicating an overall trend of performance decline; however, no differences were noted among events or between the two age groups. The quadratic trend was also significant in indicating that the overall extent of performance decline increased with age. In other words, as one ages, the pace of decline quickens. Again, no age group differences were observed, but there was, however, an event difference. The long jump was the only event for which the performance decline diminished with age, and it differed significantly from the 400 and 5000-m events. To compare these performances on age curves with cross-sectional designs, Stones and Kozma (1984) reanalyzed the data from their 1982 study using regression models. As seen in table 10.2, the cross-sectional data supported the prediction of steeper rate

■ Table 10.2
The Mean Values of the Linear and Quadratic Coefficients for Cross-Sectional and Longitudinal Data

	Linear	Quadratic
Cross-sectional	.96	.16
Longitudinal	.33	.34

of decline with little curvilinearity. In contrast, the longitudinal data are much more balanced between the linear and quadratic trends.

In 1984, Hartley and Hartley examined the differences between longitudinal and cross-sectional designs, but this time it was for the sport of swimming. Two sets of data were used: one, longitudinal information from persons who competed in the 1976 and 1981 United States national masters swimming championships (30-80 years) and, two, information from the top-ten performers in the United States in each event in 1976 and 1981. They referred to this second data set as a *repeated cross-sectional design*. For the longitudinal data, a change score was used. Performance times in 1976 were subtracted from performance times in 1981. A negative score indicated a performance decline because performances in 1976 would have been faster than those in 1981; thus, a negative number reflected a lack of improvement over time. As seen in table 10.3 for the longitudinal data set, only the youngest cohort group showed a performance improvement over the five-year period. For men in particular, the performance decline worsened as age increased.

■ Table 10.3
Average Change Score Across Cohort Groups for the Longitudinal Data

	30-39 years	40-49 years	50-59 years	60-69 years	70-79 years
Men	.01 yard/sec	.00	−.02	−.04	−.14
Women	.03	.00	−.01	.00	−.10

For the longitudinal data set, polynomial regressions were computed for both men's and women's performances. Across the four events for men (50, 100, 200, 500 yards) both the linear and quadratic components were significant, whereas across two events for women (50, 100 yards), only the linear component was significant.

The second set of data were cross-sectional in nature and represented the best-case scenario because only the top performances in each of the two years were analyzed. The dependent variable of interest was the speed in yards per second for each of the events (50, 100, 200, 500, 1,650 yards). For both men and women, speed decreased as age increased, with older cohorts showing the greatest decline in speed over the five-year period. The coefficients from all the regression analyses are presented in table 10.4. Note that for men, the cross-sectional data show the greatest change, whereas for the women, the longitudinal data show the greatest change. The fact that the longitudinal data for the women show the largest decline may be a function of the limited number of events available in the longitudinal data set (50, 100 yards). The short distance events exhibited the greatest change score; thus, those were the events analyzed.

■ Table 10.4

Linear and Quadratic Beta Coefficients for Men and Women for Longitudinal and Cross-Sectional Analyses in 1976 and 1981

	Men		Women	
1976 Data	Linear	Quadratic	Linear	Quadratic
Longitudinal	−.0005	−.0001	.0184	−.0003
Cross-sectional	.0128	−.0002	.0035	−.0002
1981 Data	Men		Women	
Cross-sectional	.0123	−.0002	.0056	−.0002

Overall, for both swimming and track and field, cross-sectional data showed the greatest rate of change.

Our recent work on both Master swimming and track and field has attempted to tie these age-related performance changes to the theory of deliberate practice and the sport expertise literature. Expertise research has traditionally examined performances only up to the point of achieving expert performance. Little work has examined the changes in practice and performance beyond the attainment of expertise. Data were collected for both track (Starkes, Weir, Singh, Hodges, & Kerr, 1999) and swimming (Weir, Kerr, Hodges, McKay, & Starkes, 2002) using retrospective recall techniques. Athletes were asked to do the following: provide information on the structure of their practice sessions, make estimates on the amount of time they spent on each component of their practice, make estimates on the amount of time they spent on activities outside of practice (school, work, social time), and provide information on their best performance time ever and their current best performance time. These performance data allowed a semilongitudinal analysis because two data points per participant were included. Cross-sectional data were gathered from Master's Web sites that contained championship performance times.

For swimming, data were collected on a number of events; however, in this chapter, we will only present the results from freestyle swimming events. Table 10.5 shows the quadratic beta coefficients from the regression analysis for age versus performance time. From table 10.5, no clear pattern appears to exist as to whether the decline is greater in the semilongitudinal analysis or the cross-sectional analysis. For the shorter events, 50 and 100 meters, the cross-sectional sample shows a greater rate of decline. However, for the longer events, 200 and 400 meters, the semilongitudinal sample shows a greater rate of decline. It is important to keep in mind that the semilongitudinal data comprise the participant's best time ever and the current best time. As such, there was no control for the amount of time that had elapsed between the two measures. Performance changes may have therefore been quite dramatic between the two measured points.

■ Table 10.5
Quadratic Beta Coefficients for Women and Men

Event	Semilongitudinal	Cross-Sectional
Women		
50 m	.007	.017
100 m	.011	.028
200 m	.345	.041
400 m	.714	.190
Men		
50 m	.007	.013
100 m	.011	.023
200 m	.066	.055
400 m	N/A	.090

The data from the track study are presented in table 10.6 for events in the 200, 400, 800, 1,500 and 5,000 meters. For all events (with the exception of the 5,000-m distance), the cross-sectional data show a greater rate of decline.

■ **Table 10.6**
Quadratic Beta Coefficients for the Male Track Athletes

Event	Semilongitudinal	Cross-Sectional
200 m	.012	.020
400 m	.009	.040
800 m	.012	.050
5,000 m	.016	.007

The most important finding from these studies is that the patterns of performance differed across age groups (and for swimming, across events). It appears then that although cross-sectional and longitudinal data may differ in the pattern of performance change they project, the actual pattern is very much influenced by the nature of the sporting event, as well as the age range and gender of the participants. Overall, cross-sectional studies do show greater performance decline with increasing age. Partitioning the relative influence of the various factors is an important goal and one we continue to pursue.

The Microstructure of Practice in Aging Athletes

Next we turn to the changes in practice patterns of Master athletes. Here we ask whether *how much* and *what* an athlete actually does in practice changes with age. An examination of the practice data from Weir et al. (in press) supports the notion that Master athletes generally spend less time practicing than younger elite swimmers (table 10.7).

That the experienced swimmers spend less time in practice than the younger swimmers is not a new or unexpected finding. Intuitively, older athletes may not be able to sustain such long workouts or simply have the time or motivation to sustain highly intensive training (Ericsson, 1991; Hagberg, Graves, Limacher, Woods, Cononie, Leggett, et al., 1989). However, what is not obvious from previous work is that when practice components are examined as a relative percentage of

■ **Table 10.7**
The Absolute Practice Time (Minutes) Spent in an Average Pool for Each of the Components of Practice Within Each Competition Level

Males	International	Junior national	Varsity	Masters
Mean age	20.4	15.5	19.8	53.0
Pool practice	128	99	109	78
Warm-up	28	24	26	14
Speed and power	26	22	29	23
Endurance	48	34	45	27
Technique	26	19	9	13

the total practice time, the differences among age and competition levels virtually disappear. When we compare young international-level swimmers to Master swimmers using cross-sectional data, the only difference appears to be the relative time spent on speed and power work (table 10.8). Across sports, a consistency also exists in the relative amount of time that athletes devote to each component of practice. As

■ **Table 10.8**
Relative Amount of Time Spent in Each Component of Track and Swimming Practice for Males

	Sport		
	Master track	Master swimming	International swimming
Warm-up	12%	19%	22%
Flexibility	5%	N/A	N/A
Speed and power	27%	30%	20%
Endurance	32%	34%	37%
Technique	4%	17%	21%
Weight training	20%	8%*	26%*

*Weight training in swimming was classified as dry-land training and is not included in the 100% category for pool practice time.

seen in table 10.8, Master swimmers and track athletes differ only with respect to technique work. It should be noted, however, that weight training in swimming was classified as dry-land training and was not included in the 100% category for pool practice time.

Although it appears that Master athletes devote less total time to practice, the structure of their practice in relative terms is quite similar to that used by the younger more elite athletes. In Weir et al. (in press) and Starkes et al. (1999), we concluded that practice patterns play a crucial role in buffering age-related effects and maintaining modestly high levels of athletic performance. The results revealed that national-level Master athletes trained 6.5 hours per week on average, which was considered to be an adequate level of training to moderate age-related effects. However, this training volume was still substantially less than the 11.2 hours of domain-specific and 7.2 hours of domain-related practice per week reported by younger expert runners (Young & Salmela, 2001). Would normal aging patterns be further moderated if researchers were able to sample athletes who had logged greater volumes of training? Some scholars would argue that older athletes are not capable of accumulating more weekly practice because their trainability is compromised physiologically by age-related mechanisms. Yet, if we return to the case of Ed Whitlock, we know he is capable of logging over two hours of training per day (McGowan, 2001). Some would claim that the motivational character of aging athletes does not belie their participation in large amounts of grueling, effortful training. Future research should certainly address this question.

Sampling, Retrospective Recall, and Why Access to Training Journals Is Important

We wish to briefly touch on a few of the current issues relevant to the research of expertise, especially in the domain of age-related performance. In the following sections, we discuss the challenge of finding appropriate subjects, and we also examine how training logs provide researchers with valuable data for reliable longitudinal research.

The Search for Truly Expert Master Athletes

The opportunity to demonstrate the dramatic moderation of normal aging patterns may be resolved by implementing novel approaches for sampling and research design. With regard to sampling, investigators must be diligent in their efforts to secure genuine older experts.

To date, the expert samples that have been examined could be recast critically as "local expert" musicians or national-level Masters athletes. To ascertain the functional relation between large amounts of maintenance training and the retardation of age-related decline, future research should target truly expert Master athletes in their specific domains. Unfortunately, if young experts are difficult to find and survey, then older experts are even more elusive. Case studies of international-level veterans may therefore be a suitable starting point for such endeavors.

The Search for Reliable Longitudinal Data

A potential criticism of much of the work to date is that data were collected using retrospective recall techniques, where athletes were asked to recall from memory their performance and practice times (Starkes, Helsen, & Jack, 2001). Given that some Master athletes have been competing since they were young adults, this method may prove problematic. However, an analysis of training journals eliminates this problem and thus allows a systematic evaluation of practice patterns across the competition span of an individual athlete. Researchers are certainly grateful that most runners keep extremely detailed training logs, even when they continue to run but no longer compete. As a result, investigators are able to draw confident conclusions as to the relation between performance and corresponding practice patterns.

Our most recent experimental protocol requires participants to consult their personal training journals to report typical weekly training volumes at serial intervals of their career—for example, every two or every five years following the beginning of systematic practice. For the same intervals, participants provide corresponding performance records in their event. To accurately extrapolate the volumes of practice, participants (again, working from their journals) supply estimates for the annual duration of their off-seasons and denote any seasons that were impaired either entirely or partially by injury or life events. All this information is then used to graphically reconstruct athletes' accumulated practice across their careers, and it is also used to speculate on how inflections in training amounts have influenced the corresponding performances. It is most useful to confine these studies to sports with a built-in metric of performance (e.g., track, swimming). Moreover, in track, scoring instruments such as the Mercier Tables (Mercier & Beauregard, 1994) allow observers to examine performance equivalencies across different distance events. To derive the Mercier Tables, the authors translated the 10th, 20th, 50th, and 100th world performances over a three-year period into fixed points and then subsequently transformed these data using linear regression. This tool has previously proven useful when assigning athletes to expert and novice performance groups (Young, 1998; Young & Salmela, 2001).

Case Studies of DR and BM

Here, the cases of two international-level Masters track athletes (DR and BM) are examined to highlight the potential of a within-subject methodological approach. The approach draws on the retrospective reconstruction protocol, and it is longitudinal in nature.

Athlete DR

DR recorded his career-best performance of 4:20 for the mile (equal to 697 Mercier points) at 41 years of age (see figure 10.2). This performance truly qualifies him as an international-level Master athlete,

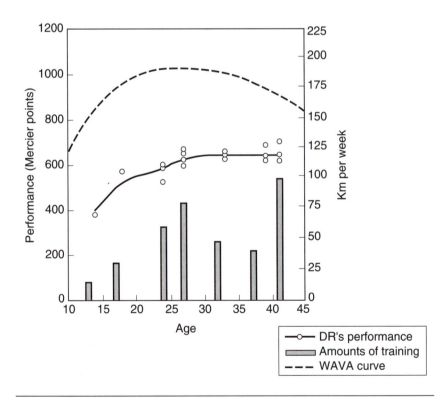

Figure 10.2   Kilometers per week run by DR and performance scores across his career. Best possible performance at each age is illustrated by the WAVA curve.

a 92% on the World Association of Veterans Athletes (WAVA) tables (WAVA, 1994). In fact, DR achieved his absolute best performance at a time in life when athletes are predicted to experience age-related decline and compromised trainability. The WAVA performance curve indicates that performance scores should decrease noticeably after 35 years of age. Schulz and Curnow (1988) noted that peak performance for runners in the mile is typically achieved much earlier at 24.8 years of age.

DR's performance has increased progressively across his running career. This trend is certainly an indicator of trainability, even into the middle ages of life. Contrary to the *preserved differentiation account* for aged expertise (Krampe & Ericsson, 1996; Salthouse, Babcock, Skovronek, Mitchell, & Palmon, 1990), the superior performance exhibited by DR does not reflect abilities that existed before the predicted onset of age-related decline. Rather, it is possible to surmise that acquired cognitive and physiological mechanisms are the prime mediator of DR's superior performance. Training data were obtained at roughly five-year intervals. DR indicated that he ceased training for a two-year period from age 20 to 22 years. Specifically, DR's investment in increasingly greater amounts of sport-specific training across his career-span, as well as his heavy investment in training (ages 40-41 years), may provide a plausible explanation for the acquisition of these mechanisms and for his substantial improvement in performance. DR invested 8.0 hours and 100 kilometers per week in training at the age of 41, which is substantially more than he devoted (5.9 hrs, 60 km per week) around the expected age of peak performance (age 30-35).

Aging patterns gleaned from cross-sectional data have been criticized for presenting decrements in performance that are much too accelerated (Weir et al., 2002; Starkes et al., 1999). Semilongitudinal within-subject data show that age-related patterns are probably moderated. DR's profile reaffirms the following notion: Age-related decline is tempered when it is observed in a subject who has maintained systematic practice that is uninterrupted across a running career.

Athlete BM

BM provides an example of superior performance in an older individual who has actively maintained continued levels of domain-specific practice. BM recorded his fastest performance times at 29 years of age (figure 10.3). However, at the age of 56, BM established a 10-km performance time of 34:23 (531 Mercier points), which is equivalent to 92%

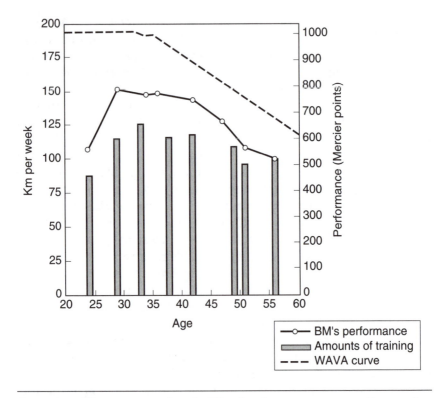

Figure 10.3   Kilometers per week run by BM and performance scores across his career. Best possible performance at each age is illustrated by the WAVA curve.

on the WAVA age-graded tables and indicative of international-level Master's status.

Whereas DR provided a remarkable profile of skill improvement in middle age, BM's profile relates more to Krampe and Ericsson's (1996) notion of selective maintenance in older age. BM's profile from the ages of 52 to 56 underscores the potential for trainability and the moderation of age-related decline in older athletes. He invested similar volumes of training at age 56 (8.33 hr and 100 km per week) as he did 30 years earlier (8.0 hr and 115 km per week). Despite being hampered by a nagging injury at 53, BM was able to rebound and heighten his training volumes at the ages of 54, 55, and 56. As a consequence, he was able to temper the effects of age-related decline. His intra-individual decrement in running performance was noticeably less than the decrements demarcated by the WAVA curve, a curve derived from cross-sectional data.

Intra-Individual Evolution of the Microstructure of Practice Across a Career

Earlier we indicated that the expertise literature has primarily focused on how much training athletes have accumulated across their career, but it has largely neglected exactly what athletes do in practice and how they go about structuring their practice environment. Once again, a numerical approach is important for outlining longitudinal aspects of athletes' investment; however, as a complement, empirical endeavors must also consider athletes' relative investment in the constituent activities of their training repertoire—that is, their microstructure of practice. Furthermore, investigators must consider how this microstructure evolves as a function of expertise.

Although research regarding practice microstructure and its acquisition is limited, an even greater dearth of research exists with respect to the training microstructure and its role in the maintenance of high-level performance. To date, only two cross-sectional studies have looked at the microstructure of training in aging athletes. These studies are static in that they fail to longitudinally trace how the microstructures evolved across years and decades of practice. Recall that Weir et al. (in press) found that Master swimmers allocated different amounts of time to the relative components of practice: 19% to warm-up, 30% to speed and power drills, 34% to endurance, and 17% to technique. When relative amounts of training were analyzed for each of the event distances, Masters swimmers continued to dedicate the largest proportion of practice to endurance activities. They devoted relatively less time to all other training components, most notably dry-land activities such as weight training.

Starkes and colleagues (1999) examined the practice microstructure of national-class Master track athletes. These athletes typically engaged in 1.5-hour training sessions that consisted of 12% warm-up, 5% flexibility, 27% speed and power drills, 32% endurance, 20% weight training, and only 4% work on special techniques. Overall, the Master athletes devoted approximately 60% of their training to aerobic activities. Young (1998) surveyed 60 young national-, provincial-, and club-level track athletes who had trained for a minimum of seven years. In contrast to Starkes and colleagues' Master athletes, the younger national-class track athletes devoted 42.2% of their total training time to aerobic activities. Provincial-class and less-skilled club athletes allocated 48.8% and 57.9% of their total practice time to aerobic activities, respectively. A comparison across these two samples of track athletes reveals that national-class Master athletes exhibit similar practice microstructures to younger, club-level athletes. Like the younger athletes, it may be that the best Master track athletes narrowly focus practice to concentrate more on aerobic activities. These types of changes in practice structure may, however, be partially dependent on the types of sport investigated. For example, track and field and swimming are more endurance-oriented sports, whereas other, more open sports may necessitate a greater preponderance of decision making and thus require different levels of anaerobic and aerobic performance.

A Longitudinal Case Study of EW's Practice Structure Over a 25-Year Period

Researchers need to conduct research on athletic expertise by tracing the intra-individual evolution of practice microstructure across an athletic career, rather than by simply observing profiles of training at static points in time. The following preliminary longitudinal case study traces the last 25 years of training for one highly skilled Master athlete. The data suggest that individual athletes may narrow the scope of their training activities over their career-span, even more than what is typically seen through cross-sectional analyses. An observation of athlete EW, a world-record holder at age 69, effectively delineates this pattern (figure 10.4).

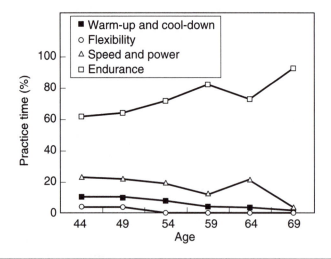

Figure 10.4   Percentage of practice time spent by EW in each of the components of track practice from 44 to 69 years of age.

Across his career EW has progressively reduced the amount of time he spends in warm-up/cool-down, flexibility, and speed and power work. At the same time, he has increased the relative proportion of time spent in endurance training to the point where at 69 years of age, it accounts for 93.8% of his total practice time.

These early findings with respect to the microstructure of practice in aging athletes once again reveal differences in data that are collected cross-sectionally with a large number of Masters athletes versus a longitudinal examination of one individual's career pattern. Cross-sectional studies indicate that Master athletes do practice much less, but the practice components are similar in terms of relative amounts performed within any one practice. EW's longitudinal data show that over time, he has narrowed his focus of practice so that it is now almost entirely endurance work. This narrowing of practice elements is not apparent in younger experts, who participate in a wide scope of training activities. If future research attests to this narrowing phenomenon, then the pursuant question should be why this happens. It is possible that Master athletes are compelled to alter their microstructure as a result of general and immutable age-related processes that compromise trainability. However, experimental studies have shown that specific physical activities can improve the functionality of virtually any physiological system, not just aerobic potential, even in older people (Spirduso, 1995).

Master athletes may alter their pattern of training to reflect changing motivational dispositions toward practice. In young athletes, experts and novices alike are well intentioned (yet a bit uninformed) in their approaches to practice (Deakin, 2001; Deakin, Starkes, & Allard, 1998; Starkes, 2000). Specifically, these athletes are far more likely to spend time on already well-learned elements than on elements needing remediation. Athletes will more typically opt for the comfort zone that the rehearsal of well-versed skills affords, rather than expending the effort to acquire or refine unstable skills. Runners' perceptions of their own training activities have indicated that endurance activities are significantly less effortful than other practice activities, such as speed and power drills or weight training (Young & Salmela, in press). A further issue to be explored is whether this narrowing actually serves to maximize trainability in older athletes.

Summary

Master athletes are a rich and untapped source for the study of expertise. They present our best hope for understanding how the natural, age-associated decline in one's performance may be tempered through continued physical training. Without a doubt, older experts can potentially retain much of their performance through what Krampe and Ericsson (1996) have termed *maintenance practice.* However, we need to be aware that data generated from cross-sectional analyses may produce a very different picture of aging and performance retention than will data that are generated from longitudinal sources. Cross-sectional data tend to overestimate the rates of decline seen in athletes over a long period. Cross-sectional analyses also illustrate that older athletes generally practice less, but the studies do not show changes in the relative amounts of what exactly is practiced. In contrast, case studies of a longitudinal nature reveal that although older athletes engage in generally lower amounts of practice than they did as younger experts, they also engage in a general narrowing of practice activities as well. Perhaps the narrowing of practice activities is related to their ability to retain performance, which may ultimately help minimize injury or maintain their level of motivation. We certainly hope that future research will help shed light on these intriguing questions.

EXPERTS' COMMENTS

Question

In this chapter, Starkes, Weir, and Young suggest that Master athletes who are experts can retain fairly high-performance levels with less practice per week (6.5 hours as opposed to 20-plus hours). They have also noted that as athletes age, they have a tendency to focus more on endurance training and less on technique, warm-up, and the like. What are your thoughts on this phenomenon?

Coach's Perspective: Nick Cipriano

My experience with high-performance wrestlers certainly confirms Starkes, Weir, and Young's findings that Master athletes who are experts can retain fairly high-performance levels with generally less practice per week. An apt example of this phenomenon is a wrestler whom I have personally coached for nearly 20 years and who is now well past his prime by at least 8 to 10 years. Yet, this individual has been a National Open finalist for the past eight years with as little as four to six hours of training a week. I marvel at his accomplishment and how gracefully he manages to defeat younger, yet equally skilled opponents, who are doing at least three times more training than he is. I believe the source of his success is largely related to his level of efficiency, superior strategy, and confidence. Although it may be different for other Master wrestlers, my observations generally confirm that older wrestlers who continue to compete beyond their peak years initiate fewer attacks—however, the attacks they do make have a high probability for success. Hence, they conserve their energy by limiting their exposure to situations that require a high expenditure of energy. In comparison to young wrestlers, older wrestlers rely less on speed and strength for successful execution of attacks and rely more on smooth, flowing tactical attacks. In essence, they appear to attack much slower, but they actually penetrate the opponent's defense with remarkable ease. Older wrestlers also make few mistakes. They exercise greater patience in carrying out a game plan, and they are less panicked by unexpected developments during the course of a match. The older athlete competes with a sense of confidence and control by reacting to developments with calmness and purpose.

Player's Perspective: Therese Brisson

Because I am closer to the end of my athletic career than the beginning, I was delighted to read this chapter by Starkes, Weir, and Young. They suggest that expert Master-level athletes can retain high levels of performance with less practice per week (6.5 hours as opposed to 20 or more hours). They also show that as an athlete ages, there is a tendency to focus more on endurance training and less on other areas. This is something that I have observed in my career and a fact of which many coaches are intuitively aware. For example, older athletes are often given more rest time than some of the younger athletes, partly because of a perception that older athletes need more rest (not sure this is true) and partly because the more experienced athletes seem to require less practice to maintain peak performance (of which I am convinced). More experienced athletes also tend to train smarter and more efficiently. They also invest more time in training that is cognitive in nature. That is, they spend less time doing physical training and more time thinking about the game and evaluating and planning performance. I find that I can accomplish more in a 40-minute workout than a less experienced athlete can accomplish in a 3-hour session.

One thing that amazes me (and that I have experienced first-hand) is the way more experienced athletes can endure more time away from training and competition and require less time to reach peak condition, compared to their less experienced counterparts. During the preparation period before the 2002 Winter Olympics, I sustained a serious concussion, which prevented me from doing any physical activity for 12 weeks. I resumed training only 7 weeks before our first game at the Olympics. The period of inactivity was so long and the symptoms of the injury were so pronounced that my training started with walking, which was humbling to say the least. I was able to make the jump from brain injury patient to Olympian in this very short period after such a long time away from training because I had 18 years of training behind me. I'm not sure that a less experienced athlete would have been ready. I think the other important element was my use of imagery training to re-hearse decision-making skills while I was injured. I complemented the imagery with live rehearsal training during competitions. I watched the games from behind the bench and followed a team-mate that played the same position I do (defense). I watched the player and made the same decisions that this player confronted during the course of the game (in effect, play the game from this player's perspective). This kind of recovery is not unusual among elite athletes. Many NHL players experience long periods away from training because of injury, yet they seem to be back in peak form within 2 weeks.

Part IV

Novel Ways of Examining the Characteristics of Expertise and Related Theories

THIS SECTION OF THE BOOK provides some novel ways of thinking about expertise that have not yet been considered. Much of our understanding of expertise has come from the study of musicians in conservatory structured learning programs or in the case of sport, from highly structured competitive youth programs typical of North American or Western European society. In Western societies, young athletes have access to facilities, coaching, and competition. Salmela and Moraes (chapter 11) consider the case of how expert athletes are produced in developing countries that may not be able to provide extensive facilities and coaching. Their examination of the development of soccer in Brazil forces us to examine preconceived notions of how best to produce top athletes.

The literature on expertise is full of examples of how experts are afforded certain performance advantages because of skill—by perceiving the correct information quickly, by making decisions more efficiently, by conserving energy in movement, and so on. Beilock, Wierenga, and Carr (chapter 12) are the first to demonstrate that expert performance also has a downside. One such aspect is that expert athletes lose the ability to recall procedural aspects of their movements. This chapter is important from a theoretical perspective because it suggests how movements may become automated, which has ramifications for our understanding of the control structures that underlie movement. As Beilock et al. note, their findings also have implications for understanding how attention is best trained and focused during performance.

The last chapter in this section by Beek, Jacobs, Daffertshofer, and Huys (chapter 13) broadens our perspective on how best to study expert performance. As has been noted on several occasions throughout the book, the vast majority of research conducted on sport expertise to date has been influenced by the cognitive approach, which has particular limitations for studying movement-based behaviors. Dynamical systems theory and ecological psychology are often viewed as difficult theories to employ in real-world situations; likewise, they are rarely viewed in conjunction. Beek et al. provide a fascinating chapter on how the theories may be used together for their metaphoric value in describing expert performance. This chapter is a wonderful tutorial on dynamical systems and ecological psychology, and it provides practical examples of how the theories may shed new light on typical situations in sport.

Chapter 11

Development of Expertise

■ ■ ■ ■ ■

The Role of Coaching, Families, and Cultural Contexts

John H. Salmela

Luiz Carlos Moraes

> To get men to do things that they don't want to do in order to achieve things that they want to achieve. That's what coaching is all about.
>
> Tom Landry, Dallas Cowboys football coach

The study of coaching in North America can be traced back over 75 years when Coleman Griffiths wrote *The Psychology of Coaching* in 1926, which was based on known psychological principles of that era and actual coaching practices. The coaching profession has been more recently studied in terms of leadership styles (Chelladurai, 1980), coaching behaviors (Smith, Smoll, & Hunt, 1977), and coaches' needs and education (Gould, Giannini, Krane, & Hodge, 1990). Researchers have also considered the field of coaching within the expertise perspective via qualitative analyses so that they can better understand perceptions of training and competition (Côté, Salmela, & Russell, 1995), organizational tasks and educational roles (Côté & Salmela, 1996; Miller & Salmela, in press), communication skills (G.A. Bloom, Schinke, & Salmela, 1998), mentoring (G.A. Bloom, Durand-Bush, Schinke, & Salmela, 1998), coaches' personal characteristics (G.A. Bloom & Salmela, 2000), gender and coaching (Edwards, 2001), and cultural effects (Moraes & Salmela, 2001). Thus, the purpose of this chapter is to bring together these diverse contributions to better understand the coaching process in relation to family influences from a broad, cross-cultural perspective and to suggest paths for the optimal development of this domain of human expertise.

Although sport coaches in most countries enjoy a position of national prestige and (in the professional ranks) a handsome salary, there is scant research that outlines the actual tasks, roles, and knowledge structures that are central to their professional success. In some earlier publications on coaching, several intuitively attractive efforts have been advanced regarding what was believed was central to both the art and science of expert coaching. For example, Worthington (1984) advanced that the coaching process involved the interaction between knowing, organizing, coaching, and observing, whereas Fairs (1987) reflected similar observations but suggested that coaching was essentially made up of observing, diagnosis, and assessment, which was followed by setting goals, planning actions, and finally implementing and evaluating the plan. These broad overviews are useful when trying to conceptualize the exact nature of the complexities of the coaching process.

So that we can better understand the coaching process from an empirical perspective, we interviewed a variety of Canadian expert coaches over a 10-year period. To do so, we used open-ended, semistructured techniques to gain knowledge on their perceptions of how they personally evolved over their careers to become outstanding leaders and teachers of exceptional performers in sport. As designated by their respective national sport governing bodies, 55 coaches participated in the various studies in the sports of gymnastics, basketball, volleyball, field hockey, ice hockey, swimming, synchronized swimming, judo, and figure skating. Each interview lasted between an hour and a half to seven hours, and each was transcribed and inductively analyzed using qualitative data analysis procedures as outlined by Côté, Salmela, Baria, and Russell (1993).

Based on the in-depth interviews with expert Canadian gymnastics coaches, a coaching model was recently suggested by Côté, Salmela, Trudel, Baria, and Russell (1995), who used a grounded, inductive approach to form it. As the result of the analyses on the daily operations of successful coaches, a mental model, or the knowledge structure of the coaching process, was advanced. With regard to the initial goal of each coach—from winning an Olympic gold medal to developing high-level athletes to creating a discovery and learning environment in youth sport—three central processes were then advanced. First, the organization of short- and long-term goals, practices, and behaviors provided the game plan for athlete development. Second, appropriate training procedures were introduced at the physical, technical, tactical, and psychological levels, which were all in line with the goals of the previous step. The results of these two phases were then tested in competition. Afterward, the loop was closed again at the organizational level through a reassessment for future adjustments in training and competition.

Given that the coaching process has a formidable interpersonal component, two peripheral processes were suggested to interact and affect the success of the aforementioned central components. The first component was simply the characteristics of the coach and the athletes with regard to the influence they hold on the coaching process. The second peripheral component comprised the cultural factors within any given country, region, or even club-level microclimate in sport, which also had an impact on the total coaching process (figure 11.1). Although many of the components of the Coaching Model are analogous to those reported by Worthington (1984) and Fairs (1987), the present contribution was not based on intuition, but on qualitative data collected from expert gymnastics coaches. It was then validated for authenticity of this model with the same interviewed coaches, and it has since been shown to be applicable, with more importance being reported to the sport environment in both team (G.A. Bloom, 1997; G.A. Bloom & Salmela, 2000) and combat sports (Moraes, 1998; Moraes & Salmela, 2001).

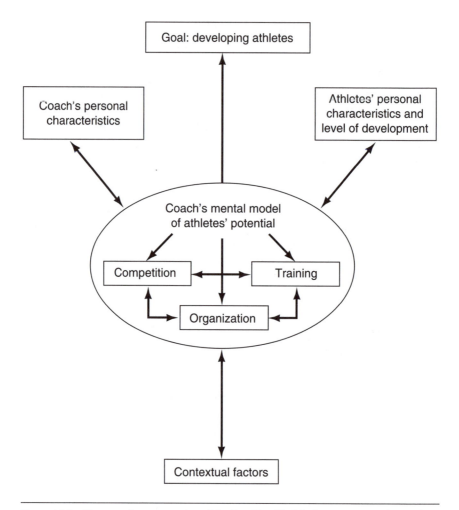

Figure 11.1 The mental representation of the Coaching Model of expert gymnastics coaches.

Adapted, by permission, from J. Côte et al., 1995, "The coaching model: A grounded assessment of expert gymnastic coaches' knowledge," *Journal of Sport and Exercise Psychology* 17: 1-17.

Coaching Within the Expert Performance Perspective

Research on the development of exceptional performance has shown that performers in sport and other domains must invest over 10 years of deliberate practice, or goal-directed practice, with the specific aim of performance improvement (Ericsson, 1996; Ericsson, Krampe, &

Tesch-Römer, 1993). Since deliberate practice is believed to be effortful and sometimes unenjoyable, athletes who engage in it must overcome the effort, resource, and motivational constraints of training. These often severe constraints limit most people's excelling in sport and other domains by their failure to carry out deliberate practice activities, which then results in a tendency for most people to drift toward more leisurely activities, such as play and games. Thus, it appears essential that one necessary condition for the attainment of superior performance is the presence of a knowledgeable and demanding monitor of daily performance activities in the form of a coach or mentor.

The argument of whether athletes are born or made has more recently leaned toward a nurturist perspective based on the seminal retrospective recall research of B.S. Bloom (1985), who interviewed 120 experts in science, the arts, and sport, as well as their parents, teachers, and coaches. The complex interplay between athletes, parents, and coaches was shown to exist during the three proposed phases of their athletic careers: during the early years of their initiation to sport, the middle years of development (when deliberate practice predominated), and the late stage when perfection of the sport activity was fine-tuned. As the athletes passed through each stage, their attitudes, activity patterns, and goals delicately (and universally) interacted with the roles of their parents and various specialized coaches.

Reconsidering the Socioeconomic Contextual Factors of Coaching and Parenting

One must now ask whether Tom Landry's definition of coaching is universally applicable within all cultural contexts. It must be remembered, for example, that in B.S. Bloom's data set, the selected athletes were either from swimming or tennis, two disciplines that are considered middle- to upper-middle-class sporting activities (Gruneau, 1999). Parents in fact did reshape their personal, family, and social lives to accommodate the demands of these time-consuming competitive sports in conjunction with providing a sound education for their children/athletes. Similarly, Côté (1999) recently reported that across the career phases of developing elite rowers, the parents showed a great deal of interest toward their child's participation, they helped them deal with setbacks, and they demonstrated differential interest for the most skilled family member—while at the same time making considerable time and financial commitments. Durand-Bush (2000), who studied multiple Olympic or World champions in Canada (along with their parents and coaches), also demonstrated that parents provided their children with the finances and guidance to attain the necessary physical and coaching resources so that they could become the best in their field, while at the same time allowing them to relocate to better coaching environments in the country. In addition, Salmela, Young, and Kallio (2000) demonstrated how the roles of the athletes, coaches, and parents evolved across their respective careers and levels of involvement in the sport within the context of "First World" sport. The luxury of such environments, where skilled coaches were readily available throughout their sporting careers and where parents were committed to redefining their lives to the demands of their child's training, might not be the norm in developing countries that are less sound, both educationally and financially.

Coaching in Developing Countries

One factor that has yet to be considered is the success of uncoached, single-parent athletes from lower socioeconomic environments—such as, for example, Central American boxers, urban American basketball players, and South American soccer players. In these situations, excellence may stem more from the potential economic benefits of success in professional sport, from greater levels of mass participation, and from needing lower resource costs. By leading practice-dominated lives in sport and by receiving the aid of unstructured peer teaching, these athletes may use these forces to overcome, or even surpass, the benefits of structured coaching.

So, it is not clear whether B.S. Bloom's (1985) middle-class model of coaching applies to sports practiced by lower socioeconomic classes, such as soccer in Brazil and in other developing countries in South America or Africa, where access to highly specialized coaching cannot be taken for granted across their athletic careers.

Recently, pre-elite Brazilian soccer players (16-18 years old) who were selected to the junior professional developmental teams of Cruzeiro, Atletico, and America in the state of Minas Gerais were studied (Moraes, Salmela, & Rabelo, 2000). This sample consisted of 22 players selected from approximately 3,000 annual tryouts. Coaches and family members were asked to detail the nature of their experiences with the players up until their selection for these professional teams (Rabelo, 2001). Moraes et al. (2000) found that most of the young soccer players who were selected to play on the junior selection sides of these three professional soccer teams reported that before being selected, they had little familial support or formal coaching, but they dedicated all of their childhood time in practicing soccer to the detriment of their participation in other play activities. However, the lack of coaching for the development of their skills appeared to be compensated by their volume of practice time and the anticipated financial rewards of a professional career. Exceptional performance seemed to emerge through the sheer volume of participating candidates, and it appeared to override their lack of coaching. Perhaps a great volume of unsupervised practice could make up for more specialized coaching over fewer hours when the outcome is so appealing and potentially lucrative.

In subsequent interviews with their current professional coaches, Rabelo (2002) discovered that these coaches had no contact with the families of the players and that most of them had little formal coaching education; however, they were all former professional players. The organization of training took place for one day yearly, along with 20-minute weekly sessions. This seeming lack of formal organization was compensated by three-hour daily practices in the morning, with two additional afternoon sessions, all without the aid of assistant coaches. In contrast, expert Canadian coaches reported that they carried out detailed daily practice planning, but they certainly could not commit their athletes, nor themselves, to the training volume seen in Brazilian soccer training (Salmela, 1996).

To put Brazilian training and support practices within a broader perspective beyond sport, a methodology previously used by Davidson, Howe, Moore, and Sloboda (1996) was modified and used with structured interviews to study the role of parents of musically skilled performers. As a comparison, the parents of female rhythmic gymnasts in an elite sport club were similarly interviewed (Vianna, Moraes, Salmela, & Mourthé, 2001). This provided a subset of upper-middle-class parents and coaches, who could then be compared with those of the soccer players studied earlier (Moraes et al., 2000). For example, within the Brazilian soccer context, the majority of these players were from poor, rural environments where 80% of the total family monthly earnings was between $150 and $375 and 65% had only primary school education. In comparison, 40% of the parents of the gymnasts had an upper-middle-class status and earned between $1,500 and $3,000 per month. Of that group, 40% earned $3,000 or more, and 25% had secondary or university education. Even though 65% of the gymnasts' parents had only primary education, their earning powers in a major city were still considerably higher than that in the rural setting of the soccer players.

Rabelo, Moraes, and Salmela (2001) also discovered, in separate interviews with the parents of this same sample of soccer players, that the players received only minimal coaching until they reached the professional ranks as juniors but that they played and practiced an enormous amount of time. In fact, 85% of them reported that playing soccer occupied all of their leisure time. In contrast, all gymnasts received specialized coaching from the beginning of their careers. During their leisure time, 75% did activities apart from gymnastics. The latter is in agreement with Durand-Bush (2000), who reported that both multiple Olympic and World champions in Canada in various sports spent their youth discovering a variety of other domains and only in a few cases were totally devoted to their selected activities. Côté (1999) described this early period as the "sampling years," during which young athletes tried out a number of sport and leisure activities and shared their downtime from sport in other domains throughout their primary sport career. Both of the latter authors agreed that sampling other sport activities, besides their primary one, allowed these athletes to develop a broader skill and fitness base and that these diversions may have contributed to their commitment to the sport.

Given that the practice and play of the soccer players was largely unsupervised, Rabelo et al. (2001) reported that 78.3% of the families said that their son's activity in soccer did not change any aspect of their daily life routines while only 17% reported making adjustments to allow them to participate in sport. In sharp contrast, 84% of the gymnasts' families indicated that they were forced to reschedule the family's daily routine to accommodate their daughter's participation in sport (Vianna et al., 2001). These results are similar to those found both by Durand-Bush (2000) and Côté (1999), who reported that there was a crucial interplay in the adjustment of daily schedules by both parents and siblings with modified meal times, transportation to practices and games, and in some cases, relocation of the athlete within or even to another city for improved facilities or coaching.

Whereas 24% of the gymnasts' parents took time to interact with the coaches regarding their daughter's progress, no interaction was reported in the case of the soccer parents since coaching was almost nonexistent, but about one third of the fathers told their sons about their previous experiences and insights in playing the game. Finally, the gymnastics parents understandably maintained daily contact with their daughters at all levels of performance whereas 50% of the soccer parents saw their sons every one to three months at the time of the interviews (because they had relocated hundreds of kilometers away to the urban metropolis).

In sum, the levels of parental involvement and the intimacy of the coaching process (during their 20 hours of weekly contact in the gym with these Brazilian gymnasts and their parents) were similar to the degree of personal investment that Davidson et al. (1996) found with elite, developing British musicians, as well as what Durand-Bush (2000) and Côté (1999) reported with expert Canadian athletes. In fact, the original results reported by B.S. Bloom (1985) with athletes, artists, and scientists showed that this close interplay between performers and their parents and coaches facilitated the achievement of their exceptional performance.

The present situation in Brazilian soccer is somewhat more intriguing. Until the athletes have reached 16 or 17 years of age, they have received little or no structured coaching, but they have dedicated their entire leisure time to playing the game in informal, often disadvantaged conditions (i.e., without a proper ball, shoes, or a playing surface). But soccer is king in Brazil, and everyone follows the game year-round on television. Tryouts for professional teams in the major cities involve thousands of candidates per semester, who often travel from the countryside at substantial family expense to the professional club, although only a handful of players are selected. Even though they did not receive supervised coaching, these soccer players did, however, practice passionately, more than most musicians in their youth. This self-directed learning seems to suggest a form of "soccer Darwinism," where only the best survive.

So, a partial disparity exists in the model of coaching expertise within the Brazilian context where soccer aspirants from lower-class backgrounds (Rabelo et al., 2001) were compared with those from upper-middle class ranks in tennis (Vianna 2002) and rhythmic gymnastics (Vianna et al., 2001). Soccer players had little formal coaching, few financial resources, and often no family support. Vianna et al. (2001), however, found that the level of parental and coaching support reported by B.S. Bloom (1985) was comparable in this upper-middle-class Brazilian environment.

Coaching in Developed Countries

Smith and Smoll (1990) found that American youth sport athletes greatly benefited from coaching and that the coach was an important factor in the development of young athletes. For example, the two observed behavioral dimensions of supportiveness and instructiveness were positively related to the players' attitudes toward their coach, sport, and teammates. Their research also revealed that trained and untrained coaches differed in their behaviors. Trained coaches communicated more effectively than untrained coaches, were evaluated more positively by players, and noted that their players acquired significant increases in self-esteem when compared with the previous year. Coaches who were interviewed in Canada were shown to be the principal providers of both physical and human resources, which allowed athletes to overcome the constraints of effort and motivation, as was demonstrated in the Coaching Model (Côté et. al, 1995). Expert coaches of elite athletes also appeared to advance through a predictable series of developmental stages from athlete (usually not as top performers) to becoming exceptional coaches (Schinke, G.A. Bloom, & Salmela, 1995). As well, no unitary quality, aside from a great passion and willingness to improve their current operational standards, appeared to tie this process together (G.A. Bloom & Salmela, 2000). Finally, while maximizing deliberate practice, they also regularly invested considerable energy in perfecting their own skills and knowledge base, and they sought further educational opportunities regarding their present coaching procedures (McPherson & Salmela, 1997; Moraes, 1996). Crucial lessons were learned from mentoring, dealing with setbacks, and creating innovative solutions to complex problems over their coaching careers.

G.A. Bloom (1997) found that the Coaching Model applied as well to expert coaches in field hockey, ice hockey, basketball, and volleyball, although the nature of the microstructure of this process, especially for the athlete and coach interactions, was extremely complex for team sports. Given the dynamics of these open-skill sports, it was clear that the nature of the ongoing coach-athlete interactions was considerably more complex than in coaching the closed sport of gymnastics, because of the number of players involved and the continual interplay among the coach, players, opposition, and even referees (Côté et al., 1995). These coach-athlete interactions included the following: the evolving personal characteristics of the coach (G.A. Bloom & Salmela, 2000), the development of communication skills (G.A. Bloom, Schinke, & Salmela, 1998), the mentoring of young assistant coaches (G.A. Bloom, Durand-Bush, Schinke, & Salmela, 1998), and team building (Schinke, Draper, & Salmela, 1997). To add to the complexity of these interpersonal relationships, these expert team-sport coaches reported a fairly consistent evolution of their personal development and the evolving nature of their interactions with athletes at various stages of their own coaching careers (Schinke, G.A. Bloom, & Salmela, 1995).

Moraes (1998) and Moraes and Salmela (2001) also found a good fit for the Coaching Model with expert judo coaches for those in Canada who originated from either Japan, Europe, or Canada. However, it was found within this sample that the contextual factors were very influential. The Japanese and European coaches had to adapt their personal beliefs and actions, forged in countries where the sport was most popular, to the demands of coaching within the more liberal, permissive Canadian judo context. The rigorous training procedures that were common to the practice of judo in other cultures were not found acceptable to Canadian judokas, and the coaches had to make personal adjustments or risk having the athletes quit the sport. The cultural influences on the contextual factors were reinforced by Kitamura, Salmela, and Moraes (2001), who found that Japanese soccer coaches conceptualized the coaching process like the Canadian coaches, except for the nature of coach-athlete relationships, where the sanctions for tardiness or social misbehaviors were much more strict within the Japanese context.

In stark contrast to coaching within the Canadian context, d'Arripe-Longueville, Fournier, and Dubois (1998) found that authoritative judo coaches in France often used what in Canada and elsewhere might be questionable interpersonal methods with their elite teams. These included inciting rivalries, giving verbal abuse, showing interpersonal indifference, demonstrating preferential treatment of judokas, and direct conflict with them. The particular context of judo in France allows such coaching behaviors because (a) they have a large pool of developing athletes, (b) the sport and its results are highly praised and rewarded in this country, and (c) they share a common goal to become and remain one of the best in the world. Although the Coaching Model still applies to French judo coaching, its dimensions differ considerably from the Canadian judo context, especially for coach-athlete relationships.

Since the field of coaching has been found to be a male-dominated domain (Weiss & Stevens, 1993), Edwards (2001) outlined an insightful, New Zealand–based perspective on the gender bias. Specifically, it centered on the predominance of males who coach female international field hockey teams. The "gender archetype" model was developed using participant observation with semistructured interviews and questionnaires. Edwards showed how this model explained the coaches' characteristics as they related to "gendered beliefs and attitudes, physical myths and realities, confidence and competence, and sex and sexuality" (p. iii). This interaction of the coaches' gender and the particular cultural context is a fascinating new area of study within the coaching process.

In developed countries, the human resource of quality coaching has been shown to be one of the best predictors of success over the careers of elite middle-distance runners (Young & Salmela, 2002). Runners who began working later in their careers with structured coaching performed less well after nine years of training than those who were required to submit themselves to rigorous training regimes during their adolescence. Middle-distance running apppears to be a somewhat boring and effortful activity when carried out at high levels of intensity. It is clear that the presence of an expert coach enabled these successful athletes to overcome the effortful constraints noted by Ericsson et. al (1993) through the provision of motivational, physical, and personal resources during effective training.

As Moraes and Salmela (2001) found, the Coaching Model was still robust when applied to coaches from extremely diverse cultures and contexts, such as Japan and Canada. However, in even more homogeneous, but nuanced contexts, such as those of Canada and the United States, Miller and Salmela (in press) found that Canadian university coaches saw their goals in coaching to be mainly directed toward an athlete's personal development, or academic achievement as an athlete-centered priority. These Canadian university coaches chose to be a person-centered teacher, rather than an outcome-focused coach, which was reported to be present in the American context (Locke & Massengale, 1978).

Although it has been demonstrated that effective youth coaching not only facilitates performance but also enhances personal development (Smith & Smoll, 1990), a case can also be made for less formalized coaching during the early years, or what Côté (1999) called the "specializing years." Carlsson (1993) demonstrated that a number of top-level international Swedish athletes in tennis (including Stefan Edberg), ice hockey, and swimming did not make their teams during early adolescence nor did they receive highly structured coaching. Nevertheless, they eventually reached the top by other means. They returned to their hometowns and continued practicing with a local-level coach, but they spent more time playing, experimenting, and having fun under light supervision in informal practice within more naturalistic settings before partaking in the "investment years" of deliberate practice.

It appears that models for the development of exceptional performance and the role of coaching in developed countries must be reconsidered within contexts where the potential rewards for exceptional performance are great, the number of participants are numerous, and the resources of both a physical and personal nature are minimal. However, consideration of the appropriate training strategies to develop effective coach-education programs that cover all cultural contexts is not very evident. Although these programs are believed to be effective for countries such as Australia, Canada, Germany, Great Britain, and the United States, the exportation of such knowledge, strategies, and skills has proven unwieldy when applied to the global community (Salmela & Durand-Bush, 2001).

Conditions for the Training of Expert Coaches

Let us consider for a moment the sufficient and necessary conditions for learning for both athletes and coaches. Within the context of athletes' learning and performing, Ericsson's (1996) suggestion cuts to the quick: ". . . that for effective learning the subject must acquire mechanisms supporting reasoning, planning, prediction, and expectation in order to generate feedback and effective error diagnosis with appropriate corrections" (p. 39). These learning demands appear to be a daunting task to carry out by oneself and beg the trained supervision of an expert coach. But, perhaps an even more challenging task within such a learning paradigm is to determine the most appropriate set of cognitive and emotional skills, effective knowledge bases, and interpersonal abilities required for expert coaching, and how they can best be transmitted to novice coaches, especially in developing societies.

Gould, Giannini, Krane, and Hodge (1990) examined a number of elite coaches' needs in coach education and coach development. One of their findings, which was particularly disturbing to most academics, was that coaching textbooks and seminars were the least important sources of coaching information. The elite coaches felt that the two most important knowledge sources that helped them develop their coaching styles were the constant adaptation of their own coaching experience and the observation of other successful coaches.

Moraes (1996) was able to reflect on the collective oral wisdom of 22 of Canada's elite coaches of team sports when asked the question: "How do you believe that we can facilitate and accelerate the learning processes of upcoming, aspiring coaches?" This simple query resulted in some elemental steps from which the educational process and its study can at least begin its journey, as expressed in their coaches' own words.

General Academic Training

It is clear that the existence of university-based schools of physical education, human kinetics, or kinesiology provide the necessary time and resources for optimal learning, especially if they include coaching programs of study. Nevertheless, the acquired bases in human anatomy, physiology, biomechanics, pedagogy, and sport psychology are only the foundations on which sport-specific knowledge must be built:

> Education is not always a panacea, but I think it has really helped me as a coach because you need that background

first. Maybe that is why I have changed so much, because I had a physical education background. But at the time, I didn't want to teach physical education, I wanted to coach. (Moraes, 1996, p. 212)

However, tertiary education is not always available for coaches, especially in developing countries, but other options are certainly available in more short-term settings.

Formal Coach-Centered Learning

Within many Western countries, the sport authorities have acknowledged that sport-centered, even sport-specific, schools of training and education are central to the development of sport achievement, from the local to the international levels. These programs are best carried out in academic, technical, and even social settings to enhance learning of all types:

> As a beginning coach I remember one of the things my colleagues constantly said to me was: "Make sure you get into the coaching certification program." The contacts made through the coaching program become very important . . . I always learn from coaching courses, and a lot of the learning comes from the people you are studying with. (Moraes, 1996, pp. 208-209)

Although classroom and social experiences provide valuable tools for the coaching process, the best coaches always emphasize the necessity of applying training theory knowledge acquired in the classroom with appropriate and supervised coaching experiences learned in the gym:

> When I did Level 3 assessment of coaches, I actually sat on their benches. I listened to what they said to the athletes at half-time and to their pre-game talks. I listened to their post-game talks and then we would sit down and I would discuss all aspects of the game. It was a real exchange of information. It is valuable for me, because I feel that I have something to contribute and recognize the growth that I have had as a coach. You don't realize that something that is automatic to you, like analyzing an opponent, is not automatic to a young coach. The opportunity to talk is valuable for me, and I think this kind of interchange between coaches needs to go on far earlier. (Moraes, 1996, p. 209)

By putting developing coaches in such educational environments, learning institutions ensure a greater probability that the coaches will have (and seek out) the multiple coaching resources that already exist in bookstores, magazines, and now on the Internet:

> I set out on a mission. I started reading everything that I could. The first book that I read was *Blitz Basketball*. The author was a long-time coach who won a lot of championships. Very up tempo, full of court pressing basketball. I think that I latched onto that because it was exciting. I was aggressive and most of the girls didn't play that style yet. I think it hid the fact that I wasn't very sound, I didn't have the fundamental background yet, so I think that I compensated by using the material from the book. (Moraes, 1996, pp. 212-213)
>
> I had this guy following me around with a video camera for three or four weeks. I remember the representative saying it was very valuable for other coaches. They see you in action, hear you, see how you take a guy aside, and deal with a problem he is having with a play and how you organize it. (Moraes, 1996, p. 213)

Unfortunately, such tools have not always been universally available, especially in developing nations where valuable reading or audiovisual materials are often in a foreign language. But with the advent of the Internet, most countries can access at a lower cost previously inaccessible materials on coaching. Still, one resource that is universally accessible in any country of the world, rich or poor, is experienced coaches who speak their native language.

Networking and Mentoring

Constant interaction with peers has been shown to be one of the best sources of learning for expert coaches (Gould et al., 1990). Sharing of knowledge with other passionate coaches provides a rich forum for better understanding the complexities of coaching, as well as testing the effectiveness of one's particular ways of interacting and behaving in practice and games:

> I think coaches have a great opportunity at tournaments to observe other coaches in action, and other teams practicing. There's a great laboratory in a lot of rinks in this city. I see some coaches taking a look at drills. It always surprises me that more coaches don't do that. (Moraes, 1996, pp. 215-216)

The field of coaching is based on sport-science principles from the hard sciences, such as biomechanics and exercise physiology, but what might be more central is the development of the artistic side of the process, which can only be learned from the close interaction with other expert coaches in the mentoring process:

> I went to the national team. The years under the influence of the Olympic coach was like going to school. It can be compared to a guy who goes to university four years and graduates with a master's degree. He taught me how to coach, what coaching was all about. (Moraes, 1996, p. 217)
>
> I do have an interest in being with master coaches. I can see the potential for enrichment because each coach at the master level has a particular quirk or particular design that they bring to the game. For instance, I can name some coaches who are among the worst people I have ever met. I have spent time with them socially, and they can be absolute bores or bullies. Yet, I went to their clinics and also found that they can be extremely organized people, applying focus and concentration, despite the repetition of practice and work overload. (Moraes, 1996, p. 221)

Finally, the task of self-reflection is crucial in honing one's methods and practices in the coaching profession. Since there is no clear set of recipes that define coaching, what appears to be essential for personal development is questioning one's current beliefs and actions:

> One of the most important statements that I have made is "Think about what you are doing and don't accept it. Once you become comfortable with the basic idea of coaching, don't be afraid to change it totally and do something that fits your team." (Moraes, 1996, p. 221)

In sum, it is clear that detailed attention must be given to various forms of coach education, both formal and informal. It has been shown that even in countries with relatively small populations, such as the former East Germany, Norway, and Australia, that this formula can produce spectacular results on a per capita basis at the Olympic level in terms of medal standings. The ideal formula appears to be one where formal postsecondary coaching education is combined with hands-on, supervised practical experiences in actual training contexts.

However, in certain developing countries, these resources may not be available; therefore, coaches must turn to their colleagues and mentors less formally through information sharing and performance monitoring. Unfortunately, this practice does not seem to be common, in Brazil at least, where "trade secrets" are rarely shared and where past playing experience appears to be the key element (Moraes et al., 2000). It would appear that the availability of unlimited information via the Internet both on sport sciences and coaching has now removed this barrier to these resources.

Summary

Coaching is undoubtedly what could be termed an *ill-defined task*. Although certain attempts have been made to provide some order to the coaching process (Côté et al., 1995), the amount of variation within each of the constituent categories is tremendous. As is the case in pedagogy (Berliner, 1986), pulling together all of the necessary elements has proven to be a daunting task. The complexity of the process increases when coaching is put within its broadest perspective on an international scale, where the access to physical and human resources may vary. In addtion, the nature of the predominant values of each culture colors the total process (Gruneau, 1999). The present chapter was an attempt to shed some light on the complexities of expert coaching from this broader cultural perspective.

EXPERTS' COMMENTS

▪ *Question*

In this chapter, Salmela and Moraes note that all research to date on sport experts has been conducted with athletes from developed countries, for whom access to coaching, facilities, and the like is readily available. They consider the case of soccer in Brazil, which has a significant grassroots participation; however, young athletes typically have no access to skilled coaching or appropriate facilities. Nevertheless, we cannot dispute the level of expertise attained by many Brazilian soccer players. You've coached in developing countries and worked with high-level athletes from impoverished areas. What role do you feel coaching and facilities play, and how do the particpants in developing countries overcome the lack of such amenities?

■ *Coach's Perspective: Nick Cipriano*

In my experience, competent coaching leadership is an important component in the overall process of developing a freestyle wrestler to a high level of expertise. Although well-equipped facilities are certainly advantageous, they are by no means vitally important. The good coach is able to improvise and make do with whatever facilities are available and will develop a training program that makes the best use of available facilities. Certainly such is the case in many countries around the world that are noted for having inadequate facilities, yet who regularly produce world and Olympic champions. More important than facilities in the development of expert wrestlers, in my judgment, is the need to create a large training group and have two or more individuals vying for the same weight-class representation—in essence, creating intragroup competition. The inherent competition within the training group creates a fertile ground for improvement to take place and for volitional qualities that include, but are not limited to, perseverance, will power, and determination to emerge. The coach plays a critical role in fostering the development of volitional qualities, in addition to inspiring the athletes to practice for the long term. Intragroup competition is likely a key component in the development of soccer players in countries such as Brazil, with the difference being that the training group has no formal membership and that training is less unstructured.

■ *Player's Perspective: Therese Brisson*

Salmela and Moraes point out that all motor expertise research to date has focused on athletes from developed countries, where access to coaching, facilities, and equipment is common. Developing nations such as Brazil have strong grassroots participation in soccer but little access to coaching, facilities, and equipment. Brazil, however, has produced many expert soccer players. These observations are important because they clearly indicate that there is no one-size-fits-all approach to developing motor expertise. For this reason, I have always been opposed to the cookie-cutter approach of developing and evaluating high-performance sport programs. What works in one sport for a given set of athletes living in a particular country and culture may not necessarily work elsewhere.

I would say that good coaching is an important factor in elite athlete development. However, many athletes never had good coaching, but they developed great skills; many athletes have quality coaching, but they never develop athletic excellence. An important factor in the development of elite athletes is the training group. The Olympic Oval in Calgary, used in the 1988 Winter Olympics, is an example of the Canadian solution to creating what I call *cultures of excellence.* Speed skaters, hockey players, bobsledders, swimmers, and track-and-field athletes all train in groups at the same facility. Athletes at similar levels in their development train together on a daily basis. The less experienced athletes learn from the more skilled, and those who are pushing to get to the top challenge the more skilled athletes on a daily basis. Developing athletes are exposed to role models. In this environment they learn how to approach training, competition, and adversity. Training groups at the Oval have high-performance coaches and sport science and sports medicine support, but the critical factor is the interaction with other athletes and the daily challenges and learning that presents. Soccer is part of Brazilian culture, and mass participation creates cultures of excellence for developing soccer expertise. I would say the same of cross-country skiing in some of the Nordic countries. An athlete needs the support of a training group or the guidance of good coaching; both of these factors together create the most ideal training situation.

Chapter **12**

Memory and Expertise

■ ■ ■ ■ ■

What Do Experienced Athletes Remember?

Sian L. Beilock • Sarah A. Wierenga
Thomas H. Carr

Examinations of the memory structures associated with novice and well-learned skill performance shed light on the cognitive substrate governing performance at high levels of skill execution across diverse cognitive and sensorimotor skill domains. From the chess studies of De Groot (1946/1978) and Chase and Simon (1973) to more recent research in the sensorimotor domains of basketball, field hockey, and dance (for a review, see Starkes, Helson & Jack, 2001), expert performers' abilities to retain and recall information within their area of expertise have been assessed in the hopes of illuminating the cognitive properties that support exceptional skill execution. These assessments have included memory for the step-by-step unfolding of performances, structured and unstructured game situations, and performance outcomes.

Why has such emphasis been placed on the memorial capacities of expert performers? One reason may be that similar to overt performance, various aspects of memory can be compared and contrasted across skill level as a means to identify unique aspects of high-level performance. For example, following a particularly challenging putt, an expert golfer might be asked to recollect their memory of the exact steps (i.e., the steps involved in assessing and analyzing the putting situation, as well as those underlying the actual mechanical act of implementing the putt) that they went through in taking their last putt. Researchers can compare this information with the same types of episodic performance recollections of less skilled golfers to ascertain whether differences as a function of skill level exist in the memories of on-line performance processes (i.e., the ability to recall the processes and properties of skill execution as it actually unfolds).

But what could be learned from such a comparison? Because episodic memory is thought to depend on explicit attention at the time of encoding (Craik, Govini, Naveh-Benjamin, & Anderson, 1996; Naveh-Benjamin, Craik, Guez, & Dori, 1998), an understanding of what expert golfers remember may lead to inferences that concern the representation of their skill in working memory (i.e., the skill information that is attended to and monitored) as performance actually occurs (Beilock & Carr, 2001). Researchers have found that a critical ingredient in the successful, explicit retrieval of information from memory is attention to this material at the time of encoding. Thus, we can examine one particular aspect of experts' and novices' memory structures (explicitly accessible memories of step-by-step instances of performance) in order to infer what these performers are paying attention to during skill execution.

Utilizing episodic memories, however, to infer explicitly attended information during real-time performance is only one strategy that may be deployed in accessing the contents of working memory. Another logic commonly proposed in the expertise literature relies on introspective reports of the conscious contents of working memory as evidence for on-line information processing (Ericsson & Simon, 1993). Concurrent verbal report protocols are often utilized in an attempt to determine what performers are thinking about as they perform a skill. Under this logic, reported thought processes are thought to reflect information heeded during skill execution and, ultimately, the representation of this skill in working memory. It is an empirical question whether these two methods designed to access the contents of working memory will produce similar conclusions regarding information attended during skill execution and ultimately the cognitive processes driving this performance. We will return to this issue later.

In this chapter we first begin with a review of past research that assessed the memorial capabilities of expert performers. Along with episodic performance recollections, three other memorial capacities have been examined in an attempt to differentiate the memory structures supporting novice and well-learned skill execution: the ability to recall performance outcomes, that is, the end result of performances (Backman & Molander, 1986); recollections for briefly presented stimulus arrays within a domain of specialization, the kinds of stimuli to which a skill is applied (for a review see, Ericsson & Lehmann, 1996); and retrospective verbal report protocols that detail high-level strategies and game plans (McPherson, 2000). We then discuss new and emerging findings that concern the relationship between the attentional processes and memory structures governing sensorimotor skill performance at various levels of learning. Finally, some implications of memory research for the acquisition and maintenance of high-level performance in real-world settings are presented.

Research on Memory and Expertise

Explorations of the memory structures that support experienced skill execution have reached across skill domains. Nonetheless, many parallel findings regarding experienced performers' memorial capabilities have emerged from these separate areas of interest. One such finding centers on experts' exceptional ability to recall task-relevant stimuli. It has been repeatedly demonstrated that when experienced performers are briefly presented with structured stimuli from within their domain of expertise, they are better able to recall this information than less skilled performers. In their classic chess studies, Chase and Simon (1973) found that chess masters were better able to recall briefly presented chess positions than were less experienced players (for confirmatory data see De Groot, 1978; and for similar results from computer programmers see Soloway & Ehrlich, 1984). Analogous results have been found in sensorimotor skill domains. In dance, for example, Starkes, Deakin, Lindley, and Crisp (1987) demonstrated that when expert and novice ballet dancers were presented with a series of choreographed movement sequences and then asked to recall these movements either verbally or physically, expert dancers were better able than their novice counterparts to do so. Across cognitive and sensorimotor skill domains, parallel findings of experts' superior memories have led to the conclusion that expertise serves to enhance memory capacity within performers' domain of specialization.

Not only do experts appear to be better at recalling task-relevant stimulus information in comparison with less skilled players, experts also appear to have superior memory for the outcome of their performance. In a study that assessed skill execution and performance memory of low- and high-skilled miniature golf players of different ages, Backman and Molander (1986) found that when asked to recollect the outcomes of particular shots, expert miniature golfers were better able to do so than were less-skilled golfers—even when these recollections were tested unexpectedly. Experts' superior memory for outcomes included successful performances, such as a hole-in-one, and also shots that missed the hole either as a result of direction or speed. Furthermore, through the examination of concurrent and retrospective verbal report protocols of novice and experienced tennis players, McPherson (2000) has found that experienced players retrieve past performance outcomes and use this information for the diagnosing and updating of subsequent performance strategies to a greater degree than less skilled individuals. The type of outcome information recalled by experienced players included information about the success of their opponents' prior shots as well as the style of shots their opponents had a tendency to make.

Such findings demonstrate quite clearly that experts have superior explicit memory for certain kinds of information within their domain of specialization, including incidental explicit memory as revealed by unexpected memory tests. So what exactly does this mean? Some have suggested that because "experts' incidental memory for task-relevant information is superior to that of novices . . . most forms of expert performance remain mediated by attention-demanding cognitive processes," (Ericsson & Lehmann , 1996, p. 291). However, despite the well-documented dependence of explicit memory on attention, it is possible that this suggestion does not apply to all types of memory processes nor does it apply to all components of high-level skill execution. Experts may have better episodic recollection for the stimuli in the environment that they operate on, for example, chess game configurations, basketball play scenarios, or choreographed dance sequences. They may also have better recollection for the perceptible changes in that stimulus environment created by the outcomes of their performance. To our knowledge, however, it has not been demonstrated that experts are better able to recall step-by-step components involved in their own superior performance as it actually unfolds in real time, such as heavily practiced mechanical aspects and low-level (or local) cognitive planning and decision strategies. Therefore, it remains an open question whether on-line production of expert performance—the sequence of operations itself, rather than the stimuli being operated on—is mediated by the kind of attended implementation of capacity-demanding knowledge structures that one might infer from the quote by Ericsson and Lehmann.

We would like to make salient a distinction about the type or mode of expert performance that we are addressing in the present chapter. Within the expertise literature, care has been taken to make a distinction between performance for the sole purpose of maximizing real-time execution and "deliberate practice" for the alteration, fine-tuning, and long-term improvement of specific skill components. These two types of performance are thought to occur in different contexts (Ericsson & Charness, 1994), with the former presumably determining the successful demonstration of expertise in current competitive situations and the latter occurring during training situations and more strongly contributing to the acquisition of high-level performance in the future. It may very well be the case that experts demonstrate superior episodic memory for performance when the goal is to explicitly analyze skill components to alter or change performance processes. Experts presumably have more experience and skill knowledge about the diagnosis and altering of performance patterns than do novices. Thus, when their goal is to attend to performance, experts may be proficient at retaining episodic memories of the skill parameters they are modifying. As will be seen in the following studies, this ability does appear to be the case, at least under some conditions. However, attending to and remembering a specific performance may not always be easy for an expert, and in situations in which an individual's goal is to perform at the current highest level possible without the added objective of attending to that performance or necessarily remembering it later, we suggest that experts' memories of step-by-step skill execution are not superior at all. Explaining why we make such a suggestion brings us to the literature on skill acquisition and automaticity.

In this literature, the unpracticed performances of novices are thought to be controlled by declarative knowledge that is held in working memory and attended step-by-step. In contrast, highly practiced or overlearned performances are thought to be automated, supported by procedural knowledge that operates without the need for explicit or attended monitoring (Anderson, 1983, 1993; Fitts & Posner, 1967). As skill level increases, information is restructured into a new type of skill representation (which is usually called a "procedure" in the domain of cognitive skills, but is often called a "motor program" in the domain of sensorimotor skills). This skill representation does not mandate the same degree of attention and control that was necessary at lower levels of practice (Brown & Carr, 1989; Keele, 1986; Keele & Summers, 1976), and it is supported by different neural structures than were active early in learning (Karni et al., 1998; Raichle et al., 1994).

Although proceduralization is one available concept about the automatization of practiced task performance, alternative explanations of automaticity have also been put forward. Logan (1988) has proposed that automaticity is based on the direct retrieval of specific past episodes or instances of performance from long-term memory, rather than the reliance on a procedure or program that can effectively and efficiently generate new performances. Performance based on retrieval of instances is thought to differ from earlier, less practiced stages of execution in which problem solutions and task performances are derived through the implementation of an explicit rule-based algorithm. From Logan's "instance theoretic" perspective, efficient, experienced skill execution is constrained by the stimuli, contexts, and problems actually encountered during practice; hence, they are stored in memory as retrievable instances of past performance. Thus, skill supported by instance retrieval is not easily transferable to new exemplars of a problem, except through simple processes of similarity-based stimulus generalization (Logan, 1988, 1990; Ericsson, 2001).

Differences exist in the predictions of the proceduralization and instance-based theories of automaticity regarding flexibility and breadth of transfer of performance. These differences have been used to argue that practiced sensorimotor skills are in fact supported by procedures rather than by the retrieval of instances (Koh & Meyer, 1991). However, despite the fact that transfer may occur in proceduralized skills, it is our view that there is a cost associated with such transfer. Specifically, if the required control parameters of high-level performance are altered by new task demands, transfer of a skill may still occur. However, if this alteration is sufficiently dramatic, experts may be forced to devote more attention to performance than they would ordinarily in an attempt to implement the new, less-proceduralized control parameters, which would result in a diminished working memory capacity during skill execution. Such attended transfer might occur without apparent performance consequences when the skill environment is not overly complicated. For example, a competitive skier who is adjusting to a new pair of racing skis may need to attend to controlling those skis to a degree not required by her old, familiar pair. Nevertheless, this skier may not exhibit performance deficits on a familiar and unchallenging race course. This scenario may not be the case, however, when this skier finds herself in a new situation with distracting attention demands or significant strategic and executional challenges. In this scenario, the skier might be forced to race on new skis and on a difficult course that she has never seen before. The added attention the skier must devote to controlling her new skis may not leave enough attentional capacity to implement the planning strategies required to race a novel course. Consequently, performance may suffer, either as a result of planning failures, control failures, or both.

If the relationship we have just described between attention and automaticity is correct—that skills automatized through proceduralization do not require constant attentional monitoring and thus rely less heavily on the active maintenance of information in working memory in comparison with less practiced skills—then memory for the on-line processes involved in skill execution may actually decrease as skill level increases, at least when novel task properties are not involved. Abernethy, Thomas, and Thomas (1993) have suggested that experienced skill execution is "automated" in just this way, not based on consciously accessible declarative knowledge. As a result, specific performances cannot be accurately described or reported through the explicit retrieval of performance rules or general principles because they were not attended or entered into working memory during skill execution—nor can specific performances be described by retrieving actual, explicitly accessible episodic memories of the performances. This deficiency is due to the fact that such memories depend on the allocation of attention to the information that must be stored, which does not actually occur during the real-time skill execution of experienced performers. Thus, although high-level performers may have superior memories for certain aspects of their skill execution (such as the stimulus situations they attend to), if they are not explicitly attending to step-by-step execution in real time, they may actually possess impoverished memories for the component details of how that performance was planned, controlled, and executed on-line. If so, then the relation between expertise and memory may be more complex than the simple notion that experts remember more. We now turn to recent findings concerning the relationship between memory and expertise that support these hypotheses.

New Findings in Memory and Expertise

In an attempt to assess the memory structures and attentional processes that govern high-level sensorimotor skill execution, Beilock and Carr (2001) conducted a series of experiments exploring generic knowledge of golf putting and episodic memories of particular putts in expert and novice golfers. "Generic" knowledge captures prescriptive information about how a skill is typically done; "episodic" knowledge captures an autobiographical record of a particular performance, a memory for a specific instance of skill execution. Golf putting was chosen as the experimental task because it is a complex sensorimotor skill that is thought to become proceduralized with practice. Although this laboratory putting task lacked many of the variables that make actual putting so difficult (e.g., changing environmental conditions, rolling terrain), individuals in a large majority of the studies performed golf putts that varied in length and angle dimensions. Thus, the putting task was similar to real-world situations because it required the mechanical instantiation of golf swing movements as well as the assessment and planning of putting processes and procedures.

Regardless of one's viewpoint regarding the attentional processes that govern skilled performance, it is generally believed that experts have more explicitly available generic or prescriptive knowledge about the domain in which they are skilled than do their novice counterparts (for reviews, see Ericsson & Smith, 1991; Proctor & Dutta, 1995; Van Lehn, 1989). Experienced golfers should, in theory, give a more detailed and systematic generic description of the steps involved in a typical golf putt than novices. In terms of episodic memories for specific instances of performance, however, the situation may be reversed. If on-line, well-learned golf putting is supported by procedural knowledge that reduces the need to attend to the specific procedures of skill execution, then expert golfers may provide diminished episodic accounts of their performance in comparison with novices, especially those aspects of performance that have been repeatedly practiced, such as mechanics and low-level (or local) planning strategies. In contrast, if expertise is indeed mediated by attention-demanding cognitive processes, expert golfers should give more extensive and descriptive episodic accounts of their performance than their novice counterparts.

In the first experiment, expert golfers (Division I intercollegiate golf team members) and novice golfers (with no previous golf experience) performed a series of putts on a carpeted indoor putting green (3.0 meters by 3.7 meters). Participants were instructed that the object of the task was to putt a golf ball as accurately as possible, making it stop at a target marked by a square of red tape that was located 1.5 meters away. A standard golf putter and golf ball were supplied. All participants took part in identical pretest, practice, and posttest conditions that consisted of 20 putts, 30 putts, and 20 putts, respectively. Putting accuracy was recorded after every putt, and an average putting accuracy was computed for each of the putting conditions. Following the pretest condition, participants were asked to produce a generic knowledge protocol—what one ought to do on a typical putt. Following the posttest condition, participants were asked to describe their episodic memory of their last putt taken—their memory of what they actually did on that specific putt (for questionnaire instructions, see figure 12.1).

The memory protocols were analyzed in two ways. First, a quantitative analysis documented the number of steps given in each protocol. Second, a qualitative analysis divided steps into three categories. The first category was *assessment,* or *planning,* and it referred to deciding how to approach a particular putt, what problems it might present, and what properties the putt ought to have. Examples include "read the green," "read the line" (from the ball to the hole or target), "focus on the line," and "visualize the force needed to hit the ball." The second category was *mechanics,* or *execution,* and it referred to the components of the mechanical act that implements the putt. Examples include "grip the putter with your right hand on top of your left," "bring the club straight back," and "accelerate through the ball," all of which deal with the effectors and the kinesthetic movements of the effectors required to implement a putt. The third category was *ball destinations,* or *outcomes,* and it referred to where the ball stopped or landed—hence, its degree of success.

Experts demonstrated superior putting accuracy in comparison to novices as measured by putting performance in both the pretest condition (experts $M = 13.89$, $SE = 0.99$; novices $M = 23.35$, $SE = 1.61$) and the posttest condition (experts $M = 8.96$, $SE = 0.79$; novices $M = 19.37$, $SE = 1.48$). In terms of the memory protocols (figure 12.2), novice golfers produced shorter generic descriptions and longer episodic recollections of specific putts, whereas the expert golfers produced an opposite pattern. Experts' generic descriptions were longer than novices', reflecting golf expertise. Additionally, experts gave less detailed

Generic Questionnaire (Experiments 1 and 2)

Certain steps are involved in executing a golf putt. Please list as many steps that you can think of, in the right order, which are involved in a typical golf putt:

Episodic Questionnaire (Experiment 1)

Pretend that your friend just walked into the room. Describe the last putt you took, in enough detail so that your friend could perform the same putt you just took:

[Note: Additional explanation was given to make it clear that what was being asked for was a recipe, or set of instructions, that would allow the putt to be duplicated in all its details by someone who had not seen it. Participants were told that the friend was not an expert golfer, but someone with an ordinary knowledge of the game. This context was provided to prevent excessive use of jargon or in-group shorthand, in an attempt to equate the need for knowledge that would be assumed by the describers across groups.]

Episodic Questionnaire (Experiment 2)

Pretend that your friend just walked into the room. Describe the last putt you took, in enough detail so that your friend could duplicate that last putt you just took in detail, doing it just like you did:

[Note: This episodic questionnaire was changed slightly from Experiment 1 in an attempt to elicit the most detailed episodic descriptions possible from participants.]

Figure 12.1 Generic knowledge and episodic memory protocol instructions for the novice and expert golfers.

episodic recollections in comparison with their generic descriptions and in comparison with the episodic recollections of the novice golfers. Beilock and Carr (2001) have termed experts' impoverished episodic recollection "expertise-induced amnesia." Expertise-induced amnesia centers on the notion that highly skilled on-line performances are controlled by automated procedural knowledge that operates largely outside the scope of attention and is therefore substantially closed to explicit analysis and report. As a result, memories for the step-by-step processes involved in performance are diminished in comparison with less skilled individuals due to the dependence of explicit memory on attention.

In terms of the types of steps given by participants, expert golfers' generic descriptions dealt considerably more with assessing and planning a putt than did novices'. This finding is consistent with research on expert performers across a wide range of task domains (Chi, Feltovitch, & Glaser, 1981; Lesgold et al., 1988; Priest & Lindsay, 1992; Proctor & Dutta, 1995). Expert golfers' episodic recollections included fewer assessment steps than did their generic descriptions. Expert golfers also made fewer references to putting mechanics in their episodic recollections than did novices (see figure 12.2). To interpret these differences, we again applied the logic described earlier, that the explicitly accessible content of an episodic recollection is a function of how attention was allocated during the experience being recollected. Thus, by this logic, both the qualitative and quantitative protocol analyses demonstrate that although experts' extensive generic knowledge of putting may be declaratively accessible during off-line reflection, it is not used or attended to during real-time performance, which is instead controlled by automated procedural knowledge.

One might worry that the experts' exclusion of assessment steps from their episodic recollections was merely an artifact of our simple and highly repetitive situation, in which assessment was not much needed after a short amount of practice on our putting green. To guard against this alternative explanation, a reanalysis of the experts' protocols was done, and it dropped from each generic protocol all assessment steps that (a) did not appear in the corresponding episodic protocol and (b) were likely to be unnecessary once multiple putts had been taken in our laboratory situation. Excluded were steps such as "read the green" and "read the lie of the ball," since neither the green nor the lie of the ball changed during the experiment. Steps that would always be necessary in order to execute a putt, such as "taking aim," were maintained. This reanalysis of assessment produced a significant

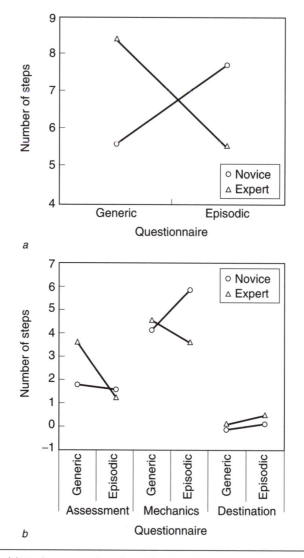

Figure 12.2 (*a*) Total mean number of steps for the generic questionnaire and the episodic questionnaire and (*b*) mean number of steps in each category for the generic and episodic questionnaire for both expert and novice golfers.

From *Journal of Experimental Psychology: General* 130: 701-725. Copyright © 2001 by the American Psychological Association. Adapted with permission.

interaction between expertise and type of protocol whose shape was the same as the original.

The results of the experiment described above support the notion that high-level skill execution is encoded in a procedural form that supports effective real-time performance without requiring continuous on-line attentional control. As a consequence, experienced golfers' memories for specific instances of performance are less complete than less skilled golfers. However, if novel task constraints are imposed, thus requiring experienced performers to alter skill execution processes, then proceduralized skill execution should be disrupted and experts should be forced to attend to step-by-step task control. Though accuracy of execution may decline, this restoration of attention should improve episodic memory.

In a second experiment, Beilock and Carr (2001) again compared putting performance and generic and episodic memory descriptions in expert and novice golfers under normal putting conditions (i.e., using a regular putter). Additionally, a subset of the expert and novice golfers performed the putting task with a "funny putter" made from a regular putter head attached to an S-shaped and arbitrarily weighted putter shaft. The design of the "funny putter" required experienced golfers to alter their well-practiced putting form to compensate for the distorted club. The idea was to force participants to allocate attention to the new task constraints.

Novice golfers with no previous golf experience and experienced golfers with either two-plus years of high school varsity golf or a PGA handicap under eight performed the same putting task as in the first experiment in a two (novice, expert) by two (regular putter, funny putter) design. All participants took part in identical pretest and practice conditions that consisted of 20 putts and 30 putts respectively, followed by two posttest conditions. The first posttest consisted of 20 putts while the second posttest consisted of 10 putts. Similar to the first experiment, putting accuracy was recorded after every putt, and an average accuracy score was computed for each condition. To ensure that the performers were not adapting to the highly repetitive task of putting from one specific spot on the green, we had all the participants in the second experiment alternately putt from nine different spots, located at varying angles and distances from the target. Following the pretest and practice conditions, participants produced a generic knowledge protocol. Following both the first and second posttest conditions, participants were asked to describe, in as much detail as possible, their episodic memories of their last putt (see figure 12.1). As in the first experiment, the first episodic memory protocol was a surprise. Just before the last putt taken prior to the second episodic memory protocol, participants were warned to attend to their performance because they would be subsequently asked to produce an episodic memory protocol of their next putt.

Results indicated that novices' putting accuracy was not affected by type of putter. This result might be expected considering that the novice golfers were not experienced with either type of putter before the experiment. Experts' putting accuracy was superior to novices, and was more accurate with the regular putter than with the "funny putter" (figure 12.3). Protocol data showed that novice golfers produced short generic descriptions and longer episodic recollections (figure 12.4). Again, the type of putter did not influence novices' protocols. Experts who used the regular putter produced an opposite pattern. These experts gave longer and more detailed generic descriptions than the novices did. In addition, experts who used the regular putter gave shorter episodic recollections in comparison with their generic descriptions and also in comparison with novices' episodic recollections, again demonstrating "expertise-induced amnesia."

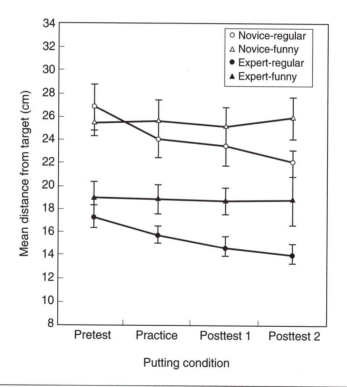

Figure 12.3   Mean distance (cm) from the target that the ball stopped after each putt in the pretest, practice, posttest 1, and posttest 2 conditions for each group. Error bars represent standard errors.

From *Journal of Experimental Psychology: General* 130: 701-725. Copyright © 2001 by the American Psychological Association. Adapted with permission.

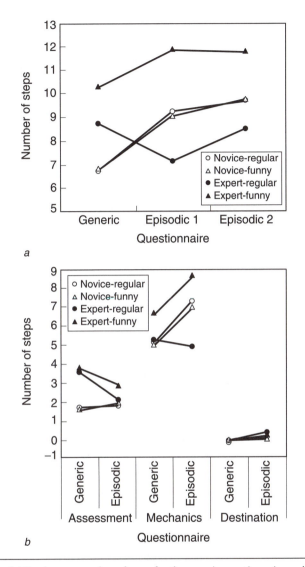

Figure 12.4   (a) Total mean number of steps for the generic questionnaire and the two episodic questionnaires and (b) mean number of steps in each category for the generic and first episodic questionnaire for each group.

From *Journal of Experimental Psychology: General* 130: 701-725. Copyright © 2001 by the American Psychological Association. Adapted with permission.

The second episodic memory test, in which participants knew in advance that they would be required to produce an episodic memory of their last putt, generated the same results. Even when forewarned of the memory test, experts using the regular putter recalled less about a specific putt than did novices. One might have thought that our earlier results arose because experts simply *choose* not to attend to performance enough to support memory unless there was a need or an incentive to remember. Instead, it is as if experts *cannot* pay enough attention to remember as well as novices, at least when performing under routine conditions so close to what they have practiced in the past.

In contrast, experts using the funny putter did not show impoverished episodic recollection. These experts provided the most elaborated generic and episodic protocols, and their episodic recollections were longer than their generic descriptions, not shorter as produced by the regular putter experts. Thus, when a proceduralized skill is disrupted by the imposition of novel task demands, "expertise-induced amnesia" disappears. Furthermore, once experts start attending to task performance, their expert knowledge allows them to remember more of what they are attending to than novices.

The qualitative analysis followed a similar pattern to that obtained in the first experiment (see figure 12.4). Assessment steps decreased in number from the generic to episodic protocol for the two experienced groups, regardless of type of putter used, whereas the opposite pattern occurred in the two novice groups. In terms of mechanics steps, the experienced golfers using the funny putter gave more mechanics steps than any other group, whereas the experienced golfers using the regular putter gave fewer mechanics steps than the other three groups. The two novice groups did not differ. Finally, regardless of putter type or expertise, ball destinations were more likely to appear in episodic recollections than generic protocols.

Thus, both the expert golfers using the regular putter and the expert golfers using the funny putter gave decreased assessment step descriptions from generic to episodic protocols, but a different pattern occurred for mechanics steps. The experienced golfers who used the funny putter gave significantly more mechanics steps in their episodic protocol in comparison with their generic description, whereas the experienced golfers who used the regular putter gave somewhat fewer steps (see figure 12.4). The design of the funny putter was intended to specifically distort the mechanical act of implementing the putt in the present experiment. Attention to the assessment and planning of the putt should not have been significantly influenced by putter type. Thus, the results demonstrating that the experienced golfers using the regular putter and the experienced golfers using the funny putter did not differ in terms of assessment steps included in their episodic memory protocols, yet did vary in their accounts of the mechanical properties involved in putting performance, is consistent with the notion that increased attention to performance as a result of novel task constraints serves specifically to enhance episodic memories for the altered parameters and components of skill execution.

In the studies just described, Beilock and Carr (2001) used measures of episodic performance memory to infer the attentional demands of on-line performance processes at different levels of expertise. As mentioned earlier, however, another approach has been utilized for the same general purpose, and it attempts to access the contents of working memory directly, rather than relying as we do on the impact of attention on the content of episodic recollections. Specifically, Ericsson and Simon (1993) have developed a framework for the collection of concurrent and retrospective verbal reports of the conscious and hence introspectable contents of working memory. These contents are thought to reflect the attended processes, or "heeded" processes (held consciously in working memory), that govern skill execution. Under this framework, instructions to verbalize conscious thoughts are distinguished from instructions to verbalize reasons and explanations for performance. Ericsson and Simon suggest that only the former type of verbalization, which focuses specifically on conscious thoughts, accurately reflects the cognitive processes supporting skill execution. This distinction is due to the fact that the latter type, which focuses on reasons and explanations, may require an individual to add information that might not otherwise be consciously processed during the actual unfolding of performance. That is, verbalizations that elicit rationales and reasons for performance may reflect reconstructions of performance elements much like what we have called "generic" protocols, rather than the information "heeded" during task deployment.

How do our two kinds of protocols relate to Ericsson and Simon's (1993) framework? It is clear that our generic protocols fall into the second category of verbalizations. Our generic protocols are descriptive and explanatory in nature, and they provide a general account of a golfer's putting knowledge. They need not and almost certainly do not correspond to a specific memory trace of any particular performance. In our experiments, we used the generic protocols to illustrate that experts do indeed have more domain-relevant knowledge than their novice counterparts, a finding that has been repeatedly upheld in the expertise literature (for a review, see Ericsson & Smith, 1991). Our experiments also illustrate that we can capture this difference within our laboratory putting paradigm.

Similar to the generic protocols, our episodic protocols are also "descriptive," and from Ericsson and Simon's (1993) perspective, it may be legitimate to worry about exactly what they are describing and why. However, in contrast to our generic questionnaire, it does not appear that our episodic questionnaire is eliciting "verbal rationales and reasons" (Ericsson & Simon, 1993, p. xviii). We formulated our episodic question under the assumption that attention leaves explicit memory traces and that one needs to explicitly attend to a stimulus to encode it and later be able to retrieve this information from memory and report it in a recall task. Such an assumption is standard fare in the memory literature, and as such, it should be uncontroversial (see, for example, Craik et al., 1996; Naveh-Benjamin et al., 1998). Nevertheless, although recall of episodic content increases in amount and accuracy when attention is paid during encoding, one must take into account the constructive nature of any recall attempt. That is, there is the possibility that recall does not represent *just* an episodic memory trace of a particular performance instance, but instead, it includes reconstructed information based on general knowledge. This possibility might be especially likely in our episodic protocols because performers were instructed to describe their memory of their last putt so that another individual could duplicate this putt. Specifically, participants in our studies may have been tempted to give a general account of their performance that included considerable generic information, perhaps highlighting what the golfers believed to be the unique characteristics of their own skills, rather than the intended memory description of a specific instance of skill deployment.

If the episodic protocols obtained in the previously mentioned studies were constructed accounts of what might have been—or worse, for our purposes, what *ought* to have been—then one would expect experts to be much more able to engage in such an exercise, because, as demonstrated in our generic protocols, they have more domain-relevant knowledge to work with in creating such a construct. However, this expectation is falsified by the results, since it predicts that experts should produce more elaborate episodic protocols, not the less elaborate ones that they did in fact produce when using the regular putter. That is, if our episodic questionnaire was eliciting a theoretical or schema-driven explanation rather than an attempt to produce a specific memory of performance, then one might hypothesize that the expert-novice differences in episodic memory protocols presented earlier in this chapter would be reversed. Experts, with their extensive domain-relevant knowledge base, certainly should be able to explain and elaborate their performance to a greater degree than novices.

A second piece of insurance against the concern that our episodic questionnaire is eliciting reasons and explanations for performance (rather than episodic memory traces reflecting information attended during on-line execution) is provided by the detailed episodic memories of performance given by the funny-putter experts in the second experiment. If reconstructed or schema-driven explanations of performance produced our results, then it is difficult to account for the differences in protocols between the experts using the regular and funny putters. That is, why would experts using the funny putter produce different memory protocols than experts using the regular putter, considering that they were given the same episodic questionnaire. Our explanation is that the accounts of the experienced golfers' memories differ because they attended to different things and hence encoded different information into memory. Again, this logic follows uncontroversially from the memory literature. Furthermore, the types of steps that were enhanced by the funny putter were mechanical in nature (see figure 12.4). These are precisely the types of steps that one would predict experts would need to attend to with the instantiation of novel mechanical parameters (i.e., the unevenly shaped and distortedly weighted funny putter).

Nevertheless, one lingering issue concerns whether or not concurrent verbal reports would have produced the same pattern of information. That is, although we have followed one logic to determine what was attended (i.e., the collection of retrospective episodic memory measures), another logic could be followed that would collect concurrent or immediately retrospective verbal reports of conscious thoughts. We do not know whether this method would produce the same results or different ones. This issue is important. One way to corroborate our retrospective memory findings might be to collect verbal report protocols following Ericsson and Simon's (1993) techniques during skill execution. A comparison could then be made between concurrent protocols based on instructions to verbalize conscious thought processes and episodic memory protocols designed to access the information attended and encoded during performance. This is a line of work that we plan to pursue in the future in collaboration with Anders Ericsson.

Finally, in an attempt to provide converging evidence on Beilock and Carr's (2001) inferences that regard the cognitive processes supporting novice and experienced skill execution (as well as to further understand the relationship between memory, attentional demands, and skill level), Beilock, Wierenga, and Carr (2002) performed an experiment that compared the single-task and dual-task performance of expert and novice golfers. If high-level performance processes do not require constant attentional control, then the addition of secondary task demands should not significantly impinge on experienced performers' primary task performance. In contrast, because of the attentional demands of novel or unpracticed performances, the addition of secondary task demands should result in a decrease in primary task performance because novices must allocate attention to skill performance processes.

Novice and experienced golfers took a series of golf putts on an indoor green using either a standard golf putter or a funny putter under single-task and dual-task putting conditions in a two (novice, expert) by two (regular putter, funny putter) by two (single-task, dual-task) design. In the single-task condition participants performed the putting task in isolation. In the dual-task condition, participants completed the putting task while simultaneously performing an auditory word monitoring task. The monitoring task consisted of a series of auditorally presented words in which participants were instructed to listen for a specified target word and, on hearing the target word, repeat it out loud. A subset of the words presented during the monitoring task were used as the basis for a subsequent recognition memory test.

In terms of putting performance, the novice groups, as well as experienced golfers using the funny putter, showed performance decrements from the single-task to the dual-task putting condition. In contrast, experts using the regular putter continued to improve in putting accuracy from the single- to dual-task condition (figure 12.5). Word recognition performance followed a similar pattern. The novice groups and the expert golfers using the funny putter showed decrements in recognition memory for words heard while putting in comparison to a single-task word recognition test given as a base-line measure. The expert golfers using the regular putter, however, did not show this decrement in word recognition performance (figure 12.6).

Thus, as illustrated by putting performance and word recognition data, performing in a dual-task environment harmed novice golfers and those experts using the funny putter, but it did not disrupt putting performance or word recognition ability in expert golfers putting under normal conditions. These results once again suggest that expertise leads to the encoding of task components in a proceduralized form that supports effective real-time performance, without the need for constant on-line attentional control. As a result, experts performing under normal, practiced conditions are better able than novices to allocate a portion of their attention to other stimuli and task demands if the situation requires it—even though these experts are less inclined and less able to allocate attention to and remember the step-by-step details of their performance, as shown by the expected and unexpected episodic memory tests of the previous two experiments.

These results also demonstrate that high-level proceduralized performance is transferable to novel task situations. Specifically, experts performing with the funny putter under single-task conditions that allowed them the attention necessary to concentrate on putting execution were able to attend to and adapt to the altered putter constraints without decrements in primary task performance. However, a decrease

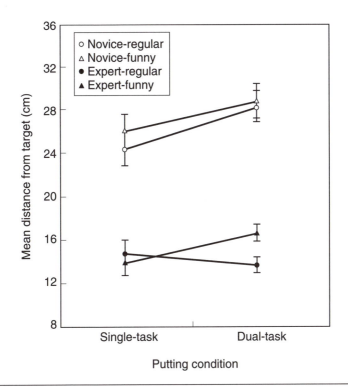

Figure 12.5 Mean distance (cm) from the target that the ball stopped after each putt in the single-task and dual-task conditions for each group. Error bars represent standard errors.

From *Journal of Experimental Psychology: General* 130: 701-725. Copyright © 2001 by the American Psychological Association. Adapted with permission of the Experimental Psychology Society.

in primary and secondary task performance occurred with the implementation of the secondary auditory monitoring task. Under dual-task conditions, the experienced golfers using the funny putter were forced to allocate attention to the altered putting task and the secondary auditory monitoring task. As a result, attentional capacity was stressed, and performance suffered—similar to what might happen when an experienced skier is forced to simultaneously attend to the parameters of her new skies and a novel, challenging race course.

In the studies discussed earlier in this chapter, episodic memory protocols, dual-task performance, and recognition memory for secondary stimuli presented during performance were used as support for the following notion: Well-learned sensorimotor skills are based on a proceduralized skill representation that (a) requires little attention to the well-practiced mechanical aspects and low-level planning strategies involved in skill execution, (b) operates largely outside of working

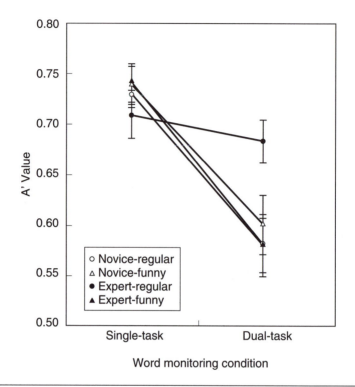

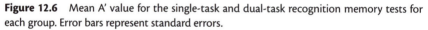

Figure 12.6   Mean A' value for the single-task and dual-task recognition memory tests for each group. Error bars represent standard errors.

From *Journal of Experimental Psychology: General* 130: 701-725. Copyright © 2001 by the American Psychological Association. Adapted with permission of the Experimental Psychology Society.

memory, and (c) is substantially closed to introspection and report. This is in contrast to novel performance processes that must be explicitly attended to in real time.

Implications for Real-World Performance

What exactly does the high-level athlete gain and lose with the changes in memory structure that accompany skill acquisition? The ability of experts when performing under normal task constraints to withstand the impact of dual-task conditions demonstrates that high-level skills may be performed at an optimal level under circumstances in which novice performance suffers. Because experienced skill execution does not mandate constant on-line attention and control, expert performers are able to encode and react to extraneous stimuli and environmental cues without decrements in primary task performance, stimuli that might very well serve to overload novice performers' attentional resources (Beilock, Carr, MacMahon, & Starkes, 2002; Beilock, Wierenga, & Carr, 2002; Leavitt, 1979; Smith & Chamberlin, 1992). Indeed, the ability of highly skilled performers to consistently perform at an exceptional level across a variety of situations, even under conditions that create added attention demands, seems to be one of the benchmarks of expert skill execution.

Expert Performers As Teachers and Coaches

It should be noted that although the cognitive processes that drive well-learned performance may contribute to optimal skill execution across a variety of attention-demanding situations, a lack of conscious attention to skill parameters may make it difficult for expert performers to reflect and introspect on past performance decisions, strategy choices, and execution processes implemented during task execution (Abernethy et al., 1993). This type of reflection may be useful for altering maladaptive strategies and processes or for correcting execution parameters that have drifted away from optimal values. Thus, difficulty in gaining access to memories of performance may harm the formulation of "deliberate practice" regimens.

Furthermore, experienced performers' inability to access explicit knowledge about performance processes carries implications for how effective experts will be in teaching their skill to others. A series of experiments (Hinds, 1999) were designed to assess the ability of experienced and less skilled individuals to predict novices' competence in solving both a Lego building task and a cellular-phone technology task. Hinds found that experts were poor predictors of novice performance and that they had difficulty understanding the types of problems that novices might face. In addition, experts were found to be ineffective in accurately recalling their own performances when they themselves were less skilled. Experts consistently underestimated their novice performance time and left out imperative steps involved in deriving the problem solution. Hinds explained experts' inability to assess novice performance as the "curse of expertise," whereby expert performers' lack of insight into their own high-level performance processes interferes with their ability to capitalize on superior task-relevant declarative knowledge in predicting the task performance of less skilled individuals.

Experts' inability to introspect on their performance has also been documented in real-world teaching settings. In Brown and Burton's (1978) assessment of the arithmetic skills of experienced elementary school math teachers, it was found that although experienced teachers were able to perform actual arithmetic operations at a high skill level, they had a great deal of difficulty in verbalizing the steps they went through in solving the math equations.

The findings of both Hinds (1999) and Brown and Burton (1978) suggest that although experts know *what* to do and are able to do it, they may not have explicit access to a detailed representation of *how* to do it that can be communicated to others (Adelson, 1984). This finding obviously carries serious implications for how experts may perform in roles as coaches, teachers, and educators. That is, although expert performers may be exceptional players, they may not necessarily make the best coaches. Can you imagine, for instance, how Michael Jordan might explain to young aspiring basketball players how he performs a dunk?

Expertise and "Choking Under Pressure"

The findings of recent memory research carry implications for high-level skill execution under pressure. "Explicit monitoring," or "execution focus," theories of choking suggest that suboptimal performance of a well-learned skill under pressure results from an attempt to exert explicit monitoring and control on proceduralized knowledge that is best run off as an uninterrupted and unanalyzed structure (Baumeister, 1984; Lewis & Linder, 1997). Thus, high-level skills based on an automated or proceduralized skill representation may be more susceptible to the negative consequences of performance pressure than less practiced performances. Beilock and Carr (2001) have found support for this notion in sensorimotor skill performance.

Participants learned a laboratory golf putting task to an asymptote in performance under different training conditions and were then exposed to single-task situations of both low and high pressure. The first training regimen involved ordinary single-task practice, which provided a baseline measure of the occurrence of choking. A second regimen involved practice under a distracting, dual-task condition (while monitoring an auditory word list for a target word), which was designed to expose performers to being distracted from the primary task by execution-irrelevant activity in working memory. The third training regimen exposed performers to the particular aspects of high-pressure situations that explicit monitoring theories of choking propose cause performance decrements. In this "self-conscious," or "skill focus," training condition, participants learned the putting task while being videotaped for subsequent public analysis by experts. This manipulation was designed to expose performers to having attention called to themselves and their performance in a way intended to induce explicit monitoring of skill execution. It was found that choking occurred for those who where trained on the putting task in a single-task, isolated environment and also for those trained in a dual-task environment that simply created distraction. Choking did not occur, however, for those trained in the self-conscious condition. This group actually improved under pressure. Beilock and Carr (2001) concluded that training under conditions that prompted attention to skill parameters served to adapt these performers to the type of attentional focus that often occurs under pressure. That is, self-consciousness training served to inoculate performers against the negative impact of pressure, which enticed them to overattend to well-learned proceduralized performance processes.

Summary

Researchers have attempted to assess a number of components that constitute the memory structures supporting skill performance so that they can illuminate the cognitive substrate that governs high-level skill execution. Extensive evidence of experts' superior memory for stimuli encountered or operated on within their domain of interest has been collected across cognitive and sensorimotor skill domains. These results have been taken as support for the notion that expert performance is mediated by reportable attention-demanding explicit cognitive processes (Ericsson & Lehmann, 1996). Recently, however, researchers have attempted to document another property of the cognitive substrate of sensorimotor skill execution—namely, the declarative accessibility, or openness to introspection and report, of real-time skill planning and execution processes at different levels of expertise. Measurements of experts' episodic memory representations permit inferences that concern the underlying control structures driving real-time performance. Namely, these results suggest that well-learned sensorimotor skill execution is controlled by proceduralized knowledge structures that are not attended to and hence not included in the memories left over from task performance. As a result, experts may have less detailed memories for some aspects of performance in comparison with less skilled performers.

However, reduction in episodic memory may not hold across all conditions of performance. In practice situations, for example, in which performers are consciously attempting to dismantle their skill and modify certain parts to more closely align their performance with desired goal states, experts may retain extremely detailed memories of performance in comparison with novices. That is, once experts do attend to performance processes, their greater knowledge base should afford them the ability to identify skill problems, derive solutions, alter performance processes, and ultimately encode this information for subsequent use to a greater degree than their novice counterparts. However, it may be difficult for experts to achieve and maintain this state of heightened attention to performance as indicated by the contrast between expert golfers' intentional memories when using a regular putter and their much-improved intentional memories when using the funny putter. These conclusions regarding skill expertise and memory are not only relevant to understanding the cognitive mechanisms that underlie expert skill execution, but they may also lend insight into the optimal conditions for exceptional performance in real-world situations.

EXPERT'S COMMENTS

■ Question

Beilock and colleagues cite evidence that being an expert presents occasional disadvantages, particularly when one has to recall individual portions of well-practiced movements. Have you seen other examples in sport where you think this might be the case?

■ Player's Perspective: Therese Brisson

Beilock, Weirenga, and Carr present the curious finding that expert golfers were not able to verbalize elements of expert performance immediately after their performances. This is an interesting finding that supports my long-held belief that recently retired hockey players who played at high levels rarely make the ideal coaches for youth hockey. They know what to do, but they can't communicate how they do it! When I run hockey camps for children, given the choice between the skilled hockey player with little instruction experience and the experienced physical education teacher with no elite playing experience, I always select the teacher. Teaching skating skills is one of those problem areas. How exactly do you skate faster? What do I need to do to execute a sharp turn and to stop? The good news is that with experience in coaching and communication, former players can learn how to break down skills and, even more important, communicate teaching points to the learner. But this comes with coaching experience, not playing experience.

Chapter 13

Expert Performance in Sport

■ ■ ■ ■ ■

Views From the Joint Perspectives of Ecological Psychology and Dynamical Systems Theory

Peter J. Beek • David M. Jacobs
Andreas Daffertshofer • Raoul Huys

E xpert performance in sport and complex perceptual-motor actions in general are an exciting and theoretically significant topic of inquiry. The study of expertise may also have a broad variety of practical implications. For example, when we understand why experienced assistant referees in soccer still often make errors in judging offside or when we know which behaviors distinguish the expert juggler from the intermediate and novice jugglers, we may be able to apply skill-specific instructions for improvement of the perceptual and motor skills in question. In this chapter, we discuss these and other real-life examples within the context of two theoretical approaches that we feel have much to offer in studying expertise in sport: ecological psychology and dynamical systems theory.

These two approaches made their respective appearances in the study of perception and coordinated movement around the year 1980. The initiation of the ecological approach was marked by the publication of J.J. Gibson's (1979) book and of various related publications (Turvey, 1977; Michaels & Carello, 1981; Turvey, Shaw, Reed, & Mace, 1981), while the dynamical systems approach to coordinated movement took off with the publication of two manifesto-like chapters written by Kugler, Kelso, and Turvey (1980, 1982), and the accompanying experimental work of Kelso (1981; Kelso, Holt, Kugler, & Turvey, 1980) on rhythmic finger and hand movements. This experimental work eventually led to a key model construct for the study of coordinated rhythmic movements formulated by Haken, Kelso, and Bunz (1985).

Ecological psychology and dynamical systems theory have several theoretical features in common. First, both approaches show a marked reluctance to resort to cognitive constructs, such as mental representations and motor programs, in explaining human behavior. Second, both approaches, broadly conceived, place great theoretical emphasis on variables that are defined over multiple components or elements that are thought to govern the perception and production of patterns, respectively. Such ensemble or collective variables are called *higher order invariants* in the case of ecological psychology and *order parameters* in the case of dynamical systems theory. Indeed, these shared theoretical features have led some scholars to present or interpret the two approaches as constituting a single theoretical perspective (e.g., Turvey, Carello, & Kim, 1990; Abernethy, Thomas, & Thomas, 1993). Although understandable from the identified coarse-grained similarities, such a roughly lumping together of theoretical approaches has a disadvantage in that the dissimilarities between the approaches, which are by no means trivial, are played down or ignored. As a result, the theoretical problems that have to be resolved for the approaches to be aligned or reconciled are overlooked (cf. Michaels & Beek, 1995).

These issues, however, are only of later concern. We are primarily interested in exploring how ecological psychology and dynamical systems theory, each in their own right, may contribute to the understanding of expertise in sport. To do so requires an introduction to the key concepts in the two approaches and to the manner in which these concepts have been expanded theoretically and methodologically to address learning and expertise in the perceptual-motor domain. In the next section, we address the question how applied sport science may benefit from the recent advances in ecological studies of perceptual learning and from the circumstances preventing or promoting it. To this end, we highlight the usefulness of the ecological notion of *education of attention*—that is, the process of learning to pick up specifying higher order invariants (rather than nonspecifying information) for performing a particular task. We subsequently discuss how sport scientists who are interested in motor expertise may benefit from using the concepts and tools of dynamical systems theory. In this context, we discuss the significance of the dynamical notion of *reduction of dimensionality*, which is the harnessing of control to the degrees of freedom that are essential for performing a particular task while abandoning residual, nonessential degrees of freedom. Finally, we briefly indicate how the two perspectives may lead to a coherent framework for studying and understanding expertise in sport. Our overall goal, however, is not so much to derive an overarching conceptual framework but rather to demonstrate how exciting questions concerning expertise in the perceptual-motor domain may be posed and addressed from the notion of low-dimensional variables.

Applying Ecological Principles in Sport Science: How to Foster Reliance on Information?

One of the cornerstones of ecological psychology is the concept of specificity. In the ecological studies of learning to be discussed later, specificity is typically considered a qualifier of the relation between variables. In this use of the concept, two variables are said to be specific to each other if the value of each can be predicted from the value of the other, under all considered circumstances. Thus, perceiving (i.e., picking up) a variable that specifies a variable of interest in a certain task allows one to make reliable judgments about this variable. In the course of learning, perceivers may converge on picking up and using information that is specific to relevant environmental properties. First, though, we need to consider the specificity of ambient energy patterns, or informational variables, and the environment.

Specificity of Information and the Environment

A key objective of ecological psychology is to reduce the theoretical burden in explaining perception and action by carefully analyzing the information available in specific task situations and the perceptually accessible environmental properties that are pertinent for achieving a particular task goal. In particular, the approach rejects the traditionally held assumption that ambient energy patterns are impoverished, or information-poor, and are therefore ambiguous with respect to the environment. It follows from this assumption that mediating concepts such as knowledge and inferences has to be introduced to resolve the alleged stimulus ambiguity (e.g., Fodor & Pylyshyn, 1981). To the extent, however, that the informational variables on which perception is based specify environmental properties, perception would not have to disambiguate them, and theorists would therefore not have to resort to mediating constructs to explain perception (e.g., Turvey, Shaw, Reed, & Mace, 1981). It seems worthwhile, then, to investigate whether information-environment specificities indeed exist. Two ideas promoted by J.J. Gibson (1950, 1966, 1979) have proven useful in this regard.

The first idea is the widely accepted refutation of elementarism (Runeson, 1994). Variables that might appear intellectually simple (say, in terms of the International System of Units) are in fact on equal ontological footing with variables that might not appear simple. Consequently, in spite of understandable inclinations to assume otherwise, perception could be equally well based on apparently complex variables, or higher-order invariants, as on apparently simple variables. Such higher-order variables could, for instance, be defined over considerable spatiotemporal intervals and over different sensory arrays. Identifying informational variables that are specific to relevant environmental properties is in many cases only feasible if one agrees to consider higher-order informational variables (e.g., Michaels & Carello, 1981).

A second crucial idea is that information-environment specificities exist by virtue of constraints. In addition to universal constraints, such as natural laws, J.J. Gibson (1979; cf. Runeson, 1988) considered ecological constraints, which might hold only in the eco-niches of particular animals. He demonstrated, for example, that the distribution of texture elements might provide information about the slant of surfaces. Careful analyses of ecological constraints have led to the identification of many information-environment specificities in many other instances as well. Yet additional constraints, including game rules and local conventions, can be said to prevail if one further narrows the considered ecology to particular task situations. It seems improbable, however, that evolution has endowed perceivers with perceptual systems that are attuned to the specificities that might be granted by the local constraints in such restricted and typically contrived (and therefore novel) task environments (Jacobs, Runeson, & Michaels, 2001). Therefore, a main question to be addressed here is whether and how perceivers *learn* to take advantage of local constraints and the information-environment specificities furnished by those constraints.

It is important to note that ecological psychologists do not claim that it has been proven that all relevant environmental properties are specified. To the contrary, the large numbers of potentially relevant constraints and higher-order variables prevailing in everyday situations severely complicate proofs or refutations of information-environment specificities. At the same time, this informational richness of sufficiently complex task ecologies motivates ecological psychologists to start from the assumption that relevant information-environment specificities exist with the concomitant expectation that further analyses can provide evidence for them (Runeson & Fryckholm, 1983; Runeson, Jacobs, Andersson, & Kreegipuu, 2001).[1]

The Education of Attention As Explanation of Perceptual Improvement

In the preceding section, we argued that informational variables that specify relevant environmental properties have been shown to exist in sufficiently constrained situations and may at least be assumed to exist in more complex ecologies. The general accuracy of perception can be explained by viewing perception as the detection of such specifying patterns: If perception is specific to information and the information is specific to relevant environmental properties, perception must be specific to those properties. In many cases, however, perception does not appear to be accurate. For instance, assistant referees in soccer often perceive an attacking player to be offside when in fact the player is not, or vice versa, they perceive the player not to be offside when in fact the player is (Oudejans, Verheijen, Bakker, Gerrits, Steinbrückner, & Beek, 2000). How can the occurrence of such flag and no-flag errors be explained? Oudejans et al. (2000) argued that the errors made by assistant referees were due to reliance on the relative retinal position of the attacking and defending players, which is an optical variable that is not specific to whether or not the attacking player is actually offside.

In other words, a player who is closer to (or farther from) the byline than an opponent player also tends to be projected as closer to (or farther from) that line on the retina, indicating that reliance on this variable can often lead to correct flagging. In a significant minority of cases, however, that depend on the position of the assistant referee, a player who is in fact closer to (or farther from) the byline is projected as farther from (or closer to) that line. In these cases, reliance on the variable would lead to errors. The existence of these cases also indicates that the variable is not one-to-one related to whether an attacking player is offside; hence, it illustrates why the authors of the studies to be discussed later would refer to it as a *nonspecifying* variable.[2]

If perceptual errors can be more generally attributed to the non-specificity of the detected variables, perceptual improvements might also be expected to reside at the level of variable use. Accordingly, J.J. Gibson (1966) suggested that perceptual improvements could be due to detection of other variables, a process he referred to as the *education of attention* (see also E.J. Gibson, 1969, and E.J. Gibson & Pick, 2000). To investigate this phenomenon, many recent studies on visual perception have analyzed which variables perceivers use at different stages in the learning process. For instance, Michaels and de Vries (1998) studied the perception of the relative pulling force exerted by human and stick-figure pullers; Smith, Flach, Dittman, and Stanard (2001) studied the timing of collision control; Jacobs, Michaels, and Runeson (2000) and Runeson, Juslin, and Olsson (2000) addressed the perception of the relative mass of colliding balls; and Jacobs and Michaels (2001) addressed the perception of the distance and size of freely falling balls. All of these studies used a pretest-practice-posttest design. Feedback was given during the practice stages but not in the pretests and posttests.

Overall, in the pretests, perceivers tended to use variables that were not specific to the properties that they were supposed or required to perceive. Novice perceivers often differed with regard to the (non-specifying) variables they used, although these individual differences stood out more in some tasks than in others. After practice with feedback, many perceivers exhibited changes in the variables that they relied on. They usually came to rely on one of the more useful variables, and sometimes they even converged on specifying information. The variables on which perceivers converged depended to a large extent on the sets of displays that were used in practice; perceivers often came to rely on variables that were useful only in those sets. Furthermore, if perceivers initially used nonspecifying variables that allowed for reasonably accurate performance in the practice phases, only few changes in variable use were observed and the convergence on specifying information proceeded slowly.[3]

Fostering Reliance on Information

The finding that the convergence on specifying variables proceeds more slowly if the initially used nonspecifying variables allow reasonably accurate perception suggests that the convergence might proceed more rapidly if the nonspecifying variables are not at all useful. Since facilitating perceptual learning is of considerable relevance to applied sport science, we describe in some detail a study about this issue. In a series of experiments (Jacobs, Runeson, & Michaels, 2001), participants practiced with feedback to visually perceive the relative mass of colliding balls. Again, a pretest-practice-posttest design was used. The practice phases of individuals differed with regard to which nonspecifying variables were rendered useless as well as to how this was achieved.

A first way in which variables were rendered useless was to keep them constant. Perceivers who rely on a variable that does not vary over trials should give the same judgment on each trial. This would lead to discouraging feedback, which might motivate perceivers to find other, perhaps more useful variables. To test such *no-variation practice*, Jacobs, Runeson, and Michaels (2001) composed a set of practice displays in which the considered nonspecifying variables (i.e., the exit-speed difference, the scatter-angle difference, and combinations of these; see the original article for details) had about the same value on every trial. Indeed, some perceivers came to rely on mass-specifying information during the practice phase. In a posttest, however, in which the nonspecifying variables were varied normally, perceivers appeared to resort to their old strategies. Thus, no-variation practice temporarily forced perceivers to use other variables, but perceivers did not seem to have learned that the initial variables were not the most useful ones.

A second way to render nonspecifying variables useless is to nullify the correlation between those variables and the property to be perceived. To test such *zero-correlation practice*, Jacobs, Runeson, and Michaels (2001) composed a set of practice displays in which the considered nonspecifying variables were varied normally but in which they were also entirely uncorrelated with relative mass. This practice condition was successful in the sense that all perceivers learned *not* to use the nonspecifying variables that they used initially, and they did not fall back to the old variables in a posttest. Several perceivers, though, did not appear to discover other variables that could lead to reasonably accurate performance. After exploring a few nonspecifying variables that did not lead to accurate performance, these perceivers appeared to give up searching for useful perceptual variables, and they thus performed badly in the posttest.

This study led Jacobs, Runeson, and Michaels (2001) to compose a different type of zero-correlation practice. In these practice conditions, only one of the nonspecifying variables did not correlate with relative mass. This type of practice had markedly different effects on the performance of different perceivers on the variables that they used before practice. Perceivers who initially relied on a variable that was useless in practice performed badly in the first practice trials and, as in the earlier zero-correlation practice, explored the other variables. Several of the other nonspecifying variables could lead to a reasonably accurate, albeit not perfect performance, which appeared to aid perceivers in exploring the available variables. In the end, all of them discovered the more useful variables, and they continued to use these in the posttest. On the other hand, performance of perceivers who relied on nonspecifying variables that were not rendered useless and could thus lead to reasonably accurate performance was hardly affected by this practice condition. These perceivers often continued to use the same nonspecifying variables throughout the experiment.

In sum, no-variation practice does not seem to be successful in that perceivers appear to revert to their old strategies after the practice phase. Zero-correlation practice in which many nonspecifying variables are rendered useless is successful in teaching perceivers not to rely on the nonspecifying variables, but it includes the risk that perceivers do not discover specifying information or any other reasonably useful variable and therefore lose their motivation. This risk can be remedied by rendering only a single nonspecifying variable useless. To be effective, however, this should be the nonspecifying variable that is used initially. Hence, these results indicate that knowledge about which variables *novices* tend to use is indispensable for the design of optimal practice conditions, which is remarkable in the light of the more common view that "a detailed understanding of the specific sources of information employed during *skilled perception* is an essential prerequisite to the development of effective perceptual training programs in sport." (Williams & Grant, 1999, p. 211, italics added). It follows from these results that different practice conditions should be used for different perceivers in tasks that show individual differences in the variables that are used by novices. It also perhaps illustrates that it might be beneficial to modify practice conditions adaptively, tracking possible changes in which variables appear to be used.

Concluding Remarks

In the preceding sections, a few key principles of the ecological approach to perception and action were highlighted in the context of recent studies on learning, which were conducted from this perspective. The development of expertise was described as the convergence on information that is suited to the demands of the task at hand. Manipulating constraints on practice conditions, and thus manipulating the usefulness of the available nonspecifying variables, was shown to affect the rate of convergence. We argued that the convergence proceeds most rapidly if one uses zero-correlation practice in which only the initially used nonspecifying variable is rendered useless. To conclude this section, we discuss how zero-correlation techniques might be applied in more practical situations and how they might be combined with other practice methods. In addition, we briefly address recent ecological studies that have proposed learning processes other than the education of attention.

Although manipulating correlations might appear difficult in more applied situations, this need not be the case. Consider the example of judging offside again (Oudejans et al., 2000). Assistant referees might rely on a nonspecifying variable in part because this variable leads to correct judgments in the majority of potential offside situations and because they do not usually receive appropriate feedback after the judgments (they typically ignore the booing of the audience because the audience always boos). We suggest that this could be one of the applied situations in which zero-correlation practice might be useful. Using, for instance, videotaped or simulated potential offside situations, one could obtain a zero-correlation set of practice displays merely by selecting situations in which the considered nonspecifying variable leads to correct judgments in about half of the trials. This would lead to a low correlation between the nonspecifying variable and whether the attacking player is offside. Generalizing the laboratory results, one would predict that if such practice were used, assistant referees would learn not to use the commonly used nonspecifying variable and, perhaps, come to rely on variables that lead to fewer errors.

In similar ways, such techniques could be applied to the anticipation of penalty kicks by goalkeepers (McMorris & Hauxwell, 1997; Williams & Burwitz, 1993; Franks & Hanvey, 1997) and to tennis players anticipating their opponents' serves (Farrow, Chivers, Hardingham,

& Sachse, 1998; Singer et al., 1994). Other techniques to foster reliance on the more useful variables have been applied in and evaluated with these tasks. Such techniques include occluding or highlighting particular variables in videotaped or computer-generated stimuli and explicitly instructing perceivers as to what variables to attend. One interesting note is that zero-correlation techniques can be applied in addition to such techniques, and they might therefore fulfill part of the need identified by Williams, Davids, and Williams (1999, pp. 245-246):

> Particularly needed is research which looks at the design of practice environments so that perception-action couplings can be quickly confirmed and exploited by learners. One exciting possibility to be researched is how the use of salient materials, objects and colours in purpose-designed dynamic learning environments could help learners pick out invariants from the surrounding array.

Further research is needed to determine which combinations of techniques most successfully foster reliance on specifying information. A possible concern with methods that aim at explaining or highlighting the variables that should be picked up and used, however, is the general ecological assumption that expert performance consists of the exploitation of higher-order informational variables. The abstract nature and spatiotemporal extendedness of such variables might complicate attempts to explain or highlight these variables.

In addition, the study of Runeson et al. (2000; cf. Jacobs, Michaels, Zaal, & Runeson, 2001) seems to suggest that telling perceivers what variables to attend to might not contribute to a rapid convergence. These authors argued that the acquisition of expertise entails a transition from an inferential mode to a perceptual mode of apprehension. In their view, fostering reliance on information implies fostering perceptual functioning. Instructing perceivers to rely on their intuition or to attempt just to *see* the property to be perceived would be more likely to invoke perceptual functioning than carefully explaining what informational variables to attend to and how to infer the "to-be-perceived" properties from these variables. This seems to be in agreement with the conclusions of Magill (1998), who argued that merely instructing perceivers what regions to attend to and letting them explore the available variables themselves might be more effective than precisely explaining to them what variables to use.

Yet another process that has figured in recent ecological learning studies is the process of calibration (Jacobs & Michaels, 2001, 2002;

McConnell, Muchisky, & Bingham, 1998; Wagman, Riley, & Turvey, 2001). The ecological approach assumes that perception is specific to ambient energy patterns, which is to say that perception is a single-valued function of such patterns. Calibration, then, can be understood as the process that adjusts the single-valued function to the task demands—as opposed to the education of attention that adjusts the operative informational variables. Knowledge about the origin of perceptual errors seems indispensable for the design of optimal practice conditions. Are the errors due to inferential functioning, to inappropriate calibration, or to the use of nonspecifying variables? The methods previously addressed would be useful only if perceivers initially rely on nonspecifying variables.

A wealth of empirical methods that might indicate whether novices use nonspecifying variables can be found in the discussed ecological studies (for other innovative methodologies, see also Michaels, Zeinstra, & Oudejans, 2001; and Zaal & Michaels, in press). We suspect that, in addition, one can predict to a certain extent whether novice perceivers will rely on nonspecifying variables by considering the naturalness of the task and the constraints that prevail in the task ecology. If these are very natural, perceivers are likely to have experience with the task, and the attention of "novices" might already be geared toward the more useful informational variables. If so, practice methods should focus on other processes than the education of attention. It has been shown, for instance, that although the education of attention appears to be evident in one-handed catching, it explains only a small part of the large improvements that are observed in this task (Jacobs & Michaels, 2002). In many situations relevant to applied sport science, however, the task and the prevailing constraints are not so natural. This means that the information in the task situation is different from the information in natural ecologies and thus that evolution and learning might not yet have endowed perceivers with perceptual systems that are sensitive to the information. Examples of such tasks are again the perception of offside and the anticipation of penalty kicks and tennis serves. In our view, practice methods for this type of task might benefit from the techniques that are emerging in ecological learning studies.

Dynamical Systems: Perceptual-Motor Learning As Pattern Formation

Phanta rei: Everything changes, and virtually everything that evolves in time is a dynamical system (Newell, Liu, & Mayer-Kress, 2001). As such, any biological system can be described formally in terms of its dynamics. It is a task, however, that is only feasible when concentrating on the most relevant properties of the system under consideration. In this spirit, one interprets coordinative structures (i.e., task-specific neuromuscular organizations constrained to act as a functional unit, see Kugler et al., 1980) as open systems—a term borrowed from thermodynamics, which refers to dissipative structures that are in permanent contact with the environment (Haken, 1996)—that is, there is a continuous exchange of energy between the system and its surroundings. Being composed of numerous components, certain classes of open systems may organize and form coherent patterns or structures as a result from interactions between the assembling subsystems. In the inanimated world, examples of such coherent structures are laser light, sand ripples on the beach, and particular types of clouds (e.g., a fleecy or mackerel sky). In the animated world, one may think of the stripe pattern on zebras or the honeycomb structures in the beehive, but one may also think of coordinated patterns of movements such as the gaits of quadrupeds. All such patterns have in common that their explicit shapes are not prescribed by any external agent or code so that their formation is said to be self-organized. A closer look on the underlying mechanism shows that in all such systems the (microscopic) components (photons, molecules, neurons, muscle fibers, and so on) cooperate with each other to generate a few (macroscopic) quantities, which reflect ordered states of the entire system. Switches between those order states or phases, reflecting qualitative changes in pattern stability owing to the appearance and disappearance of stable solutions, can be identified as so-called (nonequilibrium) phase transitions. Here, the systems' evolution can be rigorously formalized by concepts of self-organized pattern formation as stipulated in the theory of synergetics (Haken, 1977).

In brief, following the concepts of synergetics, the aforementioned macroscopic patterns are operationalized via order parameters, which evolve in time. Phase transitions are of pivotal importance in the identification of order parameters. The reason for this is that in the immediate vicinity of phase transitions, the order parameters evolve arbitrarily slow with regard to the generating subsystems, which maintain their individual finite time scales. From the viewpoint of the order parameters, all the subsystems evolve arbitrarily quick so that they can adapt instantaneously to changes of the order parameters. Because of this colossal separation of time scales, one may say that the order parameters, even though they are generated by the subsystems, enslave their procreators by imposing a structural order onto the entire system (i.e., the slaving principle). These causal transactions between microscopic components and macroscopic states are referred to as *circular causality* (Haken, 1977). As a consequence of the slaving principle, there is a profound reduction of information in that the information that is required to characterize coherent macroscopic structures is much less than the information necessary to describe the accompanying microprocesses or microstates. Hence, if one is interested in qualitative (macroscopic) changes of the systems' behavior, one can restrict studies to (low-dimensional) order parameter dynamics, provided the order parameters can be identified.

In sum, because the order parameter dynamics cover all qualitative properties of the entire (i.e., complex, high-dimensional) system by imposing a structure onto the entire set of subcomponents, an enormous reduction of information occurs.

Changes in the Stability Properties of an Existing Order Parameter: Relative Phase and Frequency

From the theoretical backdrop outlined in the preceding section, Kelso (1981) reported an experiment (which by now is paradigmatic) on finger movements that demonstrated the occurrence of phase transitions in human interlimb coordination. When subjects start to cycle their index fingers (or hands) rhythmically in antiphase (simultaneous activation of nonhomologous muscle groups) and gradually increase the cycling frequency (as prescribed by a metronome), a spontaneous, involuntary switch to the in-phase pattern (simultaneous activation of homologous muscle groups) occurs at a certain critical frequency. Beyond this critical value, only the in-phase pattern can be stably performed. In the corresponding theoretical work (Haken et al., 1985), the coordinative states are modeled mathematically by means of a single order parameter that phenomenologically coincides with the relative phase between the fingers. Specifically, the dynamics are given by a one-dimensional potential function along whose gradient the order parameter evolves (see figure 13.1). Notice that in this figure, the order parameter's evolution should be viewed as overdamped motion of a particle (ball) over a landscape (as defined by the potential function), which implies that the order parameter always relaxes to its closest valley. Valleys (local minima) reflect stable states (see figure 13.1, left panel). The deeper the valley, the more stable the corresponding state (i.e., stronger perturbations are required to "kick" the ball out of a deep valley than out of a shallow one). A phase transition is brought about by the disappearance of a minimum so that the ball will roll from there to another, still existing, valley, resulting in an abrupt, dramatic change in the system's state (figure 13.1, middle panel). The change of the landscape is induced by an externally manipulated quantity referred to as *control parameter* (here, the cycling frequency of the fingers), which consequently affects the stability properties of the order parameter without prescribing the resulting macroscopic behavior (hence, the term self-organization).

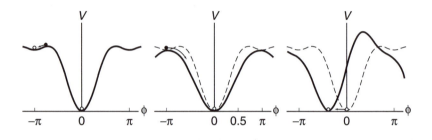

Figure 13.1   Potential landscape describing the stability features of the antiphase and in-phase modes of coordination (left panel, see also text). The stable coordination solutions are depicted by the white balls in the valleys. A black ball that rolls overdamped to its closest valley visualizes the actual state of the system. Varying the control parameter results in a change of the potential's shape so that eventually the antiphase position ($\phi = \pm\pi$) can no longer be maintained, resulting in an abrupt shift to the in-phase mode of coordination (middle panel). Right panel: An additional potential is superimposed to capture the effects of intention on the order parameter dynamics (see text).

When looking for further examples of successful studies of interlimb coordination in terms of dynamical systems, it is important to recall that the interactions between the subsystems involved are a key feature of pattern formation phenomena. During bimanual performance of multifrequency or polyrhythmic patterns (i.e., when two limbs move at different frequencies), these interactions become particularly apparent. Although the unimanual subtasks are equally simple, different frequency ratios vary considerably with regard to their difficulty of performance (e.g., Summers, Rosenbaum, Burns, & Ford, 1993), which eventually leads to abrupt transitions to other, more simple frequency ratios when the tempo of polyrhythmic performance is gradually increased (Peper, Beek, & van Wieringen, 1991, 1995). These phenomena can again be formalized as stability features of a dynamical model (Haken, Peper, Beek, & Daffertshofer 1996), which describes the differentially stable states of frequency locking as well as the transitions between these states.[4]

In contrast with experimental model systems, one might expect in more everyday situations that cyclic activities will be more independent—for instance, walking while waving a hand. Yet such activities tend *not* to be entirely independent, particularly if continued for a while. For example, most joggers notice that during steady-state running, breathing tends to lock into a fixed relationship with the step cycle with two or three steps to each inhalation cycle or perhaps three steps to two inhales. Indeed, Bramble and Carrier (1983) observed that untrained runners have little synchronization between breathing and stride. On the other hand, trained runners commonly employ the ratios 1:4, 1:3, 2:5, 1:2, 2:3, and 1:1 when running at various grades and at various speeds. That is, once it is realized that jogging with specific respiration:step ratios *is easier* and less effortful (cf. Diedrich & Warren, 1995), the jogger will select a certain frequency locking, depending on speed and externally required power. These observations illustrate that expertise is often manifested in qualitative changes in coordination modes. In this regard, multistability and the resulting flexibility may be viewed as central features of expert behavior.

To achieve this kind of expertise, considerable learning is required to gain flexibility in the face of always existing coordination tendencies. Initial attempts to address issues of learning in the context of bimanual coordination were made by Schöner and Kelso (1988), who focused on the learning of specific phase relations between rhythmic finger movements using the aforementioned potential as a starting point. Their formalization of the learning process was based on a gradient dynamics of the order parameter where the intrinsic coordination tendencies were covered by the potential shown in figure 13.1 and the desired coordination by an additional potential with a single minimum. The so-defined potential included parameters to cover the effects of both nonspecific manipulations (e.g., movement frequency as external control parameter) and coordination-specific influences (e.g., the intention to perform a certain phase relation). As such, intention might change the potential landscape and hence the stability properties of the resulting performance.

As an aside, we remark that the order parameter can still be described by a potential, provided that its dynamic either does not affect the intentional level or is much faster than the changes in intention. The latter, more realistic scenario indicates again a drastic discrepancy between time scales—however, not between micro- and macrolevels, but rather between changes in performance (fast) and intention (slow).[5]

Zanone and Kelso (1992) further elaborated these ideas in the context of an empirical study on the learning of a new phase relation (see figure 13.1, right panel). They demonstrated that the successful learning of an a priori unattractive coordination mode indeed corresponds to the emergence of a newly stable state, or, in terms of the adopted potential description, the appearance of a new valley. They also demonstrated that previously attractive modes could become unattractive when learning the new phase relation (i.e., the antiphase coordination became unattractive). The latter result implies that learning of a specific coordinative pattern may also affect the stability features of other patterns—that is, that the potential landscape changes locally as well as globally during learning (Schöner, Zanone, & Kelso, 1992).

Monotonic Reduction in Dimensionality/Number of Order Parameters

The order parameter concept is fully developed in the realm of complex systems in physics. In fact, one can make use of detailed knowledge about the microscopic components (e.g., photons in the case of laser light), allowing for unique deductions of the order parameters defined at more macroscopic levels of analysis (Haken, 1977). In the animated world, however, one is often restricted to inspired guesses regarding the relevant quantities as a result of the limited information about or inaccessibility of the subsystems. This phenomenological approach immediately leads to the question of degrees of freedom in the performance and control of movement. Apparently, one may pose this topic as a problem of discovering how the motor control system constrains the many possible combinations of joint postures to stabilize task-dependent essential variables. In this context, Scholz and Schöner (1999) proposed that variations in joint configuration, which leave the values of essential task variables unchanged, are stabilized to a lesser degree than joint configuration changes, which shift the values of the task variables. Experimentally, they studied pistol shooting at a target under various conditions (Scholz, Schöner, & Latash, 2000) and analyzed the trial-to-trial variability of the joint configurations. Throughout the entire movement, the variability of joint configurations, which affected the relevant variables, was much smaller than the fluctuations, which did not affect these variables, implying that the latter manifold becomes uncontrolled. In other words, changes of joint configurations that are irrelevant to success at the task are selectively released from control. This is an important insight because it implies that expertise is achieved by restricting control to a few relevant joint configurations while abandoning control over other configurations (rather than trying to control every possible configuration). When seeking applications of this concept, it becomes crucial to determine relevant (or irrelevant) joint configurations, or essential (or irrelevant) task variables, respectively. More important, knowing the essential task variables provides one the opportunity of promoting learning by offering knowledge of performance (or knowledge of results) in terms of those variables.

Performance of motor tasks generally involves a task-specific functional embedding of various subsystems, and one may speculate that expert performance critically depends on a task-dependent optimal embedding. Consider a soccer player's avoiding a sliding tackle while keeping control of the ball and passing it on to a teammate, which at the very least demands postural control, coordination of limbs (in avoiding the sliding and passing), and, simultaneously, anticipation of the evolving game. A variety of perceptual and motor subsystems clearly have to be set for performance to be successful, or different subsystems (including perceptual and motor components) need to be strongly correlated. The detection of correlations, or alternatively, the analysis of different degrees of variability, is of central interest, and it may elucidate principles regarding the organization of perceptual-motor tasks, the process of skill acquisition, and, by focusing on perceptual systems, the perceptual basis of the task. In fact, time-series analysis techniques are expedient tools for studying time-continuous couplings between dynamical subsystems. They are also easily applied, especially in the context of rhythmic, repetitive tasks.

Post, Daffertshofer, and Beek (2000) studied tempo-induced changes in correlations during juggling. The study was based on principal component analysis (PCA), which allows for an optimal description by means of the least number of uncorrelated variables. What is interesting to note is that the number of relevant modes was smaller for the preferred tempos than for higher tempos, with the quality of juggling being higher at the preferred tempos. Extending this line of research, Huys and Beek (2002) examined the relation between point of gaze (PG) and ball movements in three-ball cascade juggling as a function of expertise, (juggling) pattern, and tempo. Spectral analysis revealed that with increasing expertise in juggling, PG movements were reduced and often settled down in a so-called gaze through, a behavioral pattern in which the point of gaze remains bounded within a small but economically chosen region at or near the core of the pattern (see figure 13.2). Less skilled subjects predominantly showed either 1:1 or 1:2 frequency locking between ball movements and PG. In other words, juggling expertise was reflected in an overall reduction in the degree to which the balls were visually tracked. In all likelihood, the expert jugglers relied more on peripheral vision as well as on haptic and kinesthetic information than the nonexpert jugglers. These results illustrate that with increasing expertise, a gradual task-specific harnessing of the degrees of freedom associated with relevant subsystems is achieved, constituting an efficient solution to the "motor problem" at hand, to use Bernstein's (1967) apt term.

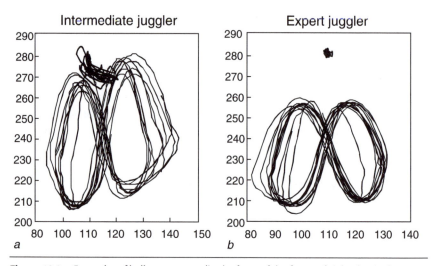

Figure 13.2   Examples of ball movements (in the form of the figure of eight that is characteristic for the cascade pattern) and PG (the trajectories near or above the zeniths of the ball trajectories) in *(a)* an intermediate and *(b)* an expert juggler. Whereas the PG of the intermediate juggler moves from ball to ball, the expert shows a clear "gaze through," or "distant stare."

Such monotonic reductions in degrees of freedom have also been a persistent finding in studies of motor learning that focus on changes in the dimensionality of movement patterns per se (e.g., Haas, 1995, using PCA; Mitra, Amazeen, & Turvey, 1998, using Abarbanel's method for state space reconstruction). It is important to note, however, that, like the research of Huys and Beek (2002), these analyses were restricted to initial (Haas, 1995; see also Haken, 1996) and intermediate (Mitra et al., 1998) stages of learning. It therefore remains an interesting and important task for researchers in this area to establish how long this reduction in dimensionality persists in the course of learning and when it levels off. It might even be the case that when expert levels of performance are reached, the dimensionality of performance again increases, reflecting a release of the number of active degrees of freedom to achieve truly superior performance. Results hinting at this possibility were reported by Ganz, Ehrenstein, and Cavonius (1996), in the context of a visual tracking task (see also Beek, 1989, for related suggestions regarding expertise in juggling). Thus, in view of the fact that expert performance is often highly flexible and adaptive, it will be crucial to actually compute the number of relevant dimensions, and, if feasible, to identify the nature of these dimensions and their functional roles. In this sense, there remains a clear need for concepts such as the uncontrolled manifold introduced by Schöner and others.

Concluding Remarks

In the preceding sections, we offered a brief (yet hopefully sufficiently succinct) survey of current developments in the study of motor learning from the perspective of dynamical systems theory. When confronted with expertise in sport tasks, the notion of potential functions may be useful for illustrating basic phenomena, such as transfer effects or the observation that an expert performer may, under certain conditions, be attracted to a previously learned but no longer desired coordinative pattern (which may still be present in the form of a local minimum in the potential landscape). An example of the latter is provided anecdotally by the case of a Dutch ice skater who suffered from an imperfection in the coordination of the push-off movement in one of the legs, but who succeeded in largely getting rid of this problem through extensive training, except that the problem tended to reemerge in competition (i.e., when under pressure). Here, one may use the notion of a potential landscape at least methaphorically, provided that due respect is paid to the distinction between methaphorical and strict operational use of dynamical concepts. When actually seeking to characterize the coordination dynamics of complex sport tasks, the notion of potential functions is presumably of little help, considering that multifrequency (as opposed to isofrequency) behavior is already too "complex" to be described in terms of evolving potential landscapes. Still, in many cyclical tasks, such as running and juggling, changes between multistable frequency-locked modes may provide a window into expert behavior. As we explained in the preceding analyses, the coherent but adaptive behavior of experts in these activities can be viewed as the result of functionally tuned interactions between relevant subsystems, such as locomotion and respiration, and gaze and stance.

Obviously, to gain more insight into the process of the formation of coordinative patterns in skilled athletes, we need to study the participating components in greater detail. In this context, it will be important to study several functional subsystems in parallel. Such an endeavor is particularly important in view of the fact that besides the nontrivial interactions, each of the functional subsystems are characterized by their own dynamical properties (i.e., intrinsic dynamics) and may evolve on individual time scales (but all shorter than those of the order parameters). Incorporating explicit dynamical properties of components into the dynamical regularities observed at the macrolevel may allow for a deeper understanding of the organizational principles between the subsystems and thus to explanations and manipulations of observed learning dynamics. For this reason, we are presently conducting an elaborate and extensive longitudinal study on learning to juggle, during which regular recordings are made of ball and hand movements, point of gaze, center of pressure, and respiration. By means of the described methods (i.e., PCA and various spectral analyses), we will then analyze the long-term changes that occurred in the interactions between the subsystems, which, in our expectation, will deepen our understanding of expertise in juggling.

Prospects of a Coherent Conceptual Framework for Understanding Expertise in the Perceptual-Motor Domain

What perceptual information do experts use? How does the information they rely on differ from the information used by less expert performers? How are motor control systems organized? How is it that experts achieve their goals with so much greater ease and so much more effectively than less expert performers? Remarkably little is known that allows us to answer such important and urgent questions. One certain reason is that perceptual and motor functioning are notoriously complicated phenomena; they are already difficult to understand in a laboratory setting, let alone in the context of everyday activities, such as those encountered in sport.

In the present chapter, we have outlined how questions regarding the perceptual and motor functioning of experts may be addressed from the perspectives of ecological psychology and dynamical systems theory, respectively. Besides a shared reluctance to invoke mediating cognitive constructs in the explanation of perceptual-motor functioning, these approaches share the more positive position that the study of perception and movement is best served by an analysis in terms of the recognition (perception) and formation (movement) of higher-order invariants or collective variables. In principle, this communality could provide the conceptual foundation for developing a coherent conceptual framework for understanding expertise in the perceptual-motor domain. For this to be achieved, however, a number of hurdles have to be taken related to epistemological and methodological differences between ecological psychology and dynamical systems theory.

Although this is not the place for an extensive treatment of these differences, it is useful to briefly highlight the main issues at stake. The first is that the ecological notion of specifying higher-order invariants is merely an epistemological assumption, whereas the order parameters in dynamical systems theory are operationally defined through the slaving principle. This implies, among other things, that neither the issue of time scales nor the issue of component dynamics plays (or can play) an essential role in ecological psychology. In our opinion, both of these aspects will prove to be indispensable when trying to come to terms with both pattern recognition and pattern formation as dynamical processes. We (or at least some of us) are therefore inclined to think that in the long run, dynamical systems theory rather than ecological psychology constitutes the more encompassing framework for studying and understanding expertise in the perceptual-motor domain. For this belief to be scientifically grounded, however, it is required that the perceptual abilities of expert performers are understood in terms of order parameters characteristic of low-dimensional percepts.

Considering the paucity of work conducted from the perspectives of ecological psychology and dynamical systems theory in the sport domain, we feel it is more productive to emphasize the shared emphasis on low-dimensional variables, whether they are called higher-order invariants or order parameters. In the present chapter, we have outlined a variety of concepts, experimental methods, and correlation techniques that may be usefully employed to identify and study the manner in which, in the development of expertise, information is collapsed in the perception of events and scenes as well as the production of coordinated movement. In addition, we have hinted at possible practical applications of these concepts and methods in the sport domain.

Summary

In this chapter, we argued the position that ecological psychology and dynamical systems theory have much to offer with regard to furthering our understanding of expertise in sport, both theoretically and methodologically. We focused on new ideas, and we alluded to the accompanying methods in passing. In particular, we highlighted the usefulness of the ecological notion of *education of attention*—that is, the process of learning to pick up specifying rather than nonspecifying information for performing a particular task. Subsequently, we introduced the dynamical notion of *reduction of dimensionality*, which is the harnessing of control to the degrees of freedom that are essential for performing a particular task while abandoning residual, nonessential degrees of freedom. Finally, we briefly discussed how these two perspectives might lead to a coherent framework for understanding expertise in sport. All in all, we hope to have illustrated how new exciting questions may be posed and addressed from the notion that expertise in both the perceptual and motor domain is characterized by information reduction.

▬ EXPERT'S COMMENTS ▬

■ Question

Beek and colleagues espouse the value of examining skilled movement from both dynamical and ecological approaches. Dynamical systems infer that certain rhythmic patterns of movement are intrinsic to the human system, whereas other patterns of movement are more difficult to acquire. Have you experienced this phenomenon in sport skills?

■ Player's Perspective: Therese Brisson

Beek, Jacobs, Daffertshofer and Huys suggest that joint perspectives of ecological, psychology, and dynamical systems theory can offer new insights on the study of motor expertise. Specifically the direction of attention and studying movement during destabilization rather than stable periods might be useful. The dynamical systems approach offers an exciting paradigm for understanding how we develop stable movement patterns and, perhaps more interesting, how we unlearn undesirable movement patterns. I have done a lot of skating instruction over the past few years, and I have always found it easier to work with children because they don't have bad habits. It is just a matter of teaching new movements. With adults, coaches need to break the bad habits first and then teach the new skill, which is something I have always found more difficult.

Unlearning undesirable but stable movement patterns can be very difficult. As a youth, I was involved in competitive swimming and had to do many timed long-distance swims. I remember the summer I was trying to change my breathing pattern for freestyle swimming. I found that I ran out of breath if I tried to breathe every fourth stroke, but breathing every second stroke was too disruptive. I concluded that breathing every third stroke would be the right balance, but this would mean breathing on both sides (bilateral breathing). So, my project for the summer was to break out of the habit of breathing on only one side and switch to the bilateral breathing. It took the whole summer of very focused and conscious attention to destabilize the old pattern and learn the new one. Much to the dismay of the lifeguards, I ended up choking and running out of breath many times. But by the end of the summer I was comfortable with the bilateral breathing. To this day, even though I don't swim very much, I use bilateral breathing, which is definitely my new stable pattern. Teaching techniques that force learners into movement patterns, such as squeezing a ball between the knees while learning the whip kick, might be useful in destabilizing undesirable movement patterns and learning new patterns.

[1]As an aside, we hesitate to accept the common argument that relevant environmental properties must be specified by ambient energy patterns because such patterns are generated lawfully. For instance, it is physically possible that different forces generate the same movement, which is to say, despite their lawful generation, movement patterns do not necessarily specify the underlying forces. The fact that ambient energy arrays are a function of environmental properties does not prove that such functions always have an inverse. Thus, although we appreciate the value and plausibility of information-environment specificity, we do not accept the lawful generation of ambient energy patterns as conclusive proof for this assumption.

[2]Note that the label "nonspecifying" is used as a qualifier of the relation between the considered variable and the property that perceivers are supposed to perceive. Thus, so-called nonspecifying variables might very well be specific to environmental properties that perceivers are not supposed to perceive. One might therefore wonder to what extent the views presented here on (non)specificity and perceptual errors are in the spirit of the philosophical foundation of ecological psychology (i.e., direct realism). These views—including the possible exploitation of nonspecifying variables—are adopted because we think they are better suited to further our understanding of perceptual learning. It could be argued that the more traditional ecological claim that perceivers always rely on specifying variables is less suited to explain the emergence of expertise, because from this position it becomes difficult to explain why the performance of perceptual tasks should be flawed in the first place. We refer the reader to a forthcoming article (Jacobs & Michaels, 2002) for more detailed treatments of such issues.

[3] We refer the reader to the appendix in the original article for details about how local constraints were manipulated to compose the different sets of displays. It is of some relevance, though, to note that the usefulness of different variables can

to a large extent be manipulated independently. Also note that the specificity of information granted by natural laws or other global constraints, which has been shown to exist in the case of the relative mass of colliding balls (e.g., Runeson et al., 2000), is not affected by the manipulation of local constraints.

[4] Unfortunately, this dynamical system cannot be nicely illustrated in terms of potential functions because it cannot be expressed as gradient dynamics. Thus, we refer the reader to the original study (Haken et al., 1996).

[5] In this line, one may be tempted to say that intention enslaves performance, but this might be a little far-fetched.

Part V

The Great Debate: Is a General Theory of Expert Performance Achievable?

N THIS BOOK, WE DO NOT SHY AWAY from debate; it's part of the scientific process we celebrate. This is best exemplified by chapters 14 (Abernethy, Farrow, & Berry) and 15 (Ericsson), and is framed by one of the most contentious issues in expertise research—whether a general theory of expertise that encompasses perceptual motor performance (as well as other domains) is attainable. Bruce Abernethy is one of the pioneers of sport expertise and a well-respected researcher, and Anders Ericsson's work has been more influential than any other researcher's in our current understanding of the acquisition of expertise. For this reason, their debate makes for a lively exchange.

Abernethy and colleagues' perspective is that our current understanding of expertise in sport has been overly influenced by the approaches of cognitive psychology. Such approaches don't necessarily account for behavior in sport, where movement is integral—where complex movements must be performed under extreme time constraints and often under conditions of physiological fatigue and competitive stress. They outline a series of shortcomings they perceive within the general theory of expertise, within the subsequent expert performance approach (Ericsson & Smith, 1991), and within the theory of deliberate practice (Ericsson, Krampe, & Tesch-Römer, 1993). For this reason, they speculate that a more general theory will only be accomplished when motor control elements are considered integral to it. Their criticisms probably reflect the concerns of many researchers in motor behavior and sport psychology.

Much of the research in sport expertise has been highly influenced by the theories and research that emerged from a group of cognitive psychology researchers at Carnegie-Mellon University in the 1970s and 1980s. To understand the theoretical directions of this group, we must briefly review a short geneology. This group was a formidable research team, as evidenced by the work of Herb Simon (Nobel laureate), Bill Chase (one of Simon's original doctoral students), and Anders Ericsson (a postdoctoral fellow working with Simon and Chase). Since Ericsson collaborated closely with Simon (Ericsson & Simon, 1980, 1984, 1993) and with Chase (Chase & Ericsson, 1981, 1982; Ericsson, Chase, & Faloon, 1980), it might seem inevitable that his collaborations and subsequent work would embrace the fundamental assumptions of human information-processing theory (e.g., fixed short-term memory capacity). However, his work on exceptional memory with Chase resulted in a direct attack on the assumptions about fixed short-term memory capacity and led eventually to the proposal of long-term working memory (Ericsson & Kintsch, 1995; see Ericsson & Kintsch, 2000, for a detailed discussion of the historical development of the new concepts).

Ericsson's publications with Simon were carefully negotiated to find a mutually acceptable theoretical framework (Ericsson & Simon, 1984, 1993, pp. 1-62) where they showed that an instantiation of the information-processing model of verbalization was possible but was by no means required nor was it the only possibility. In addition, for the purposes of the 1984 book, they agreed to avoid making claims about fixed processes and capacities so that they could reach an acceptable compromise. Since that time Ericsson, out of personal respect for Herb Simon, has tried to avoid explicitly criticizing his papers. Instead, he has concentrated on explicating his own independent views. However, one of Simon's collaborators recently published an explicit comparison between Simon and Ericsson's respective approaches (Gobet, 2000a), and this has led to a clarification of the substantial differences in assumptions (Ericsson & Kintsch, 2000; Gobet, 2000b). Given this background, it is not hard to see how others might believe that the basic tenets of Ericsson's expert performance approach might emulate those of Simon and Chase's general theory of expertise because of their close collaboration; yet, as Ericsson is the first to indicate, this is not the case.

A fundamental assumption of the general theory of expertise, proposed by Simon and Chase (1973), was that the same basic processes mediate all forms of expertise. In contrast, Ericsson and Smith (1991) proposed an inductive approach where the structure of experts' performance was empirically induced by process-tracing and experiments, which has been referred to as the *expert performance approach*. Ericsson and Smith's approach was meant as a rejection of the general theory of expertise. Reflecting on Abernethy's critique, Ericsson feels that the confusion about the role of basic information processes and fixed capacity constraints in the expert performance approach is in many ways quite understandable and possibly widely held among researchers in motor control. Ericsson's rebuttal (chapter 15) is a valuable exercise because it discusses how criticisms directed toward the general theory of expertise have been addressed by the expert performance approach. Most important, Ericsson provides his interpretation of how the expert performance approach differs from either traditional laboratory studies that test general hypotheses about basic processes or descriptive studies that attempt to elicit basic processes by designed tasks in the laboratory. He describes how the expert performance approach is committed to the study of complex behavioral phenomena and how these phenomena can be reproduced and analyzed under controlled conditions.

This debate is important because until there is consensus on what the expert performance approach proposes and how this approach differs from alternative approaches, the approach cannot be adequately evaluated. Ericsson (who should be the authoritative source on his expert performance approach) provides enlightening discussion on how his and Abernethy's interpretation of the expert performance approach differ.

Constraints and Issues in the Development of a General Theory of Expert Perceptual-Motor Performance

■ ■ ■ ■ ■

A Critique of the Deliberate Practice Framework

Bruce Abernethy
Damian Farrow • Jason Berry

A decade ago when Bruce Abernethy and Jerry and Kathi Thomas were asked to appraise the status and prospective directions of motor expertise research (Abernethy, Thomas, & Thomas, 1993), it was observed, among other things, that the field was (a) comparatively data-rich and theory-poor (see also Abernethy, 1997), (b) characterized more by descriptive work than genuine theory-driven experimentation, (c) highly influenced by research in the cognitive field (paradigmatically and theoretically) and (d) largely disconnected from key developments and issues in the motor control field and in other branches of kinesiology and exercise science. The passage of time and the excellent cross-section of ongoing motor expertise research assembled in this text provide a timely opportunity to reflect again on these issues and to make some appraisal of progress over the past decade. Some of the contributors in this volume (e.g., Janelle & Hillman, chapter 2) suggest that a number of the issues, concerns, and constraints identified previously may still remain current.

Without doubt, the perspective that has most influenced motor expertise research generally, and sport expertise research specifically, over the past decade has been that advanced by Anders Ericsson and his colleagues. The work of Ericsson and his coworkers has been influential on at least two major fronts: first, in providing a description of a general approach for the systematic study of expert performance (Ericsson & Smith, 1991) and, second, in presenting an integrated theoretical framework for the explanation of expert performance (Ericsson, 1996, 1998, 2001; this volume, chapters 3, 15). A central pillar to the theoretical framework has been the notion of deliberate practice (Ericsson, Krampe, & Tesch-Römer, 1993) and this premise, more so than others on which the theoretical framework is based, has attracted enormous research activity and debate in recent years. The position advanced by Ericsson and his colleagues—that the amount of deliberate practice is *the* limiting factor to expert performance—has almost single-handedly put the question of practice squarely back on the skill learning and expertise research agenda.

Over the past decade, the research advanced by Ericsson and colleagues—the expert performance approach, the theoretical framework, and the deliberate practice notions—has had a significant impact on motor expertise research. Given the likely prospective influence of these perspectives, it is timely to scrutinize the frameworks closely, to challenge the assumptions and premises on which the theoretical perspectives are based (as Sternberg, 1996 has also done), and through this, to determine what, if any, additional evidence or refinements to the current perspective are needed. Only through such scrutiny and challenge can theory be improved and a field be continually progressed.

This chapter attempts to provide a critique of Ericsson and colleagues' theoretical framework as it applies to the advancement of understanding motor expertise. The clear intent of the chapter is not to be iconoclastic but rather to highlight assumptions and limitations that need to be addressed explicitly and to ensure that the approach is indeed heading research in the field along a path that is likely to be illuminative, not only with respect to the description of expertise but also with respect to its explanation and prediction.

This chapter is organized into three major sections. The first section examines some of the key premises underpinning the generic expert performance approach advocated by Ericsson and Smith (1991) and the evidence available to assess the veracity of these assumptions. The second section of the chapter examines some of the central assumptions and premises that underlie the theoretical explanation of expert performance advanced by Ericsson and colleagues, particularly in the most recent elaboration of the theoretical framework provided in chapter 15 in this volume. The centrality of deliberate practice and cognitive mediation to skill learning is given particular attention. The final section examines the question of whether a theory of expertise that encompasses both cognitive and motor skills is indeed feasible or whether the quest for generality may be incompatible with the need for a theory that is both comprehensive and biologically grounded.

Issues for Experimental Analyses of Expert Performance

Ericsson and Smith (1991) have suggested the need for a three-stage approach to the understanding of expert performance. The first stage involves *in situ* observation of expert performance, the goal of which is to capture the essence of expert performance for the domain of interest and then use this to guide the design of more precise laboratory tasks. These tasks must allow the component skills of expertise to be faithfully reproduced in the laboratory setting. The rationale for commencing study with the observation of experts in their natural performance setting is that representative tasks, and ultimately also the mechanisms that underpin expert performance, can only be determined by examination of the stable performance attained by experts. If performance is unstable, the person, by definition, may not be an expert, and the underlying control mechanisms may be undergoing change as well.

The second stage proposed by Ericsson and Smith (1991) involves the more analytical and controlled search for the processes underlying the expert advantage via laboratory tasks and established investigative methodologies. The processes that mediate expert performance are assumed to be cognitive ones, and as a consequence, established methodologies from cognitive psychology are considered to be the most appropriate ones to use to trace the mediating processes. Methodologies such as those based around mental chronometry, visual search pattern measurement, and verbalization protocols are advanced as essential tools for the determination of underlying control processes and the locus of the expert advantage. A caution presented by Ericsson and Smith (see also Ericsson, chapter 15) is that laboratory tasks used with nonexperts may suggest constraints in basic information processing that simply do not apply to experts.

The final stage proposed by Ericsson and Smith (1991) involves drawing links between the putative mechanisms underpinning expert performance (as revealed through the study of representative laboratory tasks in stage two) and the type and quantity of practice and training activities undertaken by the experts over the course of their skill development. The growing number of retrospective accounts of the practice histories of experts are typical of this stage of elucidation of the expert performance approach. They include histories from experts in domains such as chess (e.g., Charness, Krampe, & Mayr, 1996), music (e.g., Krampe & Ericsson, 1996), and sport (e.g., Helsen, Starkes, & Hodges, 1998; Hodges & Starkes, 1996; Starkes, Deakin, Allard, Hodges, & Hayes, 1996; Deakin & Cobley, chapter 5; and Côté, Baker, & Abernethy, chapter 4).

Although the three-stage approach to the experimental examination of expert performance presented by Ericsson and Smith (1991) is generally accepted uncritically, some of the assumptions and rationale underpinning it nevertheless warrant critique. In the following section, three general issues arising from the so-called expert performance approach will be briefly discussed. These issues relate to the questions of whether performance must be stable for meaningful analyses to be conducted, whether typical laboratory studies misestimate (or overestimate) the processing constraints on human skill, and what types of data can provide valid and reliable insight into the control processes for perceptual-motor skills of the type displayed in many sports. The issue of whether the mechanisms affording the experts their performance advantage are necessarily cognitive ones will be addressed in a later section of the chapter. Some other related methodological issues, such as the definition of experts and the determination of appropriate control groups (which are pertinent to elements of this stage approach), have been addressed previously (Abernethy et al., 1993) and will not be repeated here.

Must Performance Be Stable for Analyses to Be Meaningful?

Ericsson (chapter 3) proposes that issues related to the essential characteristics for expert performance "can only be resolved by studying the stable performances that experts have attained after many years of practice." Without stability of performance, it is certainly questionable whether the person being studied is truly an expert (most definitions of expertise require sustained rather than occasional demonstrations of high-level performance). The absence of stability also questions whether the same underlying control processes are being used from one performance to the next. The converse, however, is not necessarily true—that is, consistent high-level performance by experts does not necessarily imply stability in the type of control processing being used nor does it imply stability in the processes that mediate expert performance.

Stable task performance (or apparently stable task performance) can potentially be achieved through factors other than a consistency in underlying control mode or an invariance in the approach taken to controlling the movements needed for the task. A number of alternative scenarios are possible. For one, true performance stability for even the simplest, most routine of motor tasks may be a rarity. The classical data of Crossman (1959), for instance, demonstrated that for even the simple task of hand-rolling cigars, components of performance continued to show measurable improvements even after many millions of trials of practice. Typical measurements of performance for the task domain may be too insensitive to detect ongoing improvements in performance that are actually taking place. It is equally possible for fundamental changes in underlying control processes to occur without affecting the overall level of task performance. In the well-documented movement equivalence phenomenon, for example, the same motor output (such as writing one's own signature) can be achieved through quite dissimilar underlying control processes—for example, the recruitment of different motor units within the hand and wrist (Rosenbaum, 1991).

Another example where stability is not representative of skill is the work of Beek and colleagues on expert jugglers (e.g., Beek et al., chapter 13; Beek & van Santvoord, 1992). This work has revealed that less skilled jugglers effectively constrain the degrees of freedom of movement; therefore, their performance "appears" to be quite stable. However, the hallmark of expert jugglers is that they can systematically "free up" degrees of freedom in movement so that even though movements are more variable, the result is a more skilled performance.

An alternative question is whether periods of performance stability are necessarily the most useful times to gain insight into the underlying control processes of expert performance, even if they can be accurately documented. In this context, it is interesting to note the emergence in the motor control field of a number of dynamical systems theories that focus on periods of transition rather than periods of stability (e.g., Haken, Kelso, & Bunz, 1985). Such theories are opposed to the cognitive and representational concepts of movement control (Carello, Turvey, Kugler, & Shaw, 1984) and are motivated by synergetics (Haken, 1983, 1990). The experimental philosophy of these approaches is that more can be learned about the underlying control processes for complex systems (such as the human nervous system) by examining these systems during periods of instability, rather than during periods of stability (Jeka & Kelso, 1989; Kelso, 1990, 1995). Proponents of dynamical systems approaches have argued that studying motor development at the cusps between the emergence of different types of dominant movement patterns (e.g., at the time of transition between crawling and walking; Clark, 1995; Kugler, 1986; Vereijken, Whiting, & Beek, 1992) can reveal new information about the organization, control, and coordination of skilled movement. Similarly, Newell (1991) has noted that the qualitative changes in movement dynamics that occur late in practice, as a function of the flexible and adaptive qualities of the skilled performer, have rarely been examined but may be potentially enlightening. He suggests that "the experimental strategy of examining the discontinuities of practice effects will also afford an understanding of their continuities" (p. 218). Extending such logic to the motor expertise field supports the contention that there would be value in using observations from periods other than the stable performance of experts to gain insight into the key processes that might ultimately mediate expert performance.

Do Laboratory Studies Misrepresent the Constraints on Human Skill?

Ericsson and Smith (1991) have concluded that typical laboratory-based estimates of information-processing constraints may significantly overstate the constraints placed on expert performers by concluding that experts are "able to acquire mechanisms that can circumvent or simply change the basic limits on information processing." Ericsson (chapter 3) further suggests that the information-processing limitations and constraints revealed by traditional laboratory studies of untrained participants are simply not valid estimates of the constraints faced by experts. The principal basis for this contention is the demonstrable changes in memory performance and memorization strategy that accompany extended practice (i.e., hundreds of hours) (Ericsson & Lehmann, 1996). A critical question in the current context is whether these statements hold true in the motor domain and for processing limitations other than those associated with memory.

The evidence in relation to this question appears somewhat mixed. It is certainly true that when laboratory tasks are chosen that are not representative of task requirements in the natural task or when they are so simplified as to deny experts access to the "smart" perceptual/ cognitive processors they may have acquired through extended practice (McLeod, McLaughlin, & Nimmo-Smith, 1985; Runeson, 1977), then the processing constraints faced by the expert in the natural setting can be dramatically overestimated. One example is the temporal accuracy of experts on simple laboratory coincidence-timing tasks, which are orders of magnitude poorer than their temporal accuracy during natural hitting and catching skills (e.g., Bootsma, 1988; Hofsten, 1987). It is also true that experts are clearly able to find ways of circumventing established information-processing constraints (Salthouse, 1991). Experts in fast ball sports, for instance, circumvent reaction time constraints through superior anticipatory skills (Abernethy, 1991), and expert players and judges or referees (Ste-Marie, chapter 7) circumvent processing demands through selectivity of processing.

What is less clear, however, is whether the basic information-processing limits are actually altered for experts. McLeod (1987), for example, has shown that even for expert cricket players, the same basic reaction time limits to unanticipated visual stimuli hold as for untrained participants. Psychological refractory period effects have been reported to remain for athletes as well as for nonathletes (e.g., Smith, 1973). Although such effects can be reduced with extended practice, they are not eliminated altogether (Gottsdanker & Stelmach, 1971). Sport experts show superior capacity for dual-task performance than do less skilled performers (e.g., Parker, 1981). Nevertheless, they still show significant single-to-dual-task decrements on secondary task performance, which indicates that automatization or proceduralization of movement control to fully release attention is rarely, if ever, obtained (Abernethy, 2001). Likewise, in studies of movement control, using classical Fitts tapping task protocols (Fitts, 1954), experience does not alter the essential linear relationship between task difficulty and movement time, although the slope (and hence the information-processing rate) may be significantly affected by practice (Kay, 1962). It is perhaps less clear for the motor domain than for the cognitive domain, and for component tasks other than memory, as to the extent to which traditional laboratory estimates of processing constraints are valid indicators of the constraints faced by expert motor performers.

Do Verbal Report Data Reflect Accurately on the Control Processes for Movement?

As noted previously, the expert performance approach presented by Ericsson and Smith (1991) places emphasis in its second stage on the use of verbal self-reporting and other tools from cognitive psychology as means of gaining insight into the nature of the control processes that mediate expert performance. Substantial and protracted debate has occured in the psychology literature as to the validity of verbal report data, and perspectives vary dramatically as to the utility (e.g., Ericsson & Simon, 1993; White, 1980) or otherwise (e.g., Le Plat & Hoc, 1981; Nisbett & Wilson, 1977) of such self-reports. At the root of debate is the extent to which performers have direct verbal access to those processes (cognitive or otherwise) that are directly responsible for the control of their skilled actions and that may provide the locus for the expert advantage. A decade ago, Abernethy et al. (1993) adopted the position that the use of verbal data may be more problematic for the study of motor experts than cognitive experts. The contention is that although there may be reliable verbal access to those aspects of cognition and control that are conscious, serial, deliberate, and effortful (after Schneider & Shiffrin, 1977), such access is unlikely for many of the rapid, automatized, or proceduralized processes that underpin skilled motor performance.

Beilock, Wierenga, and Carr (chapter 12) provide additional compelling evidence for this position by demonstrating that highly learned skills, although governed by automated or proceduralised knowledge, do not rely on conscious control during execution. The episodic memory of experts is in fact less complete and comprehensive than that of less practiced performers, which casts clear doubt on the usefulness of verbal reports as a tool for understanding the underlying control processes for movement. This new evidence is consistent with preexisting evidence of the disassociation between performance of motor skills such as bicycle riding (Runeson, 1977) and shoelace tying (Annett, 1986) and the ability to describe the required action. Such disassociation is also apparent on many cognitive tasks. For example,

Hatano (1988) found that despite their fast and accurate calculations, expert abacus users could not explain the steps involved in abacus use. Indeed "the paradox of expertise" is that "as individuals master more and more knowledge in order to do a task efficiently as well as accurately, they also lose awareness of what they know" (Johnson, 1983, p. 79).

The clear message from this evidence is that researchers need to exercise considerable caution in the use of verbal reports as data. For some (perhaps many) aspects of motor and cognitive expertise, such data may be potentially misleading and thus retard rather than accelerate understanding. To rely on the self-reports of experts as to what cues they use as the basis of, say, anticipating an opponent's action in ball sports (e.g., see Abernethy, 1990) or ensuring precise contact of the bat with the ball (e.g., see Bahill & LaRitz, 1984) would produce responses that are demonstrably false. For example, experts report "watching the ball hit the bat" when objective measurements of eye movement patterns show this to not be the case (Bahill & LaRitz, 1984).

Although it may well be reasonable to ask experts to self-report on their practice activities and other conscious decisions, it may be entirely unrealistic to expect experts to reliably self-report the coordinated neuromuscular control processes they use to hit a golf ball or execute a complex gymnastics routine. Tools different to (or at least additional to) those used for the study of conscious decision making in cognitive tasks are necessary to fully understand the processes that mediate expertise in the motor domain.

Issues for Deliberate Practice As a Theoretical Framework

Ericsson in this volume and elsewhere (Ericsson, 1996, 1998, 2001; Ericsson et al., 1993) has presented an integrated theoretical framework that builds on the expert performance approach of Ericsson and Smith (1991) by attempting to explain expert performance. This section of the chapter examines six of the key pillars and assumptions within the theory presented by Ericsson and his colleagues, and it seeks to assess the evidence regarding these assumptions and assertions.

Practice (Not Talent) Sets the Limits to Performance

The deliberate practice theory of expert performance takes the strong perspective that it is practice and experience rather than any innate talent that is the real determinant of expert performance. This perspective is one that gains support from those advocating environmental determinants of exceptional performance (e.g., Howe, 2001; Howe, Davidson, & Sloboda, 1998), but it is clearly at odds, as Janelle and Hillman note (chapter 2), with the perspectives advanced by behavioral geneticists (e.g., Rowe, 1998).

That the undertaking of extensive amounts of practice is essential for the attainment of expert performance is largely noncontroversial. In activities such as chess and music (Charness et al., 1996; Ericsson et al., 1993) and in sport (e.g., Helsen et al., 1998; Hodges & Starkes, 1996; Starkes et al., 1996; Deakin & Cobley, this volume, chapter 5; Côté et al., this volume, chapter 4), there is a general consistency of finding that those who reach expert levels of performance in competitive domains have all typically undertaken something in the order of 10 years or 10,000 hours of practice (for an exception, see van Rossum, 2000). Although some justifiable debate exists as to how accurate long-term retrospective recall (of hours of practice) may be and how accurately hours spent *at* practice equates to hours spent *in* practice (see Deakin & Cobley, chapter 5, and Starkes, Weir, & Young, chapter 10), there is little contention over the observation that experts don't become experts without an enormous investment in practice. Where contention arises is in relation to the more extreme claims that (a) any healthy individual can become an expert if they do sufficient practice and (b) genetic characteristics (or "talent") do not set limits to the attainment of expertise. Ericsson (chapter 3, p. 56), for example, argues that when one excludes "height-related characteristics, recent reviews . . . have not uncovered any firm evidence that innate characteristics are required for healthy adults to attain elite performance." He further claims that "when appropriately designed training is maintained with full concentration on a regular basis for weeks, months, or even years, inborn unmodifiable characteristics do not appear to constrain anyone from reaching high levels of performance." Addressing these claims requires resolution of whether practice is not only a necessary condition for expert performance but also a sufficient one.

It is understandably difficult to obtain solid evidence in regard to the claim that any healthy individual can become an expert if one does sufficient practice (of the right type). Nevertheless, it is possible to gain considerable improvements on the existing research base concerning the practice-expertise linkage. As Sternberg (1996, pp. 349-350) notes, it is impossible to draw causal inference regarding the link between the amount of practice and expert performance in the absence of control groups. More systematic evidence clearly needs to be collected on nonexperts than is currently the case. Even a single case of someone's undertaking the same amount and type of practice over the same extended period as does a matched expert without becoming an expert would cast significant doubt on the amount of practice as a sufficient condition for expert performance.

A growing body of evidence, however, now allows the veracity of Ericsson's claim regarding the influence (or noninfluence) of genetic factors in expert motor performance to be evaluated. Despite the assertions to the contrary, clear evidence, through controlled studies such as the HERITAGE Family Study (Bouchard et al., 1995), supports the conclusion that not only do some genetic factors account for significant variation in basal levels of parameters, such as maximal oxygen uptake (accounting for about 40% of the variance; Bouchard et al., 1998), but that different genetic factors also account for nearly half of the individual differences seen in response to extended training (20 weeks; Bouchard et al., 1999). Although some aspects of sport expertise (such as tactics and technique) may not be affected by genes, it is very difficult in the face of the growing evidence from exercise science to sustain the argument that genetic factors do not play a critical role in determining the limits to the impact of training and therefore the ultimate limits to performance levels in many sports (Singer & Janelle, 1999; Skinner, 2001). Twin studies suggest that the influence of hereditary factors is not simply restricted to physiological capacities (such as $\dot{V}O_2$max), but they may also account for a significant portion of the performance variance in more skilled-based parameters, such as choice reaction time and coincidence timing (e.g., Luciano et al., 2001).

Only Some Types of Practice Will Allow Expertise to Develop

A fundamental pillar of the Ericsson et al. theory of expert performance is that not all practice activities are equally beneficial for skill learning. It is primarily the quantity of a particular subset of possible practice activities (viz., deliberate practice) that determines whether or not expertise is ultimately achieved. Deliberate practice activities are considered by Ericsson et al. (1993) to be those activities that (a) are specifically designed to improve performance, (b) are of (apparently) high relevance to the particular domain, (c) take significant effort to complete, and (d) are not intrinsically enjoyable. These characteristics themselves suggest a range of issues for which evidence-based scrutiny is possible.

Must Practice Necessarily Be Deliberate and Purposeful to Be Beneficial?

The Ericsson et al. position is that only practice performed deliberately and with the designed intent of improving performance can be beneficial to the acquisition of expertise. Such a position consequently rules out the prospect of incidental learning (i.e., learning in the absence of an intention to learn) contributing to the acquisition of expertise. The basis for doing this is unclear, given the large body of evidence showing the possibility that significant incidental learning can take place in laboratory, real-world, and motor contexts (e.g., Kelly, Burton, Kato, & Akamatsu, 2001; Dickinson, 1978). A recent study of expert team sport players (see Abernethy, Côté, & Baker, 2002; Côté et al., this volume, chapter 4) has demonstrated the powerful effect that early experience in a range of other sports can have on the development of expertise in the specialist activity. In other words, the broader the range of other sporting experiences undertaken during the sampling years, the less deliberate practice the players need to undertake to acquire expertise. Given that these other sport involvements would have taken place without the deliberate and purposeful intent of improving performance in the activity in which expertise was ultimately attained, this finding provides an example of activities that do not qualify as deliberate practice activities within the Ericsson et al. criteria, yet which are apparently important for the development of expert performance. It would appear as a consequence that practice need not necessarily be deliberate and purposeful to contribute to the acquisition of expertise. It is perhaps more likely, as Magill (1989, p. 482) has suggested, that it "is the type of processing activity engaged in during practice that may be more important for learning than the intention to learn."

Must Practice Necessarily Require Full Concentration and Attention to Be Beneficial?

Ericsson (chapter 3) posits that practice requires "full attention and complete concentration" to allow athletes to derive the necessary benefits from practice to progress toward expertise. Again, this position is one that is not completely consistent with all of the available evidence, especially from the learning and performance psychology fields. One consideration is that full concentration may not always generate the optimal learning and performance outcome. Indeed, increasing consciousness to many actions may result in poorer (rather than better) performance—Eccles' (1972) "paralysis by analysis" problem. A second important consideration is the strong potential for implicit learning to occur—that is, improved task performance in the absence of concurrent acquisition of conscious and explicit knowledge about the performance of the skill (Maxwell, Masters, & Eves, 2000). Although both implicit and explicit processes may contribute to learning on the same task, growing evidence suggests that implicit learning may be advantageous in that it may be less subject to interference from conscious processes such as emotion and anxiety and may be more resistant to forgetting than explicit learning (Reber, 1989).

The evidence base for the efficacy of implicit-learning processes in the acquisition of perceptual-motor skills is growing (e.g., Green & Flowers, 1991; Masters, 1992; Maxwell et al., 2000). Farrow and Abernethy (2002) have recently presented evidence suggesting that one of the classical defining characteristics of expert racket sport players—the capacity to anticipate their opponent's action from movement pattern information alone—can be learned more effectively through implicit means than through more traditional explicit instruction. Indeed, some theorists (e.g., Beek, 2000) now suggest that implicit learning may be the norm, and explicit learning the exception, for the acquisition of movement skills. The fundamental hierarchical organization of the human motor system may mean that explicit learning is only possible when the task constraints are such as to permit involvement of those select, upper levels of the nervous system that have the capacity to use verbal information. In all other circumstances, implicit learning may be the only viable learning form. The important point here is that significant learning of characteristics known to be the ultimate hallmarks of expert performance seems possible in the absence of explicit concentration and attention on the features to be learned.

Must Performance in Practice Necessarily Be of High Quality to Be Beneficial?

Ericsson (chapter 3) suggests that the quality of an athlete's performance must be maintained in practice for learning of benefit to accrue. Some of the older laboratory evidence on motor learning under fatiguing conditions would suggest this need not necessarily be the case, although validation in natural settings is certainly necessary. The literature on massed practice (for a review, see Schmidt & Lee, 1999) indicates that it is possible for significant learning to occur in the absence of good performance in practice. Participants assigned to practice conditions with short rest intervals (massed practice conditions) typically perform poorly during practice as compared with participants given lengthy rest intervals (distributed practice conditions). They are, however, able to demonstrate, after suitable rest intervals, levels of learning indistinguishable from that of those practicing under less fatiguing conditions (e.g., Stelmach, 1969). Likewise, the literature on contextual interference also indicates that quality practice and learning need not be synonomous (for reviews, see Magill & Hall, 1990; Brady, 1998). Contextual interference occurs when several skills are practiced within the same practice session. Practicing one skill repeatedly for a block of trials before changing to practice another skill is considered a low-interference (blocked) practice schedule. In contrast, alternating between the two skills after each practice trial results in a high-contextual interference (random) practice condition. The research evidence indicates that although random practice typically leads to suppressed or impaired practice performance relative to blocked practice, it ultimately leads to superior learning, as assessed through retention or transfer measures (e.g., Hall, Domingues, & Cavazos, 1994). High-quality performance in practice is therefore not necessarily an essential precondition for positive learning outcomes.

Is Solitary Practice Better Than Competition As a Means of Acquiring Expertise?

The contention from the studies of chess players (Charness et al., 1996) and musicians (Ericsson et al., 1993) is that solitary practice is the best predictor of expert performance and that the consideration of time spent in competition adds nothing further to the prediction of performance variance. As Janelle (2001) observes, it would appear premature to discount experience in competition as a necessary condition for the development of expertise, at least in the sport domain, given the absence of any evidence to the contrary. Indeed, in team sports in particular, the evidence that is available (Helsen et al., 1998; Starkes et al., 1996) suggests that time spent in competition is an extremely important component on the path to expertise. Competition is certainly regarded by athletes themselves as pivotal for the development of key performance components, such as perception, decision making, and physical fitness (Baker, Côté, & Abernethy, in press).

Is Beneficial Practice Necessarily Not Intrinsically Enjoyable?

In its strictest conception, deliberate practice activities are those activities that are not only designed to improve performance, but they also have high domain-relevance, require significant effort, and are not intrinsically enjoyable (Ericsson et al., 1993). Studies of the practice activities of sport experts generally reveal very few activities of significance that simultaneously satisfy all of these criteria. The dominant practice activities reported by sport experts that are high in relevance and effort are typically regarded by the athletes as also being high in enjoyment (e.g., see Deakin & Cobley, this volume, chapter 5; Helsen et al., 1998; Hodge & Deakin, 1998; Starkes, 2000). Ericsson (1996) has proposed that the observed differences are due to differences in measurement approach and that the reported enjoyment levels by athletes relate to their enjoyment of the outcomes of practice, rather than practice per se. A recent study of team sport athletes in which the athletes were asked to rate enjoyment of practice relative to the most enjoyable activities they could imagine revealed that although enjoyment decreases in the later years, where training volume and intensity are at their peak, practice even at this time remained among the most enjoyable activities that the athletes could imagine (Abernethy et al., 2002). In sport tasks at least, it appears that practice, while highly beneficial to the ultimate development of expertise, can also be undertaken when it is inherently enjoyable. Failure to consider the enjoyable, playful elements of movement experience may well mean overlooking foundational elements that are pivotal to the development of expertise (and the maintenance of motivation), at least as it manifests itself in the domain of sport (Côté et al., chapter 4).

Is Progressive Challenge Necessary for Skill Development?

A theme developing progressively through the incremental elaborations of the deliberate practice framework is that practice must present continual challenges for skill progression to occur. This proposition is quite uncontentious, at first approximation at least, and it is one completely consistent with the kind of practical advice one can find in the majority of texts on the teaching and learning of skills, including motor skills (e.g., Ditchfield & Bahr, 1988; Robb, 1972). However, the evidence is quite limited to support the superiority in skill-learning contexts of practice activities of increasing difficulty over practice activities of constant difficulty. Although a strong body of evidence indicates that variable practice is superior in its learning outcomes to constant practice (Lee, Chamberlin, & Hodges, 2001; Schmidt & Lee, 1999), the benefits or otherwise of progressive challenge have not been as well investigated as one might expect. Coaches and teachers are frequently thought to play a key role in the provision of practice that is suitably challenging to stimulate progressive skill development, but it is clearly difficult to know with certainty whether the coach's or teacher's role in performance improvement is causal or simply correlational. The data from developing countries presented by Salmela and Moraes (chapter 11) and from a coaching perspective (Cipriano, chapter 11, p. 292) suggests that although the availability of good coaching may aid the development of expertise, it is not a necessary condition for the emergence of exceptional performance.

As with much of the current dogma on best practice for skill improvement, the development of a much stronger evidence base than currently exists is needed before a more prescriptive position can be taken on what types of practice will, and equally important will not, contribute to the development of expert performance. With respect to Ericsson's deliberate practice framework, a number of important issues clearly offer room for modification and improvement. Important considerations, not well encapsulated in the current deliberate practice framework, include the need for practice to faithfully reproduce the underlying control requirements of the performance setting and to address factors known to be limiting ones to performance. Practice that requires active problem solving (or solution generation) (Deakin & Cobley, this volume, chapter 5; Starkes, 2000) is more likely to be beneficial than practice that merely passively repeats the same actions, however relevant and effortful they may be. Similarly practice that addresses skill components known to reliably discriminate the expert performer from the nonexpert is more likely to be beneficial than practice of components that lack this discriminative characteristic (Abernethy, Baker, & Côté, 1999; Williams & Ward, this volume, chapter 9).

Mental Representations Mediate Expert Performance

Ericsson (chapter 3) concludes that expert performance "is mediated by acquired mental representations that allow the experts to anticipate, plan and reason about alternative courses of action." We have noted earlier in this chapter one particular aspect of contention with this conclusion: The contribution that implicit learning and control below the level of consciousness appear to play in at least some aspects of expert motor performance brings into question the conclusion that experts necessarily have the capacity to reason about their actions. However, a more general issue is whether expert performance is necessarily mediated by mental representations.

Over the past two decades, there has been protracted debate in the motor control and learning field as to whether a consolidated theory of movement control and learning requires mental representations and other cognitive constructs to be invoked as a basis for explanation. Theorists influenced by Gibson's perspectives on direct perception (e.g., Gibson, 1979) and Bernstein's perspectives on action (e.g., Bernstein, 1967) have argued strongly against the arbitrary nature of mental representations in particular (e.g., see Carello et al., 1984; Kelso, 1986) and have rather, under the frameworks of dynamical systems and ecological psychology, proposed alternatives that seek explanation without recourse to the use of representations. Full treatments of these alternative perspectives and their implications for the study of expertise have been given previously (e.g., Abernethy, Burgess-Limerick, & Parks, 1994; Williams, Davids, and Williams, 1999) and will not be repeated here. A critical point, in the current context, is that alternative explanations of skill to those based on mental representations are possible and, given the central place such constructs play in the Ericsson framework, a fuller consideration of the assumptions underpinning this aspect of the framework is warranted than has been undertaken to date. A second, equally important point, illustrated well by Beek et al. (chapter 13) and the work of Vereijken, Emmerik, Whiting, and Newell (1992) is that mental representations are certainly not required to account for all aspects of expert performance. Experts, for example, are able to exploit more fully gravitational and inertial forces and the intrinsic physical properties of the musculoskeletal system to control movements, thus reducing the total load that might be placed on any cognitively-mediated control system. If there is indeed a role for mental representations and other cognitive constructs in movement control (and few would dispute this), they alone are unlikely to be the sole mediators of expert performance.

Stable Performance and Automation Are the Causes of Nonexpert Performance

Ericsson (chapter 3) presents the proposition that one of the defining developmental characteristics of experts is that they do not allow their performance to stabilize and become automated; rather, what Ericsson contends is that experts maintain cognitive awareness throughout their development and that this ability permits continual refinement of their mental representations of the task. Stable performance and automaticity are conceptualized as the key factors that arrest the development of nonexperts.

For a number of reasons, as noted in one form or another earlier in this chapter, this proposition is potentially problematic, at least for expertise in the motor domain. First, it is doubtful whether experts maintain conscious awareness of many of the control processes that underpin skilled movement. Second, stability in performance does not necessarily mean consistency in the underlying control. Stability in performance and automaticity need not necessarily coexist; indeed, they are at different levels of analysis. Stabilized performance is at the descriptive outcome level whereas automaticity is at the underlying control process level. It is therefore possible to have stable performance without a skill becoming automated, and it is equally possible for a skill to become automated with performance still showing elements of variability. Implicit within Bernstein's (1967) view of coordinated movement, for instance, is the notion of variability being a necessary by-product of skilled performance. Third, and most telling, the available experimental evidence, primarily arising from dual-task studies, is that automaticity is increased in experts (e.g., Brouwer, Waterink, van-Wolffelaar, & Rothengatter, 1991; Parker, 1981; Rowe & McKenna, 2001; Beilock et al., this volume, chapter 12; for a review, see Abernethy, 2001), not decreased as the Ericsson proposition would predict. In the face of this conflicting evidence, it is difficult to sustain the proposition that resisting automaticity has a justifiable basis for inclusion in a consolidated framework directed at understanding expert performance.

Neural Adaptations Are Like Any Other Physiological Adaptation

The elaborations of the theoretical framework for expert performance by Ericsson and colleagues increasingly make reference to physiological training data. Observations from such sources are frequently used to draw inferences in relation to expert performance in skill-based domains. The tacit assumption in so doing is that valid comparisons and parallels can be drawn between physiological adaptations to training and skill adaptations to practice. Although such a comparison may indeed be valid, the evidence to support this assumption is not yet available. The neural basis for learning is still poorly understood (Beggs et al., 1999), and it is not at all clear whether the mechanisms through which the nervous system reorganizes in response to extended practice share much in common at all with the mechanisms responsible, for example, for improvements in physical capacity following endurance training. A major challenge for any theory of human performance that claims to be integrated will be to make satisfactory, biologically plausible links between a number of different levels of explanation and analysis. Given how difficult this step of integration has proven in other areas of psychology (e.g., see Cacioppo, Berntson, & Crites, 1996), there is still clearly much left to do to gain a satisfactory, integrated explanation of the interplay between neural biology, cognition, and action as it applies to expert perceptual-motor performance.

Is a General Theory of Expertise Possible?

Theory development in the field of expertise has, to date, been dominated by paradigms and approaches developed from, and for, the study of cognitive tasks. Memory-based paradigms from chess (e.g., Chase & Simon, 1973) and knowledge-based paradigms for problem solving in mathematics and physics (e.g., Anderson, 1982) have been particularly influential in shaping the research agenda in the cognitive and the motor domain. Indeed, it is not uncommon to be presented with the view that the scholarly study of expert performance has its origins in the chess studies of de Groot (1965) and then Chase and Simon (1973) (e.g., see Ericsson, chapter 3) even though a much earlier body of literature exists that is derived from the study of motor tasks such as typing and telegraphic skills (e.g., Bryan & Harter, 1899; Book, 1908).

The general theoretical framework for explaining expert performance presented by Ericsson and colleagues is strongly grounded in the cognitive tradition, and it is based on the premise that the same basic processes mediate expert performance in the motor domain of sport as in the cognitive domain of activities such as chess playing. To what extent this premise is true bears directly on the issue of the viability and plausibility of a general theory of expertise.

The strongest argument in favor of the possibility of an omnibus theory that might satisfactorily explain expertise in cognitive and motor domains is demonstration that many of the characteristics that discriminate experts from nonexperts in the cognitive domain also discriminate the expert in sport from the nonexpert (cf. Glaser & Chi, 1988; Abernethy, 1994). What is not clear, however, is whether this arises because the component processes mediating expertise are fundamentally the same in both domains or simply because the same investigative paradigms, and the inherent assumptions and biases within them, are used in both settings (Abernethy et al., 1993). Although some obvious similarities exist between the domains, it is important to recognize the existence of a number of fundamental differences in task requirements and constraints between the sport domain and the quintessential cognitive pursuits, such as chess playing. Sport tasks typically present greater temporal constraints (e.g., responses required in time windows of milliseconds, rather than minutes) and greater spatial complexity (e.g., dynamic patterns in three dimensions, rather than two). Unlike chess, the additional task complexity in many sports arises from the need to consider the concurrent actions of multiple teammates and opponents. What further complicates sport performance are the effects of physiological fatigue and the need to adaptively respond to subtle differences in performance conditions from one occasion to the next (e.g., differences in playing surfaces, wind, and other weather conditions).

The defining characteristic of performance in the motor domain is, of course, the need to produce a movement response—with the quality of the movement produced having a direct bearing on the performance outcome. What is important to note is that the addition of the need to produce a movement response may completely change the nature of the underlying control mechanisms and hence also the potential mediating variables. Sport tasks need to be conceptualized as more than simply the perception and cognition processes from chess with an action component added. In other words, it is possible that perception and cognition may be fundamentally different in motor tasks because of the need for these processes to couple with action, both dynamically and often under severe time constraints. For example, the task constraints of sport skills may favor the emergence of control processes that are fast acting, automated, and directly coupled; however, they may not be conducive to the emergence of conscious control modes and the production of verbalizable knowledge. That the relationship of the motor component of skill to the perception and cognition components is likely interactive rather than simply additive is acknowledged clearly in Gibsonian theories of perception-action coupling (Gibson, 1979), but it is also evident in some more traditional cognitive knowledge-based approaches. French and Nevett (1993), for instance, note the influence on knowledge organization of an athlete's self-perceived motor capabilities.

Because of the likelihood that the control processes underlying skilled (expert) performance in cognitive tasks and motor tasks, such as those involved in sport, may be quite different, any attempt to go beyond simple description and build an omnibus explanatory theory of expertise may be extremely difficult. A comprehensive theory of motor expertise needs a much fuller grounding in motor control elements and how these may modify with different types of practice than is currently provided in the deliberate practice framework. As Beek et al. (chapter 13) notes, and as was the case a decade ago (Abernethy et al., 1993), the challenge remains to more fully integrate theoretical advances in the motor control and learning field with premises on expertise of the type being developed by Ericsson and colleagues. Until that challenge is met, a more satisfactory explanation of motor expertise is likely to remain elusive.

Summary

The work of Ericsson and Smith (1991), in setting an operational framework for the study of expertise, and Ericsson and colleagues (Ericsson, 1996, 1998, 2001, chapters 3, 15; Ericsson et al., 1993), in developing a theoretical framework for the explanation of expert performance, has dominated conceptualization and research about expert performance for the past decade. It has placed issues related to the quantity and type of practice to the forefront of the expertise research agenda. The focus of this chapter has been an examination of some of the key assumptions and premises underpinning the expert performance approach and the deliberate practice theoretical framework. It is concluded that although the approach has many positive attributes, especially for the explanation of expertise in the cognitive domain, it has some significant shortcomings that require attention and reconceptualization if the approach is to provide a viable framework for the explanation and prediction of expertise in the motor domain. Issues viewed as particularly problematic relate to the use of verbal reports as data, the omission of the role of incidental and especially implicit learning in expert performance, the conceptualization of automaticity and proceduralization as an impediment rather than an attribute of expert performance, and the exclusive reliance on cognitive mechanisms as the locus of expertise. Resolution of these issues through a closer alignment of theory development on cognitive expertise and theory development in the motor control and learning field is important for the continued progression of motor expertise from a largely descriptive field to one in which theory building and testing is a more prevalent activity.

How the Expert Performance Approach Differs From Traditional Approaches to Expertise in Sport

■ ■ ■ ■ ■

In Search of a Shared Theoretical Framework for Studying Expert Performance

K. Anders Ericsson

I n chapter 14, Abernethy, Farrow, and Berry review recent progress in the study on motor expertise, and they focus on one approach, namely the expert performance approach. They judged this approach to have had a dominant impact on motor expertise research during the decade following the seminal book by Starkes and Allard (1993) on "cognitive issues in motor expertise." Unfortunately, their chapter is based on the incorrect assumption that the expert performance approach was a natural extension of the classic theory of expertise proposed by Simon and Chase (1973).

As Starkes explains in her introduction to this section, the expert performance approach has a complex relation to the classic theory of expertise. When the cognitive evidence on complex skills and expertise emerged in the 1980s, it forced many scientists to reject the basic theoretic assumptions of Simon and Chase's (1973) information-processing theory of expertise. In response to the demands for a new alternative framework for the study of expertise, Ericsson and Smith (1991) proposed the expert performance approach. However, Abernethy et al. (chapter 14, p. 367) describes the essence of the expert performance approach in the following incorrect manner: "The general theoretical framework for explaining expert performance by Ericsson and colleagues is strongly grounded in the cognitive tradition, and it is based on the premise that the *same basic processes* mediate expert performance in the motor domain of sport as in the cognitive domain of activities such as chess playing. To what extent this premise is true bears directly on the issue of the viability and plausibility of a general theory of expertise." The premise that the same basic processes mediate all forms of expertise describes the fundamental assumption of the general theory of expertise as proposed by Simon and Chase (1973), not the expert performance approach of Ericsson and Smith (1991). Given that the expert performance approach was proposed as a rejection of both this assumption and Simon and Chase's general theory of expertise (which was based on empirical evidence from cognitive domains of expertise), it would obviously reject any generalization to perceptual-motor domains. Consequently, the insightful criticisms of Simon and Chase's (1973) general theory of expertise and its proposed learning mechanisms articulated by Abernethy, Thomas, and Thomas (1993) are not valid when redirected toward the expert performance approach as Abernethy et al. have done in parts of chapter 14. In fact, much of their chapter's criticisms directed toward the basic learning mechanisms of the general theory of expertise indirectly support and validate an alternative, such as the expert performance approach.

Even when the distinction between the expert performance approach and the classic theory of expertise has been accepted, Abernethy et al.'s views (chapter 14) and my views still differ on how to best apply the expert performance approach to the study of motor expertise. In particular, I will emphasize in this chapter how the expert performance approach makes a firm commitment to the study of complex integrated behavioral phenomena and how these phenomena can be reproduced and examined under controlled conditions. I will then attempt to describe clearly what the expert performance approach proposes and how this approach differs from alternative approaches. Only when we have a consensual understanding of the theoretical framework for the expert performance approach is it possible to evaluate it fairly.

This chapter consists of three main parts. In the first part, I sketch the historical background to Simon and Chase's (1973) general theory of expertise and how later evidence even from cognitive domains of expertise were found to contradict its assumptions. Unfortunately, there will be some overlap with my other chapter (chapter 3), but this background is necessary for explaining how the expert performance approach fundamentally differs from traditional approaches where theoretical assumptions motivate the design of laboratory tasks and experiments. In particular, I show how the expert performance approach was developed to find reproducibly superior performance in everyday life and then capture this performance with representative tasks in the laboratory. In the second part, I show how Abernethy et al.'s (chapter 14) interpretation differs from my own in the application of the expert performance approach to sport. Finally, and most important, I will contrast the expert performance approach's focus on capturing the superior performance of experts with the traditional approach's focus on designing simple tasks to test general theoretical assumptions and hypotheses. Specifically, I discuss Abernethy et al.'s (chapter 14) claim that the expert performance approach is generally accepted, and I argue that only a small number of researchers currently conduct research with the focus on capturing the essence of expert performance in sport. (In fact, many of them have contributed chapters to this book.) In the third section, I discuss Abernethy et al.'s (chapter 14) attempts to identify generalizable claims about deliberate practice within the expert performance approach. In particular, I address his criticisms that neither the expert performance approach nor I fully appreciate the new emerging evidence for the importance of innate talent in sport. Finally, I conclude with a few comments on my own vision for future research on expert performance in sport.

The Challenge of Studying the Complex Mechanisms Mediating Expertise

In the following sections, I give a brief overview of just how complicated and challenging it is to study expertise. First, I give a review of the history of how the expert performance approach came to be. Second, I consider how crucial it is to capture and re-create the performance via the expert performance approach. Last, I discuss the factors involved in capturing expert performance in the lab, and I also touch on the difference between capturing sport and nonsport performance.

A Brief History of the Emergence of the Expert Performance Approach

Researchers of highly skilled performance often become discouraged by the daunting complexity of the mechanisms that mediate expertise. The recent boom for studies of expertise during the 1970s, '80s, and '90s can be linked to a theory-based proposal for how expertise could be easily studied with standardized tasks in the laboratory. In this description, I focus on how the seminal work by Chase and Simon (1973) offered a new laboratory paradigm for studying the memory performance of experts that was based on the assumptions of their theory of expertise (Simon & Chase, 1973). I then show how this theoretically motivated approach was criticized and how the expert performance approach was proposed to address the problems of explaining expertise within the constraints of basic processes and fixed capacities.

When de Groot (1978/1946) started his pioneering empirical studies of expertise in chess, he was interested in how expert chess players were able to find better chess moves than less skilled players. Consequently, he presented world-class and expert players with chess positions (taken from unfamiliar games among chess masters), and he asked them to pick the best move while thinking aloud. From extended analyses of the "think-aloud" protocols, de Groot found that the best players discovered their best move while they evaluated different move sequences during the planning phase. Even more surprising, he found that the best players were able to identify very good moves (not necessarily the best move) even after looking at a new position for only a few seconds. After such brief presentations, the best players could recall the locations of virtually every chess piece whereas less skilled players could recall much less. In his book, de Groot (1978/1946) gives extended analyses of the complex thoughts and mechanisms that mediate the selection of moves by world-class experts, and he describes aspects of the massive complex knowledge about chess that chess masters have acquired during years of study of chess.

It was Chase and Simon (1973) who fundamentally changed the study of expertise by intentionally avoiding the study of the complex processes that mediated the selection of moves. They instead focused on de Groot's finding that experts displayed an exceptional memory for chess positions. In contrast to de Groot's (1978/1946) interest in the incidental memory resulting from selecting a move for a presented chess position, Chase and Simon changed the task to a test of memory by instructing chess players to attempt to remember as much as possible from briefly presented chess positions. Chase and Simon's studies of memory demonstrated that highly skilled players recalled nearly all of the 25 to 30 pieces from regular chess positions whereas beginners could only recall around 4 to 6 pieces. On the other hand, when the chess pieces were randomly rearranged before the presentation, the memory of highly skilled players was reduced almost to the low level of beginners, and thus they could only recall around four to six pieces. The latter finding is crucial because it shows that skilled players' recall advantage is highly constrained and limited to meaningful chess positions.

Simon and Chase (1973) proposed a general theory of expertise based on human information-processing theory (Newell & Simon, 1972), where the key constraint for attaining expertise was the slow accumulation of patterns and chunks that mediated and thus explained superior memory for regular chess positions. The same patterns were hypothesized to mediate retrieval of moves for previously encountered chess positions from memory. Simon and Chase showed that 10 years of intense involvement in the domain was necessary to reach an international level in chess, and their analyses suggested the need to acquire some 50,000 patterns and chunks—roughly equivalent to the number of foreign words that had to be mastered in learning a new foreign language. The Chase and Simon theory thus suggested a tight relation between length of experience and attained expertise. In fact, some researchers started to define expertise in terms of sufficiently lengthy experience in the associated domain, typically 10 years or more.

The Chase-Simon memory paradigm allowed investigators to easily study expertise in laboratory settings for many different domains without analyzing and describing the complex skills and knowledge that mediate their performance in representative situations. Experts and novices could be presented with representative stimuli from the domain for recall tests, and their memory could be compared across groups as well as to recall for randomly arranged versions of the same stimuli. Numerous studies demonstrated that experts recalled more information from representative stimuli from the domain than less accomplished participants or novices with no comparable differences for "random" stimuli in sport (Starkes & Allard, 1991) and in many other domains (Ericsson & Lehmann, 1996).

The rationale for studying experts' memory performance to understand the structure of their real expertise (such as selecting the best moves) was based on a fundamental theoretical assumption. Simon and Chase (1973) assumed that the fixed capacity of short-term memory was severely limited and thus constrained how learning and pattern-based retrieval could be accomplished. Improvement in chess skill and memory for chess position had to be mediated by the same complex patterns that were acquired and stored in long-term memory. Superior chess skill would therefore logically imply superior memory for representative situations. Many different scientists, such as Abernethy et al. (1993) and Ericsson and Smith (1991), have questioned the validity of these assumptions, especially for skilled and expert performers who have engaged in years of practice.

In addition, direct empirical evidence contradicted the assumptions of Chase and Simon. For example, the memory for chess positions by some completely unfamiliar with chess was shown to improve dramatically with practice. After only around 50 hours of practice with the memory test for chess positions (Ericsson & Harris, 1990), the novice was able to match the recall performance of chess masters who had thousands of hours of chess-playing experience. In general, participants were found to react to the memory tasks with further experience. After some practice with these tasks, chess experts were able to improve their performance and even display consistently superior performance for "random" arrangements of chess pieces (for a recent review, see Ericsson, Patel, & Kintsch, 2000). After some debate (Ericsson et al., 2000; Simon & Gobet, 2000; Vicente, 2000; Vicente & Wang, 1998) an agreement emerged that the mediating memory mechanisms in expert performance are far more complex than previously theorized and that they reflect integrated skills that allow the experts to execute their performance as well as plan and reason about future actions (Ericsson & Kintsch, 1995).

Already in the late 1980s, it was becoming increasingly clear that the approach based on the general theory of expertise and its study of memory for representative stimuli was not leading to a deep understanding of expert performance. Doubts similarly increased about the fixed limits of the human information-processing and the general theory of expertise that would only permit people to attain expert performance by a couple of well-defined theoretical mechanisms. Smith and I (Ericsson & Smith, 1991) reviewed the empirical evidence on expertise and argued that expert performance is mediated by complex and tightly integrated mechanisms that are gradually acquired and refined over many years of preparation and training. If this is the case, then mechanisms that mediate expert performance cannot be determined by analysis and extrapolation from theoretical assumptions. It therefore becomes necessary to discover the characteristics of these mechanisms by descriptive empirical studies.

Capturing Reproducible Superior Performance With the Expert Performance Approach

If one is interested in studying the natural phenomenon of truly expert performance, then it is essential to capture the superior performance that truly distinguishes such performance from the norm. It is then necessary to re-create all the relevant conditions for eliciting the same performance in the laboratory. One of the best examples of this type of captured performance is de Groot's (1978/1946) pioneering work in chess, where he re-created the contexts of actual chess games by presenting all players with an actual position. He then asked them to select the best move while thinking aloud. Subsequent research has confirmed that the quality of selected moves for positions under those conditions is the best available standardized measure of chess playing under tournament conditions (Ericsson et al., 2000; Ericsson & Lehmann, 1996). More generally, it is possible to use the same method of re-creating naturally occurring situations where superior performance defines the essence of expertise in a domain. The fact that some individuals (experts) perform consistently better than less accomplished individuals is one of the primary characteristics of the expert performance approach. Once the performance of experts can be repeatedly reproduced and shown to be consistently superior to less accomplished performers, standard experimental and process-tracing techniques can then be applied to study the responsible mediating mechanisms.

Earlier reviews (Ericsson, 1996; Ericsson & Smith, 1991) show that the application of the expert performance approach is relatively rare. When participants perform representative tasks in their domains of expertise under controlled conditions, so-called experts do not always exhibit superior performance to less experienced performers (Ericsson, chapter 3; Ericsson & Lehmann, 1996). For example, when wine experts are required to detect, describe, and discriminate characteristics of a wine without knowledge of its identity (seeing the label on the bottle), their performance is only slightly better than those generated by regular wine drinkers (Gawel, 1997; Valentin, Pichon, de Boishebert, & Abdi, 2000). If the research goal is to study the structure of superior performance in the representative activities that define expertise in a given domain (such as objective evaluation of unknown wines), then the study of experts' extensive verbal knowledge of wines will be an unproductive diversion. According to the expert performance approach, researchers need to restrict themselves to domains and activities within domains where experts exhibit clearly superior and reproducible performance. When expert performers can reliably reproduce their superior performance in competitions, they should be able to do the same during training and even under laboratory conditions (a finding confirmed by a large body of research; Ericsson & Lehmann, 1996).

The requirement of reproducibly superior performance under standardized representative situations excludes most behavioral phenomena from everyday life (Ericsson, 1996; Ericsson & Smith, 1991). There are many types of habitual activities, such as walking, eating, driving a car, and tying one's shoes, where the normal execution of the behavior is not focused on maximal speed or accuracy. Instead, people want to perform these activities adequately and with the least amount of effort. When scientists attempt to induce these kinds of activities in the laboratory, the instruction to perform them fast and accurately may even interfere with their execution and reproducibility. Furthermore, efforts to measure habitual performance, such as driving a car (Groeger, 2000), have been remarkably unsuccessful in finding any reproducibly superior performance that could be captured and examined further in the laboratory. In contrast, performance in NASCAR racing and other domains with competition, such as sports, chess, and many professions, is nearly always characterized by reproducibly superior performance.

The Differences Between Traditional Laboratory Studies and Studies of Captured Expert Performance

The differences between Abernethy et al.'s interpretations (chapter 14) and my interpretations are clearly shown by their assessment that the expert performance approach has already been adopted by researchers in sport psychology. In contrast, I have felt considerable tension between the majority of more traditional researchers of perceptual-motor performance who design tasks to test theories—often very simple tasks designed to maximize experimental control—and investigators, like many of those presenting their research in this book. The traditional laboratory researchers might occasionally invite experts to perform their laboratory tasks, but there is little concern for whether their laboratory tasks capture the experts' superior performance and its mediating mechanisms. Most of these studies have shown that expert performers do not exhibit a general superiority over control groups on basic tasks when the complex representative contexts have been eliminated. Consequently, these studies tell us very little about the specific mechanisms that control and mediate the superior performance of experts.

The alternative—the expert performance approach—does not attempt to avoid the complex contexts of naturally occurring phenomena. Instead, the approach strives to re-create the conditions and demands of representative situations with sufficient fidelity where experts can repeatedly reproduce their superior performance. However, designing laboratory conditions that capture expert performance is challenging, especially in domains in sport, where real-time constraints and perceptual requirements for reproducing precise motor actions exist. In domains such as chess, chess positions can be communicated in different ways (e.g., actual chess boards with pieces or diagrams) without influencing the ability of chess players to select the best move (Ericsson et al., 2000). In direct contrast, the real-time act of hitting a ball with a bat or a racket requires perceptual input of high fidelity to allow the experts to reproduce their superior performance. In some situations, it may be possible to present the stimuli on computer displays and by film segments (see Williams and Ward, chapter 9). Many new and exciting efforts are now available to study expert performance in the natural context of competitive games (see, for example, McPherson & Kernodle, chapter 6). It is even possible to study actual performance while introducing experimental manipulations, such as occlusion with liquid crystal glasses (Abernethy, Gill, Parks, & Packer, 2001; Starkes, Edwards, Dissanayake, & Dunn, 1995) to examine the players' ability to anticipate actions.

In cognitive domains, the exact nature of motor responses has been found to be almost irrelevant. Chess players can move the pieces (or verbally report which piece should be moved) without any consequences. In contrast, instructing people to verbally describe their motor responses in sports such as squash or volleyball differs from actually executing the same behavior. Another method for studying skilled performance involves instructing athletes to predict future outcomes, such as the landing position of a ball. However, the athletes might not normally generate that information while engaging in actual play and while executing their motor responses, such as hitting or blocking a ball. Consequently, experts' verbal predictions might be mediated, at least in part, by different mechanisms than those that mediate and control actual movements during the real-time act of hitting. These types of differences might explain why experts are able to generate representative movements faster than they can generate corresponding reporting responses (cf. Shea & Paull, 1996). It may thus be necessary to present actual situations from sport and allow the athletes to produce representative full-body motor responses (Abernethy et al., 2001; Helsen & Pauwels, 1993; Helsen & Starkes, 1999).

In sum, the central goal of the expert performance approach is to describe the structure of superior performance of experts by reproducing it repeatedly in the laboratory and then by applying available methods of process-tracing and experiments to assess the mediating mechanisms. The types of phenomena selected for such research should be particularly suitable for this type of extended analysis because these phenomena reflect stable adaptations to the demands of representative tasks. The elite performers have made extended efforts to reach their best performance during an extended period of practice and preparation. Consequently, there are no known short-term methods to enhance the experts' performance beyond its current level. If such short-term performance-enhancing methods were known and available, these experts would already have attained those adjustments a long time ago as part of their efforts to reach their maximal performance. When we can reproduce their superior performance with representative tasks in the laboratory, we know that it must be mediated by the same mechanisms and thus be similarly stable at its maximal level.

With this clarification of my understanding of how the expert performance approach should be applied to sports, I will now discuss Abernethy et al.'s (chapter 14) specific criticisms and follow their chapter's organization as closely as possible to facilitate comparisons.

Stage One: Capturing Expert Performance— Stability of Performance?

Abernethy et al. (chapter 14) start their evaluation of the expert performance approach by discussing the search for consistently superior and stable performance. In doing so, they raise several issues about the assumption that the expert performance and its mediating mechanisms are stable. Their first point is that not all superior performance is stable. Even in the simplest tasks showing reproducibly superior performance, such as the hand rolling of cigars, performers' average performance still improves even after two to three million rolled cigars (roughly two years of full-time work). However, the absolute levels of improvement in rolling a cigar decrease with more experience. According to the analysis by Newell and Rosenbloom (1981), the time to roll one cigar decreases by 62.06% from the 10th to 1,010th cigar but only 0.01% from the 2,000,010th to the 2,001,010th cigar. Hence, any investigator who studies the performance for 1,000 trials of a highly experienced worker would get far more stable and interpretable results than someone who studies a beginner, such as a college student confronting an unfamiliar task in the laboratory. The claim in the expert performance approach is more general in that experts' performance often continues improving for 10 to 30 years, and this conclusion is based on the data on the ages when experts start training and when they reach the peak performance of their career. These improvements are often small and gradual, and thus for all practical purposes, the performance and underlying mechanisms remain the constant when studied under laboratory conditions for a couple of hours (or even 5 to 10 hours) under representative task conditions.

Abernethy et al.'s second point is that some type of everyday performance, such as writing, is surprisingly flexible. In fact, people can "write with a pencil held between your teeth (for example, to write a rescue note if you are held captive)" (Rosenbaum, 1991, p. 5) and write with one hand under many types of unusual constraints. Although these findings are interesting with important theoretical implications for the generalizability of mediating representations and mechanisms, it is less clear how they relate to possibilities of capturing stable superior expert performance. These phenomena in general raise questions about how to identify and capture expert performance in the domain of handwriting. My own inclination would be to search for expert stenographers (if such can still be found) who have developed methods, abbreviations, and special signs to write down speech as rapidly as possible in a manner that allows them to reproduce the words verbatim at a later time. Under standardized test conditions, these experts would probably not exhibit a lot of variability in the methods to write messages when maximal speed was emphasized. I would similarly predict that regular adults, when asked to write as rapidly and accurately as possible, would eventually settle down on preferred techniques to maximize their performance. However, given that most people have not experienced the demand for fast and accurate copying using handwriting, it is likely that the induced performance under test conditions would differ from their typical activity of handwriting and thus not capture it well. Consequently, there may be several reasons why everyday handwriting may not be an appropriate activity to study with the expert performance approach. For a discussion of similar problems and issues in capturing expert performance in reading books, the reader is directed to Wagner and Stanovich (1996).

Abernethy et al.'s third and final point is that periods of stability of performance may not provide the best opportunity to study control processes. Instead, they recommend that we study human development and the transitions between stable motor patterns, such as when a child progresses from crawling to walking. These phenomena are again interesting, but they do not seem to meet the criteria for reliably superior (i.e., expert) performance.

The primary differences between Abernethy et al.'s interpretation (chapter 14) and my own seem to concern which perceptual-motor phenomena meet the criteria for reproducible expert performance. Abernethy et al. include the whole range of perceptual-motor activities, such as handwriting and development of walking, under the traditional assumption that the study of any motor phenomenon will provide insights into a restricted set of generalizable basic processes. This finding is in stark contrast to the expert performance approach that sets out to capture the complex processes that mediate large reproducible differences between expert and novice performance. It is critical to this latter approach that the investigators successfully reproduce the superior performance in the laboratory to be able to identify the particular complex mechanisms that mediate superiority in that specific domain of activity. Which of these different approaches will turn out to be the most successful in explaining expert perceptual-motor performance, only the future can tell. All that I would request is that researchers recognize that there are several different approaches directed toward reaching the same goal.

Stage Two: Identifying the Mechanisms That Mediate Expert Performance

Abernethy et al. (chapter 14) identify two central issues that pinpoint the main differences between studies that test assumptions of a general theory of expertise and the empirical studies that are based on the expert performance approach. First, how does the laboratory represent (or misrepresent) the constraints on human skill? Second, how useful are verbal reports for the studying of expert performance in sport?

Do Laboratory Studies Misrepresent the Constraints on Human Skill?

Abernethy et al. (chapter 14) evaluate the assumption of the expert performance approach that the information-processing limitations of basic processes and capacities inferred from performance on the laboratory tasks do not provide a valid description of constraints for expert performance, especially in the motor domain. They first review evidence when basic processes and capacities do not limit expert performance. For example, they show that estimates of coincidence timing in laboratory tasks are "orders of magnitude poorer than their temporal accuracy during natural hitting and catching skills" (p. 355). They also report that experts through anticipation can circumvent information-processing constraints as shown by studies of expert racket players (Abernethy, 1991) and judges (Ste-Marie, chapter 7).

On the other hand, they also describe laboratory phenomena where cognitive limits do not seem susceptible to extended practice. They mention the classic phenomenon of the psychological refractory period, where the production of reactions to two cognitive tasks remains slower than the reacting to either task individually, even when it is physically possible to execute the two tasks simultaneously. Although it was believed for a long time that these differences could not be overcome by practice, recent research shows that with different practice methods, the serial constraint on mental processing disappears (Meyer & Kieras, 1997; Schumacher et al., 2001).

The essential issue to expert performance approach is not whether limits can be demonstrated for some laboratory task, but whether basic fixed limits actually constrain the attainment of expert performance. McLeod (1987) nicely illustrates this difference by showing that not even expert cricket players can hit certain types of balls that bounced unpredictably on a prepared rough surface. Although expert cricket players occasionally encounter such unplayable balls under game conditions, it is a relatively rare situation that such players cannot reduce the unpredictability by different coping strategies, such as approaching the bouncing ball (McLeod, 1987, p. 59). However, it is possible to design laboratory conditions with artificial rough surfaces, with balls bouncing at a critical distance from the plate, and with fixed positions of feet during batting where players will experience unplayable balls far more frequently than they would do under representative situations in any domain of expert performance. Keep in mind that these conditions deviate markedly from normal conditions, because many sports have designed courts and rackets with reasonably smooth surfaces and balls with fairly predictable bounces that provide skilled players with the possibility of anticipating events, such as ball paths. Studies that capture performance for such representative conditions have not found, at least as far as I know, that fixed cognitive limits constrain the performance attainable by experts. In fact, level of elite performance appears to keep improving during the last century in many domains. The expert performance approach in general has not made any firm claims that such limits will never be found. It does, however, claim that the identification of such potential limits will require the study and analysis of captured expert performance, where players will have ample and extended opportunities to modify or circumvent constraints to allow continued improvement of their performance.

The Usefulness of Verbal Reports for Studying Expert Performance in Sport

Through the history of psychology, and especially in psychology of sport, there has always been the temptation to ask participants and athletes to describe the factors that control their athletic performance. If athletes could give valid descriptions of their behavior and the detailed processes that mediate this behavior, then the extended and tedious work of collecting data with experimental tasks in the laboratory would not be necessary. Verbal descriptions and explanations given by athletes, however, are often inconsistent with careful observations of their actual behavior. The work by Abernethy et al. (chapter 14) and myself regarding verbal reports is in complete agreement about the problems of validity of such reports. In fact, Herb Simon and I (Ericsson & Simon, 1980, 1984, 1993, 1998) discuss several examples of inconsistencies between actual behavior and answers from interviews and questionnaires. We even give examples from sport, such as the inability of golfers to report where they are looking at the time they are hitting a golf ball with a driver (Ericsson & Simon, 1984, 1993, p. 58). Similar types of inconsistency between verbal reports and observed behavior have been frequently documented even when participants are engaged in experimental tasks and asked to explain *why* they selected one of several possible actions (for a classic review, see Nisbett and Wilson, 1977). Regarding their subsequent review of the validity of verbal report, we (Ericsson & Simon, 1980) did not challenge Nisbett and Wilson's basic findings, namely that there are situations when participants are unable to give valid explanations of their behavior. For example, when I have asked students in a cognitive psychology class to give the first word that comes to mind that starts with the letter *a*, more than half of them report the word *apple*. When you ask them to explain why they picked that particular word, they are more than willing to speculate. Some of them report that they had an apple for lunch, others say that they like apples, and yet others report that they learned the letter *a* in school with a picture of an apple. In all the cases, participants cannot report any thoughts that occurred between the request for the word and the recall of the word apple. Their proposed explanations for their behavior are generated inferences that could account for the observed behavior of other people just as well. There are many types of behaviors, especially habitual behaviors, where a behavior is emitted without any reportable thoughts that are necessary to mediate and control it. Abernethy et al. (chapter 14) mention behaviors, such as tying one's shoes, riding a bike, and walking. In some cases, people cannot even recall if they emitted the behavior and thus have to check again and again whether they locked the doors or turned off the stove.

There are, however, many types of behavior where all participants will spontaneously report mediating thoughts. When we ask college students to "think aloud" (see Ericsson and Simon, 1984, 1993, pp. 375-379, for instructions) while they mentally multiply 36 times 24, they all verbalize intermediate thoughts. For example, they might create a sequence such as the following: "4 times 6 is 24 . . . carry the 2 . . . 4 times 3 is 12 . . . 14 . . . 144 . . . 8, 6, 4 . . . 864." Without going into the theoretic model, Simon and I (Ericsson & Simon, 1980, 1984, 1993) proposed that participants are able to either report many of the mediating thoughts concurrently (think aloud) or recall the mediating thoughts immediately after the completion of the task. Based on reviews of over 100 studies, our findings showed that when the appropriate verbal reporting procedures are used, participants can then generate these types of reports without changing the structure of the underlying processes. The primary problem is that verbalizing one's thoughts takes more time than merely thinking them. Hence, when participants "think aloud," their solution times are often found to be somewhat longer than in a silent controlled condition. Consequently, the collection of retrospective reports of thinking may be preferable in tasks where athletes are limited by real-time constraints.

Abernethy et al. (chapter 14) claimed that the validity of verbal reports is still engulfed in "substantial and protracted debate" (p. 356). In contrast, I think that it is fair to say that researchers have now accepted that participants provide valid concurrent and retrospective verbal reports on their cognitive processes that match other evidence for the associated performance and process-trace data (Ericsson, 2001a; Von

Eckardt, 1998). It is, however, important to note that these recommended types of verbal reports involve a completely different procedure for eliciting reports than the direct questioning cited by Abernethy et al. (chapter 14). These verbal reports were given in response to requests to describe their use of anticipatory cues in squash (Abernethy, 1990) and to questions about where expert batters typically look during contact between the bat and the baseball (Bahill & LaRitz, 1984).

Can think-aloud and retrospective verbal reports provide information about expert performance in sport, where complex actions are often executed under time pressure? In Ericsson and Lehmann's (1996) review, we described a pioneering study by Abernethy, Neal, and Koning (1994), where expert snooker players were asked to "think aloud" while selecting a shot for series of "tables" with unique positions of the balls. They found that the higher-level players (experts) engaged in deeper planning and had better memory for the encountered positions, thus replicating the signature findings for expert chess and bridge players (Charness, 1991). The findings on snooker players are interesting in that these studies show that it is during the preparation and selection of the shot that players verbalize thoughts rather than during the brief instant of executing the shot. Recent reviews of putting and driving in golf (Ericsson, 2001b) support a similar account where expert players read the green and mentally generate predicted ball paths and thus complete their thinking before the act of executing the putt. I was really impressed by Beilock, Wierenga, and Carr's (chapter 12) discussion of the differences between their reporting procedure and the concurrent and retrospective report procedures (Ericsson & Simon, 1993). As long as we acknowledge that different verbal reporting methods will elicit different types of information and that some data will bear a closer relation to the performance on a given trial, many types of reporting techniques can be used to study skilled performance (Ericsson & Simon, 1998).

The most exciting methodology of concurrent and retrospective verbal reports has recently been adapted and applied in a series of tightly related studies to study expert tennis playing (see McPherson & Kernodle, chapter 6) and expert performance in baseball (French et al., 1996). These two lines of research show the potential of verbal reports in sport when the focus is on unobtrusively collecting the thoughts of the performers as they plan, execute, and monitor their performance. Furthermore, the demand for working memory to maintain accurate representation of the current and future game situations to guide selection and execution of actions leads expert performers to refine their mental representations and acquire long-term working memory (LTWM) for working memory support (Ericsson, 1998a: Ericsson &

Kintsch, 1995), which in turn allows elite athletes to display superior recall for representative stimuli (Ericsson et al., 2000). Future research will extend the work on expert typing and music performance and explicate the detailed mechanisms by which the mental representations of game situations in sport guide and control the execution of complex motor actions under real-time conditions.

In sum, research on expert performance in sport needs to turn away from the problematic methods of directed questioning and introspection toward the collection of concurrent and retrospective verbal reports of thinking during expert performance with representative tasks. The methodology of protocol analysis provides a tool that allows researchers to identify information that passes through expert performers' attention while they generate their behavior without any need to embrace any controversial theoretical assumptions. In support of this claim, protocol analysis has emerged as a practical tool to diagnose thinking outside the cognitive tradition. For example, researchers in behavior analysis (Austin & Delaney, 1998), designers of surveys (Sudman, Bradburn, & Schwarz, 1996), and computer software developers (Henderson, Smith, Podd, & Varela-Alvarez, 1995) regularly collect verbal reports and rely on protocol analysis.

Stage Three: The Role of Deliberate Practice and Innate Talent

The third and final stage is described by Abernethy et al. (chapter 14) as "drawing links between the putative mechanisms underpinning expert performance (as revealed through the study of representative laboratory tasks in stage two) and type and quantity of practice and training activities undertaken by the experts over the course of their skill development" (p. 352). This description summarizes my interpretation of the focus of the third stage of expert performance approach quite well. Hence, we both want to assess accounts of the developmental origin of those identified mechanisms that had been found to mediate reproducibly superior performance for representative tasks. Our recommended approaches, however, differ completely.

The expert performance approach attempts to describe the specific activities that most efficiently cause the mediating mechanisms and thus indirectly cause performance to improve. Over time, the description of these learning activities associated with specific changes in particular domains will be increasingly refined by process tracing and experimentation. General principles can eventually be induced that will allow precise predictions of the effects from engaging in these activities (deliberate practice). In contrast, Abernethy et al. (chapter 14) favor a more traditional approach where general assumptions are tested in designed experiments. However, they acknowledge that the framework for deliberate practice is not a formal theory with explicit generalizable claims. To deal with the absence of such general claims, Abernethy et al. (chapter 14) construct or derive their own general theoretical claims regarding characteristics of deliberate practice of experts and then search for counterexamples in laboratory studies of learning with mostly novices and college students as participants.

Generating and Testing General Theoretical Claims by the Designed Laboratory Studies

First, I will briefly describe several of Abernethy et al.'s (chapter 14) constructed claims for deliberate practice, and I will show why I do not agree with these claims, even if the claims can be considered as an empirical characterization of the available evidence from expert performance. Then I will discuss differences between the testing of general theories (such as the general theory of expertise) and descriptive theoretical frameworks (such as the expert performance approach and the framework for deliberate practice). I will conclude this section with some points of actual disagreement between our two positions.

Abernethy et al.'s (chapter 14) first constructed general claim states that "the Ericsson et al. position is that *only* practice performed deliberately and with the designed intent of improving performance can be *beneficial* to the acquisition of expertise" (pp. 359-360, italics added). This extraordinary claim implies that nobody can improve any aspect of performance relevant to expertise without engaging in deliberate practice. Hence, any demonstration of benefits from engaging in activities outside of deliberate practice is sufficient to falsify the claim. For example, children and adults engage in all sorts of activities (mental and physical) that do indeed lead to learning and physical adaptations. However, my position on the central idea of deliberate practice does not concern whether other types of learning are possible; instead, it focuses the comparative efficiency of various activities to induce specific changes and improvements. For example, if some specific training activities, such as deliberate practice, provide faster and more appropriate improvements in gymnastics than engagement in play or watching gymnastics on TV, then it provides a possible account of the observed differences in attained gymnastics performance and the acquisition of the mediating mechanisms.

Abernethy et al.'s (chapter 14) second constructed general claim is that "full attention and complete concentration" is necessary "to derive the necessary benefits from practice to progress toward expertise" (p. 360). They then point to cases where full concentration does not seem to lead to optimal learning. In my own chapter (Ericsson, chapter 3), I emphasized the need for the training activities to be appropriate for the desired goal. Excessive effort to extend training sessions or engage in inappropriate training activities is not just wasteful but probably harmful (Ericsson, chapter 3). In general, I do not think that the complexity of expert performance and its continued improvements by deliberate practice permits traditional universal claims such as "a higher level of characteristic A will always improve speed of learning." In fact, some evidence supports the learning benefits of even the *opposite* of full attention and complete concentration, namely complete rest and relaxation in the form of napping (Ericsson, 1996).

Abernethy et al. (chapter 14) also suggest another constructed general claim, namely that "the quality of an athlete's performance must be maintained in practice for learning of benefit to accrue" (p. 361). They then point to counterevidence in the form of demonstrations of learning in the absence of high-quality performance during practice. It is just as easy, however, to point to counterevidence for this claim: For example, I would point to the benefits of strength training with weights and other training that is designed to strain local muscle groups (Ericsson, chapter 3) where the motor actions during these brief training episodes would not need to be completely integrated within the representative activities that yield a quality performance.

The general approach of stating general claims (and laws) and then searching for even a single exception has a long history in the natural sciences. This approach is adapted to the assessment of general theories with simple well-defined mechanisms, such as the general theory of expertise (Simon & Chase, 1973; see also Richman, Gobet, Staszewski, & Simon, 1996), which makes strong claims about how learning could and could not occur. To assess the validity of such general theories, it may be legitimate to study the effects of learning in novices by forcing them to generate random letters while putting in golf (Masters, 1992). It is also reasonable to search for evidence for implicit learning in everyday life and show that peoples' memory for the orientation of faces on coins is slightly, yet reliably, better than chance (Kelly, Burton, Kato, & Akamatsu, 2001). However, there is a substantial difference between demonstrating evidence for the existence of some forms of learning and showing that they specify very good or even optimal methods for achieving increases in performance (in the context of refining complex skills of the type that mediate expert performance).

The Expert Performance Approach to the Study of Development of Expert Performance

The focus of the expert performance approach is to study how experts can gradually develop an interacting set of mechanisms of sufficient complexity to permit them to continue to improve their performance over years and decades. The approach assumes that improvements in the complex mediating mechanisms have to be made in the context of the demands of representative performance. This approach differs fundamentally from approaches that are based on the general theory of expertise that argue that expertise can be broken apart into fixed basic processes and independent component abilities. The expert performance approach (Ericsson & Smith, 1991) was based on the assumption that it will be difficult to extract and isolate component mechanisms. In particular, it will be nearly impossible to design experimental conditions that elicit a single mechanism and only its particular function in a stable and reproducible model. The expert performance approach implies that the major challenge of training involves the coordination of improvements of mediating mechanisms and that the primary challenge concerns the full integration of improved aspects within the structure of overall performance.

In my chapter (Ericsson, chapter 3), I described several types of complex mechanisms that control and interactively mediate expert performance. For example, chess skill in selecting moves is linked to the increased ability to represent chess knowledge and mentally manipulate chess positions in working memory. The ability to prepare typing actions ahead (eye-hand span) increases with increased typing speed. The ability to maintain a high level of running economy is closely related to long-distance running performance at the elite levels.

I then reviewed research that is relevant to the identifying and describing of potential practice activities. Such activities would allow performers with attained representations to monitor and control their performance to improve from the current level to a higher, not yet previously attained, level. These activities prescribe sources of feedback, such as the "correct" move selected by chess masters, which provide sufficient information to allow one to identify the necessary corrective modifications to one's mediating mechanisms; these, in turn, then enable production of the elevated level of performance. A critical aspect of these training activities is the involvement of problem solving that allow performers to find ways to improve aspects of mediating mechanisms that increase the integrated performance on representative tasks without negative side effects. Consequently, I was surprised by Abernethy et al.'s (chapter 14) criticism that deliberate practice framework did not entail "practice to faithfully reproduce the underlying control requirements of the performance setting and to address factors known to be limiting ones to performance," and "practice that requires active problem solving . . . more likely to be beneficial than practice that merely passively repeats the same actions however relevant and effortful they may be" (p. 364).

Retrospective Reports of Amounts and Characteristics of Various Types of Practice

The deliberate practice framework proposes that the difference between the attained level of performance of amateurs and experts can be accounted for in terms of the quantity and quality of engagement in demanding practice activities that are designed to improve specific aspects of performance. Abernethy et al. (chapter 14) raise several issues about some of the suggested characteristics of deliberate practice. They discuss whether these attributes can explain individual differences in the quantity and quality of engagement. The fact that recreational athletes, such as golfers and tennis players, spend essentially no time in activities that qualify as deliberate practice is not in dispute. Nor is the fact that experts, whose performance keeps improving, spend many hours per week in deliberate practice. This finding is even true for jogging and running, where elite long-distance runners regularly engage in extended runs and interval training, whereas amateur runners typically avoid those types of training activities.

If we can agree that differences between amateurs and experts can be explained mostly by differences in the engagement in deliberate practice, then how do we explain *why* some individuals engage in these activities with full concentration and effort while others tend to avoid them all together. Ericsson, Krampe, and Tesch-Römer (1993) suggested that it wasn't the process of engaging in deliberate practice that attracted the participants to it but that this type of practice allowed them to make improvements and thus indirectly gain benefits and rewards. Suppose that all athletes at all levels of skill really enjoyed the act of exerting themselves in strength training, interval training, technique training, and other activities designed to improve their current performance. Why, then, do they so rarely engage in these practice activities, and when they do, why do they so rarely perform at their maximum level of concentration and effort?

Abernethy et al. (chapter 14) point to the research that has consistently found how certain training activities that are rated as relevant for improvement are judged as highly enjoyable by all athletes—with a similar pattern for athletes at elite and lower levels of achievement. I have already tried to address this interesting and still controversial issue in Ericsson (chapter 3), but allow me make a few additions in response to Abernethy et al.'s (chapter 14) argument. Given my already discussed issues of validity of certain types of verbal reports, let me briefly expand on this in the context of verbal reports that regard enjoyment, level of concentration, and effort. Using Ericsson and Simon's (1984, 1993) model, one should not ask athletes to evaluate the enjoyment of a given practice activity in general; instead, one should ask them to report their thoughts while they are engaging in the particular activity or alternatively, recall their thoughts immediately after completing the practice activity.

At this time, we don't really know what athletes think about when they are rating their enjoyment or concentration during various practice activities while they fill out the questionnaires. The immediate enjoyment presumably varies from one training session to another—and even from one time to another during a given practice session, while engaging in the same practice activity. Some practice activities, especially effortful ones, might even be more enjoyable once the activity is completed, when the athletes can relax and think back on their practice activity. Therefore, I believe that studies of the microstructure of deliberate practice (cf. Deakin and Cobley, chapter 5) would be a much better context for collecting the athletes' thoughts and immediate judgments of enjoyment and concentration. The reported judgments of enjoyment and effort can then be compared with other indicators of effort and enjoyment, such as concurrent performance and physiological indicators (e.g., eye fixations, EMG, and heart rate). At least one pioneering study has used a diary procedure to collect ratings of practice activities immediately after the completion of practice. Hodges, Kerr, Weir, and Starkes (2002) collected diaries from 14 triathletes, who rated different specific practice sessions in terms of relevance, physical effort, concentration, and enjoyment. They replicated the earlier findings with the exception that ratings of relevance and enjoyment for practice activities were not reliably correlated. This fascinating study also correlated the reported duration of the different types of practice to assess the type of practice that would be most relevant to predict the attained performance. Their analysis found that "the most relevant activities were not enjoyable." The study by Hodges et al. (2002) has set a new standard for future research on deliberate practice.

How improvement of performance is related to characteristics of the practice activities will eventually require experimental variation for its conclusive determination. It would be interesting to follow up a recent study that was able to identify an experimental condition involving interval training that improved performance reliably more than a control condition, even when both experimental and control groups consisted of elite Norwegian soccer players (Helgerud, Engen, Wisloff, & Hoff, 2001). A replication of this study would allow investigators to monitor the crucial training activity with respect to effort, concentration, and enjoyment as well as how it differed from characteristics of the other practice activities. As researchers, we certainly hope that microanalyses of various types of practice activities will help us understand why the spontaneous engagement patterns differ across participants of different skill levels. One interesting question is, Will the verbalized thoughts differ between elite and less-accomplished athletes as they prepare before the start of the practice activity, during their engagement in it, and after the completion of it? Could these differences explain the effectiveness of practice sessions and the differential development of performance?

Given the great difficulties of conducting longitudinal case studies where athletes are continuously observed and monitored during their practice, it is reasonable to collect as much valid information as we possibly can from retrospective interviews. As long as we limit recall to information that athletes are able to recall accurately over a particular time period—such as a week, a month, or a year or more—this method should provide a useful overview that will allow subsequent studies to follow up with application of concurrent methods to address specific issues of particular interest (Côté, Ericsson, & Beamer, 2001).

Individual Differences Attributable to Genetic Endowment

In their chapter, Abernethy et al. claim that the expert performance approach and deliberate practice framework state that it is practice and not talent that sets limits. That, however, is not entirely correct, because the expert performance approach was intentionally designed to be a framework for assessing the characteristics that mediate differences in reproducible performance, whether innately determined or acquired, or by some combination of factors. When Smith and I first wrote our chapter (Ericsson & Smith, 1991), it was "obvious" to many scientists that a lot of the variability in expert performance would be attributable to innate talent. Once the framework of the expert performance approach was applied to assess the evidence critically, however, innate interindividual differences were only rarely found to determine the attainment of expert performance. In my review of un-disputed evidence for innate talent (Ericsson, chapter 3), I stated that height and body size were the only currently known factors that can-not be enhanced by training, yet I also stated that they are known to limit attainment of expert performance for healthy people in specific domains. In fact, that appraisal has not changed since my earlier re-views of the evidence (Ericsson, 1990, 1996, 1998b). On the other hand, Abernethy et al. (chapter 14) cite "clear evidence" for genetic effects on basic function as well as on the effects of training and argue that genetic factors "play a critical role in determining the limits to the im-pact of training and therefore the ultimate limits to performance lev-els in many sports." Similarly, Janelle and Hillman (chapter 2) argue that "the limits imposed are primarily genetically determined." Given these critical evaluations, it may be useful to discuss the rationale for my assessment in more detail. I will therefore examine the two studies that they cite as the best available evidence, and I will try to explain why I don't accept them as firm evidence for the role of additional genetic factors that limit attainment of expert performance.

Abernethy et al. point out that Bouchard and his colleagues in the HERITAGE study have found that over 40% of the variance in maxi-mal oxygen uptake ($\dot{V}O_2$max) is heritable (Bouchard, Daw et al., 1998). Furthermore, the same project has found that $\dot{V}O_2$max is trainable to some degree but that half of the variability of the increases in oxygen uptake in response to training is determined by heritable genetic fac-tors (Bouchard, An et al., 1999).

When I first encountered these reported findings, it was clear to me that these studies were not designed to address the question of interest to the expert performance approach; namely, will hereditary factors constrain the attainable level of $\dot{V}O_2$max for a given motivated healthy individual after a decade or more of training? This project studied people at the other extreme, mostly young and middle-aged sedentary adults, who trained for five months and only the last six weeks were at a training intensity suggested to be necessary for improvements in young adults (Bouchard, Leon et al., 1995). Furthermore, it is not clear that $\dot{V}O_2$max is the key constraint for long-distance runners. In fact, the differences in performance among highly accomplished long-dis-tance athletes are better predicted by submaximal performance—that is, running economy (Conley & Krahenbuhl, 1980) and physiological adaptations (Coyle et al., 1991) other than $\dot{V}O_2$max. In a recent review

Noakes (2000) criticizes the traditional models where exercise performance is limited by fixed capacities, such as $\dot{V}O_2max$, and he discusses the full range of physiological, metabolic, and mechanical factors that have been shown to influence endurance performance.

The central question is whether these and other findings would conclusively convince scientists, like myself, that hereditary individual differences will impose firm limits on the level of $\dot{V}O_2max$ that an individual can attain through extended training. From my reading of other research on this issue, I have found that the available evidence on hereditary control of $\dot{V}O_2max$ was more complex. In fact, Bouchard, Lesage et al. (1986) claimed a decade earlier (via a review of an extensive body of literature and an additional study of almost a hundred pairs of twins) that "a significant genetic variance has been found on dizygotic and monozygotic twin data for all variables, with the exception of $\dot{V}O_2max/kg$ FFW [$\dot{V}O_2max/kg$ controlled for fat free weight]" (p. 645). This means that the genetic influence on $\dot{V}O_2max/kg$ must be completely explained by individual differences in accumulated fat stores. Bouchard has also acknowledged that among athletes it is quite possible to increase $\dot{V}O_2max/kg$ significantly, even by as much as 40% with training (Prud'homme, Bouchard, Leblanc, Landry, & Fontaine, 1984). From this evidence, it would appear that $\dot{V}O_2max/kg$ would not be a good candidate for a factor that was constrained by heredity. However, Prud'homme et al. (1984) completed a training study where only 10 pairs of identical twins trained for 20 weeks and where the correlation between improvements of related twins was found to be statistically reliable at 5% p level, but not the 1% level. The absence of a control group with dizygotic twins made it difficult to assess the proportion of heritable variance, but one could assume a maximum of 50% heritability (under the assumption that the dizygotic twins' improvements would have been totally unrelated). However, conclusions based on the results of twin studies with small samples are notably unreliable. In fact, Bouchard and his colleagues (Bouchard, Simoneau, et al., 1986) were unable to replicate the high heritability found for the proportion of fast-twitch fibers in muscles in a famous study by Komi et al. (1977), who estimated that the proportion of muscle fibers was almost completely heritable (over 93%) for a sample of 31 pairs of twins. Bouchard, Simoneau et al. (1986) found no evidence for heritable factors for the same proportion, with a larger sample of 61 pairs of twins. They therefore estimated the heritability to be close to 0%.

A careful reading of the HERITAGE study shows that it is quite different from the earlier studies of athletes and younger twins. In fact,

Bouchard, Leon et al. (1995) recruited families with members between the ages of 17 and 65, where everyone in the family had been completely sedentary for the last 90 days—that is, "no regular physical activity over the previous 3 months" (p. 723). I will focus here on only the two most important concerns with this study.

First, the HERITAGE study uses the correlation between biologically related family members to estimate maximal values for heritability. Given that no adopted children were included and that all family members shared their environment and genes, there was no exact way to separately estimate the main effects of genes versus shared environmental influences. Bouchard, An et al. (1999) acknowledge this by referring to their estimate as the "*maximal* heritability estimate of the $\dot{V}O_2$max response to training" (p. 1007, italics added).

Second, and most important, the core challenge to any study that wishes to evaluate the effects of a fixed amount of training and practice is control of the effort and concentration necessary to induce one's body to change physiologically and yield improvements of aerobic performance. This problem is particularly well documented in studies of improvement of physical fitness by physical exercise because half of the initial participants typically drop out (Berger & McInman, 1993). Even among the participants who continue physical exercise, it is very difficult to induce and control the level of effort exerted to eliminate individual differences in the intensity of the training activity.

The HERITAGE study attempted to address these problems by way of exercise bicycles that allowed the heart rate to be measured continuously. It would automatically adjust the load on the pedals to maintain one's targeted heart rate. The training protocol gradually increased the required heart rate for the exercise, and for the last six weeks, all participants were supposed to exercise at 75% of their maximal heart rate (roughly 145 beats/minute for a max heart rate of 190) for 50 minutes, for three sessions each week. The HERITAGE study appears to have been surprisingly successful in attaining exercise adherence, which is particularly notable given that all participants were sedentary and that roughly a quarter of them were over 50 years old. Skinner et al. (2001) report that less than 13% of the 855 participants (113) did not finish the training program. Among these participants who did not complete the study, only "22 voluntarily refused to continue" (p. 1771), which led to a pure dropout rate of only 2.5%.

Given this exceptional retention record and its unusually strict protocol for ensuring a maintained heart rate of 75% maximum during training, I was surprised that I could not find detailed information on the training of their participants. In fact, I could not find out how and even if the HERITAGE study verified compliance with the strict protocol to ensure maintenance of the targeted heart rate for the whole training session. One might possibly infer that the exercise machine monitored the participants' heart rates and continuously adjusted the load, which would have thus automatically ensured compliance. However, it is clear that the automatic mechanism cannot be in effect at the start of a cycling session or just after a brief break in pedaling: When their heart rate remained below the target, the load would have kept increasing to such a level that the participants could not peddle. My crucial point is that the virtual absence of information on detailed procedures makes it possible (and even likely) that the training intensity differed among participants. Consequently, any results in improved $\dot{V}O_2$max and associated estimates of heritability might reflect individual differences in motivation and associated differences in the intensity of their training.

As a final note, even if the results from the HERITAGE study could be verified and replicated by other independent research groups, there is no accepted understanding of the associated physiological processes to determine whether different findings might be obtained if the training procedures were changed and different targets for heart rates were set and attained. Most critical is that the results might also differ if the training were initiated at younger ages—for example, during the development of children and adolescents. The results may also differ if the study were extended to six months or even a couple of years, which would further emphasize the role of individual differences in motivation.

In sum, it is unlikely that we will resolve the issues of heritable limits on expert performance until the biochemical processes that trigger gene expression and regulate synthesis of new proteins and compounds are better understood. Recent research shows that the biochemical responses of cells to various types of strain induced by vigorous activity, such as physical exercise, are very complex. A recent study has found that the levels of concentration of over a thousand genes in single-cell organisms are reliably changed when metabolism is switched from anaerobic to aerobic mode (DeRisi, Iyer, & Brown, 1997). Even more directly relevant to physical exercise is that over a hundred different genes are activated and expressed in mammalian muscle in response to intense physical exercise (Carson, Nettleton, & Reecy, 2001). Reviews show that it is rare that single genes have observable effects and that most observable characteristics are the result of a complex interaction of many different genes working as a system with many mechanisms for regulating adaptations (Wahlsten, 1999).

Even if we understood the biochemical processes of adaptation, we would also need to understand the processes that induce the strain on the cells and the body—that is, the individual's ability to sustain engagement in appropriate practice activities (cf. deliberate practice). These issues concerning deliberate practice will lead back to the fundamental issues of differences in motivation where some role of heritable differences is not controversial. My colleagues and I (Ericsson et al., 1993) wrote that "we reject an important role for innate ability. It is quite plausible, however, that heritable individual differences might influence processes related to motivation and the original enjoyment of the activities in the domain and, even more important, affect the inevitable differences in the capacity to engage in hard work (deliberate practice)" (p. 399).

Recent research on twins has shown that the same genetic endowment and the same physical environment do not in any simple manner determine attained level of expert performance. Not even a pair of identical twins who engage in extended practice in the same domain of sport expertise necessarily will attain the same, or even similar, level of performance (Klissouras et al., 2001). It is unlikely that twin studies of the acquisition of elite performance will in general ever help us resolve these issues. In fact, the frequency of twins (even a single member of a twin pair) that attain an elite level of performance in domains of expertise is remarkably low; in fact, in science, literature, and the arts, those who reach eminence are virtually never a monozygotic or dizygotic twin (Ericsson, 1998b).

In sum, there is no disagreement regarding the importance of genes in the development of the human body and expert performance. In fact, in my chapter (Ericsson, chapter 3), I proposed that the activation of genes is critical for developing the physiological adaptations of the body and the nervous system that are necessary for attaining expert performance in any domain. However, these necessary genes appear to reflect genes that are found in most everyone's DNA. Consequently, these essential genes will not reflect heritable differences in talent but a heritable potential for performance that is shared by healthy human adults.

Summary

In this chapter, I described how the expert performance approach differs from approaches based on the general theory of expertise with its simple and generalizable learning mechanisms. Throughout this chapter, I have attempted to demonstrate that my interpretation of the expert performance approach agrees with Abernethy et al.'s (chapter 14) criticisms of strictly cognitive accounts of expert performance in sport, such as the general theory of expertise. We also have full agreement that accounts based on the fixed general capacities, basic information processes, and simple learning processes will be insufficient to explain the rich and complex findings on expertise in sport. In fact, I agree with Abernethy et al.'s (chapter 14) rejection of the general claims that they generated to characterize deliberate practice. This discussion suggested, however, a fundamental difference in our expectation of what an ultimate theoretical framework, or even theory, of expertise in sport might look like.

Whereas Abernethy et al. (chapter 14) seem to favor theories based on general basic processes, the expert performance approach makes a commitment to describing and studying expert performance as reproducible phenomena involving a superior level of achievement. This approach, therefore, requires that complex phenomena first be captured by representative tasks that incorporate all the essential constraints of the naturally occurring performance. To study the mechanisms that mediate the superior performance, experts must be confronted by representative challenges where these mechanisms are required to exhibit the observed performance. In taking this approach, the methodology of expert performance research focuses on describing and examining the structure of these complex and integrated systems of mechanisms, sometimes at the level of individual experts (Ericsson, chapter 3). Once these mediating mechanisms are described, it is necessary to account for their acquisition and development. My vision is that future theories of expert performance will resemble theories in chemistry and biology with their efforts to identify general principles and systems, rather than a search for natural laws (as in the historical development of the field of physics). Consistent with that vision, my colleagues and I have attempted to describe phenomena at a sufficiently detailed level to allow identification of the mediating processes that can be validated by experiments at the level of individual experts. These processes can be biochemical, as in the case of inducing physiological adaptations by imposing strain on homeostasis by sustained intense exercise, or they can be cognitive, as in the cases of expert performance in blindfold chess and exceptional memory. Based on an analysis of the evidence from many individual cases and groups of cases, the goal is to discover or induce general principles and mechanisms, such as deliberate practice (Ericsson, 1996, 2002; Ericsson et al., 1993) and long-term working memory (Ericsson et al., 2000; Ericsson & Kintsch, 1995). In my chapter (Ericsson, chapter 3), I tried to expand on these by describing general mechanisms that should be sufficient to explain how various aspects of performance could be gradually increased through deliberate practice over extended periods. All of these proposed concepts and ideas should be viewed as conceptual tools to guide the quest for an improved understanding of the structure and acquisition of expert performance. In much the same way that expert performers in sport is continually engaged in efforts to refine the representations that mediate and control their performance, so will scientists studying expert performance need to keep developing their representations of the underlying mechanisms and processes.

My hope is that in future evaluations of the expert performance approach, we will have reached a consensus on what this descriptive inductive approach recommends and its distinctive emphasis on capturing and reproducing expert performance to allow its study under controlled laboratory conditions. It is, therefore, my sincere wish that Abernethy and his colleagues will be able to find that my interpretation of the expert performance approach provides an adequate theoretical framework for their future research on expert performance. I am hopeful that this is the case as I view Abernethy's pioneering research on expert performance as providing some of the best examples of how I feel that this approach should be applied to sport.

The expert performance approach was proposed in response to the realization that expert performance is mediated by complex mechanisms attained during an extended period of practice. These complex mechanisms cannot be understood by theoretical extrapolation of simple learning mechanisms, but they must instead be discovered and described empirically before any attempts to develop theoretical accounts of such performance will be meaningful. For many decades, coaches and athletes have accumulated knowledge about empirical phenomena related to their performance and their best methods for training. A renewed focus on description of the stable, reproducible aspects of expert performance will allow us to initiate a dialogue with coaches and master teachers as well as aspiring athletes. In their comments on the chapters in this book, Cipriano and Brisson give outstanding examples on how master coaches and elite athletes can share their expertise and help shape the research agenda. I think that the expert performance approach will provide a framework that can promote a partnership among researchers, coaches, and athletes. All three groups can contribute and benefit from a deeper understanding of the mechanisms that mediate expert performance and how performance can be best and most effectively improved. With the rapid advances in display and recording techniques, it should be possible to develop methods that combine science and application. Scientific methods can be used to measure performance improvements and to identify the most effective training environments (see Williams and Ward, chapter 9).

One has many legitimate reasons for being interested in elite performance in sport. Many coaches and their athletes might be primarily interested in how to develop athletes who win at national and international competitions, such as the Olympic Games. My own interest in expert performance in sport arises from my persuasion that any time performers are motivated to reach their highest levels of performance, they repeatedly confront obstacles and constraints. In the process of overcoming these constraints, such athletes should be able to inform the rest of us of what is humanly possible by providing researchers a source of empirical evidence on the true potential of human achievement.

EXPERT'S COMMENTS

■ Question

As a coach, what type of athlete do you prefer to work with?

■ Coach's Perspective: Nick Cipriano

Ericsson, Krampe, and Tesch-Römer's theory of deliberate practice provides reinforcement for coaches in that they do not have to subject themselves to the idiosyncrasies of the "talented athlete." As a coach, I would much prefer to work with an athlete with mediocre talent but a high work ethic versus a talented athlete with moderate commitment. The journey to expertise is a long and arduous one, littered with numerous obstacles to overcome and with many opponents to conquer. It is highly unlikely that talent coupled with a moderate work ethic will propel an athlete to achieving expertise in sport. The talented athlete who brings forth a moderate level of commitment to sport is every coach's nightmare. Unfortunately, such athletes are given every benefit of the doubt and are provided endless opportunities to take part in an enriched training and competition schedule, with the singular expectation that in time they will realize that talent in the absence of hard work will not be developed. Unfortunately, in my 20-plus years of coaching, I have yet to see an attitude transformation take place. More often than not, talented athletes who lack a strong work ethic will be underachievers whereas the athletes who lack talent, but have a high work ethic, will be overachievers. It is work ethic that

propels athletes to work through performance plateaus and resume training following a serious injury or a subpar performance
at an important competition. Simply stated, talent in isolation of a
work ethic is a wasted talent.

A familiar scenario for athletes who display an abundance of
talent but lack a strong work ethic is for them stay ahead of the
pack (those less talented, but more committed to training) until
such time that the benefits of a deliberate and structured training
program take effect. Through deliberate practice and hard work,
the less talented will narrow the performance gap, and shortly
thereafter, the talented athletes will look to assign blame for their
apparent lack of improvement and will seek out a new coach. All
too often, athletes who demonstrate exceptional talent but have
a moderate level work ethic are resistant to coaching, compared
with athletes who have less talent but a strong work ethic. Of
course, the perfect combination of talent, coachability, and deliberate practice makes for a winning combination, and all three factors
are likely a precursor to becoming an expert.

Epilogue

We hope that part of what you take from this book is the enthusiasm for sport expertise research as felt by all of our contributors. This research area is diverse in its approaches and paradigms—sometimes theoretically driven, sometimes practically driven. The findings inevitably have great significance for how we choose to select, support, and train our best athletes and coaches. In summary, we note through the course of this book the following observations:

- A great deal of information has already been gathered on what makes an expert athlete and what optimal ways of training it takes to attain peak performance.

- We have also seen that although much is known about the rise to peak performance, far less is understood about how expert athletes can maintain their performance, particularly with aging.

- We have noted that our understanding of what makes a high-level performer in sport needs to be extended beyond athletes to encompass the skills of coaches, referees, and judges.

- We have seen the pitfalls of relying on dominant research from Western societies, where youth sport can access innumerable resources. Expert athletes are often produced in countries where resources (facilities, coaches, competition) are scarce, and it is time we began to consider different paradigms to explain this phenomenon.

- Although we are aware of the performance advantages afforded by expertise, we are only just beginning to understand the potential downsides of expert behavior.

- Perhaps the weakest area of sport expertise research is the development of adequate theories that go beyond simply explaining isolated characteristics of expert behavior. This general theory is the primary quest of the next 10 years. In this book, several authors have suggested the advantages of incorporating other often newer theoretical approaches (Tenenbaum, chapter 8; Beek et al., chapter 13; Abernethy et al., chapter 14; Ericsson, chapter 15). It remains to be seen what a broadened theoretical spectrum will provide. However, given the many advancements in sport expertise research over the past 10 years, we are extremely optimistic.

References

Chapter 1

Abernethy, B. (Ed.). (1994). Expert-novice differences in sport [Special issue]. *International Journal of Sport Psychology, 25.*

Côté, J. (1999). The influence of the family in the development of talent in sports. *The Sports Psychologist, 13,* 395-417.

Côté, J., & Hay, J. (2002). Children's involvement in sport: A developmental perspective. In J.M. Silva & D. Stevens (Eds.), *Psychological foundations of sport* (2nd ed., pp. 484-502). Boston: Merrill.

Ericsson, K.A. (Ed.). (1996). *The road to excellence: The acquisition of expert performance in the arts and sciences, sports, and games.* New Jersey: Lawrence Erlbaum Associates.

Ericsson, K.A., Krampe, R.T., & Tesch-Römer, C. (1993). The role of deliberate practice in the acquisition of expert performance. *Psychological Review, 100,* 363-406.

Ericsson, K.A., & Lehmann, A.C. (1996). Expert and exceptional performance: Evidence of maximal adaptation to task constraints. *Annual Review of Psychology, 47,* 273-305.

Ericsson, K.A., & Smith, J. (1991). Prospects and limits of the empirical study of expertise: An introduction. In K.A. Ericsson & J. Smith (Eds.), *Toward a general theory of expertise* (pp. 1-38). Cambridge, UK: Cambridge University Press.

Goulet, C., Bard, M., & Fleury, C. (1989). Expertise differences in preparing to return a tennis serve: A visual search information processing approach. *Journal of Sport & Exercise Psychology, 11,* 382-398.

Helsen, W.F., & Starkes, J.L. (1999). A multidimensional approach to skilled perception and performance in sport. *Applied Cognitive Psychology, 13,* 1-27.

Housner, L.D., & French, K.E. (Eds.). (1994). Expertise in learning, performance and instruction in sport and physical activity [Special issue]. *Quest, 26,* 2.

McPherson, S.L. (2000). Expert-novice differences in planning strategies during collegiate singles tennis competition. *Journal of Sport & Exercise Psychology, 22,* 39-62.

Newell, A., & Simon, H.A. (1972). *Human problem solving.* Englewood Cliffs, NJ: Prentice Hall.

Ripoll, H. (Ed.). (1991). Information processing and decision making in sport [Special issue]. *International Journal of Sport Psychology, 3-4.*

Simon, H.A., & Chase, W.G. (1973). Skill in chess. *American Scientist, 61,* 394-403.

Starkes, J.L., & Allard, F. (Eds.). (1993). *Cognitive issues in motor expertise.* Amsterdam: North Holland.

Starkes, J.L., Helsen, W., & Jack, R. (2001). Expert performance in sport and dance. In R.N. Singer, H.A. Hausenblas, & C.M. Janelle (Eds.), *Handbook of sport psychology* (2nd ed., pp. 174-201). New York: Wiley.

Starkes, J.L., Weir, P.L., Singh, P., Hodges, N.J., & Kerr, T. (1999). Aging and the retention of sport expertise. *International Journal of Sport Psychology, 30*(2), 283-301.

Ste-Marie, D.M. (1999). Expert-novice differences in gymnastic judging: An information processing perspective. *Applied Cognitive Psychology, 13,* 269-281.

Ste-Marie, D.M., & Lee, T.D. (1991). Prior processing effects on gymnastic judging. *Journal of Experimental Pscyhology, Learning, Memory, and Cognition, 17,* 126-136.

Straub, W.F., & Williams, J.M. (Eds.). (1984). *Cognitive sport psychology.* Lansing, NY: Sport Science.

Tenenbaum, G. (Ed.). (1999). The development of expertise in sport: Nature and nurture [Special issue]. *International Journal of Sport Psychology, 2.*

Weir, P.L., Kerr, T., Hodges, N.J., McKay, S.M., & Starkes, J.L. (2002). Master swimmers: How are they different from younger elite swimmers? An examination of practice and performance patterns. *Journal of Aging and Physical Activity, 10(1),* 41-63.

Chapter 2

Abernethy, B. (1990). Expertise, visual search, and information pick-up in squash. *Perception, 19,* 63-77.

Abernethy, B., Burgess-Limerick, R., & Parks, S. (1994). Contrasting approaches to the study of motor expertise. *Quest, 46,* 186-198.

Abernethy, B., & Russell, D.G. (1987a). Expert-novice differences in an applied selective attention task. *Journal of Sport Psychology, 9,* 326-345.

Abernethy, B., & Russell, D.G. (1987b). The relationship between expertise and visual search strategy in a racquet sport. *Human Movement Science, 6,* 283-319.

Allard, F., Deakin, J., Parker, S., & Rodgers, W. (1993). Declarative knowledge in skilled motor performance: Byproduct or constituent? In J.L. Starkes & F. Allard (Eds.), *Cognitive issues in motor expertise* (pp. 95-107). Amsterdam: North-Holland.

Allard, F., & Starkes, J.L. (1980). Perception in sport: Volleyball. *Journal of Sport Psychology, 2,* 22-23.

Bandura, A. (1997). *Self-efficacy: The exercise of control.* New York: W.H. Freeman.

Bota, J.D. (1993). Development of the Ottawa Mental Skills Assessment Tool (OMSAT). Unpublished master's thesis, University of Ottawa, Ottawa, Ontario, Canada.

Bouchard, C., Dionne, F.T., Simoneau, J.A., & Boulay, M.R. (1992). Genetics of aerobic and anaerobic performances. *Exercise and Sports Sciences Reviews, 20,* 27-58.

Bouchard, C., Malina, R.M., & Pérusse, L. (1997). *Genetics of fitness and physical performance.* Champaign, IL: Human Kinetics.

Charness, N. (1992). The impact of chess research on cognitive science. *Psychological Research, 54,* 4-9.

Charness, N., Krampe, R., & Mayr, U. (1996). The role of practice and coaching in entrepreneurial skill domains: An international comparison of life-span chess skill acquisition. In K.A. Ericsson (Ed.), *The road to excellence: The acquisition of expert performance in the arts and sciences, sports and games* (pp. 51-80). Mahwah, NJ: Erlbaum.

Chase, W.G., & Simon, H.A. (1973a). The mind's eye in chess. In W.G. Chase (Ed.), *Visual information processing* (pp. 215-282). New York: Academic Press.

Chase, W.G., & Simon, H.A. (1973b). Perception in chess. *Cognitive Psychology, 4,* 55-81.

Cleary, T., & Zimmerman, B.J. (2001). Self-regulation differences during athletic practice by experts, non-experts, and novices. *Journal of Applied Sport Psychology, 13,* 185-206.

Crews, D.J., & Landers, D.M. (1993). Electroencephalographic measures of attentional patterns prior to the golf putt. *Medicine and Science in Sports and Exercise, 25,* 116-126.

Davids, K. (2000). Skill acquisition and the theory of deliberate practice: It ain't what you do it's the way that you do it! *International Journal of Sport Psychology, 31,* 461-466.

Davids, K., Williams, A.M., Button, C., & Court, M. (2001). An integrative modeling approach to the study of intentional movement behavior. In R.N. Singer, H.A. Hausenblas, & C.M. Janelle (Eds.), *Handbook of sport psychology* (2nd ed.) (pp. 144-173). New York: Wiley.

Deakin, J. (1987). Cognitive components of skill in figure skating. Unpublished doctoral dissertation, University of Waterloo, Ontario, Canada.

Deakin, J.M., & Allard, F. (1992). An evaluation of skill and judgment in basketball officiating. Paper presented at the meeting of the North American Society for the Psychology of Sport and Physical Activity, Pittsburgh, PA.

Deeny, S., Hillman, C., Janelle, C., & Hatfield, B. (in press). EEG coherence and neural efficiency in expert and non-expert marksmen. *Journal of Sport and Exercise Psychology*.

Detterman, D.K., Gabriel, L.T., & Ruthsatz, J.M. (1998). Absurd environmentalism. *Behavioral and Brain Sciences, 21*, 411-412.

Durand-Bush, N., & Salmela, J.H. (2001). The development of talent in sport. In R.N. Singer, H.A. Hausenblas, & C.M. Janelle (Eds.) *Handbook of sport psychology* (2nd ed.) (pp. 269-289). New York: Wiley.

Durand-Bush, N., Salmela, J.H., & Green-Demers, I. (2001). The Ottawa Mental Skills Assessment Tool (OMSAT-3*). *The Sport Psychologist, 15*, 1-19.

Elbert, T., Pantev, C., Weinbruch, C., Rockstroh, B., & Taub, E. (1995). Increased cortical representation of the fingers of the left hand. *Science, 270*, 305-307.

Ericsson, K.A., Krampe, R.T., & Tesch-Römer, C. (1993). The role of deliberate practice in the acquisition of expert performance. *Psychological Review, 100*, 363-406.

Ericsson, K.A., & Lehmann, A.C. (1996). Expert and exceptional performance: Evidence of maximal adaptation to task constraints. *Annual Review of Psychology, 47*, 273-305.

Ericsson, K.A., & Smith, J. (1991). Prospects and limits of the empirical study of expertise: An introduction. In K.A. Ericsson & J. Smith (Eds.), *Toward a general theory of expertise* (pp. 1-38). Cambridge, UK: Cambridge University Press.

Fawcett, A.J., & Nicholson, R.I. (1995). Persistent deficits in motor skill of children with dyslexia. *Journal of Motor Behavior, 27*, 235-240.

Fawcett, A.J., & Nicholson, R.I. (1999). Performance of dyslexic children on cerebellar and cognitive tests. *Journal of Motor Behavior, 31*, 68-78.

Fitts, P.M., & Posner, M.I. (1967). *Human performance*. Belmont, CA: Brooks/Cole.

French, K.E., & McPherson, S.L. (1999). Adaptations in response selection processes used during sport competition with increasing age and expertise. *International Journal of Sport Psychology, 30*, 173-193.

French, K.E., Nevett, M.E., Spurgeon, J.H., Graham, K.C., Rink, J.E., & McPherson, S.L. (1996). Knowledge representation and problem solution in expert and novice youth baseball performance. *Research Quarterly for Exercise and Sport, 66*, 194-201.

French, K.E., Spurgeon, J.H., & Nevett, M.E. (1995). Expert-novice differences in cognitive and skill execution components of youth baseball performance. *Research Quarterly for Exercise and Sport, 66*, 194-201.

French, K.E., & Thomas, J.R. (1987). The relation of knowledge development to children's basketball performance. *Journal of Sport Psychology, 9*, 15-32.

Gobet, F., & Simon, H.A. (1996). Recall of random and distorted positions: Implications for the theory of expertise. *Memory and Cognition, 24*, 493-503.

Gobet, F., & Simon, H.A. (1998). Expert chess memory: Revisiting the chunking hypothesis. *Memory, 6*, 225-255.

Gould, D., & Tuffey, S. (1996). Zones of Optimal Functioning research: A review and critique. *Anxiety, Stress, and Coping, 9*, 53-68.

Gould, D., Weiss, M., & Weinberg, R. (1981). Psychological characteristics of successful and non-successful Big Ten wrestlers. *Journal of Sport Psychology, 3*, 69-81.

Goulet, C., Bard, M., & Fleury, C. (1989). Expertise differences in preparing to return a tennis serve: A visual search information processing approach. *Journal of Sport & Exercise Psychology, 11*, 382-398.

Grove, J.R., & Hanrahan, S.J. (1988). Perceptions of mental training needs by elite field hockey players and their coaches. *The Sport Psychologist, 2*, 222-230.

Hanin, Y.L., & Syrjä, P. (1995). Performance affect in junior ice hockey players: An application of the Individual Zones of Optimal Functioning model. *The Sport Psychologist, 9*, 169-187.

Hanin, Y.L., & Syrjä, P. (1996). Predicted, actual, and recalled affect in Olympic-level soccer players: Idiographic assessments on individualized scales. *Journal of Sport & Exercise Psychology, 18,* 325-335.

Hardy, L., Jones, J.G., & Gould, D. (1996). *Understanding psychological preparation for sport.* Chichester, UK: John Wiley & Sons.

Hatfield, B.D., & Hillman, C.H. (2001). The psychophysiology of sport: A mechanistic understanding of the psychology of superior performance. In R.N. Singer, H.A. Hausenblas, & C.M. Janelle (Eds.), *Handbook of sport psychology* (2nd ed.) (pp. 362-388). New York: Wiley.

Hatfield, B.D., Landers, D.M., & Ray, W.J. (1984). Cognitive processes during self-paced motor performance: An electroencephalographic profile of skilled marksmen. *Journal of Sport Psychology, 6,* 42-59.

Haufler, A.J., Spalding, T.W., Santa-Maria, D.L., & Hatfield, B.D. (2000). Neuro-cognitive activity during a self-paced visuospatial task: Comparative EEG profiles in marksmen and novice shooters. *Biological Psychology, 53,* 131-160.

Hebb, D.O. (1949). *The organization of behavior: A neuropsychological theory.* New York: Wiley.

Heller, K.A., & Ziegler, A. (1998). Experience is no improvement over talent. *Behavioral and Brain Sciences, 21,* 417-418.

Helsen, W., & Pauwels, J.M. (1990). Analysis of visual search activity in solving tactical game problems. In D. Brogan (Ed.), *Visual search* (pp. 177-184). London: Taylor and Francis.

Helsen, W., & Pauwels J.M. (1993). The relationship between expertise and visual information processing in sport. In J.L. Starkes & F. Allard (Eds.), *Cognitive issues in motor expertise* (pp. 109-134). Amsterdam: North-Holland.

Helsen, W., Starkes, J.L., & Hodges, N.J. (1998). Team sports and the theory of deliberate practice. *Journal of Sport & Exercise Psychology, 20,* 13-25.

Helsen, W., Starkes, J., & Van Winckel, J. (1998). The influence of relative age on success and droupout in male soccer players. *American Journal of Human Biology, 10,* 791-798.

Highlen, P.S., & Bennett, B.B. (1979). Psychological characteristics of successful and unsuccessful elite wrestlers: An exploratory study. *Journal of Sport Psychology, 1,* 123-137.

Hillman, C.H., Apparies, R.J., Janelle, C.M., & Hatfield, B.D. (2000). An electrocortical comparison of executed and rejected shots in skilled marksmen. *Biological Psychology, 52,* 71-83.

Hodges, N.J., & Starkes, J.L. (1996). Wrestling with the nature of expertise: A sport specific test of Ericsson, Krampe, and Tesch-Römer's (1993) theory of "deliberate practice." *International Journal of Sport Psychology, 27,* 400-424.

Howe, M.J.A., Davidson, J.W., & Sloboda, J.A. (1998). Innate talents: Reality or myth? *Behavioral and Brain Sciences, 21,* 399-442.

Isaacs, K.R., Anderson, B.J., Alcantara, A.A., Black, J.E., & Greenough, W.T. (1992). Exercise and the brain: Angiogenesis in the adult rat cerebellum after vigorous physical activity and motor skill learning. *Journal of Cerebral Blood Flow and Metabolism, 12,* 110-119.

Isaacs, L.D., & Finch, A.E. (1983). Anticipatory timing of beginning and intermediate tennis players. *Perceptual and Motor Skills, 57,* 451-454.

Jack, R., Kirshenbaum, N., Poon, P., Rodgers, W., & Starkes, J. (1999). Metacognitive differences in experts and novices in self-directed learning. *Journal of Sport and Exercise Psychology, 21,* S61.

Janelle, C.M. (2002). Modification of visual attention parameters under conditions of heightened anxiety and arousal. *Journal of Sports Sciences, 20,* 237-251.

Janelle, C.M., Hillman, C.H., Apparies, R., Murray, N.P., Meili, L., Fallon, E.A., & Hatfield, B.D. (2000). Expertise differences in cortical activation and gaze behavior during rifle shooting. *Journal of Sport & Exercise Psychology, 22,* 167-182.

Janelle, C.M., Hillman, C.H., & Hatfield, B.D. (2000). Concurrent measurement of electroencephalographic and ocular indices of attention during rifle shooting: An exploratory case study. *International Journal of Sports Vision, 6,* 21-29.

Janelle, C.M., Singer, R.N., & Williams, A.M. (1999). External distraction and attentional narrowing: Visual search evidence. *Journal of Sport & Exercise Psychology, 21*, 70-91.

Jones, C.M., & Miles, T.R. (1978). Use of advance cues in predicting the flight of a lawn tennis ball. *Journal of Human Movement Studies, 4*, 231-235.

Jones, J.G., Hanton, S., & Swain, A.B.J. (1994). Intensity and interpretation of anxiety symptoms in elite and non-elite sports performers. *Personality and Individual Differences, 17*, 657-663.

Klissouras, V. (1997). Heritability of adaptive variation: An old problem revisited. *Journal of Sports Medicine and Physical Fitness, 37*, 1-6.

Konttinen, N., & Lyytinen, H. (1992). Physiology of preparation: Brain slow waves, heart rate, and respiration preceding triggering in rifle shooting. *International Journal of Sport Psychology, 23*, 110-127.

Konttinen, N., & Lyytinen, H. (1993). Individual variability in brain slow wave profiles in skilled sharpshooters during the aiming period in rifle shooting. *Journal of Sport & Exercise Psychology, 15*, 275-289.

Konttinen, N., Lyytinen, H., & Era, P. (1999). Brain slow potentials and postural sway behavior during sharpshooting performance. *Journal of Motor Behavior, 31*, 11-20.

Landers, D.M., Han, M., Salazar, W., Petruzzello, S.J., Kubitz, K.A., & Gannon, T.L. (1994). Effect of learning on electroencephalographic and electrocardiographic patterns on novice archers. *International Journal of Sport Psychology, 25*, 313-330.

Lehmann, A.C. (1997). Acquisition of expertise in music: Efficiency of deliberate practice as a moderating variable in accounting for sub-expert performance. In I. Deliege & J.A. Sloboda (Eds.), *Perception and cognition of music* (pp. 165-191). Hillsdale, NJ: Lawrence Erlbaum and Associates.

Logan, G.D. (1988). Automaticity, resources, and memory: Theoretical controversies and practical implications. *Human Factors, 30*, 583-598.

Mahoney, M.J., & Avener, M. (1977). Psychology of the elite athlete: An exploratory study. *Cognitive Therapy and Research, 1*, 135-141.

McPherson, S.L. (1993). The influence of player experience on problem solving during batting preparation in baseball. *Journal of Sport & Exercise Psychology, 15*, 304-325.

McPherson, S.L. (1994). The development of sport expertise: Mapping the tactical domain. *Quest, 46*, 223-240.

McPherson, S.L. (1999). Tactical differences in problem representations and solutions in collegiate varsity and beginner women tennis players. *Research Quarterly for Exercise and Sport, 70*, 369-384.

McPherson, S.L. (2000). Expert-novice differences in planning strategies during collegiate singles tennis competition. *Journal of Sport & Exercise Psychology, 22*, 39-62.

McPherson, S.L., & French, K.E. (1991). Changes in cognitive strategy and motor skill in tennis. *Journal of Sport & Exercise Psychology, 13*, 26-41.

Münte, T.F., Kohlmetz, C., Nager, W., & Altenmüller, E. (2001). Superior auditory spatial tuning in conductors. *Nature, 409*, 580.

Murray, N.M., & Janelle, C.M. (in press). Anxiety and performance: A visual search examination of the processing efficiency theory. *Journal of Sport and Exercise Psychology.*

Newell, K.M. (1986). Constraints on the development of coordination. In M. Wade & H.T.A. Whiting (Eds.), *Motor development in children: Aspects of coordination and control* (pp. 341-360). Dordrecht: Martinus Nijhoff.

Nougier, V., Azemar, G., Stein, J.F., & Ripoll, H. (1992). Covert orienting to central visual cues and sport practice relations in the development of visual attention. *Journal of Experimental Child Psychology, 54*, 315-333.

Nougier, V., Ripoll, H., & Stein, J. (1989). Orienting of attention with highly skilled athletes. *International Journal of Sport Psychology, 20*, 205-223.

Nougier, V., & Rossi, B. (1999). The development of expertise in the orienting of attention. *International Journal of Sport Psychology, 30,* 246-260.

Orlick, T., & Partington, J. (1988). Mental links to excellence. *The Sport Psychologist, 2,* 105-130.

Pesce Anzeneder, C., & Bosel, R. (in press). Exogenous and endogenous components of focusing of visuospatial attention: Electrophysiological evidence from participants with and without attentional expertise. *Ergonomics.*

Posner, M.J. (1980). Orienting of attention. *Quarterly Journal of Experimental Psychology, 32,* 3-25.

Radlo, S.J., Janelle, C.M., Barba, D.A., Frehlich, S.G. (2001). Event related potential activity (ERP) differences in elite versus novice baseball players in simulated batting conditions. *Research Quarterly for Exercise and Sport, 72,* 22-31.

Reilly, T., Bangsbo, J., & Franks, A. (2000). Anthropometric and physiological predispositions for elite soccer. *Journal of Sports Sciences, 18,* 669-683.

Ripoll, H., & Fleurance, P. (1985). What does keeping one's eye on the ball mean? *Ergonomics, 31,* 1647-1654.

Rossi, B., & Zani, A. (1991). Timing of movement-related decision processed in clay-pigeon shooters as assessed by event-related brain potentials and reaction times. *International Journal of Sport Psychology, 22,* 128-139.

Russell, S.J. (1990). Athletes' knowledge in task perception, definition, and classification. *International Journal of Sport Psychology, 21,* 85-101.

Rowe, D.C. (1998). Talent scouts, not practice scouts: Talents are real. *Behavioral and Brain Sciences, 21,* 421-422.

Schneider, W., & Shiffrin, R.M. (1977). Controlled and automatic information processing: I. Detection, search, and attention. *Psychological Review, 92,* 424-428.

Shank, M.D., & Haywood, K.M. (1987). Eye movement while viewing a baseball pitch. *Perceptual and Motor Skills, 64,* 1191-1197.

Simonton, D.K. (1999). Talent and its development: An emergenic and epigenetic model. *Psychological Review, 106,* 435-457.

Simonton, D.K. (2000). Methodological and theoretical orientation and the long-term disciplinary impact of 54 eminent psychologists. *Review of General Psychology, 4,* 13-24.

Singer, R.N. (2001). *Controlled versus automatic behaviors: What does it take to realize expertise in self-paced events?* Manuscript submitted for publication.

Singer, R.N., Cauraugh, J.H., Chen, D., Steinberg, G.M., & Frehlich, S.G. (1996). Visual search, anticipation, and reactive comparisons between highly skilled and beginning tennis players. *Journal of Applied Sport Psychology, 8,* 9-26.

Singer, R.N., & Janelle, C.M. (1999). Determining sport expertise: From genes to supremes. *International Journal of Sport Psychology, 30,* 117-150.

Singer, R.N., Williams, A.M., Frehlich, S.G., Janelle, C.M., Radlo, S.J., Barba, D.A., & Bouchard, L. J. (1998). New frontiers in visual search: An exploratory study in live tennis situations. *Research Quarterly for Exercise and Sport, 69,* 290-296.

Sloboda, J.A., & Howe, M.J.A. (1991). Biographical precursors of musical excellence: An interview study. *Psychology of Music, 19,* 3-21.

Spink, K.S. (1990). Psychological characteristics of male gymnasts: Differences between competitive levels. *Journal of Sports Sciences, 8,* 149-157.

Starkes, J.L. (1993). Motor experts: Opening thoughts. In J.L. Starkes & F. Allard (Eds.), *Cognitive issues in motor expertise* (pp. 3-16). Amsterdam: Elsevier.

Starkes, J.L. (2000). The road to expertise: Is practice the only determinant? *International Journal of Sport Psychology, 31,* 431-451.

Starkes, J.L., Deakin, J.M., Allard, F., Hodges, N.J., & Hayes, A. (1996). Deliberate practice in sports: What is it anyway? In K.A. Ericsson (Ed.), *The road to excellence: The acquisition of expert performance in the arts and sciences, sports, and games* (pp. 81-106). Mahwah, NJ: Lawrence Erlbaum.

Starkes, J.L., Helsen, W., & Jack, R. (2001). Expert performance in sport and dance. In R.N. Singer, H.A. Hausenblas, & C.M. Janelle (Eds.), *Handbook of sport psychology* (2nd ed.) (pp. 174-201). New York: Wiley.

Sternberg, R.J. (1996). Costs of expertise. In K.A. Ericsson (Ed.), *The road to excellence: The acquisition of expert performance in the arts and sciences, sports, and games* (pp. 347-354). Mahwah, NJ: Lawrence Erlbaum.

Sternberg, R.J. (1998). If the key's not there, the light won't help. *Behavioral and Brain Sciences, 21,* 425-426.

Stevenson, M. (1999). The use of mental skills by male and female athletes. Unpublished master's thesis, University of Ottawa, Ottawa, Ontario, Canada.

Swallow, J.G., Garland, T., Carter, P.A., Zhan, W.Z., & Sieck, G.C. (1998). Effects of voluntary activity and genetic selection on aerobic capacity in house mice (Mus domesticus). *Journal of Applied Physiology, 84,* 69-76.

Tenenbaum, G., Stewart, E., & Sheath, P. (1999). Detection of targets and attentional flexibility: Can computerized simulations account for developmental and skill-level differences? *International Journal of Sport Psychology, 30,* 261-282.

Terry, P.C. (1995). The efficacy of mood-state profiling with elite performers: A review and synthesis. *The Sport Psychologist, 9,* 309-324.

Vickers, J.N. (1992). Gaze control in putting. *Perception, 21,* 117-132.

Vickers, J.N. (1996a). Visual control while aiming at a far target. *Journal of Experimental Psychology: Human Perception and Performance, 22,* 342-354.

Vickers, J.N. (1996b). Control of visual attention during the basketball free throw. *American Journal of Sports Medicine, 24,* S93-S97.

Vickers, J., Williams, A.M., Rodrigues, S., Hillis, F., & Coyne, G. (1999). Eye movements of elite biathlon shooters during rested and fatigued states. *Journal of Sport & Exercise Psychology, 21,* s116.

Williams, A.M., & Davids, K. (1995). Declarative knowledge in sport: A by-product of experience or a characteristic of expertise? *Journal of Sport & Exercise Psychology, 17,* 259-275.

Williams, A.M., & Davids, K. (1997). Assessing cue usage in performance contexts: A comparison between eye movement and concurrent verbal report methods. *Behavior Research Methods, Instruments, and Computers, 29,* 364-375.

Williams, A.M., & Davids, K. (1998). Visual search strategy, selective attention, and expertise in soccer. *Research Quarterly for Exercise and Sport, 69,* 111-128.

Williams, A.M., Davids, K., Burwitz, L., & Williams, J.G. (1993). Visual search and sports performance. *Australian Journal of Science and Medicine in Sport, 22,* 55-65.

Williams, A.M., Davids, K., Burwitz, L., & Williams, J.G. (1994). Visual search strategies in experienced and inexperienced soccer players. *Research Quarterly for Exercise and Sport, 65,* 127-135.

Williams, A.M., Davids, K., & Williams, J.G. (1999). *Visual perception and action in sport.* London: Spon.

Williams, A.M., & Elliott D. (1999). Anxiety, expertise, and visual search strategy in karate. *Journal of Sport & Exercise Psychology, 21,* 362-375.

Williams, A.M., Vickers, J.N., Rodrigues, S., & Hillis, F. (2000). Anxiety and performance in table tennis: A test of Eysenck and Calvo's processing efficiency theory. *Journal of Sport & Exercise Psychology, 22,* s116.

Wilmore, J.H., & Costill, D.L. (1999). *Physiology of sport and exercise* (2nd ed.). Champaign, IL: Human Kinetics.

Wilson, K.R. (1999). The use of mental skills in training and competition by synchronized skaters: Are there differences? Unpublished master's thesis, University of Ottawa, Canada.

Woodman, T., & Hardy, L. (2001). Stress and anxiety. In R.N. Singer, H.A. Hausenblas, & C.M. Janelle (Eds.), *Handbook of sport psychology* (2nd ed.) (pp. 290-318). New York: Wiley.

Zani, A., & Rossi, B. (1990). Cognitive psychophysiology as an interface between cognitive and sport psychology. *International Journal of Sport Psychology, 22,* 376-398.

Chapter 3

Abernethy, B. (1991). Visual search strategies and decision-making in sport. *International Journal of Sport Psychology, 22,* 189-210.

Abernethy, B., Neal, R.J., & Koning, P. (1994). Visual-perceptual and cognitive differences between expert, intermediate, and novice snooker players. *Applied Cognitive Psychology, 18,* 185-211.

Anderson, J.R. (1982). Acquisition of cognitive skill. *Psychological Review, 89,* 369-406.

Anderson, J.R. (1987). Skill acquisition: Compilation of weak-method problem situations. *Psychological Review, 94*(2), 192-210.

Beamer, M., Ericsson, K.A., Côté, J., & Baker, J. (2001). Developmental changes in expert gymnasts' training activities: Toward a framework for the development of deliberate practice. In A. Papaioannou, M. Goudas, and Y. Theodorakis (Eds.), *In the dawn of the new millennium: Proceedings of the International Society of Sport Psychology 10th World Congress of Sport Psychology* (Vol. 2, pp. 308-310). Tessaloniki, Greece: Christodoulidi Publications.

Bloom, B.S. (1985). Generalizations about talent development. In B.S. Bloom (Ed.), *Developing talent in young people* (pp. 507-549). New York: Ballantine Books.

Chaffin, R., & Imreh, G. (1997). "Pulling teeth and torture": Musical memory and problem solving. *Thinking and Reasoning, 3,* 315-336.

Charness, N., Krampe, R.T., & Mayr, U. (1996). The role of practice and coaching in entrepreneurial skill domains: An international comparison of life-span chess skill acquisition. In K.A. Ericsson (Ed.), *The road to excellence: The acquisition of expert performance in the arts and sciences, sports, and games* (pp. 51-80). Mahwah, NJ: Erlbaum.

Chase, W.G., & Ericsson, K.A. (1981). Skilled memory. In J.R. Anderson (Ed.), *Cognitive skills and their acquisition* (pp. 141-189). Hillsdale, NJ: Lawrence Erlbaum Associates.

Chase, W.G., & Ericsson, K.A. (1982). Skill and working memory. In G.H. Bower (Ed.), *The psychology of learning and motivation* (Vol. 16, pp. 1-58). New York: Academic Press.

Chase, W.G., & Simon, H.A. (1973). The mind's eye in chess. In W.G. Chase (Ed.), *Visual information processing* (pp. 215-281). New York: Academic Press.

Chi, M.T.H., Glaser, R., & Rees, E. (1982). Expertise in problem solving. In R.S. Sternberg (Ed.), *Advances in the psychology of human intelligence* (Vol. 1, pp. 1-75). Hillsdale, NJ: Erlbaum.

Côté, J., Ericsson, K.A., & Beamer, M. (2001). *Tracing the development of elite athletes using retrospective interview methods: A proposed interview and validation procedure for reported information.* Manuscript submitted for publication.

Dawes, R.M. (1994). *House of cards: Psychology and psychotherapy built on myth.* New York: Free Press.

de Groot, A. (1978). *Thought and choice in chess.* The Hague: Mouton. (Original work published 1946).

Ericsson, K.A. (1988). Analysis of memory performance in terms of memory skill. In R.J. Sternberg (Ed.), *Advances in the psychology of human intelligence,* (Vol. 4, pp. 137-179). Hillsdale, NJ: Erlbaum.

Ericsson, K.A. (1996). The acquisition of expert performance: An introduction to some of the issues. In K.A. Ericsson (Ed.), *The road to excellence: The acquisition of expert performance in the arts and sciences, sports, and games* (pp. 1-50). Mahwah, NJ: Erlbaum.

Ericsson, K.A. (1998). The scientific study of expert levels of performance: General implications for optimal learning and creativity. *High Ability Studies, 9,* 75-100.

Ericsson, K.A. (2001). The path to expert golf performance: Insights from the masters on how to improve performance by deliberate practice. In P.R. Thomas (Ed.), *Optimising performance in golf* (pp. 1-57). Brisbane, Australia: Australian Academic Press.

Ericsson, K.A. (2002). Attaining excellence through deliberate practice: Insights from the study of expert performance. In M. Ferrari (Ed.), *The pursuit of excellence in education* (pp. 21-55). Hillsdale, NJ: Erlbaum.

Ericsson, K.A., Chase, W.G., & Faloon, S. (1980). Acquisition of a memory skill. *Science, 208,* 1181-1182.

Ericsson, K.A., & Kintsch, W. (1995). Long-term working memory. *Psychological Review, 102,* 211-245.

Ericsson, K.A., Krampe, R.T., & Tesch-Römer, C. (1993). The role of deliberate practice in the acquisition of expert performance. *Psychological Review, 100,* 363-406.

Ericsson, K.A., & Lehmann, A.C. (1996). Expert and exceptional performance: Evidence on maximal adaptations on task constraints. *Annual Review of Psychology, 47,* 273-305.

Ericsson, K.A., Patel, V.L., & Kintsch, W. (2000). How experts' adaptations to representative task demands account for the expertise effect in memory recall: Comment on Vicente and Wang (1998). *Psychological Review, 107,* 578-592.

Ericsson, K.A., & Simon, H.A. (1993). *Protocol analysis: Verbal reports as data* (Rev. ed.). Cambridge, MA: Bradford Books/MIT Press.

Ericsson, K.A., & Smith, J. (1991). Prospects and limits in the empirical study of expertise: An introduction. In K.A. Ericsson and J. Smith (Eds.), *Toward a general theory of expertise: Prospects and limits* (pp. 1-38). Cambridge: Cambridge University Press.

Fitts, P., & Posner, M.I. (1967). *Human performance.* Belmont, CA: Brooks/Cole.

French, K.E., Nevett, M.E., Spurgeon, J.H., Graham, K.C., Rink, J.E., & McPherson, S.L. (1996). Knowledge representation and problem solution in expert and novice youth baseball players. *Research Quarterly for Exercise and Sport, 67,* 386-395.

Gabrielsson, A. (1999). The performance of music. In D. Deutsch (Ed.), *The psychology of music* (2nd edition) (pp. 501-602). San Diego: Academic Press.

Gruson, L.M. (1988). Rehearsal skill and musical competence: Does practice make perfect? In J. A. Sloboda (Ed.), *Generative processes in music* (pp. 91-112). Oxford, UK: Clarenden Press.

Helsen, W.F., & Starkes, J.L. (1999). A multidimensional approach to skilled perception and performance in sport. *Applied Cognitive Psychology, 13,* 1-27.

Helsen, W.F., Starkes, J.L., & Hodges, N.J. (1998). Team sports and the theory of deliberate practice. *Journal of Sport and Exercise Psychology, 20,* 12-34.

Howe, M.J.A., Davidson, J.W., & Sloboda, J.A. (1998). Innate talents: Reality or myth? *Behavioral and Brain Sciences, 21,* 399-442.

Landy, F.J., & Farr, J.L. (1980). Performance rating. *Psychological Bulletin, 87,* 72-107.

Lehmann, A.C., & Ericsson, K.A. (1996). Music performance without preparation: Structure and acquisition of expert sight-reading. *Psychomusicology, 15,* 1-29.

Masters, K.S., & Ogles, B.M. (1998). Associative and dissociative cognitive strategies in exercise and running: 20 years later, what do we know? *The Sport Psychologist, 12,* 253-270.

Miller, G.A. (1956). The magical number seven, plus or minus two: Some limits of our capacity for processing information. *Psychological Review, 63,* 81-97.

Nevett, M.E., & French, K.E. (1997). The development of sport-specific planning, rehearsal, and updating of plans during defensive youth baseball game performance. *Research Quarterly for Exercise and Sport, 68,* 203-214.

Nielsen, S. (1999). Regulation of learning strategies during practice: A case study of a single church organ student preparing a particular work for a concert performance. *Psychology of Music, 27,* 218-229.

Robergs, R.A., & Roberts, S.O. (1997). *Exercise physiology: Exercise, performance, and clinical applications.* St. Louis, MO: Mosby-Year Book.

Salthouse, T.A. (1984). Effects of age and skill in typing. *Journal of Experimental Psychology: General, 113*, 345-371.

Simon, H.A., & Chase, W.G. (1973). Skill in chess. *American Scientist, 61*, 394-403.

Stael von Holstein, C.-A. S. (1972). Probabilistic forecasting: An experiment related to the stock market. *Organizational Behavior and Human Performance, 8*, 139-158.

Starkes, J.L., & Allard, J. (1991). Motor-skill experts in sports, dance and other domains. In K.A. Ericsson and J. Smith (Eds.), *Toward a general theory of expertise: Prospects and limits* (pp. 126-152). Cambridge: Cambridge University Press.

Starkes, J.L., & Deakin, J. (1984). Perception in sport: A cognitive approach to skilled performance. In W.F. Straub and J.M. Williams (Eds.), *Cognitive sport psychology* (pp. 115-128). Lansing, NY: Sport Science Associates.

Starkes, J.L., Deakin, J., Allard, F., Hodges, N.J., & Hayes, A. (1996). Deliberate practice in sports: What is it anyway? In K.A. Ericsson (Ed.), *The road to excellence: The acquisition of expert performance in the arts and sciences, sports, and games* (pp. 81-106). Mahwah, NJ: Erlbaum.

Chapter 4

Abernethy, B., Côté, J., & Baker, J. (2002). *Expert decision-making in team sports.* Canberra, ACT: Technical Report for the Australian Institute of Sport.

Baker, J., Côté, J., & Abernethy, B. (in press a). Sport-specific practice and the development of expert decision making in team ball sports. *Journal of Applied Sport Psychology.*

Baker, J., Côté, J., & Abernethy, B. (in press b). Learning from the experts: Practice activities of expert decision-makers in sport. *Research Quarterly for Exercise and Sport.*

Bloom, B.S. (1985). *Developing talent in young people.* New York: Ballantine.

Brustad, R.J., Babkes, M., & Smith, A.L. (2001). Youth in sport: Psychological considerations. In R.N. Singer, H.A. Hausenblas, & C.M. Janelle (Eds.), *Handbook of sport psychology* (pp. 604-635). Toronto: John Wiley & Sons.

Carlsson, R.C. (1988). The socialization of elite tennis players in Sweden: An analysis of the players' backgrounds and development. *Sociology of Sport Journal, 5*, 241-256.

Côté, J. (1999). The influence of the family in the development of talent in sports. *The Sports Psychologist, 13*, 395-417.

Côté, J. (2002). Coach and peer influence on children's development through sport. In J.M. Silva & D. Stevens (Eds.), *Psychological foundations of sport,* (pp. 520-540). Boston: Allyn and Bacon.

Côté, J., Ericsson, K.A., & Beamer, M. (2001). *Tracing the development of elite athletes using retrospective interview methods: A proposed interview and validation procedure for reported information.* Manuscript submitted for publication.

Côté, J., & Hay, J. (2002). Children's involvement in sport: A developmental perspective. In J.M. Silva & D. Stevens (Eds.), *Psychological foundations of sport* (2nd ed., pp. 484-502). Boston: Merrill.

Côté, J., Salmela, J.H., Trudel, P., Baria, A., & Russell, S. (1995). The coaching model: A grounded assessment of expert gymnastics coaches' knowledge. *Journal of Sport and Exercise Psychology, 17*, 1-17.

Deci, E.L., & Ryan, R.M. (1985). *Intrinsic motivation and self-determination in human behavior.* New York: Plenum Press.

De Knop, P., Engström, L.M., & Skirstad, B. (1996). Worldwide trends in youth sport. In P. De Knop, L-M. Engström, B. Skirstad, & M. Weiss (Eds.), *Worldwide trends in youth sport* (pp. 276-281). Champaign, IL: Human Kinetics.

Denzin, N.K. (1975). Play, games and interaction: The contexts of childhood socialization. *The Sociological Quarterly, 16*, 458-478.

Ericsson, K.A. (1996). The acquisition of expert performance: An introduction to some of the issues. In K.A. Ericsson (Ed.), *The road to excellence: The acquisition of expert performance in the arts, sciences, sports and games* (pp. 1-50). Mahwah, NJ: Erlbaum.

Ericsson, K.A. (2001). Expertise in sport and the expert performance approach: Implications of the complexity of the acquired mechanisms. *Proceedings of the 10th World Congress on Sport Psychology*, Skiathos, Greece.

Ericsson, K.A., Krampe, R.T., & Tesch-Römer, C. (1993). The role of deliberate practice in the acquisition of expert performance. *Psychological Review, 100*(3), 363-406.

Gould, D., Udry, E., Tuffey, S., & Loehr, J. (1996). Burnout in competitive junior tennis players: 1. A quantitative psychological assessment. *The Sport Psychologist, 10,* 322-340.

Helsen, W.F., Hodges, N.J., Van Winckel, J., & Starkes, J.L. (2000). The roles of talent, physical precocity and practice in the development of soccer expertise. *Journal of Sports Sciences, 18,* 727-736.

Helsen, W.F., Starkes, J.L., & Hodges, N.J. (1998). Team sports and the theory of deliberate practice. *Journal of Sport and Exercise Psychology, 20,* 12-34.

Hodge, T., & Deakin, J. (1998). Deliberate practice and expertise in the martial arts: The role of context in motor recall. *Journal of Sport and Exercise Psychology, 20,* 260-279.

Hodges, N.J., & Starkes, J.L. (1996). Wrestling with the nature of expertise: A sport-specific test of Ericsson, Krampe and Tesch-Römer's (1993) theory of "deliberate practice". *International Journal of Sport Psychology, 27,* 400-424.

Kalinowski, A.G. (1985). The development of Olympic swimmers. In B.S. Bloom (Ed.), *Developing talent in young people* (pp. 139-192). New York: Ballantine.

Klawans, H.L. (1996). *Why Michael couldn't hit, and other tales of the neurology of sports.* New York: Freeman.

Monsaas, J.A. (1985). Learning to be a world-class tennis player. In B.S. Bloom (Ed.), *Developing talent in young people* (pp. 211-269). New York: Ballantine.

Piaget, (1962). *Play, dreams, and imitation in childhood.* New York: W.W. Norton.

Ryan, R.M., & Deci, E.L. (2000). Self-determination theory and the facilitation of intrinsic motivation, social development, and well being. *American Psychologist, 55,* 68-78.

Salmela, J.H. (Ed). (1996). *Great job coach: Getting the edge from proven winners.* Ottawa, Ontario: Potentium.

Smith, P.K., Takhvar, M., Gore, N., & Vollstedt, R. (1986). Play in young children: Problems of definition, categorization and measurement. In P.K. Smith (Ed.), *Children's play: Research, developments, and practical applications* (pp. 37-54). New York: Gordon and Breach.

Soberlak, P. (2001). *A retrospective analysis of the development and motivation of professional ice hockey players.* Unpublished master's thesis, Queen's University, Kingston, Ontario, Canada.

Soberlak, P., & Côté, J. (in press). The developmental activities of professional ice hockey players. *Journal of Applied Sport Psychology.*

Sosniak, L.A. (1985). Learning to be a concert pianist. In B.S. Bloom (Ed.), *Developing talent in young people* (pp. 19-67). New York: Ballantine.

Starkes, J.L. (2000). The road to expertise: Is practice the only determinant? *International Journal of Sport Psychology, 31,* 431-451.

Starkes, J.L., Deakin, J.M., Allard, F., Hodges, N.J., & Hayes., A. (1996). Deliberate practice in sports: What is it anyway? In K.A. Ericsson (Ed.), *The road to excellence: The acquisition of expert performance in the arts, sciences, sports and games* (pp. 81-106). Mahwah, NJ: Erlbaum.

Vallerand, R.J. (2001). A hierarchical model of intrinsic and extrinsic motivation in sport and exercise. In G.C. Roberts (Ed.), *Advances in motivation in sport and exercise* (pp. 263-319). Champaign, IL: Human Kinetics.

Vygotsky, L.S. (Ed.). (1978). *Mind in society: The development of higher psychological processes.* Cambridge, MA: Harvard University Press.

Weiss, M.R. (1995). Children in sport: An educational model. In S.M. Murphy (Ed.), *Sport psychology interventions* (pp. 39-70). Champaign, IL: Human Kinetics.

Weiss, M.R., & Petlichkoff, L.M. (1989). Children's motivation for participation in and withdrawal from sport: Identifying the missing links. *Pediatric Exercise Science, 1,* 195-211.

Wiersma, L.D. (2000). Risks and benefits of youth sport specialization: Perspectives and recommendations. *Pediatric Exercise Science, 12,* 13-22.

Chapter 5

Allard, F., Starkes, J.L., & Deakin, J.M. (1998). *The microstructure of practice in wrestling.* Unpublished manuscript.

Charness, N., Krampe, R., & Mayr, U. (1996). The role of practice and coaching in entrepreneurial skill domains: An international comparison of life-span chess skill acquisition. In K.A. Ericsson (Ed.), *The road to excellence: The acquisition of expert performance in the arts and sciences, sports and games* (pp. 51-81). Mahwah, NJ: Lawrence Erlbaum Associates.

Cobley, S., & Deakin, J.M. (2001, April). Evaluating the microstructure of practice: The relationship between coach expertise and practice structure. Queen's University Annual Research Symposium, Kingston, Ontario.

Deakin, J.M., Starkes, J.L., & Allard, F. (1998). The microstructure of practice in sport. *Sport Canada Technical Report.* Ottawa, Ontario, Canada.

Ericsson, K.A. (Ed.). (1996). *The road to excellence: The acquisition of expert performance in the arts and sciences, sports and games.* Hillsdale, NJ: Lawrence Erlbaum.

Ericsson, K.A., Krampe, R.T., & Tesch-Römer, C. (1993). The role of deliberate practice in the acquisition of expert performance. *Psychological Review, 100,* 363-406.

Helsen, W.F., Starkes, J.L., & Hodges, J.L. (1998). Team sports and the theory of deliberate practice. *Journal of Sport & Exercise Psychology, 20,* 12-34.

Hodge, T., & Deakin, J.M. (1998). Expertise in the martial arts. *Journal of Sport & Exercise Psychology, 20,* 260-279.

Hodges, N.J., & Starkes, J.L. (1996). Wrestling with the nature of expertise: A sport specific test of Ericsson, Krampe, and Tesch-Römer's (1993) theory of deliberate practice. *International Journal of Sport Psychology, 27,* 400-424.

Howe, M.J.A., Davidson, J.W., & Sloboda, J.A. (1998). Innate talents: Reality or myth. *Behavioral and Brain Sciences, 21,* 399-407.

Schultetus, S., & Charness, N. (1997, May). *Skill acquisition in sport: Building a fencer.* Paper presented at the meeting of the American Psychological Society in Washington, D.C.

Starkes, J.L. (2000). The road to expertise: Is practice the only determinant? *International Journal of Sport Psychology, 31,* 431-451.

Starkes, J.L., Deakin, J.M., Allard, F., Hodges, N.J., & Hayes, A. (1996). Deliberate practice in sports: What is it anyway? In K.A. Ericsson (Ed.), *The road to excellence: The acquisition of expert performance in the arts and sciences, sports and games* (pp. 81-106). Mahwah, NJ: Lawrence Erlbaum Associates.

Chapter 6

Abernethy, B., Thomas, J.R., & Thomas, K.T. (1993). Strategies for improving understanding of motor expertise (or mistakes we have made and things we have learned!!). In J.L. Starkes & F. Allard (Eds.). *Cognitive issues in motor expertise* (pp. 317-356). Amsterdam: Elsevier Science Publishers.

Anderson, J.R. (1987). Acquisition of cognitive skill. *Psychological Review, 89,* 369-406.

Chi, M.T.H., Glaser, R., & Farr, J.J. (1988). *The nature of expertise.* Hillsdale, NJ: Erlbaum.

Ericsson, K.A. (Ed.). (1996a). *The road to excellence: The acquisition of expert performance in the arts and sciences, sports, and games*. Mahwah, NJ: Lawrence Erlbaum.

Ericsson, K.A. (1996b). The acquisition of expert performance: An introduction to some of the issues. In K.A. Ericsson (Ed.), *The road to excellence: The acquisition of expert performance in the arts and sciences, sports, and games* (pp. 1-50). Mahwah, NJ: Erlbaum.

Ericsson, K.A., & Kintsch, W. (1995). Long-term working memory. *Psychological Review, 102*, 211-245.

Ericsson, K.A., & Simon, H.A. (1993). *Protocol analysis: Verbal reports as data* (Rev. ed.). Cambridge, MA: MIT Press.

French, K.E., & McPherson, S.L. (1999). Adaptations in response selection processes used during sport competition with increasing age and expertise. *International Journal of Sport Psychology, 30*, 173-193.

French, K.E., & McPherson, S.L. (in press). Development of expertise in sport. In M. Weiss & L. Bunker (Eds.), *Developmental sport and exercise psychology: A lifespan perspective*. Morgantown, WV: Fitness Information.

McPherson, S.L. (1993). Knowledge representation and decision-making in sport. In J. Starkes & F. Allard (Eds.), *Cognitive issues in motor expertise* (pp. 159-188). Amsterdam: Elsevier.

McPherson, S.L. (1994). The development of sport expertise: Mapping the tactical domain. *Quest, 46*, 223-240.

McPherson, S.L. (1999a). Expert-novice differences in performance skills and problem representations of youth and adults during tennis competition. *Research Quarterly for Exercise and Sport, 70*, 233-251.

McPherson, S.L. (1999b). Tactical differences in problem representations and solutions in collegiate varsity and beginner women tennis players. *Research Quarterly for Exercise and Sport, 70*, 369-384.

McPherson, S.L. (2000). Expert-novice differences in planning strategies during collegiate singles tennis competition. *Journal of Sport and Exercise Psychology, 22*, 39-62.

McPherson, S.L., & French, K.E. (1991). Changes in cognitive strategy and motor skill in tennis. *Journal of Sport and Exercise Psychology, 13*, 26-41.

McPherson, S.L., French, K.E., & Kernodle M.W. (2001). *Expert-novice differences in problem representations of male professionals and novices during singles tennis competition.* Manuscript in preparation.

McPherson, S.L., & Thomas, J.R. (1989). Relation of knowledge and performance in boys' tennis: Age and expertise. *Journal of Experimental Child Psychology, 48*, 190-211.

Nielsen, T.M., & McPherson, S.L. (2001). Response selection and execution skills of professionals and novices during singles tennis competition. *Perceptual and Motor Skills, 93*, 541-555.

Starkes, J.L., Deakin, J., Allard, F., Hodges, N.J., & Hayes, A. (1996). Deliberate practice in sports: What is it anyway? In K.A. Ericsson (Ed.), *The road to excellence: The acquisition of expert performance in the arts and sciences, sports and games* (pp. 81-106). Hillsdale, NJ: Erlbaum.

Thomas, J.R., French, K.E., & Humphries, C.A. (1986). Knowledge development and sport skill performance: Directions for motor behavior research. *Journal of Sport Psychology, 8*, 259-272.

Thomas, K.T., & Thomas, J.R. (1994). Developing expertise in sport: The relation of knowledge and performance. *International Journal of Sport Psychology, 30*, 221-234.

United States Tennis Association. (2001). *National tennis rating program*. Retrieved May 1, 2001, from http://www.usta.com/usaleague/ntrp.html.

Williams, A.M., Davids, K., & Williams, J.G. (1999). *Visual perception and action in sport*. London: E & FN Spon.

Chapter 7

Abernethy, B. (1991). Visual search strategies and decision-making in sport. *International Journal of Sport Psychology, 22,* 189-210.

Abernethy, B. (1993). Searching for the minimal essential information for skilled perception and action. *Psychological Research, 55,* 131-138.

Abernethy, B. (2001). Attention. In R. Singer, H.A. Hausenblas, & C.M. Janelle (Eds.), *Handbook of sport psychology* (2nd ed., pp. 53-85). New York: Wiley & Sons.

Abernethy, B., Neal, R.J., & Konig, P. (1994). Visual-perceptual and cognitive differences between expert, intermediate, and novice snooker players. *Applied Cognitive Psychology, 8,* 185-211.

Abernethy, B., & Russel, D.G. (1987). Expert-novice differences in an applied selective attention task. *Journal of Sport Psychology, 9,* 326-345.

Abernethy, B., Thomas, K.T., & Thomas, J.R. (1993). Strategies for improving understanding of motor expertise (or mistakes we have made and things we have learned!!). In J.L. Starkes & F. Allard (Eds.), *Cognitive issues in motor expertise* (pp. 317-356). Amsterdam: North Holland.

Aberbethy, B., Wann, J., & Parks, S. (1998). Training perceptual-motor skills for sport. In B. Elliott (Ed.), *Training in sport: Applying sport science* (pp. 1-68). New York: Wiley & Sons.

Allard, F., Deakin, J., Parker, S., & Rodgers, W. (1993). Declarative knowledge in skilled motor performance: Byproduct or constituent? In J.L. Starkes & F. Allard (Eds.), *Cognitive issues in motor expertise* (pp. 95-107). Amsterdam: North Holland.

Allard, F., & Starkes, J.L. (1991). Motor-skill experts in sports, dance, and other domains. In K.A. Ericsson & J. Smith (Eds.), *Toward a general theory of expertise: Prospects and limits* (pp. 126-152). Cambridge: Cambridge University Press.

Anderson, J.R. (1982). Acquisition of cognitive skill. *Psychological Review, 89,* 369-406.

Anzai, Y. (1991). Learning and use of representations for physics expertise. In K.A. Ericsson & J. Smith (Eds.), *Toward a general theory of expertise: Prospects and limits* (pp. 64-92). Cambridge: Cambridge University Press.

Bard, C., Fleury, M., Carrière, L., & Hallé, M. (1980). Analysis of gymnastic judges' visual search. *Research Quarterly for Exercise and Sport, 51,* 267-273.

Charness, N. (1981). Search in chess: Age and skill differences. *Journal of Experimental Psychology: Human Perception and Performance, 7,* 467-476.

Chase, W.G., & Simon, H.A. (1973). Perception in chess. *Cognitive Psychology, 4,* 55-81.

Côté, J., Salmela, J.H., Trudel, P., Baria, A., & Russel, S. (1995). The coaching model: A grounded assessment of expert gymnastic coaches' knowledge. *Journal of Sport & Exercise Psychology, 17,* 1-17.

Deakin, J., & Allard, F. (1992, June). *An evaluation of skill and judgement in basketball officiating.* Paper presented at the meeting of the North American Society for the Psychology of Sport and Physical Activity, Pittsburgh, PA.

DeGroot, A.D. (1965). *Thought and choice in chess.* The Hague: Molton.

Ericsson, K.A. (1996). *The road to excellence: The acquisition of expert performance in the arts and sciences, sports, and games.* Mahwah, NJ: Erlbaum.

Ericsson, K.A., Krampe, R.T., & Tesch-Römer, C. (1993). The role of deliberate practice in the acquisition of expert performance. *Psychological Review, 100,* 363-406.

Ericsson, K.A., & Lehmann, A.C. (1996). Expert and exceptional performance: Evidence of maximal adaptations to task constraints. *Annual Review of Psychology, 47,* 273-305.

Ericsson, K.A., & Smith, J. (1991). Prospects and limits of the empirical study of expertise: An introduction. In K.A. Ericsson & J. Smith (Eds.), *Toward a general theory of expertise: Prospects and limits* (pp. 1-38). Cambridge: Cambridge University Press.

French, K.E. (2001). Development of sport expertise during childhood and adolescence. In A.

Papaioannou, M. Goudas, & Y. Theodorakis (Eds.), *Proceedings of the 10th World Congress of Sport Psychology, Vol. 38* (pp. 349-350). Greece: Christodoulidi Publications.

Goulet, C., Bard, C., & Fleury, M. (1989). Expertise differences in preparing to return a tennis serve: A visual information processing approach. *Journal of Sport & Exercise Psychology, 11*, 382-398.

Haywood, K.M. (1993). *Life span motor development* (2nd ed.). Champaign, IL: Human Kinetics.

Helsen, W.F., Hodges, N.J., Van Winckel, J., & Starkes, J.L. (2000). The roles of talent, physical precocity and practice in the development of soccer expertise. *Journal of Sports Sciences, 18*, 727-736.

Ilmwold, C.H., & Hoffman, S.J. (1983). Visual recognition of a gymnastics skill by experienced and inexperienced instructors. *Research Quarterly for Exercise and Sport, 54*, 149-155.

Jacoby, L.L. (1978). On interpreting the effects of repetition: Solving a problem versus remembering a solution. *Journal of Verbal Learning and Verbal Behavior, 17*, 649-667.

Jacoby, L.L., & Dallas, M. (1981). On the relationship between autobiographical memory and perceptual learning. *Journal of Experimental Psychology: Learning, Memory and Cognition, 110*, 306-340.

MacMahon, C. (1999). *Making sense of chaos: Decision making by high and low experience rugby referees.* Unpublished master's thesis, University of Ottawa, Ottawa, Ontario, Canada.

MacMahon, C., & Ste-Marie, D.M. (1999, October). *Decision-making in rugby officials.* Paper presented at the Canadian Society for Psychomotor Learning and Sport Psychology, Edmonton, Alberta, Canada.

Magill, R.A. (2001). *Motor learning: Concepts and applications* (6th ed.). Boston: McGraw-Hill.

McLennan, J., & Omodei, M.M. (1996). The role of prepriming in recognition-primed decision making. *Perceptual and Motor Skills, 82*, 1059-1069.

Melton, A.W. (1967). Repetition and retrieval from memory. *Science, 158*, 532.

Oudejans, R.R., Verheijer, R., Bakker, F.C., Gerrits, J.C., Steinbrückner, M., & Beek, P.J. (2000). Errors in judging "offside" in football. *Nature, 404*, 33.

Plessner, H., & Betsch, T. (2001). Sequential effects in important referee decisions: The case of penalties in soccer. *Journal of Sport and Exercise Psychology, 23*, 254-259.

Poulton, E.C. (1957). On predicting skilled movement. *Psychological Bulletin, 54*, 467-478.

Richman, H.B., Gobet, F., Staszewski, J.J., & Simon, H.A. (1996). Perceptual and memory processes in the acquisition of expert performance: The EPAM model. In K.A. Ericsson (Ed.), *The road to excellence: The acquisition of expert performance in the arts and sciences, sports, and games* (pp. 167-187). Mahwah, NJ: Erlbaum.

Ripoll, H., Kerlirzin, Y., Stein, J.F., & Reine, B. (1995). Analysis of information processing, decision making, and visual strategies in complex problem solving sport situations. *Human Movement Science, 14*, 929-938.

Salmela, J.H. (1978). Gymnastic judging: A complex information processing task (or who's putting one over on who?). *International Gymnast, 20*, 54-56, 62-63.

Salmela, J.H., Draper, S., & Laplante, D. (1993). Development of expert coaches of team sports. In S. Serpa, J. Alves, V. Ferreira, & A. Paul-Brito (Eds.), *Sport psychology: An integrated approach* (pp. 296-300). Lisbon, Portugal: FMH.

Salthouse, T.A. (1991). Expertise as the circumvention of human processing limitations. In K.A. Ericsson & J. Smith (Eds.), *Toward a general theory of expertise: Prospects and limits* (pp. 286-300). Cambridge: Cambridge University Press.

Singer, R.N., Williams, A.M., Frehlich, S.G., Janelle, C.M., Radlo, S.J., Barba, D.A., et al. (1998). New frontiers in visual search: An exploratory study in live tennis situations. *Research Quarterly for Exercise & Sport, 69*, 290-296.

Starkes, J.L., & Allard, F. (1993). *Cognitive issues in motor expertise.* Amsterdam: North Holland.

Starkes, J.L., Allard, F., Lindley, S., & O'Reilly, K. (1994). Abilities and skill in basketball. *International Journal of Sport Psychology, 25,* 249-265.

Starkes, J.L., Helsen, W., & Jack, R. (2001). Expert performance in sport and dance. In R. Singer, H.A. Hausenblas, & C.M. Janelle (Eds.), *Handbook of sport psychology* (2nd ed., pp. 174-194). New York: Wiley & Sons.

Starkes, J.L., & Lindley, S. (1994). Can we hasten expertise by video simulations? *Quest, 46,* 211-222.

Ste-Marie, D.M. (1999). Expert-novice differences in gymnastic judging: An information processing perspective. *Applied Cognitive Psychology, 13,* 269-281.

Ste-Marie, D.M. (2000). Expertise in women's gymnastic judging: An observational approach. *Perceptual and Motor Skills, 90,* 543-546.

Ste-Marie, D.M., & Lee, T.D. (1991). Prior processing effects on gymnastic judging. *Journal of Experimental Pscyhology, Learning, Memory, and Cognition, 17,* 126-136.

Taylor, M.A., Burwitz, L., & Davids, K. (1998). Coaching perceptual strategy in badminton. *Journal of Sport Sciences, 12,* 213.

Tenenbaum, G., & Bar-Eli, M. (1993). Decision making in sport: A cognitive perspective. In R. Singer, M. Murphey, & K. Tennant (Eds.), *Handbook of research on sport psychology* (pp. 171-192). New York: Macmillan.

Tenenbaum, G., & Bar-Eli, M. (1995). Personality and intellectual capabilities in sport psychology. In D.H. Saklofske & M. Zeidner (Eds.), *International handbook of personality and intelligence* (pp. 687-710). New York: Plenum Press.

Tenenbaum, G., Levy-Kolker, N., Sade, S., Lieberman, D.G., & Lidor, R. (1996). Anticipation and confidence of decisions related to skilled performance. *International Journal of Sport Psychology, 27,* 293-307.

Thomas, K.T., & Thomas, J.R. (1994). Developing expertise in sport: From Leeds to legend. *Quest, 46,* 199-210.

Treisman, A., & Gelade, G. (1980). A feature integration theory of attention. *Cognitive Psychology, 12,* 97-136.

Tulving, E., & Thompson, D.M. (1973). Encoding specificity and retrieval processes in episodic memory. *Psychological Review, 80,* 353-373.

Vickers, J.N. (1986). The resequencing task: Determining expert-novice differences in the organization of a movement sequence. *Research Quarterly for Exercise and Sport, 57,* 260-264.

Vickers, J.N. (1988). Knowledge structures of expert-novice gymnasts. *Human Movement Science, 7,* 47-72.

Williams, A.M. (2001). Perceptual expertise in sport: Some myths and realities. In A. Papaioannou, M. Goudas, & Y. Theodorakis (Eds.), *Proceedings of the 10th World Congress of Sport Psychology, Vol 38.* (pp. 206-211). Greece: Christodoulidi Publications.

Williams, A.M., & Davids, K. (1995). Declarative knowledge in sport: A byproduct of experience or a characteristic of expertise? *Journal of Sport and Exercise Psychology, 17,* 259-275.

Williams, A.M., Davids, K., Burwitz, L., & Williams, J.G. (1994). Visual search strategies in experienced and inexperienced soccer players. *Research Quarterly for Exercise and Sport, 65,* 127-135.

Williams, A.M., & Elliott, D. (1999). Anxiety and visual search in strategy in karate. *Journal of Sport Psychology, 21,* 362-365.

Williams, A.M., & Grant, A. (1999). Training perceptual skill in sport. *International Journal of Sport Psychology, 30,* 194-220.

Chapter 8

Abernethy, B. (1987a). Anticipation in sport: A review. *Physical Education Review, 10,* 5-16.

Abernethy, B. (1987b). Selective attention in fast ball sports: II. Expert-novice differences. *Australian Journal of Science and Medicine in Sport, 19,* 7-16.

Abernethy, B. (1993). Attention. In R. Singer, M. Murphey, & L. Tennant (Eds.), *Handbook of research on sport psychology* (pp. 127-170). New York: Macmillan.

Abernethy, B., & Russell, D.G. (1987). Expert-novice differences in selective attention task. *Journal of Sport and Exercise Psychology, 9*, 326-345.

Alain, C. (1991). Existence of independent priming types and their longevity characteristics. *International Journal of Sport Psychology, 22*, 334-359.

Alain, C., & Proteau, L. (1979). Perception of objective probabilities in motor performance. In B. Kerr (Ed.), *Human performance and behavior* (pp. 1-5). Alberta, Canada: Banff.

Alain, C., & Sarrazin, C. (1985). Prise de décision et traitement de l'information en squash [Decision-making and information processing in squash]. *Revue des Sciences et techniques des A.P.S., 6*, 49-59.

Allard, F., & Burnett, N. (1985). Skill in sport. *Canadian Journal of Sport Psychology, 39*, 294-312.

Baddeley, A.D. (1986). *Working memory.* Oxford: Oxford University Press.

Bandura, A. (1997). *Self-Efficacy: The exercise of control.* New York: W.H. Freeman.

Bard, C., & Fleury, M. (1976). Analysis of visual search activity during sport problem situation. *Journal of Human Movement Studies, 3*, 214-222.

Bard, C., Fleury, M., Carrière, L., & Halle, M. (1980). Analysis of gymnastics judges' visual search. *Research Quarterly for Exercise and Sport, 51*, 267-273.

Beitel, P.A. (1980). Multivariate relationship among visual perceptual attributes and gross-motor tasks with different environmental demands. *Journal of Motor Behavior, 12*, 29-40.

Bloom, B.S. (1985). Developing talent in young people. New York: Ballantine Books.

Borgeaud, P., & Abernethy, B. (1987). Skilled perception in volleyball defense. *Journal of Sport Psychology, 9*, 400-406.

Casteillo, V., & Umilta, C. (1992). Orientation of attention in volleyball players. *International Journal of Sport Psychology, 23*, 301-310.

Cave, K.R., & Bichot, N.P. (1999). Visuospatial attention: Beyond a spotlight scheme. *Psychonomic Bulletin & Review, 6*(2), 204-223.

Chase, W.G., & Simon, H.A. (1973). Perception in chess. *Cognitive Psychology, 4*, 55-81.

Coles, M.G.H. (1989). Modern mind-brain reading: Psychophysiology, physiology, and cognition. *Psychophysiology, 26*, 251-269.

Coles, M.G.H., Gratton, G., Bashore, T.R., Eriksen, C.W., & Donchin, E. (1985). A psychophysiological investigation of the continuous flow scheme of human information processing. *Journal of Experimental Psychology: Human Perception and Performance, 11*, 529-553.

Cox, R.H. (1985). *Sport psychology: Concepts and applications.* Dubuque, IA: Brown.

De Groot, A.D. (1965). *Thought and choice in chess.* The Hague: Mouton.

Downing, C.J. (1988). Expectancy and visual-spatial attention: Effects of perceptual quality. *Journal of Experimental Psychology: Human Perception and Performance, 14*, 188-202.

Downing, C.J., & Pinker, S. (1985). The spatial structure of visual attention. In M.I. Posner & O.S.M. Marin (Eds.), *Attention and performance XI: Mechanisms of attention* (pp. 171-187). Hillsdale, NJ: Erlbaum.

Ericsson, K.A. (1996). *The road to excellence: The acquisition of expert performance in arts and sciences, sports and games.* Mahwah, NJ: Erlbaum.

Ericsson, K.A., & Charness, N. (1994). Expert performance: Its structure and acquisition. *American Psychologist, 49*, 725-747.

Ericsson, K.A., & Kintsch, W. (1995). Long term working memory. *Psychological Review, 102*, 211-245.

Ericsson, K.A., & Lehmann, A.C. (1996). Expert and exceptional performance: Evidence of maximal adaptation to task constraints. *Annual Review of Psychology, 47*, 273-305.

Eriksen, C.W., Coles, M.G.H., Morris, L.R., & O'Hara, W.P. (1985). An electromyographic examination of response competition. *Bulletin of Psychonomic Society, 23*, 165-168.

Eriksen, C.W., & Murphy, T.D. (1987). Movement of attentional focus across the visual field: A critical look at the evidence. *Perception and Psychophysics, 42,* 299-305.

Fisher, A.C. (1984). Sport intelligence. In W.F. Straub & J.M. Williams (Eds.), *Cognitive sport psychology* (pp. 42-50). Lansing, MI: Sport Science.

French, K.E., & McPherson, S.L. (1999). Adaptations in response selection processes used during sport competition with increasing age and expertise. *International Journal of Sport Psychology, 30,* 173-193.

Gentile, A.M., Higgins, J.R., Miller, E.A., & Rosen, B.M. (1975). The structure of motor tasks. In C. Bard, M. Fluery, & J.H. Salmela (Eds.), *Movement: Actes du 7 Canadien en appretissage psychomoteur et psychologie du sport* (pp. 11-28). Quebec, Canada: Association of Professionals in Physical Education of Quebec.

Hanin, Y. (Ed.). (2000). *Emotions in sport.* Champaign, IL: Human Kinetics.

Henderson, J.M., & MacQuistan, A.D. (1993). The spatial distribution of attention following an exogeneous cue. *Perception and Psychophysics, 53,* 221-230.

Holender, D. (1980). Le concept de preparation a reagir dans le traitement de l'information [The concept of préparation and reaction in information processing]. In J. Requin (Ed.), *Anticipation et comportement* (pp. 29-46). Paris: Edition du Centre National de la Recherche Scientifique.

Keele, S.W. (1982). Component analysis and conceptions of skill. In A.S. Kelso (Ed.), *Human motor behavior: An introduction* (pp. 29-61). Hillsdale, NJ: Erlbaum.

Landers, D.M., Wang, M.Q., & Courtet, P. (1985). Peripheral narrowing among experienced and inexperienced rifle shooters under low- and high-time stress conditions. *Research Quarterly for Exercise and Sport, 56,* 122-130.

Millslagle, D.G. (1988). Visual perception, recognition, recall and mode visual search control in basketball involving novice and experienced basketball players. *Journal of Sport Behavior, 11,* 32-44.

Moran, A.P. (1996). *The psychology of concentration in sport performers: A cognitive analysis.* East Sussex, UK: Psychology Press.

Neisser, U. (1967). Cognitive psychology. New York: Appelton-Century-Crofts.

Nougier, V., Stein, J.F., & Bonnel, A.M. (1991). Information processing in sport and "orienting of attention." *International Journal of Sport Psychology, 22,* 307-327.

Prinz, W. (1977). Memory control of visual search. In S. Dornic (Ed.), *Attention and performance VI* (pp. 441-462). Hillsdale, NJ: Erlbaum.

Ripoll, H. (1979). Le traitement de l'information de donnes visuelles dans les situations tactiques en sport: L'exemple du basketball [Information processing of visual data in tactical situations in sport: example from basketball]. *Travaux et Recherches en ESP, 4,* 99-104. (Plus English translation as per APA.)

Ripoll, H. (1988). Utilisation d'un dispositif videooculographique d'enregistrement de la direction du regard en situation sportive [Utilization of a video occulograpic device in recording gaze direction in sport situation]. *Science et Motricite, 4,* 25-31.

Ripoll, H. (Ed.). (1991). Information processing and decision making in sport [Special issue]. *International Journal of Sport Psychology, 3-4,* 187-406.

Starkes, J.L. (2000). The road to expertise: Is practice the only determinant? *International Journal of Sport Psychology, 31,* 431-451.

Straub, W.F., & Williams, J.M. (Eds.) (1984). *Cognitive sport psychology.* Lansing, MI: Sport Science.

Temprado, J.J. (Ed.) (1999). Perceptual-motor coordination in sport [Special issue]. *International Journal of Sport Psychology, 4,* 417-580.

Tenenbaum, G. (Ed.) (1999). The development of expertise in sport: Nature and nurture [Special issue]. *International Journal of Sport Psychology, 2,* 113-301.

Tenenbaum, G., & Bar-Eli, M. (1993). Decision making in sport: A cognitive perspective. In

R.N. Singer, M. Murphey, & L.K. Tennant (Eds.), *Handbook of research on sport psychology* (pp. 171-192). New York: McMillan.

Tenenbaum, G., & Bar-Eli, M. (1995). Personality and intellectual capabilities in sport psychology. In D. Sakulufske & M. Zeidner (Eds.), *International handbook on personality and intelligence* (pp. 687-710). New York: Plenum.

Tenenbaum, G., Levy-Kolker, N., Bar-Eli, M., & Weinberg, R. (1994). Information recall among skilled and novice athletes: The role of display complexity, attentional resources, visual exposure duration, and expertise. *Journal of Sport Psychology, 12*, 529-534.

Tenenbaum, G., Levi-Kolker, N., Sade, S., Lieberman, D., & Lidor, R. (1996). Anticipation and confidence of decisions related to skilled performance. *International Journal of Sport Psychology, 27*, 293-307.

Tenenbaum, G., Sar-El, L., & Bar-Eli, M. (2000). Anticipation of ball locations in low and high skill performers: A developmental perspective. *Psychology of Sport and Exercise, 1*, 117-128.

Tenenbaum, G., Tehan, G., Stewart, G., & Christensen, S. (1999). Recalling a floor routine: The effects of skill and age on memory for order. *Applied Cognitive Psychology, 13*, 101-123.

Tsal, Y., & Lavie, N. (1993). Location dominance in attending to color and shape. *Journal of Experimental Psychology: Human Perception & Performance, 19*, 131-139.

Williams, A.M., Davids, K., & Williams, J.G. (1999). *Visual perception and action in sport.* Routledge: London.

Chapter 9

Abernethy, B. (1988). The effects of age and expertise upon perceptual skill development in a racquet sport. *Research Quarterly for Exercise and Sport, 59*(3), 210-221.

Abernethy, B. (1990). Expertise, visual search, and information pick-up in squash. *Perception, 19*, 63-77.

Abernethy, B., Gill, D.P., Parks, S.L., & Packer, S.T. (2001). Expertise and the perception of kinematic and situational probability information. *Perception, 30*, 233-252.

Abernethy, B., & Russell, D.G. (1984). Advance cue utilisation by skilled cricket batsmen. *Australian Journal of Science and Medicine in Sport, 16*(2), 2-10.

Abernethy, B., Wann, J. & Parks, S. (1998). Training perceptual-motor skills in sport. In B. Elliott & J. Mester (Eds.), *Training in sport* (pp. 1-69). Chichester, West Sussex: John Wiley & Sons.

Abernethy, B., Wood, J.M., & Parks, S. (1999). Can the anticipatory skills of experts be learned by novices? *Research Quarterly for Exercise and Sport, 70(3),* 313-318.

Adolphe, R.M., Vickers, J.N., & Laplante. G. (1997). The effects of training visual attention on gaze behaviour and accuracy: A pilot study. *International Journal of Sports Vision, 4*(1), 28-33.

Alain, C., & Proteau, L. (1980). Decision making in sport. In C.H. Nadeau, W.R. Halliwell, K.M. Newell, & G.C. Roberts (Eds.), *Psychology of motor behavior and sport* (pp. 465-477). Champaign, IL; Human Kinetics.

Alessi, S.M. (1988). Fidelity in the design of instructional simulators. *Journal of Computer-Based Instruction, 15*, 40-47.

Allard, F., Graham, S., & Paarsalu, M.L. (1980). Perception in sport: Basketball. *Journal of Sport Psychology, 2*, 14-21.

Allard, F., & Starkes, J.L. (1980). Perception in sport: Volleyball. *Journal of Sport Psychology, 2*, 22-33.

Allerton, D.J. (2000). Flight simulation: Past, present and future. *Aeronautical Journal, 104* (1042), 651-663.

Andersson, R.L. (1993). A real experiment in virtual environments: A virtual batting cage. *Presence: Teleoperators and Virtual Environments, 2*, 16-33.

Andrews, D.H. (1988). Relationship among simulators, training devices, and learning: A behavioral view. *Educational Technology, 28*(1), 48-54.

Avis, N.J. (2000). Virtual environment technologies. *Minimal Invasive Therapies & Allied Technology, 9*(5), 333-340.

Burroughs, W. (1984.) Visual simulation training of baseball batters. *International Journal of Sport Psychology, 15,* 117-126.

Chamberlin, C.J., & Coelho, A.J. (1993). The perceptual side of action: Decision-making in sport. In J.L. Starkes & F. Allard (Eds.), *Cognitive issues in motor expertise* (pp. 135-157). Amsterdam: Elsevier.

Charlesworth, R. (1994). Designer games. *Sport Coach, 17,* 30-33.

Christina, R.W., Barresi, J.V., & Shaffner, P. (1990). The development of response selection accuracy in a football linebacker using video training. *The Sport Psychologist, 4,* 11-17.

Damron, C.F. (1955.) Two and three dimensional slide images used with tachistoscopic training techniques in instructing high school football players in defenses. *Research Quarterly, 26,* 26-43.

Davids, K., Savelsbergh, G.J.P., Bennett, S.J., & van der Kamp, J. (Eds.). (2002). *Vision and interceptive actions in sport.* London: Taylor & Francis.

Davids, K., Williams, A.M., Button, C., & Court, M. (2001). An integrative modeling approach to the study of intentional movement behavior. In R.N. Singer, H.A. Hausenblas, & C.M. Janelle (Eds.), *Handbook of sport psychology* (2nd ed.) (pp. 144-173). New York: John Wiley & Sons.

Day, L.J. (1980). Anticipation in junior tennis players. In J. Groppel & R. Sears (Eds.), *Proceedings of the International Symposium on the Effective Teaching of Racquet Sports* (pp. 107-116). Champaign, IL: University of Illinois.

Decety, J., & Ingvar, D.H. (1990). Brain structures participating in mental simulation of motor behavior: A neuropsychological interpretation. *Acta Psychologica, 73,* 13-34.

de Crock, M.B.M., van Merriënboer, J.J.G., & Paas, F.G.W.C. (1998). High versus low contextual interference in simulation-based training of troubleshooting skills: Effects on transfer performance and invested mental effort. *Computers in Human Behavior, 14*(2), 249-267.

Ericsson, K.A. (Ed.). (1996). *The road to excellence.* New Jersey: Lawrence Erlbaum Associates.

Ericsson, K.A., Krampe, R.T., & Tesch-Römer, C. (1993). The role of deliberate practice in the acquisition of expert performance. *Psychological Review, 100,* 363-406.

Farrow, D., Chivers, P., Hardingham, C., & Sachse, S. (1998). The effect of video-based perceptual training on the tennis return of serve. *International Journal of Sport Psychology, 29*(3), 231-242.

Finke, R.A. (1986). Mental imagery and the visual system. *Scientific American, 3,* 76-83.

Franks, I.M., & Hanvey, T. (1997, May/June). Cues for goalkeepers: High-tech methods used to measure penalty shot response. *Soccer Journal,* 30-38.

French, K.E., & McPherson, S.L. (1999). Adaptations in response selection processes used during sport competition with increasing age and expertise. *International Journal of Sport Psychology, 30,* 173-193.

French, K.E., & Thomas, J.R. (1987). The relation of knowledge development to children's basketball performance. *Journal of Sport Psychology, 9,* 15-32.

Gibson, J.J. (1979). *An ecological approach to visual perception.* Boston, MA: Houghton-Mifflin.

Goebal, R., Linden, D.E.J., Lanfermann, H., Zanelle, F.E., & Singer, W. (1998). Functional imaging of mirror and inverse reading reveals separate coactivated networks for occulomotion and spatial transformations. *Neuroreport, 9*(4), 713-719.

Goldstone, R.L. (1998). Perceptual learning. *Annual Review of Psychology, 49,* 585-612.

Goodale, M.A., & Milner, A.D. (1992). Separate visual pathways for perception and action. *Trends in Neuroscience, 15,* 20-25.

Grant, A., & Williams, A.M. (1996). *Training cognitive decision making in intermediate youth soccer players.* Unpublished manuscript, Liverpool John Moores University.

Groom, N.R., & Paull, G.C. (2001). Perceptual training in youth soccer: A preliminary investigation. *Journal of Sports Sciences, 19*, 79.

Hardy, L., Mullen, R., & Jones, G. (1996). Knowledge and conscious control of motor actions under stress. *British Journal of Psychology, 87*, 621-636.

Haskins, M.J. (1965.) Development of a response-recognition training film in tennis. *Perceptual Motor Skills, 21*, 207-211.

Helsen, W.F., & Starkes, J.L. (1999a). A multidimensional approach to skilled perception and performance in sport. *Applied Cognitive Psychology, 13*, 1-27.

Helsen, W.F., & Starkes, J.L. (1999b). A new training approach to complex decision making for police officers in potentially dangerous interventions. *Journal of Criminal Justice, 27*(5), 395-410.

Hughes, M., & Franks, I. (1997). *Notational analysis of sport.* London: E. & F.N. Spon.

Jeannerod, M. (1999). The 25th Bartlett lecture. To act or not to act: Perspectives on the representation of actions. *Quarterly Journal of Experimental Psychology, 52A*, 1-29.

Jones, C.M., & Miles, T.R. (1978). Use of advance cues in predicting the flight of a lawn tennis ball. *Journal of Human Movement Studies, 4*, 231-235.

Jordet, G. (2001). Perceptual training in professional football: A young Norwegian player breaking through internationally. In A. Papaioannou, M. Goudas, & Y. Theodorakis (Eds.), *Proceedings of the 10th World Congress of Sport Psychology, Vol. 4: In the dawn of the new millennium* (pp. 158-160). Skiathos, Hellas: International Society of Sport Psychology.

Junyent, L.Q., & Fortó, J.S. (1995). Visual training programme applied to precision shooting. *Opthalmic and Physiological Optics, 15*, 519-523.

Kluka, D.A., Love, P.A., Hammack, G., & Wesson, M.D. (1996). The effect of a visual skills training program on selected female intercollegiate volleyball athletes. *International Journal of Sports Vision, 3*, 1.

Kosslyn, S.M., Behrmann, M., & Jeannerod, M. (1995). The cognitive neuroscience of mental imagery. *Neuropsychologica, 33*(11), 1335-1344.

Lee, T.D., Chamberlin, C.J., & Hodges, N.J. (2001). Practice. In R.N. Singer, H.A. Hausenblas, & C.M. Janelle (Eds.), *Handbook of sport psychology* (2nd ed.) (pp. 115-143). New York: John Wiley & Sons.

Londerlee, B. R. (1967.) Effect of training with motion pictures versus flash cards upon football play recognition. *Research Quarterly, 38*(2), 202-207.

Loomis, J.M., Blascovich, J.J., & Beall, A.C. (1999). Immersive virtual environment technology as a basic research tool in psychology. *Behavior, Research Methods, Instruments, & Computers, 31*(4), 557-564.

Loran, D.F.C., & MacEwen, C.J. (Eds.). (1995). *Sports vision.* Oxford: Butterworth Heinemann.

Magill, R.A. (1998). Knowledge is more than we can talk about: Implicit learning in motor skill acquisition. *Research Quarterly for Exercise and Sport, 69*(2), 104-110.

Masters, R.S.W. (1992). Knowledge, knerves, and know-how. *British Journal of Psychology, 83*, 343-358.

Maxwell, J.P., Masters, R.S.W., & Eves, F.F. (2000). From novice to know-how: A longitudinal study of implicit motor learning. *Journal of Sports Sciences, 18*, 111-120.

McMorris, T. (1999). Cognitive development and the acquisition of decision-making skills. *International Journal of Sport Psychology, 30*(2), 151-172.

McMorris, T., & Hauxwell, B. (1997). Improving anticipation of soccer goalkeepers using video observation. In T. Reilly, J. Bangsbo, & M. Hughes (Eds.), *Science and football III* (pp. 290-294). London: E. & F.N. Spon.

McPherson, S.L., & Thomas, J.R. (1989). Relation of knowledge and performance in boys' tennis: Age and expertise. *Journal of Experimental Child Psychology, 48,* 190-211.

Michaels, C.F., & Carello, C. (1981). *Direct perception.* Englewood Cliffs, NJ: Prentice Hall.

Millslagle, D.G. (1988). Visual perception, recognition, recall and mode of visual search control in basketball involving novice and inexperienced basketball players. *Journal of Sport Behavior, 11,* 32-44.

Milner, D.A. (1998). Streams and consciousness: Visual awareness and the brain. *Trends in Cognitive Science, 2*(1), 25-30.

Milner, D.A., & Goodale, M.A. (1995). *The visual brain in action.* Oxford: Oxford University Press.

Oslin, J.L., Mitchell, S.A., & Griffin, L.L. (1998). The game performance assessment instrument (GPAI): Development and preliminary validation. *Journal of Teaching Physical Education, 17*(2), 231-243.

Phillips, W.A., & Christie, D.F.M. (1977). Interference with visualisation. *Quarterly Journal of Experimental Psychology, 29,* 637-650.

Proteau, L. (1992). On the specificity of learning and the role of visual information for movement control. In L. Proteau and D. Elliott (Eds.), *Vision and motor control* (pp. 67-101). Amsterdam: Elsevier Science Publishing.

Psokta, J. (1995). Immersive training systems: Virtual reality and education and training. *Instructional Science, 23,* 405-431.

Romano, D.M., & Brna, P. (2001). Presence and reflection in training: Support for learning to improve quality decision-making skills under time limitations. *CyberPsychology & Behavior, 4*(2), 265-277.

Schmidt, R.A., & Lee, T.A. (1998). *Motor control and learning: A behavioral emphasis.* Champaign, IL: Human Kinetics.

Scott, D., Scott, L.M., & Howe, B.L. (1998). Training anticipation for intermediate tennis players. *Behavior Modification, 22*(3), 243-261.

Singer, R.N., Cauraugh, J.H., Chen, D., Steinberg, G.M., Frehlich, S.G., & Wang, L. (1994). Training mental quickness in beginning/intermediate tennis players. *The Sport Psychologist, 8,* 305-318.

Starkes, J.L., & Allard, F. (1993). *Cognitive issues in motor expertise.* Amsterdam: Elsevier Science Publishing.

Starkes, J.L., & Deakin, J. (1984). Perception in sport: A cognitive approach to skilled performance. In W.F. Straub & J.M. Williams (Eds.), *Cognitive sport psychology* (pp. 115-128). Lansing, NY: Sport Science Associates.

Starkes, J.L., & Lindley, S. (1994). Can we hasten expertise by video simulations? *Quest, 46,* 211-222.

Steinberg, G.M., Chaffin, W.M., & Singer, R.N. (1998). Mental quickness training: Drills that emphasize the development of anticipation skills in fast-paced sports. *Journal of Physical Education, Recreation and Dance, 69*(7), 37-41.

Tayler, M.A., Burwitz, L., & Davids, K. (1994). Coaching perceptual strategy in badminton. *Journal of Sports Sciences, 12,* 213.

Tendick, F., Downes, M., Goktekin, K. Cavusoglu, M.C., Feygin, D., Wu, X., et al. (2000). A virtual environment testbed for training laparoscopic surgical skills. *Presence: Teleoperators and Virtual Environments, 9*(3), 236-255.

Tenenbaum, G. (Ed.). (1999). The development of expertise in sport: Nature and nurture [Special issue]. *International Journal of Sport Psychology, 30*(2).

Thorpe, R. (1996). Telling people how to do things does not always help them learn. *Supercoach, 8,* 7-8.

Todorov, E., Shadmehr, R., & Bizzi, E. (1997). Augmented feedback presented in a virtual environment accelerates learning of a difficult motor task. *Journal of Motor Behavior, 29,* 147-158.

Vickers, J.N. (1992). Gaze control in putting. *Perception, 21,* 117-132.

Ward, P., & Williams, A.M. (in press). Perceptual and cognitive skill development in soccer: The multidimensional nature of expert performance. *Journal of Sport and Exercise Psychology.*

Ward, P., Williams, A.M., & Bennett, S.J. (2002). Visual search and biological motion perception in tennis. *Research Quarterly for Exercise and Sport, 73*(1), 107-112.

Ward, P., Williams, A.M., & Loran, D.F.C. (2000). The development of visual function in elite and sub-elite soccer players. *International Journal of Sports Vision, 6,* 1-11.

Wilkinson, S. (1992). Effects of training in visual discrimination after one year: Visual analyses of volleyball skills. *Perceptual and Motor Skills, 75,* 19-24.

Williams, A.M. (2000). Perceptual skill in soccer: Implications for talent identification and development. *Journal of Sports Sciences, 18,* 737-750.

Williams, A.M. (Ed.). (2002). Visual search behaviours in sport [Special issue]. *Journal of Sports Sciences, 20.*

Williams, A.M., & Burwitz, L. (1993). Advance cue utilisation in soccer. In T. Reilly, J. Clarys, & A. Stibbe (Eds.), *Science and football II* (pp. 239-244). London: E. & F.N. Spon.

Williams, A.M., & Davids, K. (1995). Declarative knowledge in sport: A byproduct of experience or a characteristic of expertise? *Journal of Sport and Exercise Psychology, 7*(3), 259-275.

Williams, A.M., & Davids, K. (1998). Visual search strategy, selective attention, and expertise in soccer. *Research Quarterly for Exercise and Sport, 69*(2), 111-128.

Williams, A.M., Davids, K., Burwitz, L., & Williams, J.G. (1994). Visual search strategies of experienced and inexperienced soccer players. *Research Quarterly for Exercise and Sport, 5*(2), 127-135.

Williams, A.M., Davids, K., & Williams, J.G. (1999). *Visual perception and action in sport.* London: E. & F.N. Spon.

Williams, A.M., & Elliott, D. (1999). Anxiety and visual search strategy in karate. *Journal of Sport and Exercise Psychology, 21,* 362-375.

Williams, A.M., & Grant, A. (1999). Training perceptual skill in sport. *International Journal of Sport Psychology, 30,* 194-220.

Williams, A.M., & Reilly, T. (Eds.). (2000). Talent identification in soccer [Special issue]. *Journal of Sports Sciences, 18.*

Williams, A.M., Ward, P., & Chapman, C. (2003). Training perceptual skill in field hockey: Is there transfer from the laboratory to the field? *Research Quarterly for Exercise and Sport, 74,* 98-103.

Williams, A.M., Ward, P., Knowles, J.M., & Smeeton, N. (2002). Perceptual skill in a real-world task: Training, instruction, and transfer in tennis. *Journal of Experimental Psychology: Applied, 8,* 259-270.

Wilson, J.R. (1997). Virtual environments and ergonomics: Needs and opportunities. *Ergonomics, 40*(10), 1057-1077.

Wood, J.M., & Abernethy, B. (1997). An assessment of the efficacy of sports vision training programs. *Optometry and Vision Science, 74*(8), 646-659.

Chapter 10

Charness, N., Krampe, R.T., & Mayr, U. (1996). The role of practice and coaching in entrepreneurial skill domains: An international comparison of life-span chess skill acquisition. In K.A. Ericsson (Ed.), *The road to excellence: The acquisition of expert performance in the arts and sciences, sports, and games* (pp. 51-80). Mahwah, NJ: Lawrence Erlbaum and Associates.

Deakin, J.M. (2001). What they do versus what they say they do: An assessment of practice in figure skating. *Proceedings of the International Society of Sport Psychology, Skiathos Island, Greece, 3,* 153.

Deakin, J.M., Starkes, J.L., & Allard, F. (1998). *The microstructure of practice in sport.* Sport Canada Technical Report.

Ericsson, K.A. (1991). Peak performance and age: An examination of peak performance in sports. In P.B. Baltes & M.M. Baltes (Eds.), *Successful aging: Perspectives from the behavioral sciences,* (pp. 164-196). Cambridge: Cambridge University Press.

Ericsson, K.A., Krampe, R., & Tesch-Römer, C. (1993). The role of deliberate practice in the acquisition of expert performance. *Psychological Review, 100,* 363-406.

Hagberg, J., Graves, J., Limacher, M., Woods, D., Cononie, C., Leggett, S., et al. (1989). Cardiovascular responses of 70-79 year old men and women to exercise training. *Journal of Applied Physiology, 66,* 2589-2594.

Hartley, A.A., & Hartley, J.T. (1984). Performance changes in champion swimmers aged 30-84 years. *Experimental Aging Research, 10*(3), 141-148.

Helsen, W.F., Starkes, J.L., & Hodges, N.J. (1998). Team sports and the theory of deliberate practice. *Journal of Sport and Exercise Psychology, 20,* 12-34.

Hodge, T., & Deakin, J.M. (1998). Deliberate practice and expertise in the martial arts: The role of context in motor recall. *Journal of Sport and Exercise Psychology, 20,* 260-279.

Hodges, N.J., & Starkes, J.L. (1996). Wrestling with the nature of expertise: A sport-specific test of Ericsson, Krampe and Tesch-Römer's (1993) theory of deliberate practice. *International Journal of Sport Psychology, 27,* 400-424.

Krampe, R.T., & Ericsson, K.A. (1996). Maintaining excellence: Deliberate practice and elite performance in young and older pianists. *Journal of Experimental Psychology: General, 125*(4), 331-359.

McGowan, M. (2001, February 17). The prime of the ancient marathoner. *Saturday Night,* 18-23. Toronto: National Post Co.

Mercier, D., & Beauregard, S. (1994). *Mercier scoring tables.* Ottawa, Ontario: Athletics Canada.

Salthouse, T.A., Babcock, R.L., Skovronek, E., Mitchell, D.R.D., & Palmon, R. (1990). Age and experience effects in spatial visualization. *Developmental Psychology, 26,* 128-136.

Schulz, R., & Curnow, C. (1988). Peak performance and age among superathletes: Track and field, swimming, baseball, tennis and golf. *Journal of Gerontology: Psychological Sciences, 43,* 113-120.

Simonton, D.K. (1996). Creative expertise: A life-span developmental perspective. In K.A. Ericsson (Ed.), *The road to excellence: The acquisition of expert performance in the arts and sciences, sports, and games* (pp. 227-254). Mahwah, NJ: Lawrence Erlbaum and Associates.

Spirduso, W.W. (1995). *Physical dimensions of aging.* Champaign, IL: Human Kinetics.

Starkes, J.L. (2000). The road to expertise: Is practice the only determinant? *International Journal of Sport Psychology, 31*(4), 431-451.

Starkes, J.L., Helsen, W.F., & Jack, R. (2000). Expert performance in sport and dance. In R.N. Singer, H.A. Hausenblas, & C.M. Janelle (Eds.), *Handbook of sport psychology* (pp. 174-201).

Starkes, J.L., Weir, P.L., Singh, P., Hodges, N.J., & Kerr, T. (1999). Aging and the retention of sport expertise. *International Journal of Sport Psychology, 30*(2), 283-301.

Stones, M.J., & Kozma, A. (1982). Cross-sectional, longitudinal, and secular trends in athletic performances. *Experimental Aging Research, 8,* 195-198.

Stones, M.J., & Kozma, A. (1984). Longitudinal trends in track and field performances. *Experimental Aging Research, 10*(2), 107-110.

Weir, P.L., Kerr, T., Hodges, N.J., McKay, S.M., & Starkes, J.L. (2002). Master swimmers: How are they different from younger elite swimmers? An examination of practice and performance patterns. *Journal of Aging and Physical Activity, 10*(1), 41-63.

World Association of Veteran Athletes (WAVA). (1994). *1994 Age-graded tables.* Van Nuys, CA: National Masters News.

Young, B.W. (1998). *Deliberate practice and the acquisition of expert performance in Canadian middle distance running.* Unpublished masters thesis, University of Ottawa, Ottawa, Canada. School of Human Kinetics.

Young, B.W., & Salmela, J.H. (2001). Diary analyses of practice and recovery activities for elite and intermediate middle distance runners. *Proceedings of the International Society of Sport Psychology Abstracts, Skiathos Island, Greece, 4,* 19.

Young, B.W., & Salmela, J.H. (2002). Perceptions of training and deliberate practice of middle distance runners. *International Journal of Sport Psychology, 33(2),* 167-181.

Chapter 11

Berliner, D.C. (1986). In pursuit of the expert pedagogue. *Educational Researcher, 15,* 5-13.

Bloom, B.S. (Ed.). (1985). *Developing talent in young people.* New York: Ballantine.

Bloom, G.A. (1997). *Characteristics, knowledge and strategies of expert team sport coaches.* Unpublished doctoral dissertation, Faculty of Education, University of Ottawa, Ottawa, Ontario, Canada.

Bloom, G.A., Durand-Bush, N., Schinke, R.J., & Salmela, J.H. (1998). The importance of mentoring in the development of coaches and athletes. *International Journal of Sport Psychology, 29(3),* 267-281.

Bloom, G.A., & Salmela, J.H. (2000). Personal characteristics of expert sport coaches. *Journal of Sport Pedagogy, 6(2),* 56-76.

Bloom, G.A., Schinke, R.J., & Salmela, J.H. (1998). The development of communication skills by elite basketball coaches. *Coaching and Sport Science Journal, 2(3),* 3-10.

Carlsson, R. (1993). The path to national level in sports in Sweden. *Scandinavian Journal of Medicine and Science in Sports, 3,* 170-177.

Chelladurai, P. (1980). Leadership in sports organizations. *Canadian Journal of Applied Sport Sciences, 5,* 226-231.

Côté, J. (1999). The influence of the family in the development of talent in sport. *The Sport Psychologist, 13,* 395-417.

Côté, J., & Salmela, J.H. (1996). The organizational tasks of high performance gymnastic coaches. *The Sport Psychologist, 10(3),* 247-260.

Côté, J., Salmela, J.H., Baria, A., & Russell, S.J. (1993). Organizing and interpreting unstructured qualitative data. *The Sport Psychologist, 7,* 127-137.

Côté, J., Salmela, J.H., & Russell, S.J. (1995). The knowledge of high performance gymnastic coaches: Competition and training considerations. *The Sport Psychologist, 9,* 76-95.

Côté, J., Salmela, J.H., Trudel, P., Baria, A., & Russell, S.J. (1995). The coaching model: A grounded assessment of expert gymnastic coaches' knowledge. *Journal of Sport and Exercise Psychology, 17,* 1-17.

d'Arripe-Longueville, F., Fournier, J.F., & Dubois, A. (1998). The perceived effectiveness of interactions between expert French judo coaches and elite female athletes. *The Sport Psychologist, 12,* 317-372.

Davidson, J.W., Howe, M.J.A., Moore, D.G., & Sloboda, J.A. (1996). The role of parental influences in the development of musical performance. *British Journal of Developmental Psychology, 14,* 399-412.

Durand-Bush, N. (2000). *The development and maintenance of expert athletic performance: Perceptions of Olympic and World champions, their parents and coaches.* Unpublished doctoral dissertation, Faculty of Education, University of Ottawa, Ottawa, Ontario, Canada.

Edwards, M.G. (2001). *Gendered coaching: The impact of gender on roles and qualities of elite women's field hockey coaches.* Unpublished doctoral dissertation, Massey University, New Zealand.

Ericsson, K.A. (1996). The acquisition of expert performance: An introduction to some of the issues. In K.A. Ericsson (Ed.), *The road to excellence: The acquisition of expert performance in the arts and sciences, sports, and games* (pp. 1-50). Mahwah, NJ: Erlbaum.

Ericsson, K.A., Krampe, R.T., & Tesch-Römer, C. (1993). The role of deliberate practice in the acquisition of expert performance. *Psychological Review, 100*(3), 363-406.

Fair, J.R. (1987). The coaching process: The essence of coaching. *Sports Coaching, 11*, 17-19.

Gould, D., Giannini, J., Krane, V., & Hodge, K. (1990). Educational needs of elite U.S. National Team, Pan American and Olympic coaches. *Journal of Teaching in Physical Education, 9*, 332-344.

Griffith, C.R. (1926). *Psychology of coaching*. New York: Scribners.

Gruneau, R. (1999). *Class, sports, and social development*. Champaign, IL: Human Kinetics.

Kitamura, K., Salmela, J.H., & Moraes, L.C. (2001). Perceptions of coaching concepts of expert soccer coaches in Japan. *Proceedings of the 10th World Congress of the International Society of Sport Psychology, Skiathos, Greece.*

Locke, L.F., & Massengale, J.D. (1978). Role conflict in teacher/coaches. *Research Quarterly, 49*(2), 162-174.

McPherson, T.L., & Salmela, J.H. (1997). Deliberate practice content in expert coaching [Abstract]. *28th Annual SCAPPS Conference, 11*, Windsor, Ontario.

Miller, P.S., & Salmela, J.H. (in press). Educational roles of varsity team sport coaches. *International Journal of Sport Psychology.*

Moraes, L.C. (1996). Looking back & thinking ahead: Reflections and recommendations. In J.H. Salmela (Ed.), *Great job coach: Getting the edge from proven winners* (pp. 207-229). Ottawa, Ontario, Canada: Potentium.

Moraes, L.C. (1998). *Beliefs and actions of expert Canadian judo coaches*. Unpublished doctoral dissertation, Faculty of Education, University of Ottawa, Ottawa, Ontario, Canada.

Moraes, L.C., & Salmela, J.H. (2001). Influences of the Canadian context on beliefs of expert Canadian, Japanese and European judo coaches. In M. Pirritano & A. Cei (Eds.), *Psicologia dello sport (Psychology of Sport)* (pp. 61-74). CONI (School of Sport): Rome.

Moraes, L.C., Salmela, J.H., & Rabelo, A.S. (2000). O desenvolvimento de desempenho exceptional de jogadores jovens do futebol mineiro [The development of performance of young Mineiro soccer players]. *Anais do primeiro congresso cíentifico Latíno-Americano.* Fundep: São Paulo.

Rabelo, A.S. (2002). *The role of families in the development of aspiring expert soccer players*. Unpublished masters thesis. Federal University of Minas Gerais, Brazil.

Rabelo, A., Moraes, L.C., & Salmela, J.H. (2001). The role of parents in the development of young Brazilian athletes in soccer. *Association for the Advancement of Applied Sport Psychology Conference Proceedings, Orlando, Florida*, 52-53.

Salmela, J.H. (Ed.). (1996). *Great job coach!: Getting the edge from proven winners*. Ottawa, Ontario, Canada: Potentium.

Salmela, J.H., & Durand-Bush, N. (2001). Pedagogical and psychological factors for coaching gymnastics. *FIG coaching academy curriculum* (pp. 1-111). FIG: Moutier, Switzerland.

Salmela, J.H., Young, B.W., & Kallio, J. (2000). Within career transitions of the athlete-coach-parent triad. In P. Wylleman & D. Lavallée (Eds.), *Career transitions in sport: A sourcebook for practitioners and researchers* (pp. 181-193). Morgantown, WV: FIT Publications.

Schinke, R.J., Bloom, G.A., & Salmela, J.H. (1995). The career stages of elite Canadian basketball coaches. *Avante, 1*, 48-62.

Schinke, R.J., Draper, S.P., & Salmela, J.H. (1997). A conceptualization of team building in high performance sport coaches as a season-long process. *Avante, 3*(2), 57-72.

Smith, R.E., & Smoll, F.L. (1990). Self-esteem and children's reactions to youth sport coaching behaviors: A field study of self enhancement processes. *Developmental Psychology, 26*, 987-993.

Smith, R.E., Smoll, F.L., & Hunt, E.B. (1977). A system for the behavioral assessment of athletic coaches. *Research Quarterly, 48*, 401-407.

Vianna, N.S., Jr. (2002). *The role of families and coaches in the development of aspiring expert tennis players*. Unpublished masters thesis, Federal University of Minas Gerais, Brazil.

Vianna, N.S., Moraes, L.C., Salmela, J.H., & Mourthé, K. *The Role of Parents in the Development of Young Brazilian Athletes in Rhythmic Gymnastics.*

Weiss, M.R., & Stevens, C. (1993). Motivation and attrition of female coaches: An application of social exchange theory. *The Sport Psychologist, 7*, 244-261.

Worthington, E.S. (1984). Knowing, organising, observing and coaching. In F.S. Pyke (Ed.), *Towards better coaching* (pp. 239-262). Canberra: Australian Government Publishing Service.

Young, B.W., & Salmela, J.H. (2000). Perceptions of training and deliberate practice of middle distance runners. *International Journal of Sport Psychology, 33* (2), 167-181.

Chapter 12

Abernethy, B., Thomas, K.T., & Thomas, J.T. (1993). Strategies for improving understanding of motor expertise (or mistakes we have made and things we have learned!!). In J. L. Starkes and F. Allard (Eds.), *Cognitive issues in motor expertise* (pp. 317-356). Amsterdam, Netherlands: Elsevier Science Publishers.

Adelson, B. (1984). When novices surpass experts: The difficulty of a task may increase with expertise. *Journal of Experimental Psychology: Learning, Memory, and Cognition, 10*, 483-495.

Anderson, J.R. (1983). *The architecture of cognition.* Cambridge, MA: Harvard University Press.

Anderson, J.R. (1993). *Rules of mind.* Hillsdale, NJ: Lawrence Erlbaum.

Backman, L., & Molander, B. (1986). Effects of adult age and level of skill on the ability to cope with high-stress conditions in a precision sport. *Psychology and Aging, 4*, 334-336.

Baumeister, R.F. (1984). Choking under pressure: Self-consciousness and paradoxical effects of incentives on skillful performance. *Journal of Personality and Social Psychology, 46*, 610-620.

Beilock, S.L., & Carr, T.H. (2001). On the fragility of skilled performance: What governs choking under pressure? *Journal of Experimental Psychology: General, 130*, 701-725.

Beilock, S.L., Carr, T.H., MacMahon, C., & Starkes, J.L. (2002). When paying attention becomes counterproductive: Impact of divided versus skill-focused attention on novice and experienced performance of sensorimotor skills. *Journal of Experimental Psychology: Applied, 8*, 6-16.

Beilock, S.L., Wierenga, S.A., & Carr, T.H. (2002). Expertise, attention, and memory in sensorimotor skill execution: Impact of novel task constraints on dual-task performance and episodic memory. *The Quarterly Journal of Experimental Psychology: Human Experimental Psychology, 55*, 1211-1240.

Brown, J.S., & Burton, R.R. (1978). Diagnostic models for procedural bugs in basic mathematical skills. *Cognitive Science, 2*, 155-192.

Brown, T.L., & Carr, T.H. (1989). Automaticity in skill acquisition: Mechanisms for reducing interference in concurrent performance. *Journal of Experimental Psychology: Human Perception and Performance, 15*, 686-700.

Chase, W.G., & Simon, H.A. (1973). Perception in chess. *Cognitive Psychology, 4*, 55-81.

Chi, M.T., Feltovich, P.J., & Glaser, R. (1981). Categorization and representation of physics problems by experts and novices. *Cognitive Science, 5*, 121-152.

Craik F.M., Govini R., Naveh-Benjamin M., & Anderson N.D. (1996). The effects of divided attention on encoding and retrieval processes in human memory. *Journal of Experimental Psychology: General, 125*, 159-180.

De Groot, A. (1978). *Thought and choice in chess*. The Hague: Mouton. (Original work published in 1946)

Ericsson, K.A. (2001). The path to expert golf performance: Insights from the masters on how to improve performance by deliberate practice. In P.R. Thomas (Ed.), *Optimizing performance in golf*. Brisbane, Australia: Australian Academic Press.

Ericsson, K.A., & Charness, N. (1994). Expert performance—Its structure and acquisition. *American Psychologist, 49*, 725-747.

Ericsson, K.A., & Lehmann, A.C. (1996). Expert and exceptional performance: Evidence of maximal adaptation to task constraints. *Annual Review of Psychology, 47*, 273-305.

Ericsson, K.A., & Simon, H.A. (1993). *Protocol analysis: Verbal reports as data*. Cambridge, MA: MIT Press.

Ericsson, K.A., & Smith, J. (1991). *Toward a general theory of expertise*. Cambridge: Cambridge University Press.

Fitts, P.M., & Posner, M.I. (1967). *Human performance*. Belmont, CA: Brooks/Cole.

Hinds, P.J. (1999). The curse of expertise: The effects of expertise and debiasing methods on predictions of novice performance. *Journal of Experimental Psychology: Applied, 5*, 205-221.

Karni, A., Meyer, G., Rey-Hipolito, C., Jezzard, P., Adams, M.M., Turner, R., & Ungerleider, L.G. (1998). The acquisition of skilled motor performance: Fast and slow experience-driven changes in primary motor cortex. *Proceedings of the National Academy of Science, 95*, 861-868.

Keele, S.W. (1986). Motor control. In K.R. Boff, L. Kaufman, & J.P. Thomas (Eds.), *Handbook of perception and human performance* (Vol. 7). New York: John Wiley and Sons.

Keele, S.W., & Summers, J.J. (1976). The structure of motor programs. In G.E. Stelmach (Ed.), *Motor control: Issues and trends* (pp. 109-142). New York: Academic Press.

Koh, K., & Meyer, D.E. (1991). Function learning: Induction of continuous stimulus-response relations. *Journal of Experimental Psychology: Learning, Memory and Cognition, 17*, 811-836.

Leavitt, J. (1979). Cognitive demands of skating and stick handling in ice hockey. *Canadian Journal of Applied Sport Sciences, 4*, 46-55.

Lesgold, A., Robinson, H., Feltovitch, P., Glaser, R., Klopfer, D., & Wang, Y. (1988). Expertise in a complex skill: Diagnosing X-ray pictures. In M.T.H. Chi, R. Glaser, & M.J. Farr (Eds.), *The nature of expertise*. Hillsdale, NJ: Erlbaum.

Lewis, B., & Linder, D. (1997). Thinking about choking? Attentional processes and paradoxical performance. *Personality and Social Psychology Bulletin, 23*, 937-944.

Logan, G.D. (1988). Toward an instance theory of automatization. *Psychological Review, 95*, 492-527.

Logan, G.D. (1990). Repetition priming and automaticity—Common underlying mechanisms. *Cognitive Psychology, 22*, 1-35.

McPherson, S.L. (2000). Expert-novice differences in planning strategies during collegiate singles tennis competition. *Journal of Sport and Exercise Psychology, 22*, 39-62.

Naveh-Benjamin, M., Craik, F.I., Guez, J., & Dori, H. (1998). Effects of divided attention on encoding and retrieval processes in human memory: Further support for an asymmetry. *Journal of Experimental Psychology: Learning, Memory, and Cognition, 24*, 1091-1104.

Priest, A.G., & Lindsay, R.O. (1992). New light on novice-expert differences in physics problem solving. *British Journal of Psychology, 83*, 389-405.

Proctor, R.W., & Dutta, A. (1995). *Skill acquisition and human performance*. Thousand Oaks, CA: Sage Publications.

Raichle, M.E., Fiez, J.A., Videen, T.O., Macleod, A.M.K., Pardo, J.V., Fox, P.T., & Petersen, S.E. (1994). Practice-related changes in human brain functional-anatomy during nonmotor learning. *Cerebral Cortex, 4*, 8-26.

Smith, M.D., & Chamberlin, C.J. (1992). Effect of adding cognitively demanding tasks on soccer skill performance. *Perceptual and Motor Skills, 75,* 955-961.

Soloway, E., & Ehrlich, K. (1984). Empirical studies of programming knowledge. *IEEE Transactions on Software Engineering, SE-10,* 595-609.

Starkes, J.L., Deakin, J.M., Lindley, S., & Crisp, F. (1987). Motor versus verbal recall of ballet sequences by young expert dancers. *Journal of Sport Psychology, 9,* 222-230.

Starkes, J.L., Helson, W., & Jack, R. (2001). Expert performance in sport and dance. In R. Singer, C. Janelle, & H. Hausenblas (Eds.), *Handbook of sport psychology* (2nd ed.). New York: Macmillan.

Van Lehn, K. (1989). Problem solving and cognitive skill acquisition. In M.I. Posner (Ed.), *Foundations of cognitive science* (pp. 527-580). Cambridge, MA: The MIT Press.

Chapter 13

Abernethy, B., Thomas, K.T., & Thomas, J.T. (1993). Strategies for improving understanding of motor expertise (or mistakes we have made and things we have learned!!). In J.L. Starkes & F. Allard (Eds.), *Cognitive issues in motor expertise* (pp. 317-356). Amsterdam: North-Holland.

Beek, P.J. (1989). Timing and phase-locking in cascade juggling. *Ecological Psychology, 1,* 55-96.

Bernstein, N.A. (1967). *The coordination and regulation of movements.* London: Pergamon.

Bramble, D.M., & Carrier, D.R. (1983). Running and breathing in mammals. *Science, 219,* 251-256.

Diedrich, F.J., & Warren, W.H. (1995). Why change gaits? Dynamics of the walk-run transition. *Journal of Experimental Psychology: Human Perception and Performance, 21,* 183-202.

Farrow, D., Chivers, P., Hardingham, C., & Sachse, S. (1998). The effect of video-based perceptual training on the tennis return of serve. *International Journal of Sport Psychology, 29,* 231-242.

Franks, I.M., & Hanvey, T. (1997, May/June). Cues for goalkeepers: High-tech methods used to measure penalty shot response. *Soccer Journal,* 30-38.

Fodor, J.A., & Pylyshyn, Z. (1981). How direct is visual perception? Some reflections on Gibson's "ecological approach." *Cognition, 9,* 139-196.

Ganz, R.E., Ehrenstein, W.H., & Cavonius, C.R. (1996). Dynamic complexity of visuo-motor coordination: An extension of Bernstein's conception of the degrees-of-freedom problem. *Biological Cybernetics, 75,* 381-387.

Gibson, E.J. (1969). *Principles of perceptual learning and development.* New York: Appleton-Century-Crofts.

Gibson, E.J., & Pick, A. (2000). *An ecological approach to perceptual learning and development.* New York: Oxford University Press.

Gibson, J.J. (1950). *The perception of the visual world.* Boston: Houghton Mifflin.

Gibson, J.J. (1966). *The senses considered as perceptual systems.* Boston: Houghton Mifflin.

Gibson, J.J. (1979). *The ecological approach to visual perception.* Boston: Houghton Mifflin.

Haas, R. (1995). *Bewegungserkennung und Bewegungsanalyse mit dem synergetischen Computer [Motion recognition and analysis with a synergetic computer].* Doktorarbeit [Ph.D. thesis]. Universität Stuttgart, Germany: Shaker.

Haken, H. (1977). *Synergetics: An introduction.* Heidelberg, Germany: Springer Verlag.

Haken, H. (1996). *Principles of brain functioning. A synergetic approach to brain activity, behavior and cognition.* Berlin: Springer Verlag.

Haken, H., Kelso, J.A.S., & Bunz, H. (1985). A theoretical model of phase transitions in human hand movements. *Biological Cybernetics, 51,* 347-356.

Haken, H., Peper, C.E., Beek, P.J., & Daffertshofer, A. (1996). A model for phase transitions in human hand movements during multifrequency tapping. *Physica D, 90,* 179-196.

Huys, R., & Beek, P.J. (2002). The coupling between point of gaze and ball movements in three-ball cascade juggling: The effects of expertise, pattern and tempo. *Journal of Sport Sciences, 20*, 171-186.

Jacobs, D.M., & Michaels, C.F. (2002). On the apparent paradox of learning and realism. *Ecological Psychology, 14*, 127-139.

Jacobs, D.M., & Michaels, C.F. (2001). Individual differences and the use of nonspecifying variables in learning to perceive distance and size: Comments on McConnell, Muchisky, and Bingham (1998). *Perception & Psychophysics, 63*, 563-571.

Jacobs, D.M., & Michaels, C.F. (in press). The education of attention and calibration in one-handed catching. *Journal of Experimental Psychology: Human Perception and Performance.*

Jacobs, D.M., Michaels, C.F., & Runeson, S. (2000). Learning to perceive the relative mass of colliding balls: The effects of ratio-scaling and feedback. *Perception & Psychophysics, 62*, 1332-1340.

Jacobs, D.M., Michaels, C.F., Zaal, F.T.J.M., & Runeson, S. (2001). Developing expertise: Mode transition or mere change in variable use? In G.A. Burton and R.C. Schmidt (Eds.), *Studies in Perception and Action VI* (pp. 181-184). Poster Book of the International Conference on Perception and Action XI. Hillsdale, NJ: Lawrence Erlbaum Associates.

Jacobs, D.M., Runeson, S., & Michaels, C.F. (2001). Learning to visually perceive the relative mass of colliding balls in locally and globally contrained task ecologies. *Journal of Experimental Psychology: Human Perception and Performance, 27*, 1019-1038.

Kelso, J.A.S. (1981). On the oscillatory basis of movement. *Bulletin of the Psychonomic Society, 18*, 63.

Kelso, J.A.S., Holt, K.G., Kugler, P.N., & Turvey, M.T. (1980). On the concept of coordinative structures as dissipative structures: II. Empirical lines of convergence. In G.E. Stelmach & J. Requin (Eds.), *Tutorials in motor behavior* (pp. 49-70). Amsterdam: North-Holland.

Kugler, P.N., Kelso, J.A.S., & Turvey, M.T. (1980). On the concept of coordinative structures as dissipative structures: I. Theoretical lines of convergence. In G.E. Stelmach & J. Requin (Eds.), *Tutorials in motor behavior* (pp. 3-74). Amsterdam: North-Holland.

Kugler, P.N., Kelso, J.A.S., & Turvey, M.T. (1982). On the control and coordination of naturally developing systems. In J.A.S. Kelso & J.E. Clark (Eds.), *The development of movement control and coordination* (pp. 5-78). New York: Wiley.

Magill, R.A. (1998). Knowledge is more than we can talk about: Implicit learning in motor skill acquisition. *Research Quarterly for Exercise and Sport, 69*, 104-110.

McConnell, D.S., Muchisky, M.M., & Bingham, G.P. (1998). The use of time and trajectory forms as visual information about spatial scale in events. *Perception & Psychophysics, 60*, 1175-1187.

McMorris, T., & Hauxwell, B. (1997). Improving anticipation of soccer goalkeepers using video observation. In T. Reilly, J. Bangsbo, & M. Hughes (Eds.), *Science and Football II* (pp. 290-294). London: E. EN. Spon.

Michaels, C.F., & Beek, P.J. (1995). The status of ecological psychology. *Ecological Psychology, 7*, 259-278.

Michaels, C.F., & Carello, C. (1981). *Direct perception.* Englewood Cliffs, NJ: Prentice Hall.

Michaels, C.F., & de Vries, M.M. (1998). Higher order and lower order variables in the visual perception of relative pulling force. *Journal of Experimental Psychology: Human Perception and Performance, 24*, 526-546.

Michaels, C.F., Zeinstra, E.B., & Oudejans, R.R.D. (2001). Information and action in timing the punch of a falling ball. *Quarterly Journal of Experimental Psychology, 54A*, 69-93.

Mitra, S., Amazeen, P.G., & Turvey, M.T. (1998). Intermediate motor learning as decreasing active (dynamical) degrees of freedom. *Human Movement Science, 17*, 17-65.

Newell, K.M., Liu Y.-T., & Mayer-Kress, G. (2001). Time scales in motor learning and development. *Psychological Review, 108*, 75-82.

Oudejans, R.R.D., Verheijen, R., Bakker, F.C., Gerrits, J.C., Steinbrückner, M., & Beek, P.J. (2000). Errors in judging "offside" in football. *Nature, 404,* 33.

Peper, C.E., Beek, P.J., & van Wieringen, P.C.W. (1991). Bifurcations in bimanual tapping: In search of Farey principles. In J. Requin and G.E. Stelmach (Eds.), *Tutorials in motor neuroscience* (pp. 413-431). Dordrecht, Netherlands: Kluwer.

Peper, C.E., Beek, P.J., & van Wieringen, P.C.W. (1995). Multifrequency coordination in bimanual tapping: Asymmetrical coupling and signs of supercriticality. *Journal of Experimental Psychology: Human Perception and Performance, 21,* 1117-1138.

Post, A.A., Daffertshofer, A., & Beek, P.J. (2000). Principal components in three-ball cascade juggling. *Biological Cybernetics, 82,* 143-152.

Runeson, S. (1988). The distorted room illusion, equivalent configurations, and the specificity of static optic arrays. *Journal of Experimental Psychology: Human Perception and Performance, 14,* 295-304.

Runeson, S. (1994). Psychophysics: The failure of an elementaristic dream. *Behavioral and Brain Sciences, 17,* 761-763.

Runeson, S., & Frykholm, G. (1983). Kinematic specification of dynamics as an informational basis for person and action perception: Expectation, gender recognition, and deceptive intention. *Journal of Experimental Psychology: General, 112,* 585-615.

Runeson, S., Jacobs, D.M., Andersson, I.E.K., & Kreegipuu, K. (2001). Specificity is always contingent on constraints: Global versus individual arrays is not the issue. *Behavioral and Brain Sciences, 24*(1).

Runeson, S., Juslin, P., & Olsson, H. (2000). Visual perception of dynamic properties: Cue heuristic versus direct-perceptual competence. *Psychological Review, 107,* 525-555.

Scholz, J.P., & Schöner, G. (1999). The uncontrolled manifold concept: Identifying control variables for a functional task. *Experimental Brain Research, 126,* 289-306.

Scholz, J.P., Schöner, G., & Latash, M.L. (2000). Identifying the control structure of multijoint coordination during pistol shooting. *Experimental Brain Research, 135,* 382-404.

Schöner, G., & Kelso, J.A.S. (1988). A synergetic theory of environmentally-specified and learned patterns of movement coordination: I. Relative phase dynamics. *Biological Cybernetics, 58,* 71-80.

Schöner, G., Zanone, P.G., & Kelso, J.A.S. (1992). Learning as change in coordination dynamics: Theory and experiment. *Journal of Motor Behavior, 24,* 29-48.

Singer, R.N., Cauraugh, J.H., Chen, D., Steinberg, G.M., Frehlich, S.G., & Wang, L. (1994). Training mental quickness in beginning/intermediate tennis players. *The Sport Psychologist, 8,* 305-318.

Smith, M.R.H., Flach, J.M., Dittman, S.M., & Stanard, T. (2001). Monocular optical constraints on collision control. *Journal of Experimental Psychology: Human Perception and Performance, 27,* 395-410.

Summers, J.J., Rosenbaum, D.A., Burns, B.D., & Ford, S.K. (1993). Production of polyrhythms. *Journal of Experimental Psychology, 19,* 416-428.

Turvey, M.T. (1977). Preliminaries to a theory of action with reference to vision. In R. Shaw & J. Bransford (Eds.), *Perceiving, acting, and knowing* (pp. 211-265). Hillsdale, NJ: Lawrence Erlbaum Associates.

Turvey, M.T., Carello, C., & Kim, N.-G. (1990). Links between active perception and the control of action. In H. Haken & M. Stadler (Eds.), *Synergetics of cognition* (pp. 269-295). Berlin: Springer Verlag.

Turvey, M.T., Shaw, R.E., Reed, E.S., & Mace, W.M. (1981). Ecological laws of perceiving and acting: In reply to Fodor and Pylyshyn (1981). *Cognition, 9,* 237-304.

Wagman, J.B., Riley, M.A., & Turvey, M.T. (2001). Perceptual learning: An evaluation of attunement and calibration. In G.A. Burton and R.C. Schmidt (Eds.), *Studies in Perception and Action VI* (pp. 189-192). Poster Book of the International Conference on Perception and Action XI. Hillsdale, NJ: Lawrence Erlbaum Associates.

Williams, A.M., & Burwitz, L. (1993). Advance cue utilisation in soccer. In T. Reilly, J. Clarys, & A. Stibbe (Eds.), *Science and Football I* (pp. 290-294). London: E. EN. Spon.

Williams, A.M., Davids, K., & Williams, J.G. (1999). *Visual perception and action in sport.* Londen: E. & EN. Spon.

Williams, A.M., & Grant, A. (1999). Training perceptual skill in sport. *International Journal of Sport Psychology, 30,* 194-220.

Zaal, F.J.M., & Michaels, C.F. (in press). The information for catching fly balls: Judging and intercepting virtual balls in a CAVE. *Journal of Experimental Psychology: Human Perception and Performance.*

Zanone, P.G., & Kelso, J.A.S. (1992). The evolution of behavioral attractors with learning: Nonequilibrium phase transitions. *Journal of Experimental Psychology: Human Perception and Performance, 18,* 403-421.

Part V

Chase, W.G., & Ericsson, K.A. (1981). Skilled memory. In J. R. Anderson (Ed.), *Cognitive skills and their acquisition* (pp. 141-189). Hillsdale, NJ: Lawrence Erlbaum Associates.

Chase, W.G., & Ericsson, K.A. (1982). Skill and working memory. In G. H. Bower (Ed.), *The psychology of learning and motivation* (Vol. 16, pp. 1-58). New York: Academic Press.

Ericsson, K.A., Chase, W.G., & Faloon, S. (1980). Acquisition of a memory skill. *Science, 208,* 1181-1182.

Ericsson, K.A., & Kintsch, W. (1995). Long-term working memory. *Psychological Review, 102,* 211-245.

Ericsson, K.A., & Kintsch, W. (2000). Shortcomings of generic retrieval structures with slots of the type that Gobet (1993) proposed and modeled. *British Journal of Psychology, 91,* 571-588.

Ericsson, K.A., Krampe, R.T., & Tesch-Römer, C. (1993). The role of deliberate practice in the acquisition of expert performance. *Psychological Review, 100,* 363-406.

Ericsson, K.A., & Smith, J. (1991). Prospects and limits in the empirical study of expertise: An introduction. In K.A. Ericsson & J. Smith (Eds.), *Toward a general theory of expertise: Prospects and limits* (pp. 1-38). Cambridge: Cambridge University Press.

Ericsson, K.A., & Simon, H.A. (1980). Verbal reports as data. *Psychological Review, 87,* 215-251.

Ericsson, K.A., & Simon, H. A. (1984). *Protocol analysis: Verbal reports as data.* Cambridge, MA: Bradford Books/MIT Press.

Ericsson, K.A., & Simon, H.A. (1993). *Protocol analysis; Verbal reports as data* (revised edition). Cambridge, MA: Bradford books/MIT Press.

Gobet, F. (2000a). Some shortcomings of long-term working memory. *British Journal of Psychology, 91,* 551-570.

Gobet, F. (2000b). Retrieval structures and schemata: A brief reply to Ericsson and Kintsch. *British Journal of Psychology, 91,* 591-594.

Simon, H.A., & Chase, W.G. (1973). Skill in chess. *American Scientist, 61,* 394-403.

Chapter 14

Abernethy, B. (1990). Anticipation in squash: Differences in advance cue utilization between expert and novice players. *Journal of Sport Sciences, 8,* 17-34.

Abernethy, B. (1991). Visual search strategies and decision-making in sport. *International Journal of Sport Psychology, 22,* 189-210.

Abernethy, B. (1994). The nature of expertise in sport. In S. Serpa, J. Alves, & V. Pataco (Eds.), *International perspectives on sport and exercise psychology* (pp. 57-68). Morgantown, WV: FIT Press.

Abernethy, B. (1997, November 3-5). Perception-action relationships and the development of motor expertise. *Proceedings of the ACTES du VIIth Congres International des Chercheurs en Activites Physiques et Sportives, Marseille, France.*

Abernethy, B. (2001). Attention. In R.N. Singer, H.A. Hausenblas, & C. Janelle (Eds.), *Handbook of research on sport psychology* (2nd ed.) (pp. 53-85). New York: John Wiley.

Abernethy, B., Baker, J., & Côté, J. (1999, Sept. 27-29). Expertise in sport. In K. Roth, T. Pauer, & K. Reischle (Eds.), *Dimensions and Visions of Sports: Proceedings of the 14th Annual Conference of the German Association of Sports Science, Heidelberg* (pp. 158-162). Auflage Hamburg: Czwalina Verlag.

Abernethy, B., Burgess-Limerick, R., & Parks, S. (1994). Contrasting approaches to the study of motor expertise. *Quest, 46,* 186-198.

Abernethy, B., Côté, J., & Baker, J. (2002). Expert decision-making in team sports [Report to the Australian Sports Commission]. Canberra, Australia: Australian Sports Commission.

Abernethy, B., Thomas, K.T., & Thomas, J.R. (1993). Strategies for improving understanding of motor expertise. In J.L. Starkes & F. Allard (Eds.), *Cognitive issues in motor expertise* (pp. 317-356). Amsterdam: Elsevier.

Anderson, J.R. (1982). Acquisition of cognitive skill. *Psychological Review, 89,* 369-406.

Annett, J. (1986). On knowing how to do things. In H. Heuer & C. Fromm (Eds.), *Generation and modulation of action patterns* (pp. 187-200). Berlin: Springer-Verlag.

Bahill, A.T., & LaRitz, T. (1984). Why can't batters keep their eyes on the ball? *American Scientist, 72,* 249-253.

Baker, J., Côté, J., & Abernethy, B. (in press). Learning from the experts: Practice activities of expert decision-makers in sport. *Research Quarterly for Exercise and Sport.*

Beek, P.J. (2000). Toward a theory of implicit learning in the perceptual-motor domain. *International Journal of Sport Psychology, 31,* 547-554.

Beek, P.J., & van Santvoord, A.A.M. (1992). Learning the cascade juggle: A dynamical systems analysis. *Journal of Motor Behavior, 24,* 85-94.

Beggs, J.M., Brown, T.H., Byrne, J.H., Crow, T., LeDoux, J.E., LeBar, K., & Thompson, R.F. (1999). Learning and memory: Basic mechanisms. In M.J. Zigmond, F.E. Bloom, S.C. Landis, J.L. Roberts, and L.R. Squire (Eds.), *Fundamental neuroscience* (pp. 1411-1454). San Diego, CA: Academic Press.

Bernstein, N. (1967). *The co-ordination and regulation of movements.* Oxford: Pergamon Press.

Book, W.F. (1908). The psychology of skill. In *University of Montana Studies in Psychology* (Vol. 1.). Reprinted, New York: Gregg, 1925.

Bootsma, R.J. (1988). *The timing of rapid interceptive actions.* Amsterdam: Free University Press.

Bouchard C., An, P., Rice, T., Skinner, J.S., Wilmore, J.H., Gagnon, J., et al. (1999). Familial aggregation of $\dot{V}O_2$max response to exercise training: Results from the HERITAGE family study. *Journal of Applied Physiology, 87,* 1003-1008.

Bouchard, C., Daw, E.W., Rice, T., Pérusse, L., Gagnon, J., Province, M.A., et al. (1998). Familial resemblance for $\dot{V}O_2$max in the sedentary state: The HERITAGE family study. *Medicine and Science in Sports and Exercise, 30,* 252-258.

Bouchard, C., Leon, A.S., Rao, D.C., Skinner, J.S., Wilmore, J.H., & Gagnon, J. (1995). The HERITAGE family study: Aims, design, and measurement protocol. *Medicine and Science in Sports and Exercise, 27,* 721-729.

Brady, F. (1998). A theoretical and empirical review of the contextual interference effect and the learning of motor skills. *Quest, 50,* 266-293.

Brouwer, W.H., Waterink, W., van-Wolffelaar, P.C., & Rothengatter, T. (1991). Divided attention in experienced young and older drivers: Lane tracking and visual analysis in a dynamic driving simulator. *Human Factors, 33,* 573-582.

Bryan, W.L., & Harter, N. (1899). Studies on the telegraphic language: The acquisition of a hierarchy of habits. *Psychological Review, 6,* 345-375.

Cacioppo, J.T., Berntson, G.G., & Crites, S.L., Jr. (1996). Social neuroscience: Principles of psychophysiological arousal and response. In A.T. Higgins & A.W. Kruglanski (Eds.), *Social psychology: Handbook of basic principles* (pp. 72-101). New York: Guilford Press.

Carello, C., Turvey, M.T., Kugler, P.N., & Shaw, R.E. (1984). Inadequacies in the computer metaphor. In M. Gazzaniga (Ed.), *Handbook of cognitive neuroscience* (pp. 229-248). New York: Plenum.

Charness, N., Krampe, R.T., & Mayr, U. (1996). The role of practice and coaching in entrepreneurial skill domains: An international comparison of life-span chess skill acquisition. In K.A. Ericsson (Ed.), *The road to excellence: The acquisition of expert performance in the arts and sciences, sports, and games* (pp. 51-80). Mahwah, NJ: Erlbaum.

Chase, W.G., & Simon, H.A. (1973). The mind's eye in chess. In W.G. Chase (Ed.), *Visual information processing* (pp. 215-282). New York: Academic Press.

Clark, J.E. (1995). On becoming skillful: Patterns and constraints. *Research Quarterly for Exercise and Sport, 66,* 173-183.

Crossman, E.R.F.W. (1959). A theory of the acquisition of speed skill. *Ergonomics, 2,* 153-166.

de Groot, A.D. (1965). *Thought and choice in chess.* The Hague, Netherlands: Mouton.

Dickinson, J. (1978). Retention of intentional and incidental motor learning. *Research Quarterly, 49,* 437-441.

Ditchfield, M., & Bahr, W. (1988). *Coaching soccer the progressive way.* Englewood Cliffs, NJ: Prentice Hall.

Eccles, J.C. (1972). *The understanding of the brain.* New York: McGraw-Hill.

Ericsson, K.A. (1996). The acquisition of expert performance: An introduction to some of the issues. In K.A. Ericsson (Ed.), *The road to excellence: The acquisition of expert performance in the arts and sciences, sports, and games* (pp. 1-50). Mahwah, NJ: Erlbaum.

Ericsson, K.A. (1998). The scientific study of expert levels of performance: General implications for optimal learning and creativity. *High Ability Studies, 9,* 75-100.

Ericsson, K.A. (2001). The path to expert golf performance: Insights from the masters on how to improve performance by deliberate practice. In P.R. Thomas (Ed.), *Optimising performance in golf* (pp. 1-57). Brisbane, Australia: Australian Academic Press.

Ericsson, K.A., Krampe, R.T., & Tesch-Römer, C. (1993). The role of deliberate practice in the acquisition of expert performance. *Psychological Review, 100,* 363-406.

Ericsson, K.A., & Lehmann, A.C. (1996). Expert and exceptional performance: Evidence on maximal adaptations on task constraints. *Annual Review of Psychology, 47,* 273-305.

Ericsson, K.A., & Simon, H.A. (1993). *Protocol analysis: Verbal reports as data* (Rev. ed.). Cambridge, MA: Bradford Books/MIT Press.

Ericsson, K.A., & Smith, J. (1991). Prospects and limits in the empirical study of expertise: An introduction. In K.A. Ericsson and J. Smith (Eds.), *Toward a general theory of expertise: Prospects and limits* (pp. 1-38). Cambridge: Cambridge University Press.

Farrow, D., & Abernethy, B. (2002). Can anticipatory skills be learned through implicit video-based perceptual training? *Journal of Sports Sciences, 20,* 471-485.

Fitts, P.M. (1954). The information capacity of the human motor system in controlling the amplitude of movement. *Journal of Experimental Psychology, 47,* 381-391.

French, K.E., & Nevett, M.E. (1993). The development of expertise in youth sport. In J.L. Starkes & F. Allard (Eds.), *Cognitive issues in motor expertise* (pp. 255-270). Amsterdam: Elsevier.

Gibson, J.J. (1979). *The ecological approach to visual perception.* Boston: Houghton-Mifflin.

Glaser, R., & Chi, M.T.H. (1988). Overview. In M.T.H. Chi, R. Glaser, & M.J. Farr (Eds.), *The nature of expertise* (pp. xv-xxviii). Hillsdale, NJ: Erlbaum.

Gottsdanker, R., & Stelmach, G.E. (1971). The persistence of psychological refractoriness. *Journal of Motor Behavior, 3,* 301-312.

Green, T.D., & Flowers, J.H. (1991). Implicit versus explicit learning processes in a probabilistic, continuous fine-motor catching task. *Journal of Motor Behavior, 23,* 293-300.

Haken, H. (1983). *Synergetics: An introduction* (3rd ed.). Berlin: Springer-Verlag.

Haken, H. (1990). Synergetics as a tool for the conceptualization and mathematization of cognition and behaviour—How far can we go? In H. Haken & M. Stadler (Eds.), *Synergetics of cognition*. (pp. 2-31). Berlin: Springer-Verlag.

Haken, H., Kelso, J.A.S., & Bunz, H. (1985). A theoretical model of phase transitions in human hand movements. *Biological Cybernetics, 51,* 348-356.

Hall, K.G., Domingues, D.A., & Cavazos, R. (1994). Contextual interference effects with skilled baseball players. *Perceptual and Motor Skills, 78,* 835-841.

Hatano, G. (1988). Social and motivational bases for mathematical understanding. In G.B. Saxe & M. Gearhart (Eds.), *Children's mathematics: New directions for child development* (Vol. 41, pp. 51-70). San Francisco: Jossey-Bass.

Helsen, W.F., Starkes, J.L., & Hodges, N.J. (1998). Team sports and the theory of deliberate practice. *Journal of Sport and Exercise Psychology, 20,* 12-34.

Hodge, T., & Deakin, J.M. (1998). Expertise in the martial arts. *Journal of Sport and Exercise Psychology, 20,* 260-279.

Hodges, N.J., & Starkes, J.L. (1996). Wrestling with the nature of expertise: A sport specific test of Ericsson, Krampe and Tesch-Römer's (1993) theory of "deliberate practice." *International Journal of Sport Psychology, 27,* 400-424.

Hofsten, C. von (1987). Catching. In H. Heuer & A.F. Sanders (Eds.), *Perspectives on perception and action* (pp. 33-46). Hillsdale, NJ: Erlbaum.

Howe, M.J.A. (2001). *Genius explained.* Cambridge, UK: Cambridge University Press.

Howe, M.J.A., Davidson, J., & Sloboda, J.A. (1998). Innate talents: Reality or myth. *Behavioral and Brain Sciences, 21,* 399-407.

Janelle, C.M. (2001). Expert sport performance: An overview of critical issues and research directions. In A. Papaioannou, M. Goudas, & Y. Theodorakis (Eds.), *Proceedings of the 10th World Congress of Sport Psychology.* Thessaloniki, Greece: Christodoulidi Publications.

Jeka, J.J., & Kelso, J.A.S. (1989). The dynamic pattern approach to coordinated behavior: A tutorial review. In S.A. Wallace (Ed.), *Perspectives on the co-ordination of movement* (pp. 3-45). Amsterdam: North-Holland.

Johnson, P.E. (1983). What kind of expert should a system be? *The Journal of Medicine and Philosophy, 8,* 77-97.

Kay, H. (1962). Channel capacity and skilled performance. In F.A. Geldard (Ed.), *Defence psychology.* New York: Macmillan.

Kelly, S.W., Burton, A.M., Kato, T., & Akamatsu, S. (2001). Incidental learning of real-world irregularities. *Psychological Science, 12,* 86-89.

Kelso, J.A.S. (1986). Pattern formation in multi-degree of freedom speech and limb movements. *Experimental Brain Research Supplement, 15,* 105-128.

Kelso, J.A.S. (1990). Phase transitions: Foundations of behavior. In H. Haken & M. Stadler (Eds.), *Synergetics of cognition* (pp. 249-268). Berlin: Springer-Verlag.

Kelso, J.A.S. (1995). *Dynamic patterns.* Cambridge, MA: MIT Press.

Krampe, R.T., & Ericsson, K.A. (1996). Maintaining excellence: Deliberate practice and elite performance in young and older pianists. *Journal of Experimental Psychology: General, 125,* 331-359.

Kugler, P.N. (1986). A morphological perspective on the origin and evolution of movement patterns. In M.G. Wade & H.T.A. Whiting (Eds.), *Motor development in children: Aspects of coordination and control* (pp. 459-525). The Hague: Nijhoff.

Lee, T.D., Chamberlin, C.J., & Hodges, N.J. (2001). Practice. In R.N. Singer, H.A. Hausenblas, & C.M. Janelle (Eds.), *Handbook of Sport Psychology* (2nd ed., pp. 115-143). New York: Wiley.

Le Plat, J., & Hoc, J-M. (1981). Subsequent verbalisation in the study of cognitive processes. *Ergonomics, 24,* 743-756.

Luciano, M., Wright, M., Smith, G.A., Geffen, G.M., Geffen, L.B., & Martin, N.G. (2001). Genetic covariance among measures of information processing speed, working memory, and IQ. *Behavioral Genetics, 31,* 581-592.

Magill, R.A. (1989). *Motor learning: Concepts and applications* (3rd ed.). Dubuque, IA: Wm. C. Brown.

Magill, R.A., & Hall, K.G. (1990). A review of the contextual interference effect in motor skill acquisition. *Human Movement Science, 9,* 241-289.

Masters, R.S.W. (1992). Knowledge, knerves and know-how: The role of explicit versus implicit knowledge in the breakdown of a complex motor skill under pressure. *British Journal of Psychology, 83,* 343-358.

Maxwell, J.P., Masters, R.S.W., & Eves, F.F. (2000). From novice to no know-how: A longitudinal study of implicit motor learning. *Journal of Sports Sciences, 18,* 111-120.

McLeod, P.N. (1987). Visual reaction time and high-speed ball games. *Perception, 16,* 49-59.

McLeod, P.N., McLaughlin, C., & Nimmo-Smith, I. (1985). Information encapsulation and automaticity: Evidence from the visual control of finely timed actions. In M.I. Posner & O. Marin (Eds.), *Attention and performance XI* (pp. 391-406). Hillsdale, NJ: Erlbaum.

Newell, K.M. (1991). Motor skill acquisition. *Annual Review of Psychology, 42,* 213-237.

Nisbett, R.E., & Wilson, T.D. (1977). Telling more than we can know: Verbal reports on mental processes. *Psychological Review, 84,* 231-259.

Parker, H. (1981). Visual detection and perception in netball. In I.M. Cockerill & W.W. MacGillivary (Eds.), *Vision and sport* (pp. 42-53). London: Stanley-Thornes.

Reber, A.S. (1989). Implicit learning and tacit knowledge. *Journal of Experimental Psychology: General, 118,* 219-235.

Robb, M.D. (1972). *The dynamics of motor-skill acquisition.* Englewood Cliffs, NJ: Prentice Hall.

Rosenbaum, D.A. (1991). *Human motor control.* San Diego, CA: Academic Press.

Rowe, D.C. (1998). Talent scouts, not practice scouts: Talents are real. *Behavioral and Brain Sciences, 21,* 421-422.

Rowe, R.M., & McKenna, F.P. (2001). Skilled anticipation in real-world tasks: Measurement of attentional demands in the domain of tennis. *Journal of Experimental Psychology: Applied, 7,* 60-67.

Runeson, S. (1977). On the possibility of "smart" perceptual systems. *Scandinavian Journal of Psychology, 18,* 172-179.

Salthouse, T.A. (1991). Expertise as the circumvention of human processing limitations. In K.A. Ericsson & J. Smith (Eds.) *Toward a general theory of expertise: Prospects and limits.* (pp. 286-300). New York: Cambridge Press.

Schmidt, R.A., & Lee, T.D. (1999). *Motor control and learning: A behavioral emphasis.* (3rd ed.). Champaign, IL: Human Kinetics.

Schneider, W., & Shiffrin, R.M. (1977). Controlled and automatic human information processing: I. Detection, search, and attention. *Psychological Review, 84,* 1-66.

Singer, R.N., & Janelle, C.M. (1999). Determining sport expertise: From genes to supremes. *International Journal of Sport Psychology, 30,* 117-150.

Skinner, J.S. (2001). Do genes determine champions? *Sports Science Exchange, 14*(4), 83-90.

Smith, C.B. (1973). An investigation of the psychological refractory period of athletes and non-athletes (Doctoral dissertation, Indiana University, 1972). *Dissertation Abstracts International, 33,* 4160-A.

Starkes, J.L. (2000). The road to expertise: Is practice the only determinant? *International Journal of Sport Psychology, 31,* 431-451.

Starkes, J.L., Deakin, J., Allard, F., Hodges, N.J., & Hayes, A. (1996). Deliberate practice in sports: What is it anyway? In K.A. Ericsson (Ed.), *The road to excellence: The acquisition of expert performance in the arts and sciences, sports, and games* (pp. 81-106). Mahwah, NJ: Erlbaum.

Stelmach, G.E. (1969). Efficiency of motor learning as a function of intertrial rest. *Research Quarterly, 40,* 198-202.

Sternberg, R.J. (1996). Costs of expertise. In K.A. Ericsson (Ed.), *The road to excellence: The acquisition of expert performance in the arts and sciences, sports, and games* (pp. 347-354). Mahwah, NJ: Erlbaum.

van Rossum, J.H.A. (2000). Deliberate practice and Dutch field hockey: An addendum to Starkes. *International Journal of Sport Psychology, 31,* 452-460.

Vereijken, B., Emmerik, R.E.A. van, Whiting, H.T.A., & Newell, K.M. (1992). Free(z)ing degrees of freedom in skill acquisition. *Journal of Motor Behavior, 24,* 133-142.

Vereijken, B., Whiting, H.T.A., & Beek, W.J. (1992). A dynamical systems approach to skill acquisition. *Quarterly Journal of Experimental Psychology, 45A,* 323-344.

White, P.A. (1980). Limitations on verbal reports of internal events: A refutation of Nisbett and Wilson and of Bem. *Psychological Review, 87,* 105-112.

Williams, A.D., Davids, K., & Williams, J.G. (1999). *Visual perception and action in sport.* London: Spon.

Chapter 15

Abernethy, B. (1990). Anticipation in squash: Differences in advance cue utilization between expert and novice players. *Journal of Sport Sciences, 8,* 17-34.

Abernethy, B. (1991). Visual search strategies and decision-making in sport. *International Journal of Sport Psychology, 22,* 189-210.

Abernethy, B., Gill, D.P., Parks, S.L., & Packer, S.T. (2001). Expertise and the perception of kinematic and situational probability information. *Perception, 30,* 233-252.

Abernethy, B., Neal, R.J., & Koning, P. (1994). Visual-perceptual and cognitive differences between expert, intermediate, and novice snooker players. *Applied Cognitive Psychology, 18,* 185-211.

Abernethy, B., Thomas, K.T., & Thomas, J.R. (1993). Strategies for improving understanding of motor expertise. In J.L. Starkes & F. Allard (Eds.), *Cognitive issues in motor expertise* (pp. 317-356). Amsterdam: Elsevier.

Austin, J., & Delaney, P.F. (1998). Protocol analysis as a tool for behavior analysis. *Analysis of Verbal Behavior, 15,* 41-56.

Bahill, A.T., & LaRitz, T. (1984). Why can't batters keep their eyes on the ball? *American Scientist, 72,* 249-253.

Berger, B.G., & McInman, A. (1993). Exercise and the quality of life. In R.N. Singer, M. Murphey, and L.K. Tennant (Eds.), *Handbook of research on sport psychology* (pp. 729-760). New York: Macmillan.

Bouchard, C., An, P., Rice, T., Skinner, J. S., Wilmore, J. H., Gagnon, J., et al. (1999). Familial aggregation of VO_2max response to exercise training: Results form the HERITAGE family study. *Journal of Applied Physiology, 87,* 1003-1008.

Bouchard, C., Daw, E.F., Rice, T., Perusse, L., Gagnon, J., Province, M.A., et al. (1998). Familial resemblance for VO_2max in the sedentary state: The HERITAGE family study. *Medicine and Science in Sports and Exercise, 30,* 252-258.

Bouchard, C., Leon, A.S., Rao, D.C., Skinner, J.S., Wilmore, J.H., & Gagnon, J. (1995). The HERITAGE family study: Aims, design, and measurement protocol. *Medicine and Science in Sports and Exercise, 27,* 721-729.

Bouchard, C., Lesage, R., Lortie, G., Simoneau, J.-A., Hamel, P., Boulay, M.R., et al. (1986). Aerobic performance in brothers, dizygotic and monozygotic twins. *Medicine and Science in Sports and Exercise, 18,* 639-646.

Bouchard, C., Simoneau, J.A., Lortie, G., Boulay, M.R., Marcotte, M., & Thibault, M.C. (1986). Genetic effects in human skeletal muscle fiber type distribution and enzyme activities. *Canadian Journal of Physiology and Pharmacology, 64,* 1245-1251.

Carson, J.A., Nettleton, D., & Reecy, J.M. (2001). Differential gene expression in the rat soleus muscle during early work overload-induced hypertrophy. *FASEB Journal, 15,* U261-U281.

Charness, N. (1991). Expertise in chess: The balance between knowledge and search. In K.A. Ericsson & J. Smith (Eds.), *Toward a general theory of expertise: Prospects and limits* (pp. 39-63). New York: Cambridge University Press.

Chase, W.G., & Simon, H.A. (1973). The mind's eye in chess. In W.G. Chase (Ed.), *Visual information processing* (pp. 215-281). New York: Academic Press.

Conley, D.L., & Krahenbuhl, G.S. (1980). Running economy and distance running performance of highly trained athletes. *Medicine and Science in Sports and Exercise, 12,* 357-360.

Côté, J., Ericsson, K.A., & Beamer, M. (2001). *Tracing the development of elite athletes using retrospective interview methods: A proposed interview and validation procedure for reported information.* Manuscript submitted for publication.

Coyle, E.F., Feltner, M.E., Kautz, S.A., Hamilton, M.T., Montain, S.J., Baylor, A.M., et al. (1991). Physiological and biomechanical factors associated with elite endurance cycling performance. *Medicine and Science in Sports and Exercise, 23,* 93-107.

de Groot, A. (1978). *Thought and choice in chess.* The Hague, Netherlands: Mouton. (Original work published 1946)

DeRisi, J.L., Iyer, V.R., & Brown, P.O. (1997). Exploring the metabolic and genetic control of gene expression on a genomic scale. *Science, 278,* 680-686.

Ericsson, K.A. (1990). Peak performance and age: An examination of peak performance in sports. P.B. Baltes and M.M. Baltes (Eds.), *Successful aging: Perspectives from the behavioral sciences* (pp. 164-195). New York: Cambridge University Press.

Ericsson, K.A. (1996). The acquisition of expert performance: An introduction to some of the issues. In K.A. Ericsson (Ed.), *The road to excellence: The acquisition of expert performance in the arts and sciences, sports, and games* (pp. 1-50). Mahwah, NJ: Erlbaum.

Ericsson, K.A. (1998a). The scientific study of expert levels of performance: General implications for optimal learning and creativity. *High Ability Studies, 9,* 75-100.

Ericsson, K.A. (1998b). Basic capacities can be modified or circumvented by deliberate practice: A rejection of talent accounts of expert performance. A commentary on M.J.A. Howe, J.W. Davidson, and J.A. Sloboda "Innate Talents: Reality or Myth?" *Behavioral and Brain Sciences, 21,* 413-414.

Ericsson, K.A. (2001a). Protocol analysis in psychology. In N. Smelser and P. Baltes (Eds.), *International Encyclopedia of the Social and Behavioral Sciences* (pp. 12256-12262). Oxford, UK: Elsevier.

Ericsson, K.A. (2001b). The path to expert golf performance: Insights from the masters on how to improve performance by deliberate practice. In P.R. Thomas (Ed.), *Optimising performance in golf* (pp. 1-57). Brisbane, Australia: Australian Academic Press.

Ericsson, K.A. (2002). Attaining excellence through deliberate practice: Insights from the study of expert performance. In M. Ferrari (Ed.), *The pursuit of excellence in education* (pp. 21-55). Hillsdale, NJ: Erlbaum.

Ericsson, K.A., & Harris, M.S. (1990, November 17). *Expert chess memory without chess knowledge: A training study.* Poster presented at the 31st Annual Meeting of the Psychonomic Society, New Orleans, Louisiana.

Ericsson, K.A., & Kintsch, W. (1995). Long-term working memory. *Psychological Review, 102,* 211-245.

Ericsson, K.A., & Kintsch, W. (2000). Shortcomings of generic retrieval structures with slots of the type that Gobet (1993) proposed and modeled. *British Journal of Psychology, 91,* 571-588.

Ericsson, K.A., Krampe, R.T., & Tesch-Römer, C. (1993). The role of deliberate practice in the acquisition of expert performance. *Psychological Review, 100*, 363-406.

Ericsson, K.A., & Lehmann, A.C. (1996). Expert and exceptional performance: Evidence on maximal adaptations on task constraints. *Annual Review of Psychology, 47*, 273-305.

Ericsson, K.A., Patel, V.L., & Kintsch, W. (2000). How experts' adaptations to representative task demands account for the expertise effect in memory recall: Comment on Vicente and Wang (1998). *Psychological Review, 107*, 578-592.

Ericsson, K.A., & Simon, H.A. (1980). Verbal reports as data. *Psychological Review, 87*, 215-251.

Ericsson, K.A., & Simon, H.A. (1984). *Protocol analysis: Verbal reports as data.* Cambridge, MA: Bradford Books/MIT Press.

Ericsson, K.A., & Simon, H.A. (1993). *Protocol analysis: Verbal reports as data* (Rev. ed.). Cambridge, MA: Bradford Books/MIT Press.

Ericsson, K.A., & Simon, H.A. (1998). How to study thinking in everyday life: Contrasting think-aloud protocols with descriptions and explanations of thinking. *Mind, Culture, & Activity, 5*(3), 178-186.

Ericsson, K.A., & Smith, J. (1991). Prospects and limits in the empirical study of expertise: An introduction. In K.A. Ericsson and J. Smith (Eds.), *Toward a general theory of expertise: Prospects and limits* (pp. 1-38). Cambridge: Cambridge University Press.

French, K.E., Nevett, M.E., Spurgeon, J.H., Graham, K.C., Rink, J.E., & McPherson, S.L. (1996). Knowledge representation and problem solution in expert and novice youth baseball players. *Research Quarterly for Exercise and Sport, 67*, 386-395.

Gawel, R. (1997). The use of language by trained and untrained experienced wine tasters. *Journal of Sensory Studies, 12*, 267-284.

Groeger, J.A. (2000). *Understanding driving: Applying cognitive psychology to a complex everyday task.* Philadelphia: Psychology Press.

Helgerud, J., Engen, L.G., Wisloff, U., & Hoff, J. (2001). Aerobic endurance training improves soccer performance. *Medicine and Science in Sports and Exercise, 33*, 1925-1931.

Helsen, W., & Pauwels, J.M. (1993). The relationship between expertise and visual information processing. In J.L. Starkes & F. Allard (Eds.), *Cognitive issues in motor expertise* (pp. 109-134). New York: Elsevier.

Helsen, W.F., & Starkes, J.L. (1999). A multidimensional approach to skilled perception and performance in sport. *Applied Cognitive Psychology, 13*, 1-27.

Henderson, R.D., Smith, M.C., Podd, J., & Varela-Alvarez, H. (1995). A comparison of the four prominent user-based methods for evaluating the usability of computer software. *Ergonomics 39*, 2030-2044.

Hodges, N.J., Kerr, T., Weir, P.L., & Starkes, J.L. (2002). *Predicting performance from deliberate practice hours for the multi-sport athlete* [Abstract]. Presentation to be delivered at the European Congress of Sport Science.

Kelly, S.W., Burton, A.M., Kato, T., & Akamatsu, S. (2001). Incidental learning of real-world irregularities. *Psychological Science, 12*, 86-89.

Klissouras, V., Casini, B., Di Salvo, V., Faina, M., Marini, C., Pigozzi, F., et al. (2001). Genes and Olympic performance: A co-twin study. *International Journal of Sports Medicine, 22*, 250-255.

Komi, P.V., Viitasalo, J.H.T., Havu, M., Thorstensson, A., Sjodin, B., & Karlsson, J. (1977). Skeletal muscle fibres and muscle enzyme activities in monozygotic and dizygotic twins of both sexes. *Acta Physiologica Scandinavica, 100*, 385-392.

Masters, R.S.W. (1992). Knowledge, knerves and know-how: The role of explicit versus implicit knowledge in the breakdown of a complex motor skill under pressure. *British Journal of Psychology, 83*, 343-358.

McLeod, P.N. (1987). Visual reaction time and high-speed ball games. *Perception, 16*, 49-59.

Meyer, D.E., & Kieras, D.E. (1997). A computational theory of executive cognitive processes and multiple-task performance: Part 2. Accounts of psychological refractory-period phenomena. *Psychological Review, 104,* 749-791.

Newell, A., & Rosenbloom, P.S. (1981). Mechanisms of skill acquisition and the law of practice. In J.R. Anderson (Ed.), *Cognitive skills and their acquisition* (pp. 1-55). Hillsdale, NJ: Erlbaum.

Newell, A., & Simon, H.A. (1972). *Human problem solving.* Englewood Cliffs, NJ: Prentice Hall.

Nisbett, R.E., & Wilson, T.D. (1977). Telling more than we can know: Verbal reports on mental processes. *Psychological Review, 84,* 231-259.

Noakes, T.D. (2000). Physiological models to understand exercise fatigue and the adaptations that predict and enhance athletic performance. *Scandinavian Journal of Medicine & Science in Sports, 10,* 123-145.

Prud'homme, D., Bouchard, C., Leblanc, C., Landry, F., & Fontaine, E. (1984). Sensitivity of maximal aerobic power to training is genotype-dependent. *Medicine and Science in Sports and Exercise, 16,* 489-493.

Richman, H.B., Gobet, F., Staszewski, J.J., & Simon, H.A. (1996). Perceptual and memory processes in the acquisition of expert performance: The EPAM model. In K.A. Ericsson (Ed.), *The road to excellence: The acquisition of expert performance in the arts and sciences, sports, and games* (pp. 167-187). Mahwah, NJ: Erlbaum.

Rosenbaum, D.A. (1991). *Human motor control.* San Diego, CA: Academic Press.

Schumacher, E.H., Seymour, T.L., Glass, J.M., Fencsik, D.E., Lauber, E.J., Kieras, D.E., & Meyer, D.E. (2001). Virtually perfect time sharing in dual-task performance: Uncorking the central cognitive bottleneck. *Psychological Science, 12,* 101-108.

Shea, J.B., & Paull, G. (1996). Capturing expertise in sports. In K.A. Ericsson (Ed.), *The road to excellence: The acquisition of expert performance in the arts and sciences, sports, and games* (pp. 321-335). Mahwah, NJ: Erlbaum.

Simon, H.A., & Chase, W.G. (1973). Skill in chess. *American Scientist, 61,* 394-403.

Simon, H.A., & Gobet, F. (2000). Expertise effects in memory recall: Comment on Vicente and Wang. *Psychological Review, 107,* 593-600.

Skinner, J.S., Jaskolski, A., Jaskolska, A., Krasnoff, J., Gagnon, J., Leano, A.S., et al. (2001). Age, sex, race, initial fitness and response to training: The HERITAGE family study. *Journal of Applied Physiology, 90,* 1770-1776.

Starkes, J.L., & Allard, J. (1991). Motor-skill experts in sports, dance and other domains. In K.A. Ericsson and J. Smith (Eds.), *Toward a general theory of expertise: Prospects and limits* (pp. 126-152). Cambridge: Cambridge University Press.

Starkes, J.L., & Allard, F. (Eds.). (1993). *Cognitive issues in motor expertise.* Amsterdam: North Holland.

Starkes, J.L., Edwards, P., Dissanayake, P., & Dunn, T. (1995). A new technology and field test of advance cue usage in volleyball. *Research Quarterly for Exercise and Sport, 66,* 162-167.

Sudman, S., Bradburn, N.M., & Schwarz, N. (Eds.). (1996). *Thinking about answers: The application of cognitive processes to survey methodology.* San Francisco, CA: Jossey-Bass.

Valentin, D., Pichon, M., de Boishebert, V., & Abdi, H. (2000). What's in a wine name? When and why do wine experts perform better than novices? *Abstracts of the Psychonomic Society, 5,* 36.

Von Eckardt, B. (1998). Psychology of introspection. In E. Craig (Ed.), *Routledge encyclopedia of philosophy* (pp. 842-846). London: Routledge.

Vicente, K.J. (2000). Revisting the constraint attunement hypothessi: Reply to Ericsson, Patel, and Kintsch (2000) and Simon and Gobet (2000). *Psychological Review, 107,* 601-608.

Vicente, K.J., & Wang, J.H. (1998). An ecological theory of expertise effects in memory recall. *Psychological Review, 105,* 33-57.

Wagner, R.K., & Stanovich, K.E. (1996). Expertise in reading. In K.A. Ericsson (Ed.), *The road to excellence: The acquisition of expert performance in the arts and sciences, sports, and games* (pp. 189-225). Mahwah, NJ: Erlbaum.

Wahlsten, D. (1999). Single-gene influences on brain and behavior. *Annual Review of Psychology, 50,* 599-624.

Index

Page locators followed by an italicized *f* or *t* indicate information contained in figures or tables.

About the Editors

Janet L. Starkes, PhD, is a professor and chair of the department of kinesiology at McMaster University in Ontario, Canada. She earned her postdoctorate in clinical neuropsychology at Mt. Sinai Hospital, and has been doing research in the area of expert performance since 1975. Dr. Starkes is an International Fellow of the American Academy of Kinesiology & Physical Education and has served as president of the Canadian Society for Psychomotor Learning and Sport Psychology (1994), president of the North American Society for Psychology of Sport and Physical Activity (1997), and president of the Canadian Council of University Physical Education and Kinesiology Administrators (1999). Dr. Starkes has been invited to speak about sport expertise in 10 different countries and was keynote speaker on the topic at the World Congress of Sport Psychology in 2001. This is her second edited book in the area of expert performance.

K. Anders Ericsson, PhD, Conradi Eminent Scholar and professor of psychology at Florida State University, has greatly influenced the current direction of expertise research. In 1976, he received his PhD in psychology from the University of Stockholm, Sweden, followed by a postdoctoral fellowship at Carnegie-Mellon University. He is a Fellow of the American Psychological Association and of the Center for Advanced Study in the Behavioral Sciences. Dr. Ericsson delivered the 2001 Distinguished Scholar Lecture Series at the University of Alberta in Canada. Currently he studies the cognitive structure of expert performance in domains such as music, chess, and sports and how expert performers acquire their superior performance by extended deliberate practice. He co-edited *Toward a General Theory of Expertise* and edited *The Road to Excellence: The Acquisition of Expert Performance in the Arts and Sciences, Sports, and Games.*

About the Contributors

Bruce Abernethy, PhD, is professor and head of the School of Human Movement Studies at The University of Queensland in Brisbane, Australia. Professor Abernethy holds a bachelors degree from the University of Queensland and a PhD from the University of Otago. He is an International Fellow of the American Academy of Kinesiology and Physical Education and a Fellow of Sports Medicine Australia. Professor Abernethy has published extensively on the topic of movement expertise and skill learning and has a particular research interest in perceptual aspects and visual control of skilled movement. His research work has attracted competitive grant funding from the Australian Research Council, the Australian Sports Commission, the Australian Cricket Board, the Australian Football League, the National Occupational Health and Safety Commission, and the Motor Accident Insurance Commission.

Joseph Baker, MEd, is a graduate student with the School of Physical and Health Education at Queen's University, Canada. His research examines the factors that influence the development of elite sport performance. Currently, he is completing his doctoral dissertation investigating the development of expertise in Ironman triathletes.

Peter J. Beek, PhD, is professor in coordination dynamics at the Faculty of Human Sciences, Vrije Universiteit, Amsterdam. His research interests include the dynamics of bimanual rhythmic coordination, the relationships between perception and movement, and the learning and development of perceptual-motor skills. Building on his early studies of juggling and other bimanual skills, he is seeking applications of dynamical systems theory to the study of learning of expertise in the domain of sport.

Jason Berry is a first-class honors graduate in applied science from the University of Ballarat. Currently completing his PhD studies at the University of Queensland in Brisbane, Australia, Berry has a particular interest in expertise in team ball sports, especially Australian football in which he has extensive experience as both a player and a coach. His doctoral studies on the development and training of expert decision-making in Australian football are funded by a grant from the Australian Football League to himself and his supervisor, Professor Bruce Abernethy.

Sian L. Beilock, MA, is a doctoral candidate in the departments of kinesiology and psychology at Michigan State University. Her research focuses on the acquisition and maintenance of complex skills across both cognitive and sensorimotor skill domains, with a particular emphasis in expert performance in high-pressure and attention-demanding situations. In collaboration with Thomas H. Carr, Beilock is examining skill performance across a number of different task types and performance environments in order to gain a better understanding of the nature of successful skill execution and why, at times, it fails to occur.

Therese Brisson earned a PhD in 1995 from Université de Montréal and served as an assistant professor at the University of New Brunswick from 1995-2000, where she taught courses in motor control and learning, neural control of movement, and research methods. The focus of her research was with the cognitive processes undertaken by subjects while learning motor tasks. Brisson has been a member of the Canadian National Women's Hockey Team since 1993, serving as team captain for three seasons. Highlights of her career include winning five World Championships (1994, 1997, 1999, 2000, 2001), a silver medal at the 1998 Nagano Winter Olympics, and a gold medal at the 2002 Salt Lake City Winter Olympics. Brisson serves on the board of directors of several sport organizations and is actively involved in athlete representation in Canada. She is currently an MBA candidate at the Schulich School of Business in Toronto.

Thomas H. Carr, PhD, is a professor in the department of psychology at Michigan State University where he does cognitive-psychological and cognitive-neuroscientific research on attention, perceptual recognition, and motor control as components of complex real-time skills. The largest part of his work has focused on reading and writing, but since beginning his collaboration with Sian Beilock he has begun to study real-world sensorimotor skills and how they compare to the kinds of cognitive skills he was already investigating. Carr has served as editor of *Journal of Experimental Psychology: Human Perception and Performance,* associate editor of *Cognitive Psychology,* and is the incoming editor of *Perception & Psychophysics.*

Nick Cipriano, MSc, is an associate professor in the department of kinesiology at McMaster University. He started coaching freestyle wrestling shortly after Canada announced that it would boycott the 1980 Moscow Olympics. Over the past 22 years, he has been a member of Canada's National Team coaching staff, in addition to serving as head coach of the McMaster University men's varsity wrestling team. In 1996, he started coaching women wrestlers as well. Career highlights include coaching at three Olympic Games (1988, 1992, 1996), two Pan American Games (1987, 1995), and numerous World Championships. His greatest coaching thrill to date took place at the 1992 Barcelona Olympics when one of the athletes whom he had coached for nearly 10 years achieved his best possible performance and was one controversial scoring action away from advancing to the medal rounds. His greatest disappointment to date involves the same athlete, but took place some eight years earlier in his career when he was easily winning the gold medal match at the National Championship, only to get caught and pinned with a very basic technique.

Stephen Cobley, MA, is an active sporting individual and coach who originates from Rotherham, England. This area of the United Kingdom also provided the starting point of Steve's sporting and academic career. From 1996-2001 Steve graduated from Loughborough (UK) and Queen's (Canada) where his sport science work began. Today, Steve is presently developing his career in the United Kingdom as a lecturer, with special regard to sport and exercise psychology.

Jean Côté, PhD, is an associate professor in the school of physical and health education at Queen's University in Kingston, Canada. His research interests focus on the developmental and psychosocial factors that affect sport performance and participation. He has published numerous articles on youth and elite sport including studies on athletes, parents, coaches, and referees. Dr. Côté has been a visiting academic in Australia and the United States studying the development of expert athletes in these countries.

Andreas Daffertshofer, PhD, is an associate professor at the Faculty of Human Movement Sciences, Vrije Universiteit, Amsterdam. He received his PhD in theoretical physics at Stuttgart University in 1995. His primary interest is in complex dynamics in biological systems and its formal and conceptual assessment in terms of synergetics. At present, his research activities focus on spatio-temporal aspects of neural synchronization phenomena during perceptual-motor tasks.

Janice M. Deakin, PhD, is the director of the school of physical and health education at Queen's University in Kingston, Canada. A central theme of her research program continues to be the exploration of the constituent components underlying exceptional levels of performance. The influence of skill level has been examined in a variety of sport settings including, figure skating, the marital arts, basketball, and volleyball. Investigations into the relationship between the level of expertise in coaching and practice structure are recent additions to her research program.

Damian Farrow, PhD, earned his PhD in 2002 from the University of Queensland in Brisbane, Australia, where he completed a doctoral thesis on expertise and the acquisition of perceptual-motor skill under the supervision of Professor Bruce Abernethy and with the support of a grant from the Australian Sports Commission. The holder of bachelors and masters degrees from Deakin University, Farrow held a lecturing position at the University of Ballarat before undertaking his doctoral studies. He is currently the inaugural appointee to the position of Skill Acquisition Specialist at the Australian Institute of Sport in Canberra—a position in which he supplies evidence-based sport science support to elite-level athletes and coaches seeking to improve the design of practice and other aspects of skill learning.

Charles H. Hillman, PhD, is an assistant professor of kinesiology and psychology at the University of Illinois at Urbana-Champaign. He is co-director of the exercise and sport psychophysiology laboratory and mainly conducts research on psychophysiological aspects of physical activity effects on cognition and emotion in older adults. In addition, he conducts research on neuroelectric concomitants of elite performance states. His research has been funded by the National Institutes of Mental Health and the National Institute on Aging, and he has lectured to coaches and athletes at the United States Olympic Training Center on the psychophysiology of elite marksmanship.

Raoul Huys is a PhD student at the Faculty of Human Movement Sciences, Vrije Universiteit, Amsterdam. The primary focus of his research project, supervised by Peter Beek, is the assembly of multiple subsystems (i.e., visual, manual, postural, and respiratory) into a functional dynamical organization during the acquisition of juggling skills.

David M. Jacobs, PhD, earned his PhD in 2002 with a thesis entitled "On perceiving, acting and learning: Towards an ecological approach anchored in convergence." The central topic of interest of this doctoral work was the convergence of perceptual learners onto the variables that are most informative for accomplishing specific perceptual or perceptual-motor tasks. After his doctorate, David enrolled as a student of mathematics at the University of Salamanca, Spain.

Christopher M. Janelle, PhD, is an assistant professor in sport and exercise psychology in the department of exercise and sport sciences at the University of Florida. His research interests primarily surround the interactive nature of emotion and attention as related to human performance and health issues, and he is currently funded by the National Institutes of Mental Health for his work in these areas. He has published numerous scientific articles and book chapters and has made presentations worldwide dealing with these topics. He also co-authored the *Handbook of Sport Psychology* (Wiley, 2001). He reviews papers for each of the leading journals in the field and currently serves as the program chair for Division 47 of the American Psychological Association.

Michael W. Kernodle, PhD, is an associate professor at Appalachian State University in Boone, North Carolina where he teaches under-graduate motor learning, motor development, and a graduate class in sport sociology. He played tennis at the university and professional level, is the chairperson of the ITA National Sports Science Committee, and is a member of the USTA National Sports Science Committee. His research interests are in computer-assisted distance learning, learning styles, and multiple intelligences as well as the tactics and strategies involved in the sport of tennis.

Sue L. McPherson, PhD, is an associate professor of motor behavior in the physical therapy department at Western Carolina University in Cullowhee, North Carolina. Currently, she teaches scientific inquiry and motor behavior courses. Previously, she taught graduate and un-dergraduate motor behavior and sport psychology courses in kinesi-ology departments. She studies expertise and player development in sport domains and motor learning interventions in injury prevention and rehabilitation. She is currently serving as chair of the Motor Devel-opment Academy for the National Association for Sport and Physical Education. She was a former certified tennis teaching professional and collegiate tennis coach.

Luiz Carlos Moraes, PhD, is a professor in sport psychology and director of the center for excellence in sport at the Federal University of Minas Gerais in Belo Horizonte, Brazil. He completed his doctoral studies at the University of Ottawa in Canada. He was a former na-tional team champion in judo in Brazil, trained in Japan for one year, and continues his applied work in the martial arts. Dr. Moraes has presented his research on the beliefs and actions of judo coaches in Europe, Canada, the United States, and Brazil, and his current projects are centered on the roles of family in the development of expertise in Brazilian athletes from different socioeconomic backgrounds.

John H. Salmela, PhD, is a former national team champion in both football and gymnastics in the United States and Canada. He was a professor of sport psychology, motor learning, and motor development at Laval University and the universities of Montreal and Ottawa in Canada. He is presently a visiting professor at the Federal University of Minas Gerais in Belo Horizonte, Brazil. He has worked as a performance consultant for the national men's gymnastics team for 20 years and has attended two Olympics and six world championships in this capacity. His research initially focused on talent identification but later was directed toward talent development, especially on the roles of expert coaches and families on the teaching and nurturing processes that are central to the development of exceptional performance in sport. He served as chairman of the Social Sciences and Humanities Research Council of Canada and was vice president of the International Society of Sport Psychology.

Diane Ste-Marie, PhD, is the current director of the school of human kinetics at the University of Ottawa. Her expertise research has been motivated through her experiences in gymnastics as a competitor, coach, and judge. Both her master's (MSc in human biodynamics) and doctoral studies (PhD in cognitive psychology) were earned at McMaster University in Canada and concentrated on the cognitive processes of memory and perception. Funding through the Natural Sciences and Engineering Research Council of Canada has enabled her to continue research on memory and perception, with a specific emphasis on these processes in judging aesthetic sports, a topic directly related to the expertise chapter developed in this text. Funding through the Social Sciences and Humanities Research Council of Canada has allowed her to investigate the importance of cognitive processes in the two motor learning techniques of modeling and contextual interference.

Gershon Tenenbaum, PhD, is a professor of sport and exercise psychology at Florida State University. He is a graduate of the University of Chicago in measurement and statistics. He is the editor of the *International Journal of Sport and Exercise Psychology* and the past president of the International Society of Sport Psychology (ISSP). His main areas of research are cognitive processes during competitive events, determination of performance-related emotional zones, and the social-cognitive determinants of perseverance behaviors. Dr. Tenenbaum received several awards for his research and scientific contributions. He has worked with Australian and US athletes and currently provides scientific services to athletes world wide. He is married and has three children and two dogs.

Paul Ward, PhD, is a postdoctoral research associate in the department of psychology and the Institute for Simulation and Training at the University of Central Florida. He received his PhD in 2002 from the Research Institute for Sport and Exercise Sciences at Liverpool, John Moores University, United Kingdom. His thesis specifically focused on the study of expert human performance. Dr. Ward has recently authored papers on the development of perceptual-cognitive expertise, training perceptual-cognitive skills, and the visual search characteristics of experts. His interests are in the cognitive structure of expertise in applied domains, specifically as it relates to contemporary theories of working memory and cognition, the acquisition of expert levels of performance through deliberate practice, and more recently, in examining expertise as a mitigator of task-related stress.

Patricia L. Weir, PhD, is an associate professor of kinesiology at the University of Windsor. Her motor control research focuses on the planning and control of goal-directed aiming and prehension movements, in both two- and three-dimensional situations. Her recent work has examined the effector/target relationship. From a more applied perspective she is interested in the factors that contribute to the maintenance of high-level athletic performance in older Master athletes.

Sarah A. Wierenga is currently a doctoral candidate in the professional counseling program at Argosy University in Phoenix, Arizona. Wierenga is a graduate of the psychology and criminal justice departments at Michigan State University, where she studied high-level skill execution and performance under pressure in collaboration with Sian Beilock and Thomas Carr.

A. Mark Williams, PhD, is professor of motor behavior at the Research Institute for Sport and Exercise Sciences, Liverpool, John Moores University. Dr. Williams has contributed almost 40 journal articles to the field in publications such as *Research Quarterly for Exercise and Sport, Journal of Motor Behavior, Journal of Sport and Exercise Psychology, Journal of Experimental Psychology: Applied,* and *The Lancet.* He has written 5 books, 15 book chapters, and more than 40 coaching and professional articles. He has also made more than 70 conference presentations worldwide. He currently acts as the cognitive sport psychology section editor for the *International Journal of Sport Psychology* and is shortly to become section editor for the *Journal of Sports Sciences.* In 2001, Dr. Williams was awarded the International Society of Sport Psychology Early Career Distinguished Scholar Award and received the same award from the North American Society for the Psychology of Sport and Physical Activity in 2002. Dr. Williams is also involved with high-level sport and is a sports science adviser for the English Football Association as well as several Premier League football clubs.

Bradley W. Young is a doctoral candidate in the department of kinesiology at McMaster University. His research focuses on the acquisition and maintenance of expert performance and issues of talent development in sport. As head coach of the McMaster varsity cross-country running team, he takes a vested interest in the application of these empirical avenues to coaching science. In collaboration with Janet Starkes, Bradley is examining the career patterns of skill acquisition for aged competitors from various athletic domains in order to gain a better understanding of how these athletes can best organize their training and psychosocial resources to maintain remarkable levels of skilled performance.

*You'll find
other outstanding
sport psychology resources at*

www.HumanKinetics.com

In the U.S. call

1-800-747-4457

Australia.............................. 08 8277 1555
Canada 800-465-7301
Europe...................... +44 (0) 113 255 5665
New Zealand.......................... 09-523-3462